MW00398939

Yale Agrarian Studies Series

JAMES C. SCOTT, SERIES EDITOR

The Agrarian Studies Series at Yale University Press seeks to publish outstanding and original interdisciplinary work on agriculture and rural society—for any period, in any location. Works of daring that question existing paradigms and fill abstract categories with the lived experience of rural people are especially encouraged.

—James C. Scott, *Series Editor*

James C. Scott, *Seeing Like a State: How Certain Schemes to Improve the Human Condition Have Failed*

Steve Striffler, *Chicken: The Dangerous Transformation of America's Favorite Food*

James C. Scott, *The Art of Not Being Governed: An Anarchist History of Upland Southeast Asia*

Timothy Pachirat, *Every Twelve Seconds: Industrialized Slaughter and the Politics of Sight*

Andrew Sluyter, *Black Ranching Frontiers: African Cattle Herders of the Atlantic World, 1500–1900*

Brian Gareau, *From Precaution to Profit: Contemporary Challenges to Environmental Protection in the Montreal Protocol*

Kuntala Lahiri-Dutt and Gopa Samanta, *Dancing with the River: People and Life on the Chars of South Asia*

Alon Tal, *All the Trees of the Forest: Israel's Woodlands from the Bible to the Present*

Felix Wemheuer, *Famine Politics in Maoist China and the Soviet Union*

Jenny Leigh Smith, *Works in Progress: Plans and Realities on Soviet Farms, 1930–1963*

Graeme Auld, *Constructing Private Governance: The Rise and Evolution of Forest, Coffee, and Fisheries Certification*

Jess Gilbert, *Planning Democracy: Agrarian Intellectuals and the Intended New Deal*

Jessica Barnes and Michael R. Dove, eds., *Climate Cultures: Anthropological Perspectives on Climate Change*

Shafqat Hussain, *Remoteness and Modernity: Transformation and Continuity in Northern Pakistan*

Edward Dallam Melillo, *Strangers on Familiar Soil: Rediscovering the Chile-California Connection*

Devra I. Jarvis, Toby Hodgkin, Anthony H. D. Brown, John Tuxill, Isabel López Noriega, Melinda Smale, and Bhuwon Sthapit, *Crop Genetic Diversity in the Field and on the Farm: Principles and Applications in Research Practices*

Nancy J. Jacobs, *Birders of Africa: History of a Network*

Catherine A. Corson, *Corridors of Power: The Politics of U.S. Environmental Aid to Madagascar*

Kathryn M. de Luna, *Collecting Food, Cultivating People: Subsistence and Society in Central Africa through the Seventeenth Century*

Carl Death, *The Green State in Africa*

For a complete list of titles in the Yale Agrarian Studies Series, visit yalebooks.com/agrarian.

The Green State in Africa

Carl Death

Yale UNIVERSITY PRESS

New Haven & London

Published with assistance from the Louis Stern Memorial Fund.

Yale University Press books may be purchased in quantity for educational, business, or promotional use. For information, please e-mail sales.press@yale.edu (U.S. office) or sales@yaleup.co.uk (U.K. office).

Set in Adobe Garamond type by IDS Infotech, Ltd.
Printed in the United States of America.

ISBN 978-0-300-21583-0 (hardcover : alk. paper)

Library of Congress Control Number: 2016932026

A catalogue record for this book is available from the British Library.

This paper meets the requirements of ANSI/NISO Z39.48-1992 (Permanence of Paper).

10 9 8 7 6 5 4 3 2 1

Contents

Acknowledgments, vii

List of Abbreviations, xi

Introduction, 1

1 Global Environmental Governance and the Green State, 19

2 Postcolonial Theory and the Green State in Africa, 44

3 Green Land and State Territory, 69

4 Green Citizens and Problematic Populations, 108

5 Green Economies and Environmental Markets, 152

6 Green African States and International Relations, 193

7 Afro-Ecologism, 233

Notes, 247

Bibliography, 285

Index, 337

Acknowledgments

This book has emerged at a pedestrian pace, and in it I walk through a wide range of literatures, issues, and debates. At times I lost my way and had to retrace my steps, and the tracks of those errant footprints are probably still visible here. There may well be other places, not evident to me, in which the path veers down blind alleys or meanders frustratingly. But I hope you come along for the journey anyway.

Some walks are better with companions, and this book owes much to the many people who have shaped its course. Elements of the argument have been presented in seminars at Birmingham, Cape Town, Kent, King's College London, Manchester, Oxford Brookes, SOAS, Sheffield, Stellenbosch, the Western Cape, and Yale as well as at conferences in Dodoma ("Green Economy in the Global South," 2014), London (BISA, 2015), and Oxford ("Twenty Years of South African Democracy," 2014). Chapter drafts or versions of the argument in some form were read and commented upon by anonymous reviewers for Yale University Press as well as by Rita Abrahamsen, William Beinart, Dan Brockington, Ian Bruff, Bram Büscher, Olaf Corry, Aharon DeGrassi, Rosaleen Duffy, Clive Gabay, Julia Gallagher, Toni Haastrup, Sophie Harman, Alder Keleman, Keri Lambert, Gediminas Lesutis, Laura MacLeod, Aoileann Ní Mhurchú, Pete Newell, Louiza Odysseos, Chuks Okereke, Mat Paterson, Maano Ramutsindela, Adrienne Roberts, Dave Richards, Jim Scott, Stuart Shields, Gabriel Siles-Brügge, David Simon,

Hayley Stevenson, Paul Tobin, Mark Whitehead, Rorden Wilkinson, Huw Williams, Japhy Wilson, Maja Zehfuss, and Andreja Zevnik. I am very grateful for their help, and I apologise to those I have mistakenly omitted. I have gained a great deal from participating in the Global Political Economy research cluster, the Society and Environment Reading Group, and the Social Movements Reading Group at the University of Manchester. It was a privilege to present a chapter of the book to the Yale Agrarian Studies Program colloquium, which was both a rewarding intellectual experience and an excuse to spend an enjoyable month reading, walking, and learning about pigs in New Haven. I am indebted to Jean Thomson Black, Samantha Ostrowski, Margaret Otzel, Lawrence Kenney, Enid L. Zafran, and others at Yale University Press who encouraged me at the start, helped me improve it during the writing, and produced a physical object—a book!—at the end.

The research was informed by a number of trips I have made to South Africa and Tanzania since 2006 and conversations with a large number of activists, academics, bureaucrats, journalists, diplomats, trade unionists, and others from across the continent and beyond who gave generously of their time, energy, and emotion. They include Gottlieb Arendse, Bryan Ashe, Bernard Baha, Magdalena Banasiak, Judy Beaumont, Patrick Bond, Sarah Bracking, Mathew Burkhi, Anton Cartwright, Ines Ceruti, Sharad Chari, Blandina Cheche, Fantu Cheru, Jacklyn Cock, Brian Cooksey, Scarlett Cornelissen, Rick de Satgé, Nicci Diedrichs, Des D'Sa, Linda Engström, Saliem Fakir, David Fig, Andre Fourie, Pieter Fourie, Lorraine Gerrans, Stephen Granger, Anique Greyling, Andy Gubb, Ruth Hall, Ralph Hamann, Samantha Hargreaves, Arend Hoogervoorst, Christophe Huegel, Thabit Jacob, Rebecca Karpul, Elana Keef, Nick King, Kyaruzi Ladislaus, Muna Lakhani, John Ledger, J. P. Louw, Enkingo Makembe, Amon Manyama, Andrew Marquand, Teboho Mashota, Masupha Mathenywa, Mandisa Mbali, Dale McKinley, Mary Metcalfe, Benedict Mongula, Mapitso Muambadzi, Victor Munnik, Alan Murphy, Werner Myburgh, Obert Ncube, Patrick Ndaki, James Ngana, Trevor Ngwane, Lungisile Ntsebeza, Bheki Ntshalintshali, Lubabalo Ntsholo, Chippy Olver, Sheryl Ozinsky, Zarina Patel, Bobby Peek, Mashile Phalame, Sarah Piel, Stefano Ponte, Deborah Posel, Olivia Radebe, Sebataolo Rahlao, Tumelo Ramolefi, Britta Rennkamp, Debra Roberts, Longinus Rutasitara, Labia Said, Stephanie Schwartner, Richard Sherman, Kushmika Singh, Andy Smith, Karen Smith, Janis van der Westhuizen, Chris van Rooyen, Ahmed Veriava, Alf Wills, Jessica Wilson, Richard Worthington, Laskarina Yiannakaris, and Gina Ziervogel. Again, I apologise to those I have mistakenly omitted. The fact that the book ended up being so long I blame in part on the many interesting discussions and avenues of research I was introduced to along the way.

Footfalls are a way of seeing the landscape, according to Robert Macfarlane. This is true not only for the landscapes of the environments in which we live, but also for the landscapes of the written page. Walking has always helped me think through the twists and turns of an argument, and I am most grateful and appreciative to those who have walked with me. That is why this book owes most to Aoileann, who came walking with me in Dar es Salaam and Durban and many places in between. I am at my happiest, and most optimistic for the future, when setting out on our next walk together.

Abbreviations

AfDB	African Development Bank
AGN	African Group of Negotiators
AMCEN	African Ministerial Conference on the Environment
ANAW	Africa Network for Animal Welfare
ANC	African National Congress (South Africa)
AU	African Union
CAADP	Comprehensive Africa Agriculture Development Programme
CAMPFIRE	Communal Areas Management Programme for Indigenous Resources (Zimbabwe)
CBNRM	Community-Based Natural Resource Management
CBO	Community-Based Organisations
CDM	Clean Development Mechanism
CO_2e	carbon dioxide equivalent
COP	conference of the parties (to the UNFCCC)
CSR	corporate social responsibility
DAC	Development Assistance Committee
DBSA	Development Bank of South Africa
DRC	Democratic Republic of the Congo
EACJ	East African Court of Justice
EIA	environmental impact assessments
EPI	Environmental Performance Index (Yale University)
EU ETS	European Union Emissions Trading Scheme

FAO	Food and Agriculture Organisation
FoEI	Friends of the Earth International
G77	Group of 77
GDP	gross domestic product
GHG	greenhouse gas
GMO	genetically modified organism
HDI	Human Development Index
HPI	Happy Planet Index
IAS	invasive alien species
IFI	international financial institution
ILO	International Labour Organisation
IPCC	Inter-Governmental Panel on Climate Change
IR	international relations
IUCN	International Union for the Conservation of Nature
KAZA-TFCA	Kavango–Zambezi Trans-Frontier Conservation Area
KNP	Kruger National Park
LDC	least-developed country
LHWP	Lesotho Highlands Water Project
MEC	minerals–energy complex
MEND	Movement for the Emancipation of the Niger Delta
MOSOP	Movement for the Survival of the Ogoni People
MW	megawatt
NGO	nongovernmental organisation
NEPAD	New Partnership for African Development
OAU	Organisation of African Unity
OECD	Organisation for Economic Cooperation and Development
PACJA	Pan-African Climate Justice Alliance
PES	Payments for Ecosystem Services
PPF	Peace Parks Foundation
PRSP	Poverty Reduction Strategy Papers
R	South African rand
REDD+	Reducing Emissions from Deforestation and Forest Degradation
RE IPPPP	Renewable Energy Independent Power Producer Procurement Programme (South Africa)
SADC	Southern African Development Community
SANP	South African National Parks
SAP	structural adjustment programme
SDCEA	South Durban Community Environmental Alliance
SSI	Sustainable Society Index
tCO_2	ton of carbon dioxide

TFCA	Trans-Frontier Conservation Area
TFP	trans-frontier park
TNC	transnational corporation
UNCTAD	United Nations Conference on Trade and Development
UNEP	United Nations Environment Programme
UNESCO	United Nations Educational, Scientific and Cultural Organisation
UNFCCC	United Nations Framework Convention on Climate Change
USAID	United States Agency for International Development
WWF	World Wildlife Fund
ZANU-PF	Zimbabwe African National Union–Patriotic Front

Introduction

> I owe my being to the hills and the valleys, the mountains and the glades, the rivers, the deserts, the trees, the flowers, the seas, and the ever-changing seasons that define the face of our native land.
>
> —Thabo Mbeki, *I am an African*

> In seeking restoration for my continent, I am quite literally restoring myself—as, I believe, is every African—because who we are is bound up in the rivers and streams, the trees and the valleys.
>
> —Wangari Maathai, *The Challenge for Africa*

Environmental politics is right at the beating green heart of the contemporary African condition. Instead of seeing the environment as a side issue or a concern which arises once poverty has been addressed, in this book I argue that we cannot understand African politics without understanding the political governance and contestation of environmental issues: of land, peoples, animals, plants, forests, natural resources, energy supplies, water, and crops. How to live with and within our nonhuman surroundings is a shared global concern. Yet despite this, environmental politics is sometimes regarded as a peripheral concern within the fields of both international politics and African studies. Certainly from a state-centric view of politics, environmental issues are generally regarded as low priorities and environmental ministries are rarely centres of power, either in Africa or beyond. While growing awareness of impending climate chaos is receiving increasing attention within the field of international politics, many students of African politics still tend to regard the green agenda as well below issues of conflict, security, poverty, development, etc. In contrast, I want to show that environmental politics is central to the production and transformation of states in Africa, and it has been a crucial element of the governance and contestation of land, people, economies, and international relations. Moreover, understanding environmental politics in Africa also helps us to understand processes of international change, transnational resistance, and escalating environmental crises that have genuinely global significance. This is a book about environmental politics in Africa, but it encompasses issues which should be of concern to all those interested in international politics: sovereignty, territory, subjectivity, identity, race, biopolitics, political economy, gender, conflict, and cooperation.

This is a book explicitly and directly about states in Africa, somewhat in contrast to much of the excellent empirical work on African environments from disciplines such as environmental history, geography, anthropology, and development studies. One of the purposes of the book is to draw upon the empirical research from these fields in order to make a contribution to state theory in an African context. The argument, to be brief, is that over the longue durée and even more intensively in recent decades the African state has been produced and transformed through the governance and contestation of environmental issues. In fact, what we have come to call the African state is actually the effect of the governance and contestation of territories, populations, economies, and international relations through green discourses and practices. All African states are, in some ways, green states. John Iliffe has suggested that "the central themes of African history are the peopling of the continent, the achievement of human coexistence with nature, the building up of enduring societies, and their defence against aggression from more favoured regions."[1] As this quote illustrates, environmental discourses and practices are not the only ones which have produced African states: development, security, accumulation, and nationalism are all clearly important. However, there are environmental aspects to all of these too, and once a broader conception of the environment as "where we all live" is adopted, then it becomes clear that all states are fundamentally shaped by attempts to govern land and water, flora and fauna, populations and natural resources in certain ways.

African states are not the only states to be produced through environmental politics. All states could be thought of, in some way, as an effect of the governance and contestation of territories, populations, economies, and international relations through green discourses and practices. This is as true of Saudi Arabia, Mexico, and Japan as it is of Egypt and South Africa. So what, then, is specifically African about the green states I examine in this book? Iliffe captures a key feature of popular perceptions of what it means to be African when he describes their chief contribution to history as the colonization of a hostile environment and the achievement of human coexistence with nature. This well-known quote is both enthralling and problematic in ways which will become clearer in the following chapters. My argument is somewhat different: there are four main distinguishing features of green states in Africa. First, the politics of land and conservation are of more central importance to contemporary African green state effects than to many states elsewhere in the world. Second, the biopolitics of rural under- and overpopulation—the so-called peasant question—is more prominent in Africa than elsewhere. Third, in that the continent is the least economically developed region (according to modernisation theorists), natural resource extraction and rapid, muscular green growth and modernisation are fundamental to understanding green economies in Africa. Finally, discourses and practices of African solidarity and Pan-African unity have shaped the international relations of African environmental politics to a degree rarely seen elsewhere. These are rather grand generalisations, ones which may not hold true in every specific context, but in the rest of the book I will seek to put empirical meat on these hypothetical bones. The key starting point is that if we can see all states, to some degree, as the effect of green discourses and practices, the most important question becomes: How have particular green state effects been produced, through what discourses and practices, and with what political implications? This book provides a framework for answering this question in the context of Africa.

What is at stake in such a project? Understanding how states are similar or different in their governance of environmental issues is important for comprehending processes of state transformation more generally in international politics. Accordingly, there is an intellectual and analytical importance to this research. Even more importantly, however, this research is politically vital. Environmental issues have always been crucial for human survival: safe and sufficient food and water and shelter from the elements are basic needs, and a meaningful cultural relationship with nonhuman nature, including flora, fauna, and the geophysical landscape, is part of what builds societies and communities. But the scale of environmental transformations in recent decades, principally but not solely related to climate change, has caused social, economic, racial, gendered, and other forms of environmental injustice and insecurity to such a degree that questions of how we govern and conduct our environmental politics, and the role states play in that process, have never been more crucial. As Naomi Klein argues forcefully and persuasively, "This changes everything."[2] Forging new ways of living with each other on this planet more sustainably, securely, and equitably will require revolutionary upheaval of existing ways of life, changes that will threaten entrenched elites, the profit motive, continual economic growth, and anthropocentric conceptions of development as well as many other things our political systems have tended to take for granted.

It has become popular to frame this as a politics of the Anthropocene: a new geological epoch in which the human species and our forms of political and economic and social life are transforming the very planet and its biosphere. However, this has tended to focus debates on the precise dating of geological eras and to produce rather homogenous conceptions of humanity and political agency, implying we are all in this together.[3] Yet we do not all bear equal responsibility for harms nor do we have equal vulnerabilities and capabilities. This book focuses attention on a more manageable but politically even more crucial scale: the ways in which states have governed environmental issues, popular and activist resistance to them, and how this political contestation has in turn reshaped and reproduced states themselves. The twenty-first century will be a century of spiraling climate chaos and (in all likelihood) increasingly dramatic, desperate attempts to govern an unpredictable climate and redesign existing socioeconomic and political systems. States are among the most complex and powerful of these systems, and in forthcoming decades they will be central to all attempts to govern both climatic and other environmental changes and crises. Just as the state has been at the heart of the socioeconomic and political systems which have produced the so-called Anthropocene—through settled agriculture, capitalism, the industrial revolution, military machines, imperialism, and colonialism—so state formations must be part of whatever solutions we can devise.[4] This is true for environmental politics in many countries globally, but Africa is particularly vulnerable to these changes as well as being the region most associated with state failure and weakness. As such, it is a hard case in which to look for examples of green states. One of the main contributions of this book, therefore, is to bring African cases into dialogue with the existing literature on green states in global environmental politics.

Doing so is not uncontroversial. To put it bluntly, many commentators and analysts see the African state as the root of many of the continent's problems rather than the solution.[5] Such analyses are not always wide of the mark. Indeed, much of the argument in this book is that paying closer attention to the production and transformation of green states in Africa reveals more worrying political dynamics and implications than some of the more optimistic and positive appraisals of green states elsewhere. Green states can be colonial, racist, and authoritarian, and it is a mistake to position the green state as the next step in a progressive project which (so the story goes) began with the liberal state in the nineteenth century and was transformed into the welfare state in the twentieth century.[6] This European, modernist outlook blinds us not only to the many ways in which environmental issues have been at the heart of state governance for a long time but also to the intrinsically *political* and contingent character of environmental governance in Africa (as well as elsewhere).

Nevertheless, it is true that responding to the challenges of climate chaos, social injustice and inequality, sustainable development, and the challenge of human flourishing alongside other species will require the production and transformation of state formations in some way. States have both the capacity in terms of the practices and technologies of governance and the potential legitimacy in terms of governmental rationalities such as democracy, liberalism, socialism, and the developmental state to effect large-scale, potentially radical changes in a manner which few other political institutions or assemblages can match. It is crucial to subject to critical examination questions concerning "the extent to which we have the sorts of political institutions able to contain crises and steer positive and progressive change."[7] Despite continued stereotypes and deep-rooted assumptions about the failed or failing African state, progressive changes require engagement with African states, not rejection of them. We do not need to accept uncritically the modernisation discourses of "Africa Rising" to treat assumptions about weak states and governance failures as oversimplifications of complex African realities.[8] Although much of this book is highly critical of the green state effects being produced in Africa, it shows how some manifestations of environmental politics—whether radical land reforms, renewable energy schemes, environmental education programmes, or transnational social movement solidarity—can be seen as positive African examples. The mainstream perspective of an Africa always lagging behind the globalising West or East needs to be challenged.

This book therefore focuses on Africa because it is a continent poorly understood by scholars of global environmental politics and because of the compelling fact that it is the continent most vulnerable to but least responsible for global climate change, overconsumption, and the degradation of ecosystems through chronic pollution. It is also a continent in which the state has been seen as a most unlikely vehicle for progressive politics. Even more important—and, again, contrary to many assumptions about the continent as being cut off or isolated—Africa is highly connected to transnational and international processes of state production and transformation.[9] Hence African examples can be used to illustrate with particular clarity important transnationally driven dynamics of the production of green state effects in all their similarities and differences. The book concludes that it is these dynamics which will profoundly shape the degree to which our world of states is able to navigate future challenges in ways which are socially just and ecologically sustainable.

CHANGING AFRICAN ENVIRONMENTS

The starting point for this research is a range of empirical observations about environmental governance in Africa, where there are a wide range of interesting, eye-catching developments. To mention just a few examples: fifty-three African countries submitted pledges for climate action (or Intended Nationally Determined Contributions in UN parlance) in advance of the landmark negotiations in Paris in December 2015, and African voices were some of the most prominent in demanding multilateral, ambitious, effective action on mitigation, adaption, and the provision of climate finance to developing countries. The African Group of Negotiators (AGN) has been one of the most prominent continental blocs within the conferences of the parties (COPs) to the United Nations Framework Convention on Climate Change (UNFCCC) and the Kyoto Protocol. South Africa hosted a climate change conference in Durban in 2011 (COP17) and is part of the coalition which agreed the Copenhagen Declaration in 2009 (along with Brazil, India, China, and the United States), and the eventual success of COP21 in producing the Paris Agreement was attributed by some to the use of African-style meetings, or indabas, to forge an international consensus. Some of the biggest and most ambitious new renewable energy and hydropower developments in the world are taking place in Algeria, Morocco, Ethiopia, Kenya, South Africa, and the Democratic Republic of the Congo (DRC), among others. The forested Congo Basin is one of the largest potential global sources of carbon credits for reduced and avoided deforestation, under the Reducing Emissions from Deforestation and Forest Degradation (REDD+) programme, and Ghana is set to begin construction on the Nzema solar photovoltaic plant, which would be Africa's largest and the fourth largest of its kind in the world. The United Nations Environment Programme (UNEP), based in Nairobi, has driven international discourses on conservation, biodiversity protection, and the green economy, and the UN conference on New and Renewable Sources of Energy was held in Nairobi in 1981. Countries like Rwanda, Ethiopia, and South Africa have developed high-profile interventionist national green economy strategies ostensibly designed to stimulate environmentally sustainable and socially inclusive economic growth. In a study measuring the long-term sustainable development of thirty-one countries worldwide by Standard Chartered Bank in 2013, Ghana, Uganda, Egypt, and Nigeria all came in the top ten for progress over 2000–12 in an array of sustainable development indicators. On Yale University's Environmental Performance Index (EPI), which ranks those states which have improved most over a ten-year period in terms of indicators on human health and protection of ecosystems, in 2014 Niger came in first, Sierra Leone fifth, Namibia sixth, and Congo seventh. The Sustainable Society Index (SSI) rankings for environmental well-being in 2014 put Malawi in second place, Mozambique in fourth, Rwanda in seventh, and Tanzania at number eleven. Sub-Saharan Africa has over eleven hundred national parks and reserves, thirty-six of which are designated as World Heritage Sites, and the Kavango–Zambezi Transfrontier Conservation Area in southern Africa is one of the largest protected areas in the world.[10] The Fédération Démocratique des Ecologistes du Sénégal held the Global Green Congress for green parties from around the world in Dakar in March and April 2012, the first time it has been held in Africa, and it was attended by six hundred delegates from seventy-six countries. From 2009 to 2015 Kumi Naidoo was the international executive director of Greenpeace International, and Nnimmo Bassey was chair of Friends of the Earth International (FoEI) in 2008–12; the two men were the first African heads of these prominent environmental organisations. African green parties have supplied government ministers in Kenya, Burkina Faso, the Congo, and Madagascar. Encapsulating this optimism and echoing Iliffe's admiration for African coexistence with nature, the former secretary-general of the UN Kofi Annan declared in 2014 that "the time has come to unleash Africa's green and blue revolutions."[11]

Such apparently positive features of environmental politics in Africa are rarely remarked upon, yet they are all at least potentially interesting sites of exemplary environmental governance. More familiar, however, are the many examples of contradictions, crises, and injustices associated with African environmental politics. According to Oliver C. Ruppel, the coordinating lead author on the Africa chapter of the 5th Assessment Report of the Inter-Governmental Panel on Climate Change (IPCC), Africa is the region of the world that will suffer the most from climate change and that struggles the most when it comes to capacity to manage present and future disaster risks.

According to the African Development Bank and the World Wildlife Fund (WWF), Africa as a continent was in biocapacity deficit by 2015, in that its consumption exceeds the resources (food, fuel, water, etc.) available within its borders. Famines continue to threaten several countries—including Somalia, Mali, Malawi, Zimbabwe, and South Sudan in recent years—as conflicts intersect with increased climate vulnerability, and in 2012 floods claimed 363 lives in Nigeria and 65 in Niger. Many African countries failed to meet the Millennium Development Goals, including those relating to hunger and food security, child mortality, maternal health, water and sanitation, and across the region forest cover is shrinking (very rapidly in some places). South Africa has one of the highest per capita rates of greenhouse gas (GHG) emissions in the world, higher than the United States, the United Kingdom, India, Brazil, and China, and is building two of the largest new coal-fired power stations in the world at Kusile and Medupi. In 2013 South Africa was placed last in the Standard Chartered Bank sustainable development index owing to a fall in life expectancy over the review period 2000–2012 and worries about the long-term sustainability of its environment. Land grabs for export crops and biofuels are resulting in the further marginalisation of subsistence farmers as worldwide demand for cheap food and low carbon fuel rises. This has led some to talk of carbon colonialism as Africa contributes 70 percent, or forty-five million hectares, of the global land leased or purchased by foreign enterprises to produce agricultural crops for food and biofuels. Strip mining for gold and precious metals is devastating the land, polluting air and water, and impoverishing communities from North Africa and Ghana down through the DRC and Zambia to South Africa. The Niger Delta is one of the world's most oil-polluted ecosystems after decades of intensive drilling and gas flaring, and the struggle against global oil companies led to the execution of Ken Saro-Wiwa, one of the most well-known environmental campaigners and political dissidents of the 1990s. The Rwandan green party has experienced political harassment and violent disruption in an attempt to prevent it from contesting elections, and the party's vice president, André Kagwa Rwisereka, was beheaded during the election campaign of 2010. A report by Global Witness in 2014 on the massive surge in deaths of environmental activists from 2002 to 2012 noted underreporting and difficulties in verifying killings in countries such as the Central African Republic and Zimbabwe. Mozambique and Tanzania are ranked at 157 and 159 in the EPI of most improved countries, and most African countries do badly in the New Economics Foundation's Happy Planet Index (HPI), which measures long and happy lives per unit of environmental input: Sierra Leone is at 139, South Africa at 142, Niger at 144, and Botswana is at the bottom of the table at 151.[12]

This initial survey of African environmental politics generates a number of questions and research puzzles. There are examples of innovations and impressive performers in environmental governance, alongside laggards, calamities, and abuses. What explains the similarities and differences across African countries and across environmental issue areas in forms of governance, resistance, and levels of environmental performance? To what degree are these similarities and differences driven by international factors or by local and national policies? What role do African states and politicians play in environmental governance and policy, in contrast to transnational actors, civil society, social movements, international organisations, aid donors, and the private sector? To what degree do these observable events and processes support hypotheses of ecological modernisation or degradation? What are the political implications of these changes? What do these processes imply for the capacity of developing states to respond to environmental challenges? And what are the opportunities and challenges for building more equitable, socially justice, safe, secure, and sustainable societies in some of the poorest parts of the world?

1. "Chief More's Funeral, GaMogopa," Santu Mofokeng (b. 1956). © Santu Mofokeng, 1989 silverprint edition 5. Images courtesy Lunetta Bartz, MAKER, Johannesburg.

As should be obvious from these questions, the scope of this book is wide-ranging and ambitious. It neither summarises progress on Africa's environmental targets and the challenges ahead nor presents the results of lengthy empirical fieldwork or quantitative analysis.[13] Rather, the book is an empirically informed, theoretical exploration of how we might establish a framework and set of questions for examining the relationship between the production and transformation of African states and the governance and contestation of African environments. The initial way into these questions is through the concept of the green state as deployed by scholars of global environmental politics.

THE GREEN STATE

The book takes its title from a relatively recent set of debates within global environmental politics which centre upon the role of developmental, liberal, or postliberal states in governing and responding to environmental changes and challenges. Although there are many differences of interpretation as well as different policy implications, much of this literature converges on the notion of a green state as one in which the governance of environmental issues has become central and is closely linked to core imperatives of survival, maintenance of domestic order, generation of finance, capital accumulation, and political legitimation.[14] Such green states are often held to be qualitatively different from earlier bourgeois, liberal, neoliberal, communist, and welfare states, and the most plausible potential candidates are usually assumed to be Germany, Sweden, Norway, and others in Western Europe and Scandinavia. The central question of this book is, What is the green state in Africa?

To answer this question one must begin by exploring the ways in which the governance of environmental issues forges new links to core state imperatives. However, it is soon clear that many older state forms and many illiberal, authoritarian states are also centrally concerned with the governance of environmental issues.[15] Rather than approaching environmental politics from a modernisation perspective, which inevitably tends to accord African states a backward or underdeveloped role, the research here shows how the governance and contestation of environmental issues have produced African states over the longue durée and are currently transforming African states in ways that have significant political implications.

The major reasons for the neglect of African cases by green state theorists stem from the Weberian roots of the concept of the state on which they draw and from modernisation assumptions that environmental values are adopted only once basic needs are fulfilled. I reject this theoretical starting point and approach the green state debates from the perspective of postcolonial theory. This means looking at environmental practices, rationalities, technologies, and worldviews which together produce the state as "the mobile effect of a regime of multiple governmentalities."[16] The argument is that states are the biopolitical effect of forms of environmental governance and contestation, particularly organised around the production of territories, populations, economies, and international relations.

The book draws upon a postcolonial governmentality perspective, and the analysis proceeds by questioning what things are made visible and invisible by the governing practices under study; what technologies and forms of technique are deployed; which regimes of knowledge are invoked; and how subjects and agents are produced.[17] Discourses of environmentalism, including community-based conservation, sustainable agriculture, the green economy, and environmental aid, are shown to be transforming the practices of long-standing state interventions in the policing of borders, securing of bodies, regulation of markets, and international cooperation and conflict. The level of the argument is accordingly pitched in generalised, wide-ranging terms rather than engaging in chapter-length empirical case studies. However, this general discussion is empirically informed and illustrated, and there are detailed, critical discussions of cases, including land reform and peace parks, environmental education and green citizenship policies, green economy strategies and ecosystem services programmes, and international environmental negotiations and transnational activism. Examples and illustrations are drawn from a broad spectrum of African countries, including Angola, Botswana, Congo, the DRC, Egypt, Ethiopia, Ghana, Kenya, Lesotho, Madagascar, Malawi, Mozambique, Namibia, Niger, Nigeria, Rwanda, Senegal, Sierra Leone, South Africa, Sudan, Tanzania, Uganda, Zambia, and Zimbabwe. There is certainly a predominance of Anglophone countries here, reflecting the biases of the English-language academic literature, but this also reflects the relative importance of conservation and green politics in eastern and southern Africa.[18] More generally, the argument should be judged on its logic and plausibility rather than on a claim to exhaustiveness or comprehensive coverage. There is an affinity here to Mahmood Mamdani's argument that "the commonality of the African experience" is encapsulated in shared histories of colonialism and state formation.[19] Part of the aim of this book is to show the commonalities—or at least the strong similarities—across Africa in the governance and contestation of environmental issues. Yet my overall and ultimate aim is to devise and illustrate a theoretical framework in order to answer the central question: What is the green state in Africa? Another way of putting this question is, How are the production and transformation of African states related to the governance and contestation of African environments? The stakes inherent in such questions are both intellectual and political: understanding transnational processes of state transformation as well as how state forms might and should transform in order to better govern ecological challenges in the developing world.

OUTLINE OF THE BOOK

In chapter 1 I argue that the state continues to be a central conceptual anchor of global environmental governance, despite the critiques of statist analysis from ecologist and anarchist, anti-instrumentalist, eco-Marxist, neoliberal, and globalisation perspectives. The green state literature—associated with the work of Robyn Eckersley and John Dryzek (and colleagues)—is therefore entirely right to focus our attention on the continued importance of the state in global environmental politics.[20] This literature, however, has neglected states in the developing world for problematic reasons, including assumptions about state weakness and the hierarchy of needs. These can be contested empirically through examples of various social movements as well as through programmes of environmental regulation and intervention from across the continent. The Weberian assumptions of ecological modernisation theory have meant it is difficult to understand the highly diverse context and history of African states, and in order to provide a fuller, more interesting, more historically informed, and more politically astute explanation of the relationship between the production and transformation of African states and the governance and contestation of African environments, an alternative theoretical conception of the state is required. The chapter ends, therefore, by making the case for a postcolonial approach to the green state in Africa.

Chapter 2 takes the second key step in the argument by articulating a different approach to state theory, drawing upon postcolonial authors to suggest that state can be treated as the effect of governing rationalities, an assemblage brought into being by reiterated practices, rationalities, and technologies and held together via discourses of sovereignty and the myth of the state. The chapter thus draws upon Michel Foucault's contributions to state theory as well as those of authors such as Achille Mbembe, Jean-François Bayart, Jean and John Comaroff, Mitchell Dean, James C. Scott, Bob Jessop, and Timothy Mitchell. From this postcolonial perspective the green state is regarded as the effect of an assemblage of environmental rationalities, discourses, and technologies of government through which the governance and contestation of territories, populations, economies, and international relations have been brought within the scope of sedimented power relations. This approach rejects many of the assumptions of modernisation theory and highlights some of the political dangers of green state practices. Green states are the effects of the governance of certain issues, practices, and fields in ways which explicitly invoke environmental or ecological discourses.

Chapter 3 begins the more empirically oriented analysis by examining the production of territories, borders, and frontiers in Africa, starting with a recent dispute between Tanzania and the East African Court of Justice over the legality of a proposed road through the Serengeti. The main argument in this chapter is that green state effects in Africa are primarily and quintessentially bound up with the government of land and territory to a far greater extent than in green states elsewhere.[21] These effects can be expressed in terms of the exclusive or hybrid territorialisations produced by practices of conservation, land grabs, and the forms of resistance they have stimulated. For example, having over 30 percent of its land under some form of protection and deriving substantial financial and symbolic capital from its wildlife, the green state in Tanzania can be seen as a type of conservation state. Namibia, Zambia, and Botswana have even higher proportions of land under protection. These cases can help explain why the court was able to refuse permission to build a road through the Serengeti. There are strong commonalities across Africa in the forms of land governance and resistance to it, but the chapter also explores a key political disparity between more exclusive modes of territorialisation (fortress conservation and land grabs, for example) and more inclusive or hybrid territorialisations (such as community-based conservation or wild urban spaces). These two modes of territorialisation—the exclusive and the hybrid—are useful for comparing and categorising the ways in which green states in Africa are brought into being through the governance of land. The chapter holds that rather than representing a trend from exclusive to hybrid modes of territorialisation or vice versa, environmental politics in Africa is characterised by a dynamic interplay between the two forms. This dynamic is central to the politics of green states in Africa, whether they are authoritarian conservation states committed to fortress preservation or boundless, neoliberal states creating flexible spaces attractive to investment and facilitating the free movement of animals and tourists.

In chapter 4 I discuss how green state effects in Africa have also been produced through the governance of people and their bodies as populations, consumers, and citizens. States have always been about control over a particular population, but the governance of nonhuman populations is also a central element of the biopolitics of African environmentalism. This theme is explored in the chapter through the repeated trope of the tree planter as the ideal of the responsible African environmental subject, encapsulated by Wangari Maathai's Green Belt Movement. Three central problem-subjects and their corresponding solution-subjects are identified: the uneducated peasant and the entrepreneurial farmer, the teeming urban mob and the responsible environmental consumer, and the foreign body and the green citizen. Alongside all of these exists the figure of the environmental dissident: the activist, politician, or troublemaker, exemplified by Maathai, which shows that environmental governance remains vitally political. The green state in Africa is therefore an effect of the biopolitical governance of multiple heterogeneous populations that are deeply gendered, racialized, class-inscribed, and hierarchically defined. Whether by means of the production of game and forest stewards in South Africa, enlightened farmers in Ethiopia, female tree planters in Kenya, or environmental activists in Cameroon, the green state in Africa is being built through the constitution of the bodies and populations—that is, the life—of those within its ambits and the sometimes violent exclusion of forms of life that lie outside.

Chapter 5 contends that green growth is the currently dominant global discourse of green economic intervention and is working to legitimise a new era of big infrastructural modernisation projects in African agricultural and natural resource sectors. But it is also possible to see evidence of discourses of resilience, transformation, and even revolution, which all function to coproduce green state effects and green economies. South Africa's ongoing plans to introduce a carbon tax is an entry point to discuss how markets, commodities, and economies are the products of political action, the correlative of modern forms of government. While recent analysis of the green economy has tended to present it as a win–win consensus, here I disaggregate the concept into discourses of green revolution, green transformation, green growth, and green resilience, each of which is illustrated through a range of initiatives and programmes in various African countries. Ethiopia, Rwanda, South Africa, and Tanzania all have prominent green economy strategies, many of which involve mobilising large infrastructure investment projects—dams, commercial agriculture, mining, and power plants—under the legitimising discourse of green growth. The creation of markets in carbon credits and ecosystem services, the deployment of "green mining" programmes, and the stimulation of economies through agricultural investment and employment programmes are crucial ways in which state institutions are seeking to relegitimate interventions into local, national, and global economies alongside private capital. Yet more revolutionary forms of state intervention in the economy also exist, such as Zimbabwe's Fast Track Land Reform process. As more internationally acceptable programmes of green growth and green transformation fail to achieve widespread poverty reduction and social justice, the public enthusiasm for more radical interventions is likely to grow. Like the governance of territory and populations, the intensification of green state effects in economic governance is shown to have a range of political consequences both potentially progressive and politically dangerous.

In chapter 6 I describe how international and transnational practices and discourses of cooperation and conflict—such as practices and discourses of diplomacy, nation branding, competitiveness indexing, development aid, and security—work to produce exemplary leaders and inspirational examples, on the one hand, alongside environmental laggards and pollution enclaves on the other. This produces a fundamentally lumpy, heterogeneous topography for green states in Africa, in contrast to images of a smooth, globalising, homogenous international. There is potential for this unevenness to be mitigated through projects of transnational environmental solidarity, but such practices are also constitutive of African green state effects. The central point, however, is that international politics is crucial to explaining African environmental politics and the production of Africa's green states in all their similarity and variety. Two central examples are used to illustrate this argument: South African climate and conservation leadership alongside activist hot spots in South Durban, and the so-called pollution enclave of the Niger Delta, which has also produced particular transnational environmental linkages. Although far from secure or robust, and not without their own dangers, these examples of emerging transnational environmental solidarity could provide a powerful vision of a postcolonial political project for Pan-Africanism in the twenty-first century.

The final chapter emphasises the argument that the green state in Africa is not the next stage in a modernisation project or the successor to liberal or welfare states but the effect of an assemblage of environmental rationalities, discourses, and technologies of government through which the governance of territories, populations, economies, and international relations have been brought within the scope of sedimented power relations. All states in Africa—and indeed all states everywhere—can be thought of as green states in these terms. But Afro-ecologism is more centrally concerned with the politics of land and conservation; the biopolitics of rural under- and overpopulation; natural resource extraction and rapid, muscular green growth and modernisation; and discourses and practices of African solidarity and Pan-African unity.

In the African cases studied here, green states mobilise relatively exclusive or hybrid practices of territorialisation; produce populations as uneducated, overconsuming, or foreign; invoke discourses of economic resilience, growth, transformation, or revolution; and produce green leaders and inspirational examples together with environmental laggards and pollution enclaves. This framework constitutes a powerful analytical grid for identifying and contrasting Africa's green state effects and thereby highlights the twin dynamics at the heart of this book's argument: that environmental governance and contestation are central to the production of state effects, and that state assemblages are central to environmental politics in Africa. Moreover, this framework is appropriate for the study of developing states well beyond Africa, enabling the empirical study of environmental politics in a more genuinely global manner than has been possible to date.

A CRITICAL INTERNATIONAL POLITICS OF AFRICAN ENVIRONMENTS

This book offers a critical assessment of the relationship between state formation and environmental governance and seeks to show some familiar things in a different light and some unfamiliar things more brightly than usual. Those looking for rigorously tested solutions may be disappointed, although many sections of the book discuss the pros and cons of various policy initiatives and programmes. The primary aim of the book is broader and deeper, though, and it is a response to the challenge set for critical approaches to African politics.[22] Critical approaches do not accept conventional framings of the problem or commonplace assertions of what "we" must do to solve "their" problems. Critical approaches require metatheoretical reflection upon the nature of the data and the role of the observer and a commitment to tackling big picture questions which refuse the usual boundaries between disciplines and fields. Critical approaches should be political and draw attention

2. "Winter in Tembisa," Santu Mofokeng (b. 1956). © Santu Mofokeng, 1991 silverprint edition 5. Images courtesy Lunetta Bartz, MAKER, Johannesburg.

to conflicts and contradictions, and theorists should engage in questions, issues, and problems because they care and because the answers matter. For this reason, the final note to be struck in this introduction is to reassert the irreducibly political character of African environmental politics. It is not right to shut down debate and critical enquiry by saying these issues are too important and urgent to permit theoretical reflection. It is not right to demand consensus and claim in the face of ecological insecurity that "we're all in this together." It is not right to say that such issues should be left to the technical experts, the invisible hand of the market, or the national plebiscite.

Rather, the struggle for a future which is more just, secure, and sustainable is exactly that: a struggle. I attempt to clarify and illuminate some of the power relations and dynamics of that struggle, and a number of potential political and normative implications emerge from the argument. There is a pressing need to marshal political resources and struggles in support of African attempts to build green states through practices of hybrid territorialisations; the production of dissenting environmental citizens; discourses of green transformation and revolutionary economic interventions; and relations of transnational environmental solidarity.

Ultimately, however, the struggle for the future takes place between people, ideas, and social forces. The types of green state produced and transformed in Africa, like those anywhere else, will depend on the individuals, discourses, and movements which contest them. It is a struggle with a great deal at stake: our relations with each other, relations between rich and poor, male and female, black and white, and our relations with the other species that inhabit our planet. It is a struggle, however, in which we can learn from past campaigns and from African examples. This book contains powerful examples of inspirational individuals such as Ken Saro-Wiwa, Nnimmo Bassey, Kumi Naidoo, Wangari Maathai, Phyllis Omido, and Des D'Sa. None of these individuals are perfect or should be uncritically lionised, and I am not advocating a form of politics based around hero-worship or "celebritisation."[23] On the other hand, the stories we tell are important, and stories involve actors and characters who can inspire, frustrate, and mobilise. Africa has many stories to contribute to the global struggle for more just and sustainable patterns of development. In April 2014 Archbishop Desmond Tutu drew an explicit link between the inspiration of the "South African miracle" in overturning apartheid and the struggle against environmental degradation. He called upon "people of conscience . . . to break their ties with corporations financing the injustice of climate change," proclaiming that "we need an apartheid-style boycott to save the planet."[24] The South African story of conflict and reconciliation, however partial, problematic, and contested it may be, is just one example of the many sites of resistance which can be mined to fuel the defining struggle of the twenty-first century against ecological injustice. If nothing else, this book aims to convince that there are sites of resistance everywhere and that resistance is fertile.[25]

CHAPTER I

Global Environmental Governance and the Green State

I have come to tell you that the modern man who feels a need to reconcile himself with nature has a lot to learn from the African man who has lived in harmony with nature for millennia.

—Nicholas Sarkozy, "Address at the University of Cheikh Anta Diop"

We did that often, asking each other questions whose answers we already knew. Perhaps it was so that we would not ask the other questions, the ones whose answers we did not want to know.

—Chimamanda Ngozi Adichie, *Purple Hibiscus*

Whose questions count, and whose answers have authority? Before we can begin to explore Africa's green states, we must reflect both upon the positions from which questions are asked and answers delivered and upon the interlocutors with whom the conversation is conducted. Knowledge production is not neutral or objective, and as my intent in this book is to theorise environmental politics in Africa, it is important to acknowledge at the outset Robert Cox's well-known dictum that "theory is always *for* someone and *for* some purpose."[1] In order to clarify and explain the relationship between African states and environmental politics, it is necessary to facilitate a critical, radical, progressive, postcolonial, and political analysis of how the African state has been produced and transformed through the governance and contestation of environmental issues. In terms of subject-position, I am a white, male, British academic situated within a long tradition of other academics (often white, male, and British too) writing about African politics, and yet I hope the arguments offered here provide some tools for questioning and destabilising some of these entrenched power relations of race, gender, nationality, and class. This chapter locates the approach of the book within the context of the existing literature on states and global environmental politics, while remaining cognisant of the fact that this literature is written by people occupying particular institutional and societal positions.[2]

As a point of departure, consider one of the defining framings of global environmental governance and the African state. One of the institutional gatekeepers of IR, Robert Keohane, asks us to "imagine two maps of the world. One displays the relative severity of environmental problems—air pollution, soil and water degradation, desertification, destruction of habitat—and therefore of biodiversity. The other map shows the capabilities that governments have to cope with these problems: the material resources at their disposal, the level of education of their people, the competence and honesty of their governments. Juxtaposing these maps would graphically reveal that environmental problems are most serious in those parts of the world with least capacity to deal autonomously with them."[3] This quote opens an introductory chapter in a book on environmental institutions and vividly illustrates the widely prevalent argument that countries in Africa and elsewhere in the developing world lack effective institutions to deal with their manifold environmental problems. Rich countries should realise that "preaching to poor countries will not solve the problem" and must develop "financial transfer institutions for the environment" to help build state capacity in Africa and elsewhere.[4]

Building state capacity is the predominant theme of much literature within global environmental governance when it comes to the developing world. It is the question whose answer we already know. It was also the answer advanced by then-President Nicholas Sarkozy of France during an official visit he made to Senegal in 2007. In this now infamous speech Sarkozy presented a view of Africa as characterised by tradition and in harmony with nature, existing outside History understood in Hegelian terms as the grand sweep of historical progress. While patronising, ill-considered, and borderline racist, it is a peculiarly backhanded compliment from an environmental point of view, as he seems to be suggesting that Africa possesses something the West has lost and that many seek to regain. Yet he concluded by asking whether Africans wanted the state to "fulfil its responsibilities," to "be liberated from parasitism and clientism," and whether "the rule of law should govern everywhere." If so, he argued, then "France will be at your side."[5] In this vein, the success of authoritarian regimes in countries like Ethiopia and Rwanda in delivering on tangible development goals and reducing extreme poverty led many in international development to praise "effective states," "developmental patrimonialism," and strong "developmental states."[6] The fear that Islamic insurgents are gaining ground in Africa has prompted extensive Western spending on state building and security on the continent since 2001, and the global financial crisis that began in 2008 has also powerfully relegitimated the central role of states in regulating and intervening in the economy to prevent financial collapse. Many regard the construction of more effective green states as essential to addressing global environmental crises, in particular climate change.[7]

For these reasons, among others, this book takes the concept of the green state as its focus. The analysis begins by examining the role of the state within the field of global environmental politics. It is a theoretical discussion which sets out the conceptual terrain and vocabulary for the alternative theorisation of the state that follows in chapter 2 and the more empirically oriented analysis in chapters 3 to 6. Yet starting with the state is not unproblematic, and many critical theorists have articulated compelling critiques of the assumptions and implications of the sorts of arguments presented by powerful individuals such as Keohane and Sarkozy. In Crawford Young's memorable metaphor, the colonial state in Africa came to be known as *bula matari,* "he who crushes rocks," vividly capturing both the dominating masculine power of an alien hegemon as well as the nakedly antiecological character of the state as an institution.[8] Over the past three decades the lure of the state has also been challenged by transnational networks, sub- and supranational institutions, private actors, and civil society groups. Therefore I start here by looking at the various manifestations of what could be loosely termed antistatist perspectives before explaining why the state remains a central conceptual anchor for critical approaches to global environmental governance. The next step is to consider why so little attention has so far been focused on the role of African states within global environmental politics, and why this is a mistake. However, rather than simply make the case for Africa taking its place within modernisation narratives—heeding Sarkozy's "call to reason and to the universal conscience"—the chapter ends by insisting that an alternative conception of the state is needed to address the relationship between the production and transformation of African states and the governance and contestation of African environments.[9]

ANTISTATIST PERSPECTIVES IN GLOBAL ENVIRONMENTAL POLITICS

For many of those thinking about, participating in, and writing about global environmental politics—of all hues, from the dark greens of the deep ecologists, bioregionalists, and ecoanarchists to the light greens, browns, and reds of many political ecologists, eco-Marxists, and environmental justice activists—the state is a troubling, anachronistic, and sometimes downright dangerous institution. A frequent complaint is that it is too small to solve the big problems and too big to solve the small problems.[10] Others, critical of the neo-Weberian account of the rise of the modern, autonomous, bureaucratic state, claim that states are too administrative, too rationalist, too bureaucratic, too coercive. Those who reject the neo-Weberian story in favour of a more structuralist account regard the state as the instrument of capitalist, patriarchal, and anthropocentric interests. If the state is at the heart of modern, Enlightenment narratives of progress and politics—and if it is these very narratives that have directly led to or at least contributed to the environmental crisis—it makes little sense to hope that green(er) states will be capable of making an effective response.

Of course, not everyone means the same thing when they refer to the state. One important distinction is between those who use the term "state" to refer to the administrative structure of government and those who invoke the concept of the nation-state in the sense of a sovereign unit of international politics. In the first usage, a country like Tanzania has a police force, tax collectors, a parliament, etc., which together comprise a state distinct from the rest of Tanzanian society, whereas in the second sense Tanzania is itself a state which has identity and agency within international society. In this book I am primarily interested in how other academics and activists imagine and represent the state and what political and environmental implications these representations have, but when I refer to the African state or the green state in more abstract terms I mean to encompass both domestic institutions and international cooperation and conflict as practices which constitute the state (see chapter 2).

The following sections consider various manifestations of what could be termed antistatist perspectives, including critiques of the state in both its narrower governmental aspect and as a broader sovereign entity. Deep green ecologists have pointed out the lack of fit between the fluid geographies of environmental issues (organised around watersheds, air and water currents, climatic zones, and even the biosphere itself) and the static, bounded geographies of the nation-state. Anti-instrumentalist perspectives have tended to associate the modern state with some of the worst excesses of the Enlightenment: the "iron cage" of bureaucratisation, instrumental ethics, and rationalisation. For many political ecologists or eco-Marxists the state is nothing more than the dictatorship of a greedy and environmentally destructive bourgeoisie locked into the treadmill of production or the contradictions of capitalism. Finally, an awareness of apparently ever-greater globalisation since at least the 1990s has led many to maintain that the sovereignty, authority, and legitimacy of the state have dwindled or been actively eroded by neoliberal reforms to a point where the nation-state no longer has the capacity to protect citizens against environmental harms.

The Green Ecologist Critique

Many ecological theorists—particularly the deep greens, who see an intrinsic and almost spiritual value in pristine nature, but also the bioregionalists, conservationists, and environmental scientists, who have a deep respect for nature's form and laws—regard the state as a profoundly *unnatural* construction. As a bureaucracy, the state seems to stand profoundly at odds with the fluidity, fecundity, and creativity of nature. Although the state is regrettably necessary, at least in the establishment of order and the maintenance of security in farms and cities, many of these ecologists and naturalists would prefer not to see its trappings—roads, buildings, power lines, pollution, military training facilities, border fences—in the pristine wild. Even where it plays a potentially important role in the creation and maintenance of protected areas and national parks, such self-restraint is seen as an imperfect and unfortunately necessary act on behalf of the state and the developmental imperative it embodies.[11]

This perspective is rooted in a stark distinction between the sociopolitical and the natural. Ontologically opposed, these categories nevertheless overlap and interpenetrate. The fluid boundaries of watersheds, river systems, floodplains, air currents, climatic zones, biodiversity regions, habitats, and so on cut across the imposed boundaries of nation-states, administrative areas, municipalities and regions, and areas of human habitation.[12] On the grandest scale, such as when viewed from space, the biosphere gives our small, fragile planet a unity that contrasts markedly with the divisions among nation-states. "The earth is one, but the world is not," as the report of the World Commission on Environment and Development (known as the Brundtland Report) asserted in 1987.[13] Thus the basic form and character of the state are an affront to the fluidity and fecundity of nature, and the imperative of the state to control and accumulate has ridden roughshod over older, more natural forms of the wild. Mick Smith, in an influential engagement with and critique of the green state literature, is fundamentally concerned with "the biopolitical dangers to ecology and politics that sovereignty itself represents," and he demands that we refuse to turn nature into an object of governance.[14] The imprints of such ideas can be seen even in authors who would not usually be described as deep ecologists, such as Peter Haas, who writes that "strong centralised institutions are fundamentally unecological," and Oran Young, who warns, "Some institutions are hollow shells exploited by authoritarian leaders to mask oppressive and destructive practices carried out in the name of the state."[15]

There is not the space here to provide a detailed genealogical analysis of green thought and its antipathy to the state. This antipathy certainly was a central element of the North American frontier mentality and the wilderness ethic of environmentalists like John Muir and Aldo Leopold as well as of the valorisation of Nature and the sublime in the English romantic poets. In its more contemporary form, however, it may well be, at least in part, a backlash against the authoritarian statist politics of prominent environmentalists from the 1970s like William Ophuls, Robert Heilbroner, and Garrett Hardin. The neo-Malthusian concerns of these authors—emphasising the perils of unchecked population growth, rampant resource use, the tragedy of the commons, and the need for "lifeboat ethics"—led them to call for a strong state authority willing to enforce environmentally austere policies. The rejection of ecofascist politics and the strong democratic character of contemporary environmental discourses have produced an ecological attitude in which, for some, even green parties have become somewhat suspect due to their close association with the state and formal political processes and institutions.[16]

The Anti-Instrumentalist Critique

Elements of this ecological critique have been taken up and combined with a broader philosophical scepticism towards modernity and the Enlightenment project to produce an anti-instrumentalist critique of the state. Most evident in the seminal work of the Frankfurt School of Critical Theory and recent incarnations by writers such as Ulrich Beck, this perspective has evinced a damning attitude towards the state's "iron cage of rationality."[17] The rationalism, efficiency, and cold logic of Enlightenment science threaten to lead, in the view of these critiques, to a value system in which life is weighed, calculated, and valued instrumentally rather than inherently. For Adorno and Horkheimer, "The fully enlightened Earth radiates disaster triumphant."[18] This warning was foreseen by Max Weber and seemed for many to be borne out in the mid-twentieth century in the horrors of total war, civilian bombardment, the atrocities of the concentration camp, and colonial enslavement and brutality.

That states were both the emblems and agents of this instrumental attitude seemed painfully obvious during the struggles between liberalism and totalitarianism. Modern European states were born in war and designed for warfare, and the most well-known component of the Weberian definition of the state was its monopoly on the legitimate deployment of violence. Charles Tilly argued that war making and state making are "quintessential protection rackets with the advantage of legitimacy" and are "our largest examples of organised crime."[19] The strong pacifist and Quaker currents within modern environmentalism, the sympathies with feminist and civil rights movements, and the links to contemporary struggles against nuclear weapons and the Vietnam War meant that an antistatist stance was a comfortable one for the environmental movement. It was a reaction against the way in which the state has become "the hegemonic concept for ordering the modern world."[20] One of the most articulate environmental critiques of the state was put forward by Murray Bookchin, who saw the state as an institutionalised system of coercion, and the only hope for human survival was to end the reign of the state.[21]

Such a fear seemed borne out by the ability of modern science in the second half of the twentieth century—supported, funded, and directed by states, often in times of war—to produce nuclear power, weaponry, advanced chemical compounds and industrial processes, to geo-engineer vast swathes of land and water, and even to map and modify the genetic building blocks of life itself. Such developments are described by Arturo Escobar as a period of "unprecedented gluttony in the history of vision and knowledge."[22] While state science's potential to advance standards of living, forms of travel, life expectancy, diets, and so on is acknowledged, so is their dark side. Names like Hiroshima and Nagasaki, Chernobyl and Three Mile Island, Bhopal and Baikal, the Exxon Valdez, Torrey Canyon, and Deepwater Horizon resonate through the environmental movement. Many environmentalists, whether inside or outside the academy, therefore regard the modern administrative state as being deeply bound up within the Enlightenment project and its accompanying dangers. As Ken Conca frames it, modern states "[have] been a key social innovation along the road to planetary environmental peril."[23] In his conclusion to a volume on sustainability governance, Tim O'Riordan reflects the sentiments of many environmentalists suspicious of the modern state when he writes that, in terms of designing pathways to sustainability, "the real virtue may be anarchic. It may lie in the hearts, minds and spirits of citizens, beyond government and maybe even governance."[24]

The Political Ecology Critique

Some of the most systematic and theoretically refined critiques of the modern state have been deployed from perspectives influenced by Marxist political economy. Drawing on accounts of the exploitation and alienation of nature alongside labour, the critical political ecology literature has tended toward the notion of the state as a political superstructure reinforcing capitalist and patriarchal systems with crisis-tending environmental implications. Put bluntly, the Marxist tradition challenges the Weberian ideal of the state as an autonomous entity, distinct from the rest of society. In the famous formulation of the Communist Manifesto, "The executive of the modern state is but a committee for managing the affairs of the whole bourgeoisie."[25] Although there have been heated debates within Marxist theory over the nature of the relationship between the state and society in modern capitalism (such as in the 1970s between the instrumentalist position of Ralph Miliband and the structuralist stance of Nicos Poulantzas), Marxist theory has tended to see the state as acting in the interests of the capitalist class, either directly, when captured by the bourgeoisie, or indirectly through the very structural form and character of the state itself. This close relationship between the state and society is encapsulated in Antonio Gramsci's striking formulation: "The state = political society + civil society."[26] The concept of hegemony denotes the degree to which the state acts to buttress capitalism as a social system; its flip side is the coercive force the state is willing to unleash when capitalist interests are directly threatened, for example, through attacks on private property. Internationally, the dominance of the United States and the degree of alignment between the American state and capital have prompted many to regard American hegemony as a form of statist, capitalist imperialism that has potentially disastrous consequences for the global environment.[27]

The eco-Marxist, political ecology critique of the state is thus rooted in a critique of capitalism. This has been most clearly articulated in James

O'Connor's account of the "second contradiction of capitalism," whereby capitalist accumulation produces environmental degradation as well as social dislocation and exploitation, which undermine the conditions of production.[28] The role of modern states in driving large developmental and industrial projects like mega-dams, provision of roads and airports, the support of financial markets which channel vast flows of trade and investment and pay little regard to social and environmental consequences, and the trampling or suppression of indigenous or social movement or trade union resistance is thus characteristic of their antienvironmental character. Matthew Paterson argues that "states should be seen as themselves part of a globalising capitalist dynamic, which is fundamentally ecologically problematic" and that new forms of environmental governance have been increasingly employed to channel capitalism in new and more profitable directions rather than to resolve these fundamental contradictions.[29] Stewart Davidson adds, "Put simply, the fiscal capacity and thereby legitimacy of the state is dependent upon a level of economic growth incompatible with ecological sustainability."[30]

These three lines of critique of the state—deep green, anti-instrumental, and eco-Marxist—all reveal close interlinkages as well as parallel and overlapping themes. Many of them draw upon the critiques of liberalism developed within feminist thought, in particular the separation of the public from the private and the placing of such issues as the family, religion, consumption, and lifestyle beyond the scope of the political.[31] Furthermore, many of these perspectives look to social movements, indigenous peoples, and grassroots environmentalists—what Doherty and Doyle term "emancipatory environmental movements"—rather than to institutions like the state and international organisations as sources of progressive green politics.[32] Paterson's caustic conclusion in 2000 was that "the state is not only unnecessary from a green point of view, it is positively undesirable. . . . [T]he dominant political prescription within green politics is for a great deal of decentralisation of power to communities much smaller in scale than nation states."[33]

The Neoliberal or Globalist Critique

These critical perspectives on the role of the state in global environmental governance come from a direction very different from that of the most widely known ideological attacks on the state in recent years: neoliberal advocates of the free market and the so-called Washington Consensus. The demand to roll back the welfare state was led by ardent antistatists from the Chicago School and political leaders like Margaret Thatcher and Ronald Reagan and was then taken up in a modified form under third way centrists like Tony Blair and Bill Clinton. Whether the state was actively emasculated—for example, in the slashing of environmental budgets in many countries, both developing and developed—or refashioned as a provider of targets, oversight, and essential services—which saw the government providing the targets or goals and encouraged citizen action or consumer choice on all manner of social and environmental issues—these reformers stressed the benefits of global markets and unfettered innovation. Simply put, however, for ardent theorists of neoliberal globalisation the state is no longer, if it ever was, an effective, efficient, or productive actor, and most problems are better solved through market mechanisms in which rational interest-maximising individuals trade clearly and freely priced goods.[34]

Some theorists of globalisation were critical of the spread of neoliberal markets and others welcomed them enthusiastically, but what these competing viewpoints tended to share was a view that the growing power of transnational corporations and footloose capital plus the speed and flexibility of global communications were eroding the power of the nation-state. For Beck, "The global operation of the economy is sapping the foundations of national economies and national states," and the welfare state is being "swept away" by globalisation.[35] Susan Strange wrote, "State authority has leaked away, upwards, sideways, and downwards," meaning that, while not exactly obsolete, states were "increasingly becoming hollow, or defective, institutions."[36] States appeared as anachronistic dinosaurs, withering away and either in decline or in crisis as capital, trade, knowledge, and even citizens traversed their borders with increasing ease and impunity. As global actors like international investment banks, multinational corporations, and major nongovernmental organisations (NGOs), aided and abetted by state-based organisations such as the World Trade Organisation and international investment law, squeezed the state off the top spot from above, states were pressured from below by citizens' groups, local NGOs, community movements, and subnational governments.[37]

In the arena of environmental politics, the simultaneous growth of such bodies as the Global Environmental Facility, UN agencies, the IPCC, and the increasing proliferation of international environmental law, together with the rise of local movements and bodies like the Local Agenda 21 movements, environmental NGOs, citizens' groups, private companies involved in corporate social and environmental responsibility partnerships and the importance of local governments in designing and implementing environmental regulations, meant that the state's central role in environmental protection seemed to be waning. The widespread environmental slogan Think Global, Act Local offered little sign of where the nation-state was to fit into this new age of environmental activism.[38]

More recent and arguably more sophisticated analyses of the character and role of states in an era of globalisation have denied the implied zero-sum and linear power relationship between states and private actors. Rather, they point to the important role of nation-states as agents of globalisation, for example, in accelerating free trade, economic integration, the spread of knowledge and technology, often invoking the metaphor of steering, not rowing. As Ian Clark writes, "Globalisation needs also to be understood as a number of changes within the state, and not simply as a set of external forces set against it."[39] Drawing on the increasingly nuanced literature on environmental governance, Adger and Jordan suggest that if governing refers to those activities which seek to "guide, steer, control or manage," then governance is the pattern that emerges from a wide range of actors who engage in governing, including, but not limited to, states.[40] This notion is echoed by Susan Baker, who points out that "the state still remains the primary actor in global environmental governance, even if it now plays that role in close collaboration with other actors."[41]

Despite this increasing sophistication and the awareness of the mutually constitutive relationship between states and globalisation, it is widely argued that the old sovereign nation-state is an inappropriate central category for political analysis. Thus it was possible for Mark Berger to assume at the outset of a book review essay that "we are in the midst of a crisis of the nation-state system as a whole and, thus, of the vast majority of its constituent polities."[42] To the editors of an influential reader on the state, "The state's role as 'power container' appears to have been perforated; it seems to be leaking, and thus the inherited model of territorially self-enclosed, state-defined societies, economies or cultures is becoming highly problematic."[43]

These diverse globalist perspectives as well as the deep green, anti-instrumentalist, and eco-Marxist critiques all rest upon certain conceptual images of what the state actually is. In all of them the state is seen as more of a threat to environmental protection than a source of it: whether it is a social construction cast as antithetical to and destructive of natural environments; or as an embodiment of the Enlightenment project of control and instrumental rationality which ends in the concentration camp and the nuclear bomb;

or as the tool of capitalist hegemony and the driver of an accumulation urge which inevitably leads to environmental degradation; or as a dwindling, weakened, and increasingly ineffective relic of a preglobalised age. In fact, in all of these portrayals the state stands as a proxy for or an embodiment of something else. To the green ecologist the state represents the social as opposed to the natural; to anti-instrumentalists it is an embodiment of the Enlightenment project of rationalisation; to political ecologists it is the organised expression of bourgeois class interests; and to the globalists it stands for Fordist ideals of control and regulation, contrasted to postmodern or globalist visions of flexibility in an increasingly borderless world. As such, they are somewhat at odds with Weber's classic approach to the state as a bureaucratic organisation standing apart from social institutions. It is this Weberian conception of the state which dominates the increasingly widespread literature on green states and ecological modernisation and which is the most influential response to these antistatist perspectives.

GREEN STATES AND ECOLOGICAL MODERNISERS

The concept of the green state in the fields of global environmental politics and international relations (IR) has arisen partly in response to these cogent appraisals of statism. Indeed, it is noticeable that the disciplines of political science and IR—those traditionally focused on the sovereign, autonomous state as a core conceptual category—are most amenable to the idea of a green state.[44] Yet the green state literature has drawn upon debates within other disciplines, such as philosophy, economics, sociology, the natural sciences, and technology studies. Some authors seem to have reevaluated their earlier stance on the dangers of state-based governance given the urgency of the climate crisis, while others see climate change as a new site of struggle between leviathan and behemoth.[45] One of the key arguments of this chapter—and indeed of this book—is that the growing literature on green states is entirely right to focus attention on the continued importance of the state within global environmental politics.

The literature on green states has tended to follow one of two paths: states as they might be or states as they are. The division between normative and empirical research is never clear-cut or definitive, but these two fields have pursued different research questions. The normative group have tended to ask, What should a green state look like? whereas more empirical researchers have explored questions related to why, and with what effects, have states implemented green policies and created environmental institutions? The theory of ecological modernisation has been influential in both normative and empirical research agendas and has provided a wider theoretical framework within which the concept of the green state has so far been located.

Green States: The Normative Dimension

The most important normative theorist of the green state is Robyn Eckersley. Her work essentially argues that the state is one of the institutions best able to work towards ideals of justice, equality, order, legitimacy, and accountability in modern politics. Moreover, she imagines a democratic state able to institutionalise substantive and procedural green norms: respect for future generations; respect for environmental limits; respect for nonhuman nature. In fact, she contends that "there are still few social institutions that can match the same degree of capacity and potential legitimacy that states have to redirect societies and economies along more ecologically sustainable lines."[46] She claims not that green states are an actually existing phenomenon but that green political theory opens a way to imagine what a green, democratic state might look like. She also insists that progress towards environmental goals will be unlikely unless we are able to reform existing state institutions in the direction of green states, and she has reflected that multilateral (or *minilateral*) fora might enable state-based international climate negotiations to move forward more effectively.[47]

Eckersley's version of green political thought is ostensibly postliberal and responds to many of the arguments posed by deep greens, anti-instrumentalists, and eco-Marxists. Rather than seeing their attacks as directed against the state per se, however, she suggests they are really directed at the liberal state. A truly democratic green state, according to Eckersley, would require moving beyond many of liberalism's core principles: its anthropocentrism, the public / private division, and the separation of nature and society. Eckersley thinks green political theory demands "the politicisation of the private good as well as the re-politicisation of the public good."[48] The radicalism of her proposals becomes clear when she writes that the "opportunity to participate or *otherwise be represented in* the making of risk-generating decisions should literally be extended to *all* those potentially affected, regardless of social class, geographic location, nationality, generation, or species."[49] Eckersley's conception of the state thus differs considerably from those encapsulated above. Rather than seeing the state as the embodiment or expression of underlying interests or social drives, Eckersley sees it as inherently political and capable of far greater autonomy and agency, including the potential to transcend some of the most ecologically damaging features of private capital accumulation.[50] In the ideal world of political theory, she envisages a state able to act to advance certain environmental values and provide a protected space for democratic practices.

Such a conception has been taken up by many others who also see environmental reforms most likely arriving through democratic, radical, environmentally responsible, or scientifically enlightened states.[51] One influential defence of such a proposition comes from two theorists, Newell and Paterson, previously associated with critical perspectives on the state. Starting by noting the seriousness of the climate challenge, they call for enlisting the power of financial markets to challenge extractive fossil fuel sectors. Crucially, they demand heavily regulated markets in environmental services (such as carbon credits), regulation that includes "ensuring states" but goes beyond formal institutions to include civil and activist groups.[52] Ultimately, however, they propose a form of "climate Keynesianism" involving a "New Marshall Plan" for the climate and the South and "A Green New Deal."[53] They are far more prosaic than President Sarkozy in his continental paean to the state as the embodiment of European civilisation, but there is a shared intellectual family tree in which Eckersley, Newell and Paterson, and Sarkozy all follow divergent branches but nevertheless trace their roots to the Hegelian view of the state as "the ultimate attainment of the human spirit."[54]

Green States: The Empirical Dimension

A more empirical strand of research into green states also exists, one which does not so explicitly defend an ideal environmental state but instead seeks to categorise and explain the various types of environmental policies and institutions states have introduced. Much work here has converged on the notion that environmental states are ones in which the governance of environmental issues has become central and is closely linked to core imperatives of survival, maintenance of domestic order, generation of finance, capital accumulation, and political legitimation. Some researchers propose typologies of green states, using criteria ranging from radical to reformist and light green to dark green. A variety of features are regarded as evidence of "state greening," including some explicit recognition of environmental limits, entrenching the polluter pays and the precautionary principle, explicit concern with the inheritance of future generations and the concept of global public goods and the global commons, participatory environmental policies, and the provision of environmental information.[55] In a study of thirty countries' environmental reforms, Helmut Weidner seeks evidence of broader public knowledge of and commitment to environmental values, interdepartmental / ministerial coordination, an "innovative environmental business sector," and "highly visible damage for which feasible solutions are available."[56]

The crucial task of such research is explaining why some states enact these reforms and others do not. Three levels of explanation can be identified from the outset. First, most work within the green state literature emphasises domestic factors such as regime type and social movement pressure. Most notable here is a body of work largely associated with John Dryzek and a range of collaborators. Focusing on case studies in Europe and North America, they have maintained that so-called green states are most likely to emerge in countries where there is "an emerging connection of environmental values to both economic and legitimation imperatives," contingent on the presence of "an active oppositional public sphere."[57] They propose a typology of states as "either *exclusive* or *inclusive* towards social interests" and "either *passive* or *active* in their orientation to who gets represented," and they stress the importance of domestic social movements in pushing states to internalise environmental imperatives.[58]

A second level of theoretical explanation—one most sceptical toward the emergence of green states in practice—comes from the realist tradition of international relations scholarship. The starting point here is the timeless truth of sovereign state rivalry in an anarchic international system. Principles of self-help, great power rivalry, security dilemmas, and balancing ensure the centrality of states to international politics. Thus environmental issues are likely to attract serious state attention only when they become linked to security agendas. Fear of water wars, climate chaos, peak oil, and food insecurity have all led to environmental issues being prioritised by some states at some stages and have manifested in high-level debates at the UN Security Council. The title of Tony Brenton's book, *Greening Machiavelli,* nicely encapsulates this perspective, and as an ex-diplomat he is categorical that the "centres of decision remain in national capitals."[59] For other realists, however, environmental issues are likely to remain softer political topics, always at risk of displacement from the international agenda by harder questions of national interest. Thus to realists the sovereign nature of statehood in an anarchic international system militates against the likelihood that environmental problems—the degradation of the shared commons—will be resolved.

A third explanation for the greening of states is offered by liberal and institutionalist IR theorists, for whom state sovereignty implies the capacity of states to enter into negotiations and devise institutions that can mitigate international action and produce common action on questions like global and transnational environmental degradation. Thus writers like Young have charted the ever-expanding range of international regimes associated with environmental protection, drawing in ever-larger numbers of states in more comprehensive webs of international norms and institutions.[60] According to Edith Weiss, from the early 1970s to the early 1990s the international community produced nearly nine hundred international legal instruments either directed primarily toward or containing important environmental provisions.[61] Weidner's study observes that "environmental policy is being globalised in political response to challenges of economic globalisation."[62] This evolving web of global environmental governance has lent credence to claims that some states can be regarded as ecological modernisers. Keohane writes that "[we] should not be satisfied to show how political constraints make effective action difficult, but should also point where and how it is possible for dedicated people and well-structured organisations to make a difference."[63]

These three levels of explanation—domestic social movements, security in international anarchy, and international institutions—are all grounded in a Weberian or neo-Weberian tradition which views the state as an autonomous entity characterised by its institutional and organisational form. In this they fundamentally disagree with the antistatists with which this chapter opened, all of whom interpret the state as fundamentally representing *something else.* The Weberian tradition of state theory is encapsulated by Michael Mann's classic article which defined states as "[1] A *differentiated* set of institutions and personnel embodying; [2] *centrality* in the sense that political relations radiate outwards from a centre to cover; [3] a *territorially demarcated area,* over which it exercises; [4] a monopoly of *authoritative binding rule-making,* backed up by a monopoly of the means of physical violence."[64] This Weberian tradition comprises an intellectual framework for conceptualising state transformation and for identifying new forms of state. The most familiar examples of transformation arise from the blurring or interpenetration of territorial borders, such as within the European Union (EU) and regional economic blocs, and the fracturing of the monopoly on legitimate means of violence as seen in the proliferation of international peacekeeping missions and private security contracts. Most literature on green states builds upon this tradition, alongside arguments about emerging "competition states," "transnational states," "globalised states," "spatially promiscuous states," "the global state," "governance states," and other transformations of statehood in contemporary global politics.[65]

Ecological Modernisation: State and Society

The transformation of the Weberian state can therefore be situated within a broader theoretical framework of ecological modernisation. This perspective implies that the ecological problems to which modernity has given rise, including pollution, resource use and degradation, health risks, and others, can be solved by *more modernity,* reflexive modernity, rather than by a reaction against modernity. Thus the modern state, along with modern science, technology, advanced capitalist markets, and an engaged citizenry, can all function as part of the solution to environmental problems. Indeed, "ecological modernisation processes are a reflection of policy environments that are made possible through the restructuring (or 'modernisation') of the state."[66]

Beyond this common core, ecological modernisation implies very different things to theorists. Buttel, for example, identifies four strands of the ecological modernisation framework: a sociological account of modernisation and societal development; a discursive label for policies of environmental reform; a synonym for strategies of industrial or technological management and development; and references to almost any environmental policy innovation or environmental improvement.[67] It is certainly true that under the common banner of ecological modernisation there are some radically variant images of the state and the state–society relationship.

Nicholas Ashford's portrayal of ecological modernisation identifies a rather sceptical attitude toward the state, at least in its command-and-control manifestations, and he holds that ecological modernisers have faith that reflexive, "enlightened industrial actors can succeed in advancing the material well-being of citizens, contribute to their nation's competitiveness, and can also contribute to the necessary scientific and technological changes (innovations) in products, processes, and services to adequately meet the environmental challenges."[68] Others stress the reflexive and steering role of green states within an ecological modernisation framework. Rosalind Warner, for example, argues that within ecological modernisation literature "state decision-making is less a driver than a coordinator of forces arising from within and outside of these societies."[69] Mol and Sonnenfeld focus on how the nature of the state is transforming thanks to processes of ecological modernisation in which "more decentralised, flexible and consensual styles of governance emerge, with less top-down, national command-and-control environmental regulation."[70] "Under conditions of globalisation," they maintain, "the 'environmental state' is changing its modes of operation."[71] All of these theorists share a central commitment to the principle that more modernisation rather than less is the solution to environmental problems, and the Weberian state in some form is a necessary driver or enframer of this process.

THE AFRICAN LACUNA

A notable omission from these debates about ecological modernisation and green states (both normative and empirically focused) is any sustained discussion of developing states, particularly in Africa. Indeed, a shared assumption seems to be that there is little of interest taking place in the developing world with regard to environmental governance and state transformation. Sometimes the largest and richest developing countries, such as China, Brazil, India, and South Africa, are discussed, but even here there is nothing like the wealth of literature focusing on Europe, for example. Eckersley typifies this lacuna, for while her conclusion recognises that "the most serious challenge to global sustainability" lies in the problems of poverty, underdevelopment, and historical injustice, she proposes that the EU is one of the best hopes for an evolving green transnational state and expresses the belief that as states become greener they will start to care more about environmental injustice and poverty.[72] No serious discussion of questions of development or the role of African states can be found in Eckersley's work or in the broader literature on ecological modernisation. Barry and Eckersley conclude their edited collection with the explicit claim that "most of the promising developments are emerging from the developed world."[73] Two key authors on ecological modernisation conclude that "developing countries in sub-Saharan Africa are barely touched by emerging global political institutions and agreements aiming at environmental reform."[74] To Arthur Mol, as to many others, "It is the western industrialised societies that are leading the way in creating, designing and governing global environmental institutions and in 'determining' environmental-induced transformations in all kinds of social practices and institutions."[75]

There are a number of reasons for this neglect of the African state by green state theorists. African countries tend to do rather badly on most indexes of environmental performance and governance, such as Yale's EPI or Columbia University's Environmental Sustainability Index. The top performers in most of these indexes are a set of usual suspects: Norway, Finland, and other Scandinavian countries, Germany, the Netherlands, Japan, and sometimes, on some indicators, Canada, Australia, the United Kingdom, and the United States. Even on the HPI, African countries score badly despite their lower ecological footprint due to lower life expectancies (see chapter 6).

Most theorists, however, have resisted defining green states in terms of objective measures of environmental performance and instead focus on the relative centrality of environmental (resource conservation) or ecological (respect for the inherent value of nature) imperatives within the state. These tend to be situated within a broader framework of ecological modernisation in which Africa, almost by definition, is defined as traditional, premodern, and backward. This was expressed most bluntly by Sarkozy: "The tragedy of Africa is that the African has not fully entered into History. The African peasant, who for thousands of years has lived according to the seasons, whose life ideal was to be in harmony with nature, only knew the eternal renewal of time, rhythmed [*sic*] by the endless repetition of the same gestures and the same words."[76] Modernisation theorists explicitly or implicitly highlight two mechanisms in explaining this African lack of progress. First is an assumption or assertion that African state structures are weak, failing, or underdeveloped; and, second, environmentalism is regarded as a postmaterialist concern unlikely to achieve much salience outside of more developed societies and economies.

Weak States

The weak state argument is borrowed from modernisation theory more broadly and places the African state much further behind the rest of the world on a linear path toward the modern, bureaucratic, Westphalian nation-state. The state in Africa was a colonial imposition only weakly embedded in local societies. The postcolonial nation-building project was beset with difficulties, ranging from the existence of competing domestic powers and authority, imposed and arbitrary borders, continued close economic and political ties with the former colonial power, Cold War support for predatory and neopatrimonial elites, and the emasculation of state structures through neoliberal structural adjustment programmes (SAPs). For Jonathan Joseph, as for many political theorists, African societies "lack stable bodies like the state," and the African state is commonly described as, among other things, parasitic, a shadow, vampiric, neopatrimonial.[77] As such, the African state is generally regarded as lacking in capacity, expertise, stable structures, the rule of law, and as altogether unsuitable for progression toward the post-Westphalian transnational environmental or ecological state.

This argument is assumed to hold true for most developing countries, since even the largest and richest—again, China, Brazil, India, South Africa—are seen as having a relatively weak capacity and expertise base to coordinate long-term, far-reaching environmental reforms, the scale of which many developed countries are only beginning to grapple with. Their role is to try to "copy and adapt" the best innovations from the developed world.[78] The situation is assumed to become even more self-evidently true, however, as one progresses down the scale of weak, fragile, failing, and collapsed states. Indeed, by definition a failing or collapsed state, such as Somalia, for example, does not have the resources or capacity, let alone the political structures or legitimacy, to implement environmental reforms. The assumption is therefore that so-called strong states have the capacity, if they wish, to introduce environmental reforms and that weak or failing states do not.

The notion that most African states are weak or failing and thus do not correspond to the Weberian ideal of a modern bureaucratic authority is one that lies behind a much broader marginalisation of African states within political science and IR. Peter Evans's offhand comment that "in some parts of the developing world, most dramatically Africa, real eclipses of the state, in the sense of full-blown institutional collapse, took place" is symptomatic of the way in which the continent is usually dismissed.[79] Mann writes, "Deeply troubled states in Africa seem to be fragmenting for premodern rather than postmodern reasons."[80] These contentious assertions about statehood underpin much of the lack of interest in green states in Africa.

Postmaterialist Environmentalism

The second argument advanced by theorists of ecological modernisation is that environmentalism is a postmaterialist concern and hence of less political salience in societies in which basic needs like personal security, employment, health care, food, water, and shelter remain unsatisfied. The process of ecological modernisation emphasises the emergence of new social movements in Western Europe and North America in the 1960s and 1970s to agitate for, among other things, gendered and sexual rights and freedoms, artistic expression and youth representation, peace and antiracism, environmental protection and nuclear disarmament. As economies grew and gained technical expertise these advanced states responded to environmental social movements' concerns by decoupling economic and social development from environmental degradation.[81]

Following the logic of this account, it is often assumed that developing countries lack modern environmental movements either because they have more pressing economic, social, and political problems or because their populations are regarded as too poor, uneducated, and downtrodden to campaign on environmental issues. Moreover, in the case of authoritarian states, the argument is often made that even if the population does have an interest in environmental reforms, they have no means to hold government accountable to those desires. Mol, for example, notes the weakness of civil society organisations and popular environmentalism in Africa.[82] The apparent solution is more development and more wealth creation, until the point that postmaterial values start to emerge among the population and environmentalism becomes a salient goal.

Some empirical evidence seems to support these claims. As noted above, African countries tend to perform poorly on environmental performance and governance indexes: South Africa and Nigeria, the continent's wealthiest states, are ranked 72 and 134, respectively, on the EPI for 2014.[83] A survey of attitudes toward climate change in Africa concluded that "African citizens' response to climate change is hampered by a fundamental shortage of relevant, useful information for African audiences."[84] Luke Patey's account of environmental regulation, monitoring, and enforcement in Sudan could apply to many cases across the continent: "Environmental impact assessments are often substandard, only conducted after operations have already begun, and shelved upon completion with little follow-up."[85]

Yet this picture underestimates the importance of environmental governance to the evolution and transformation of the state in Africa. The ecological modernisation argument has limited purchase and utility in Africa, and important modifications to both the failed state and postmaterialist arguments are required. Moreover, a perspective informed by critical postcolonial theory is better at capturing the long-standing centrality of environmental and ecological imperatives to the production of the African state (see chapter 2).

MODERNITY IN AFRICA?

Even in terms of the logic of the arguments of these commentators, the empirical validity of the modernisation thesis when applied to Africa can be questioned. First, the image of the failed African state is at best a caricature.

In 2015 eight of the twenty fastest growing economies in the world were in Africa, and the African Development Bank (AfDB) claims that by 2060 most African countries are projected to reach upper-middle-income status.[86] Moreover, states like Egypt, South Africa, Sudan, Nigeria, Ghana, and Ethiopia have long histories of large modernist development projects, often with the aim of managing more sustainable resource use, mitigating environmental threats, and protecting sites of natural and national heritage. These include programmes of agricultural reform and tree planting, urban planning and resettlement schemes, irrigation projects and dams, massive conservation projects, disease eradication, and public health programmes.[87] Contemporary examples of modernist, state-led development projects which claim green credentials are not hard to find. North African countries are aiming to become major renewable energy suppliers to Europe, with Algeria planning to invest $60 billion by 2030, and Morocco, supported by the AfDB and the Climate Investment Fund, is developing one of the largest concentrated solar plants in the world at the Ouarzazate solar complex. The Nzema photovoltaic plant in Ghana has been billed as Africa's largest solar power farm. The Lagos Urban Transport Project for Nigeria has created the first Bus Rapid Transit system in sub-Saharan Africa, and the Lake Turkana Wind Power Project is billed as one of the largest investments in wind energy in Africa and the largest single private investment in Kenya's history. Ethiopia has set out a strategy for a Climate Resilient Green Economy which would establish food security, expand renewable energy, stimulate reforestation, and leapfrog to modern and energy-efficient technologies in transport, industrial sectors, and buildings. Other prominent green economy strategies have been developed in Rwanda, Mozambique, and South Africa. The Grand Inga dam in the DRC is projected to become the world's largest source of hydropower when completed. Such projects imply there is much on the continent to interest ecological modernisation theorists.

Second, the ecological modernisation account of the growth of modern environmentalism is widely contested. Richard Grove sees the environmental movement as emerging not from postwar Western activism but from the encounter between Europe and the colonial world, especially in the tropics.[88] Moreover, there are many movements outside the West, albeit often with very different framings and in diverse cultural contexts, which are centrally concerned with environmental issues, broadly defined. A brief list of some of the most prominent examples includes the Chipko Indians, the Green Belt Movement in Kenya, Gandhian movements for voluntary simplicity, the

Movement for the Survival of the Ogoni People in the Niger Delta, indigenous peoples movements, La Via Campesina, peasant anti–genetically modified organism (GMO) movements, climate justice networks, Inuit movements for Arctic protection, and many forms of Buddhism and other religious ecologisms. Doherty and Doyle have argued that the development of FoEI has "increasingly been driven by the major concerns of its southern members," and the twelve African branches have played especially significant roles through individuals like Nnimmo Bassey.[89] Sowers's study of environmental politics in Egypt shows that people do care about environmental issues, state capacity to intervene on environmental issues is not inconsiderable, and substantial mobilisations around ecological grievances have occurred in recent years.[90] Green political parties exist in thirty African countries (although they are often very small), and, as noted earlier, the Global Green Congress was held in Dakar in March and April 2012.

Such developments could perhaps be explained by ecological modernisation theorists as the belated arrival of African environmental movements and states. Supporting this interpretation, the EPI ranking for most improved

3. "Prayer Service at the Altar on the Easter Weekend at Motouleng Cave," Santu Mofokeng (b. 1956). © Santu Mofokeng, 2006 silverprint edition 5. Images courtesy Lunetta Bartz, MAKER, Johannesburg.

states over the past decade includes Niger, Sierra Leone, Namibia, and Congo in the top ten.[91] But this picture of belated improvement underestimates the centrality of environmental governance to the historical evolution of the African state. The environmental state in Africa is not a recent emergence, and recognising the importance of practices of resource governance and species protection to the historical production of African states is meaningful for the concept of the green state more generally. This requires a different theoretical approach to the concept of the green state than that posited by modernisation theorists (see chapter 2).

I began this chapter by noting the prominence of antistatist perspectives in global environmental politics from a wide variety of theoretical traditions. Yet for a number of reasons states remain powerful political actors. Globalisation has not made states irrelevant. The financial crisis relegitimated active and intensive state regulation in the economy; and even erstwhile antistatist theorists have become so worried by the impending climate crisis they have demanded concerted state regulation of climate capitalism. The normative arguments of theorists like Eckersley are hard to reject entirely: few social institutions have the capacity and democratic legitimacy of the state, and states could transform in ways to mitigate some of the criticisms posed by environmentalists. The contradictory but powerful arguments of realist and institutionalist IR theorists remain important: in the absence of supranational authority, sovereign states occupy the pinnacles of international politics, and increasingly complex webs of international law, governance, norms, and shared values inscribe and reproduce the special status of states in international society.

Any serious response to climate or broader environmental crises—or to social and economic crises for that matter—will require some involvement by or contestation of states. As Lyuba Zarsky writes, "Far from making nation-states irrelevant, globalisation makes new and difficult demands on them."[92] Yet, contrary to the apparent assumptions of many participants in the green state debates, these challenges are not faced solely by great powers and developed states. African states also regulate their environments and undertake environmental initiatives. Green projects have proliferated in Africa in recent years, but this is not simply belated modernisation. Notwithstanding President Sarkozy's characterisation of Africans as existing outside History, African states have been produced through political strategies for coping with and moulding demanding environments. Contrary to Keohane's contention, their capacities to manage difficult environments are neither as weak as is often assumed nor necessarily just a product of the material resources at their disposal, the level of education of their people, or the competence and honesty of their governments. From a modernisation perspective, African states will always be perpetually running to catch up with the path laid out by the West. But this is to ask a question to which we already know the answer; a more interesting and troubling question is, What role has environmental governance played in the production of African states? In order to provide a fuller, more historically informed, and more politically astute answer as to how the production and transformation of African states are related to the governance and contestation of African environments, an alternative theoretical conception of the state is required.

CHAPTER 2

Postcolonial Theory and the Green State in Africa

> We should therefore venerate the state as an earthly divinity, and realize that, if it is difficult to comprehend nature, it is an infinitely more arduous task to understand the state.
>
> —Georg Wilhelm Friedrich Hegel, *Elements of the Philosophy of Right*

> We have to find ways to make government feel the heat to do something. And government only feels the heat when people on the ground are challenging it.
>
> —Bobby Peek, Director of Groundwork South Africa

The first chapter began with objections to focusing on the state in environmental politics and posed the green state as a response. However, theories of ecological modernisation are ill-suited to understanding and explaining the state in Africa. Thus we require an alternative theoretical conception of the green state. But what is the state? Deliberations on the concept of the state dominate both political theory and strategies of political activism: many environmental activists frame their role in terms of applying pressure to states in order to persuade them to regulate, legislate, and enforce environmental protections. This view of the state as an autonomous institution is rooted in the Weberian tradition described in chapter 1, whereas this chapter moves towards an alternative, postcolonial approach to the state as the product or effect of a set of practices and technologies of power which permeate all of society. This provides a theoretical framework for the four more empirically focused chapters which follow.

This argument involves four stages: the first is to locate this book amidst the broader forest of texts concerned with state theory more generally, while the second stage examines the utility and shortcomings of these approaches in dealing with the problem of the African state. This section ends with a consideration of postcolonial approaches to the state in Africa, such as those associated with Jean-François Bayart and Achille Mbembe, and points toward an alternative theoretical conception of the state inspired by Foucault. The third section therefore draws upon such theorists as Thom Kuehls, Jean and John Comaroff, Timothy Mitchell, Bob Jessop, and Mitchell Dean to advance a more Foucauldian approach to the state as a set of practices, assemblages, and effects. The fourth and final stage sets out the theoretical framework which will structure the subsequent empirical explorations, in which the green state is conceptualised as an assemblage produced by the government of territories, populations, economies, and international relations. This section highlights some of the key questions and concepts which will be addressed in subsequent chapters.

THEORIES OF THE STATE

The question, What is the state?—or even, Does the state exist?—is a central problem for many political theorists. I have already discussed antipathy towards the state (see chapter 1), and indeed a theoretical scepticism towards the state as a useful concept dominated much of the political science of the second half of the twentieth century, particularly in the United States. In the 1980s and 1990s, however, there were a number of efforts to "bring the state back in," while in other theoretical traditions the state had never gone away. In order to contextualise the discussion that follows and to clarify the distinctiveness of the perspective I adopt in this book, it is first necessary to examine the mainstream and most influential conceptions of the state in the fields of political science, political sociology, and IR.[1]

In chapter 1 the Weberian conception of the state was introduced as a seminal influence on the ecological modernisation approach and most green state theorists. Weber's foundational definition is that "a state is a human community that (successfully) claims the *monopoly of the legitimate use of physical force* within a given territory."[2] Following his example, many state theorists have sought to identify the central attributes of statehood conceived as a relatively autonomous entity. Hedley Bull describes a state as that which possesses "a government and asserts sovereignty in relation to a particular proportion of the earth's surface and a particular segment of the human population."[3] Some combination of these elements—institutions, community, government, sovereignty, law, legitimacy, violence, territory, and population—is usually taken to be a core element of statehood and a means of distinguishing states from other social and political entities such as businesses, the church and religious orders, and empires. John Dryzek and colleagues, working directly on the green state, begin with a conception of the state as being animated by five central tasks or imperatives: maintaining order, competing internationally, raising finances, securing economic growth, and legitimising this system.[4]

These approaches constitute the mainstream conception of the state in political science. They begin with ideal-typical characteristics of statehood and assess how far these are met (or, indeed, failed) by empirical candidates for statehood. They stress the autonomy of the state vis-à-vis society, and they can sometimes appear quite formalistic and descriptive. Sometimes they either explicitly or implicitly suggest that the state is a neutral institution, mediating power relations but also standing above and beside them. In contrast, a more relational and explicitly *political* approach to the state is provided by Marx and those working with and after him, including theorists like Gramsci and Poulantzas. Marxist perspectives establish the role of the state and the state system in the reproduction and regulation of capital accumulation as well as the state's implication in a range of power relations in society.[5]

Marx and Engels argued that "the form of the state is a reflection of the economic base of society and that its interventions are a reflection of the needs of the economy and / or of the balance of economic class forces."[6] Thus the state is neither autonomous nor distinct from the rest of society but reflects dominant class interests: it is an instrument of class rule. Gramsci famously described the state as "an outer ditch" behind which society was "a powerful system of fortresses and earthworks."[7] Much subsequent work in the Marxist tradition has sought to avoid or mitigate the tendency toward deterministic arguments that reduce the state to an epiphenomenon of underlying economic interests. Jessop, for example, sympathises with Poulantzas's argument that, rather than simple instrumentalism, the state is "the factor of cohesion in the social formation."[8] To Jessop, "the state comprises a plurality of institutions (or apparatuses) and their unity, if any, far from being pregiven, must be constituted politically."[9] He concludes that the "core of the state apparatus comprises a distinct ensemble of institutions and organisations whose socially accepted function is to define and enforce collectively binding decisions on members of a society in the name of their common interest or general will."[10]

In addition to foregrounding the role of the state in maintaining and perpetuating broader social power relations, especially between labour, land, and capital, one of the most important contributions of Marxist (and post-Marxist) state theory has been to show how divisions such as those between public and private or the economy and politics are a creation of power relations rather than ontologically prior to them. To Weberian theorists these distinctions appear more self-evident, and Weber famously argued that politics was a vocation which "follows quite different laws" to those of making money (or doing science).[11] In contrast, the scholarship on Marxist political economy has shown how class politics and contestations over production and consumption are articulated in contingent ways through state assemblages to produce apparently separate realms such as the economy and the state. Feminist political economy has also been important in highlighting the power-laden, patriarchal effects of the constitution of private and public as distinct domains of social life. In one of the most compelling articulations of this line of argument, Timothy Mitchell argued that the state–society distinction "must be taken not as the boundary between two discrete entities, but as a line drawn internally within the network of institutional mechanisms through which a social and political order is maintained."[12] In contrast to ideologies of neoliberalism, which articulate the free market as a natural idea or basic law of human interaction which needs to be protected and enabled by politics, critical political economists have shown how this obscures dense webs of power relations between capital and labour as well as within the patriarchal family, between racial and ethnic groups, and between society and nature.[13]

Another crucial politically constructed binary which has acquired a life beyond its constitution is that between national and international politics. Kenneth Waltz claimed that "national politics is the realm of authority, administration, and of law. International politics is the realm of power, of struggle and of accommodation."[14] Warfare, diplomacy, great power relations, and international law are commonly regarded as key institutions of the international society of states, and the discipline of IR provides the third major approach to the theorising of the state. Different branches of IR are influenced by both Weberian and Marxist sociology, but all tend to emphasise the constitutive role of warfare and international interaction in state formation. The typical image of the state within mainstream IR theory is the billiard ball which interacts with other states but is internally coherent and homogenous (or at least can be usefully conceptualised as such, or black-boxed, in order to explain important features of international politics).

The assertion of the political primacy of the international and a resultant justification of the need for a separate discipline with distinct tools and concepts, namely, IR itself, has been articulated by a number of theorists but has been resisted by many working within political sociology and Marxist theory. This perhaps explains Jessop's reluctance to even discuss the role of international politics in state assemblages: "Nor do I feel inclined to apologise for neglecting international relations. They are certainly an important site of social practices but there is no more reason to accord them a special theoretical status than the 'micro-physics of power' relations."[15] However, recognising that the dualistic divide between international and national politics is a product of power relations, like that between the economy and politics, does not mean that relations between states are not meaningful sites of practices and institutions which help to produce contemporary states. Indeed, more close-grained attention to practices and norms of sovereignty and to the challenges to sovereignty under conditions of globalisation are two critical areas where IR theory can help lead to a better understanding of the state.

It is the unique claim to sovereignty that in many ways produces the state as a distinct political entity, at least in conventional geopolitical imaginaries. According to most IR textbook accounts, the emergence of modern sovereignty and the modern state system can be dated to the Treaty of Westphalia (1648), in which the warring parties agreed the principle of noninterference by princes in matters of religion in other realms; the signatories agreed to recognize the terms of the Peace of Augsburg of 1555 and the principle of *cuius regio, eius religio* ("whose realm, his religion").[16] In Hirst's and Thompson's account, "Governments pledged to cease to support foreign co-religionists in conflict with their states," and thus "to a significant degree the capacity for sovereignty came from *without,* through agreements between states in the newly emerging society of states."[17] To Bull, "The kingdoms and principalities of Western Christendom (Europe) in the Middle Ages were not states: they did not possess internal sovereignty because they were not supreme over authorities within their territory and population; and at the same time they did not possess external sovereignty since they were not independent of the Pope, or in some cases, the Holy Roman Empire."[18] Notwithstanding the many problems with this account of the emergence of international relations and the mythic but dubious foundational status of Westphalia, the crucial point here is that states are states because they interact with other states.

Sovereignty has internal and external dimensions, therefore, and it is perceptual, mythical, and imagined as well as juridical and empirical. If no one believes in it, then it does not exist; but that is not to say it is not highly significant. Like paper money, sovereignty is fascinating because it is nothing while being everything. The idea of the state—and mutual recognition by states of the "stateness" and sovereignty of other members of international society—is a constitutive element of statehood. Moreover, again, the comparison with money is illuminating, because state sovereignty as an idea and a practice is a driving factor behind many of the environmental challenges and crises we face. This includes the sovereign right of states to cut down trees and emit carbon dioxide and the difficulty of getting 192 member states of the United Nations to agree on new and binding legal regimes. As Kuehls phrases it, "The state's attempts at creating territories capable of providing for its population," within what he terms a sovereign governmentality, "have greatly contributed to the ecocrises we now face."[19]

The corollary to sovereignty could perhaps be stated, in shorthand, as globalisation. It is through an analysis of the changing forms of communication, interaction, and governance on global and transnational scales that IR theory can also contribute to understanding how contemporary states are being transformed. Jessop recognises as much in his analysis of how the Keynesian welfare national state is being replaced by what he terms "a Schumpeterian workfare post-national regime," one of the facets of which is a tendential shift "from the primacy of the national scale in determining the economic and social functions of the extra-economic towards a postnational relativisation of scale."[20] Others, drawing on Saskia Sassen, have written about "partial 'disassembling'" of national states and the corresponding development of new "global assemblages" of authority cutting across global and local, public and private.[21] Such shifts pose profound challenges to some of the foundational categories and assumptions of IR theory, for example, the distinction between national and international politics and Weberian / Westphalian states as the basic unit of international politics. Beck opines that "globalisation means one thing above all else: *de*nationalisation—that is, erosion of the national state, but also its possible transformation into a transnational state"—a transnational state which is "non-national" and "non-territorial."[22]

Yet globalisation cannot and should not be assumed to be a late twentieth-century phenomenon. The globalising age began in the fifteenth century, and, as Robbie Shilliam contends, we must recognise the *global* rather than just the Western production of modernity and the constitutive role of colonialism and imperialism in producing capitalist globalisation, including, for example, the trade of slaves, rubber, gold, and diamonds out of Africa.[23]

Diplomacy, international law, and warfare have constituted some of the most important social relations through which states have produced themselves and each other, and all of these are long-standing historical practices. State production is a protracted historical dynamic and always involved transformation through interaction with other states and nonstate societies in a heterogeneous, uneven international. These relations are central to understanding contemporary state forms in Africa.

These three broad theoretical traditions, Weberian, Marxist, and realist / idealist IR, have engendered some of the most influential and coherent work on theorising the state, and the issues and questions they raise will prove useful in mapping the empirical scope of the analysis to follow in the rest of the book. The discussions so far imply that any account of the green state in Africa must include issues like territory, population, violence, government, warfare, the economy, sovereignty, and diplomacy. But a recurring critique of these approaches is that they present a Eurocentric account of the state, taking one story of the emergence of states in Europe and the spread of these states by conquest and emulation across the world and assuming it has universal applicability.[24] To what degree do the pictures of the state created so far carry any analytical or descriptive utility in parts of the world such as Africa?

THE STATE IN AFRICA

Bayart restates this problem precisely, if a little awkwardly: "The fundamental problem . . . is to know what extent the adequacy (or inadequacy) of sub-Saharan political configurations, based on the Weberian model, allow (or more probably do not allow) us to speak of them as 'States.' "[25] Weber, Bayart makes clear, would not have recognised African states as modern states with rational legal systems, bureaucracies, and competent civil servants. Jeffrey Herbst has argued that central state authority barely penetrates much of rural Africa.[26] Fredrick Cooper describes African states as typically gatekeepers: "They stood astride the intersection of the colonial territory and the outside world," deriving revenue mainly from "duties on goods that entered and left its ports" but "had trouble extending their power and their command of people's respect, if not support, inward."[27] While such claims are deeply disputable and in some cases downright incorrect, nevertheless, the African state looks quite different from the models presented in mainstream political science and sociology. Christopher Clapham paints a vivid picture of African states: "Precariously perched on top of shifting societies, bobbing about on the currents of a globalised economy, they often need the skills of an acrobat to stay upright. As the relative stability of the agreement to maintain the postcolonial order continues to erode, the new Africa is likely to owe as much to its precolonial origins, with zones of reasonable effective government interspersed with ones in which anything as readily identifiable as a 'state' is hard to discern, as to the misleading grid of states with apparently clearly demarcated boundaries bequeathed by the colonial cartographers."[28] Thus in African politics states "are not to be taken for granted."[29] In the three main areas highlighted above, of autonomous institutions, expressions of class politics, and sovereign international actors, the African state is deeply problematic.

Many African state institutions are in crisis and have been for decades. Over much of the continent formal colonialism lasted for only a few generations, and indirect rule through traditional authorities did not build the bureaucratic state structures associated with the Weberian conception of the state. Control over territory has often been partial and fragmentary, with large swathes of countries like Somalia, DRC, and even northern Nigeria outside central control. Legitimate violence is often not the sole prerogative of the state, and states struggle to prevent traditional authorities, religious groups, and well-established criminal and shadow networks from enforcing their version of the law. Populations, especially "uncaptured peasants" in rural areas, often exist with little direct intervention from or loyalty to the nation-state, and affinities are framed in ethnic and religious terms. Economies are divided between the formal, that is, registered and tax-paying, and the real or informal, in which the economic activity of the majority of people is located.[30] The responses from scholars in the Weberian tradition tend to follow two diagnoses: that African states function as neopatrimonial regimes and that state structures in Africa are failed or failing.

The neopatrimonial label is given to societies in which authority is primarily still located in patrimonial relations like family, religion, ethnicity, and patron–client relations, but where these exist alongside and permeate modern bureaucratic institutions such as the civil service, judiciary, and the education system. Such systems are often described as quasi-states in which corruption and the predominance of private interests mean big man rule prevails at the expense of rational state bureaucracies. Whereas the verdict of some analysts is that "Africa Works" through such neopatrimonial relations, an alternative verdict is that African states are failed or failing. State failure is variously defined as "a state's loss of control over the use of force" or an "inability to perform development functions"; "a political entity that lacks the institutional capacity to implement and enforce policies" or a decline in "the capacity of state to command loyalty," that is, "the right to rule."[31] This verdict emphasises the foreign imposition of the state in Africa, superficially rooted in local societies and often in conflict with established and rival centres of power. Sometimes the state is seen as foreign or parasitic, either in its institutions or in the very idea of it. From this perspective it is not just, or even, the state which is in crisis in Africa but the very idea of the state and modern political order.[32]

Both the neopatrimonial and failed state discourses have been heavily criticised despite their intuitive appeal and influence on policy makers. The reasons include analytical fuzziness and imprecision, normative ambiguity, and the tendency to pathologise developing states in general and African states in particular. While it is true that over half the states typically characterised as fragile by organisations like the Organisation for Economic Cooperation and Development (OECD) are located in Africa, many African states, especially in recent decades, have demonstrated state strength and capacity in terms of economic growth, regime stability, hold on military power, and the governance of territory and populations (see chapter 1).

Moreover, as Jonathan Fisher's work on Uganda shows, the fragile states agenda has "provided important opportunities for 'weak state' governments to secure agency in the international system" through eliciting foreign aid and military support.[33] Bayart comes to a similar verdict on corruption and neopatrimonialism and deploys the concept of extraversion to explain how African elites mobilize "resources derived from their (possibly unequal) relationship with the external environment."[34]

The key point here is that the weakness of some state institutions should not be interpreted as a vacuum of authority in Africa. The absence or weakness of some institutions or the existence of alternative state structures does not mean the absence of political order and structured power relations, and states in Africa do exist and have even demonstrated surprising longevity and endurance. Alternative forms of political order—even if they bear little resemblance to Weberian rational bureaucracies—constitute historically produced, sedimented, and often relatively stable sets of power relations. Therefore, "states must be seen as historical processes that include and span the pre-colonial, colonial and post-colonial periods."[35] Crucially, African cases make it obvious that these historically produced systems of order and hierarchy are not confined to state institutions narrowly defined. Alternative actors and institutions are implicated within networks and assemblages which run alongside, past, and through African states. As Abrahamsen and Williams observe, international financial institutions (IFIs) and donors "have achieved an ever-stronger ability to influence policy formation and decision-making on the continent," and "international NGOs are increasingly 'state-like' in their functions and influences, possessing resources and providing services that frequently outstrip anything on offer from African states."[36] As a result, narrowly Weberian institutional approaches, which emphasise the existence of ideal-typical autonomous state structures, are not best placed to understand African states.

The second major theme in state theory, the utility of Marxist frames of reference in Africa, has been long debated. Marxist theorists like Gramsci and Poulantzas as well as Marx himself spent little time considering African states. The African state is not a capitalist state or welfare state in the same way that the European and North American states are. Formal models of class analysis tend to founder on the absence of large proletariats, the widespread existence of subsistence agriculture, and the importance of ethnic and religious politics, all mediated through a patron–client system in which the state is both an active player and a site of conflict. As Bayart notes, "As soon as one adopts a rigorous definition of class societies, one in effect disqualifies African societies from the definition. For, south of the Sahara, class relations are in no way the primary source of conflict, despite the acuteness of social inequality."[37]

On the other hand, approaches to power relations that stress material interests and patterns of accumulation and production hold considerable purchase in explaining African politics. Concepts like dependency and the existence of a capitalist world system have contributed to our understanding of the legacies of colonialism and the continuing existence of neocolonial trading and economic relations. The empires of Britain, France, Portugal, Germany, and Belgium derived vast wealth from their African colonies, and as Neumann shows in Tanzania in some detail, "Securing control over access to, and the benefits derived from, natural resources was a critical process in the early formation of the colonial state."[38] In the 1980s and 1990s SAPs promoted wide-ranging, socially ambitious policies of rolling back the state in all areas of social and political life and can be interpreted as part of the project of Western neoliberalism in securing open markets in the periphery. Yet one-sided accounts of African subjugation and exploitation have underestimated the degree of African agency and extraversion and of the productive power of transnational encounters. It is inescapably true that the degree of Africa's penetration by global economic markets has driven its deprivation rather than its isolation and marginalisation, yet it is also true, as Bayart asserts, that "dependence is a historical experience in which people create themselves as subjects."[39] Moreover, economically determinist accounts of the African state which neglect or underestimate the importance of tradition, religion, ethnicity, the occult, and shadow politics are insufficient for understanding political culture in Africa. Thus Mbembe sees the African postcolonial state / society as emerging from colonialism and colonial violence, but in addition it is "chaotically pluralistic" and characterised "by a distinctive style of political improvisation, by a tendency to excess and lack of proportion."[40] Accordingly, Marxist and radical worldviews have tended to be combined with elements of postcolonial theory in critical accounts of African states and societies.[41]

The final major theoretical approach to state theory comes from IR, and it is true that African states are in no small part the products of international and transnational relations. State structures and institutions were often designed by colonial powers and inherited by postcolonial regimes, and the recognition afforded to newly independent state-nations by international society played a crucial role in enabling these structures to survive. What Christopher Clapham referred to as "letter-box sovereignty" to describe the prerogative of whoever inhabited the presidential palace to use international spaces to acquire valuable resources and prestige enabled many fragile African regimes like those of Mobutu Sese Seko to survive far longer than they would have otherwise.[42] This leads to what Ayoob represented as the schizophrenia of states in the developing world: combining the newcomer's desire for radical structural change to international society with a "vested interest in the preservation of predictable norms of state behaviour."[43] External or juridical sovereignty, in short, is central to understanding African states.

Other core insights of IR theory seem to travel less well to Africa. The anarchic international system, differentiated from domestic order, does not seem to fit most African experiences of politics, in which postcolonial trade, race, and aid relations produce a profoundly hierarchical international order, and competing networks and sources of local power often seem to tend toward domestic anarchy. IR's fundamentally Weberian assumptions about isomorphic black-boxed states do not capture the way in which colonial and postcolonial African states are, for the most part, not smooth, homogenous territories but complex, overlapping spheres of competing jurisdictions, indirect rule, and religious, ethnic, lineage, and mercantile territories. Changing forms and drivers of globalisation continue to complicate this picture, and what has been labelled contemporary globalisation is "simply an element in the ongoing formation of the state."[44] These nuances pose challenges for IR theories of the state generally, but they are particularly profound and evident in African settings. As a result, Kevin Dunn observes that "the African state is not failing as much as is our understanding of the state."[45] For this reason, within IR theory, as in the cases of the Marxist tradition and international political sociology, postcolonial perspectives on the state have been increasingly drawn upon to make sense of African politics.

Building upon these debates within state theory, two of the most influential accounts of the African state may be found in Bayart's and Mbembe's work. Both emphasise the polyvalent, heterogeneous registers of African political life, which refuses to remain cast within firm categories of public–private, labour–capital, national–international. Bayart asserts an alternative distinction in African political societies between "on the one hand, a *pays légal,* a legal structure which is the focus of attention for multilateral donors and western states, and, on the other hand, a *pays réel,* where real power is wielded."[46] He cites the continuing chaos in Somalia—to which one might add the prominence of militant Islamists across the Sahel—as evidence that "even a woebegone African country is able to defy the superpower of the international system."[47] To Bayart, drawing on Deleuze, the state should be thought of as a rhizome: it "is not one-dimensional, formed around a single genetic trunk, like a majestic oak whose roots are spread deep into the soil of history. It is rather an infinitely variable multiplicity of networks whose underground branches join together the scattered points of society."[48] The metaphor of the rhizome, alongside those of the shadow state or phantom state, is a recurring one in analyses of African politics and complicates some of the more straightforward assumptions of distinct binaries. As Mbembe remarks, "The postcolonial relationship is not primarily a relationship of resistance or of collaboration but can best be characterised as illicit cohabitation," meaning "we need to go beyond the binary categories used in standard interpretations of domination, such as resistance v. passivity, autonomy v. subjection, state v. civil society, hegemony v. counter-hegemony, totalisation v. detotalisation."[49]

FOUCAULT, STATE ASSEMBLAGES, AND AN "ANALYTICS OF GOVERNMENTALITY"

In view of the shortcomings of the most influential theories of the state when it comes to comprehending African politics, an alternative methodology is needed to study green states in Africa. My approach begins with specific, concrete practices, technologies, and discourses that are empirically identifiable and uses these to build up a picture of the green state in Africa. An approach like this should not be confused with value-neutral objectivism or a fetishisation of fieldwork. Rather, it is a theoretically informed orientation toward constitutive micropractices inspired by anthropological and ethnographic interpretations of Foucault's work. To Foucault, the "state is a practice. The state is inseparable from the set of practices by which the state actually became a way of governing, a way of doing things, and a way too of relating to government."[50]

Such an interpretation of the state therefore starts from the position that it should be studied as an assemblage of practices, technologies, and discourses. Mitchell regards the state as "an effect of detailed processes of spatial organisation, temporal arrangement, functional specification, and supervision and surveillance, which create the appearance of a world fundamentally divided into state and society."[51] Jessop, drawing on Poulantzas, describes the state as "an ensemble of distinct circuits of power, networks and apparatuses which pursue a multiplicity of diversified micropolicies."[52] Yet this diversity and heterogeneity is only part of the picture, as there is also what Jessop refers to as the "whole–part paradox," which is that "the state is just one institutional ensemble among others within a social formation; but it is peculiarly charged with overall responsibility for maintaining the cohesion of the social formation of which it is a part."[53] Thus the state is both "a dispersed ensemble of institutional practices and techniques of governance" as well as "the great enframer of our lives."[54]

Exploring some of the issues and implications that arise from viewing the state in this way requires an explanation of the role of the state in Foucault's work. A tension exists here, as Foucault famously sought to evade the trap of the state, or to "cut off the king's head" in political theory by moving away from sovereign conceptions of legitimacy.[55] He declared, "I must do without a theory of the state, as one can and must forgo an indigestible meal."[56] Yet Foucault's antipathy to the state has been overemphasised, as the publication in English of various lecture series from the late 1970s shows. Not antistatist per se or uninterested in the state and its role in politics, Foucault instead resolutely avoided formulating a top-down theory of the state. He advised focusing on microlevel practices and technologies of governance and seeking to account for the ways in which binaries such as public and private, state and civil society, national and international are produced, reified, transgressed, eroded, and reformed. Authors like Jessop have drawn attention to the similarities between Foucault's work and that of other state theorists, such as Poulantzas, and their shared approach to the state as a set of social and political relations. To Jessop, states "depend on a wide range of micro-political practices dispersed throughout society but also concentrated and condensed in the state."[57]

Explicating the role of the state in Foucault's thought can be done most clearly through his work on governmentality. There is a growing body of literature on governmentality in global politics, and two main uses of the term stand out. For some, governmentality is seen quite narrowly as synonymous with neoliberalism and refers to the rationalities or mentalities of government associated with promoting individual freedom and the rule of the market. For others, governmentality is a broader study of rationalities of rule more generally and includes the mentalities and practices deployed and articulated within conservative, liberal, biopolitical, socialist, and even authoritarian forms of rule. I have argued for the utility of the second approach and have sketched out how an "analytics of government" can comprehend "all rationalised and calculated regimes of government, which conduct the conduct of (at least partially) free and multiple subjectivities through specific techniques and technologies, within particular fields of visibility."[58] Such an outlook can highlight the similarities or homologies in rationalities and power relations across very different fields of government without reducing everything to the pernicious effects of neoliberalism. In addition, it can show how new political rationalities emerge and are conducted with various political effects.

One of the advantages of a governmentality framework lies in avoiding a statist scheme which explicitly or implicitly casts Africa and developing countries more broadly as pathologised, backward, and lacking great powers and strong sovereign states. Rather, attention to governmentality highlights diverse micropractices of power which exist broadly throughout society, not just in state institutions. As such, it has often been assumed to prioritise nonstate actors and steadfastly refuses to equate politics with state institutions, political parties, and the headquarters of power. However, rather than avoiding the state, the concept of governmentality is useful to show the ways in which governmental power relations blur the distinctions between state and nonstate actors, public and private, domestic and international. These micropractices of power transgress and overlap realms formally identified as state and society; for example, technologies of auditing and self-regulation are prolific within public administrations, international institutions, private companies, NGOs, and even families. International practices of sovereignty, including migration policies, border management and diplomatic exchanges, are crucial to the production of states and other transnational actors. As Mitchell Dean suggests, governmentality studies of contemporary international politics would do well to "bring sovereignty back in."[59] The production of states and state effects through governmentality is a crucial issue somewhat neglected in much Foucauldian work, and it deserves attention from those interested in thinking about new, more progressive, and ecologically sustainable rationalities of government.

In one of his lectures in the 1978–79 series *The Birth of Biopolitics,* Foucault spoke at some length on the question of how practices and rationalities of governmentality were linked to the existence of the state:

> The state is not a universal nor in itself an autonomous source of power. The state is nothing else but the effect, the profile, the mobile shape of a perpetual statification [*étatisation*] or statifications, in the sense of incessant transactions which modify, or move, or drastically change, or insidiously shift sources of finance, modes of investment, decision-making centres, forms and types of control, relationships between local powers, the central authority, and so on. In short, the state has no heart, as we well know, but not just in the sense that it has no feelings, either good or bad, but it has no heart in the sense that it has no interior. The state is nothing else but the mobile effect of a regime of multiple governmentalities.[60]

Thus Foucault was concerned not with the *étatisation* of society but with the governmentalisation of the state. To Foucault, "The state is not a cold monster; it is the correlative of a particular way of governing."[61] States are produced at particular historical moments through practices, discourses, and technologies alongside territories, economies, and populations. Foucault was interested in the manner in which the German and American forms of neoliberalism in the postwar period produced "a state under the supervision of the market rather than a market supervised by the state," beside and in parallel to *Homo oeconomicus* as "someone who is eminently governable."[62]

One of the implications of bringing Foucault into a discussion of environmental politics and the green state is to introduce a theme of caution and critical scepticism often missing from the ecological modernisation approaches. For example, Foucault's work on biopolitics can work to highlight some of the more troubling aspects of the green state, including their potentially racist, gendered, and fascist attributes. Foucault sees biopower as "the set of mechanisms through which the basic biological features of the human species became the object of a political strategy, of a general strategy of power."[63] To Dean, biopolitics is "a form of politics entailing the administration of the processes of life of populations" and the regulation of "the social, cultural, environmental, economic and geographic conditions under which humans live, procreate, become ill, maintain health or become healthy, and die."[64] From this perspective environmental concerns have been central to forms of governance since the earliest political communities: the pursuit of a safe, healthy living environment; food and water security; the preservation of cultural and natural landscapes; regulations to protect against communicable diseases; sustainable utilization of resources, and so on. Yet environmental concerns can also be mobilized in exclusionary and violent ways which threaten individual rights and communal identities.

This is not to say that techniques of biopolitical environmental governance have not changed over time. Certainly it is possible to identify dramatic changes in forms of biopower, for example, in the administration of the circulation of food, disease, and people in European towns and cities in the nineteenth century and in the formation and expansion of environmental ministries, international organisations, regulatory regimes, scientific networks and movements from the 1960s and 1970s onwards.[65] Foucault, however, sees such shifts not as transformations in the nature or essence of the state, as in the shift from a liberal to a welfare state and then on to a green state, but as changing assemblages of practices, technologies, and discourses.

Taking this biopolitical view together with seeing the state as an effect produced by particular ways of governing, we can suggest that the green African state is actually a product of particular attempts to govern land, species, human populations, and water resources. In this sense, the green African state is not "of quite recent origin" but the effect of long-standing, deep-rooted endeavors to govern environmental resources.[66] This includes efforts by colonial and postcolonial states to administer natural resources more profitably and efficiently, as in agricultural reform and modernisation, dam building, and forestry schemes, but it also encompasses more ecological imperatives which seek to protect and sustain species, both human and nonhuman, which can flourish in their environments. What are vaccination campaigns for livestock and humans, the creation and management of biodiversity enclaves, urban sanitation reforms, programmes to eliminate invasive alien species (IAS), and antipoaching drives if not, to repeat Dean's words, "a form of politics entailing the administration of the processes of life of populations?"[67] As Raymond Bryant and Sinéad Bailey point out, "The historical development of states has been closely intertwined with the management of the local environments on which those states, and the people they govern, have been dependent."[68]

Two examples, from colonial Egypt and apartheid South Africa, illustrate the presence of environmental and ecological imperatives at the core of state practices of government over long periods of time. They are not meant to imply that the practices have remained static over time or that they are the same in diverse contexts and countries. The racial politics of apartheid South Africa, for example, was a form of biopolitics (regulating marriages and classifying and segregating populations) that differs greatly from that in contemporary South Africa (intensive species management for rhinos and elephants and public health campaigns and human rights discourses for human populations). However, the two examples highlight certain homologies or similarities in the arts of government across disparate social domains.[69]

The Biopolitics of Colonial Egypt

Egypt's dependence on the Nile River and the relationship between the river and the desert are central to any account of the consolidation of power and authority in the region, both historically and in more contemporary interstate disputes over the Nile's waters. Mitchell's detailed accounts of state building and colonialism in Egypt draw attention to the management of environmental resources and impacts and their role in producing, performing, and representing the Egyptian state. He notes that, while control of the Nile River Valley from Cairo was not new, "from the nineteenth century for the first time political power sought to work in a manner that was continuous, meticulous and uniform" and to enter into the "process of production" itself rather than simply impose levies on agricultural produce.[70] The disciplining of society was undertaken through conscription programmes and the creation of planned villages on a staggering scale and should be understood as an attempt to model society and individuals through control and regulation of the environments in which they lived. Like their European counterparts, town planners in late nineteenth-century Egypt were obsessed with miasma and stench. Cemeteries, sewers, effluences, and cesspools were problems to be solved by light, cleanliness, air, and proper planning. One scheme, proposed in 1880, decreed that "the towns must restore to the countryside in the form of fertiliser the equivalent of what they receive in the form of consumption [i.e., human excrement]. . . . Every rotten smell in the house, in the street, in the town, signifies . . . a loss of fertiliser in the countryside."[71] Contemporary movements for Transition Towns in the United Kingdom may well sympathise with such ecologically minded notions; irrespective of their feasibility, such ideas reveal a pervasive interest in governing lived environments, waste, and life processes.[72]

After 1882 colonial authorities sought to map Egypt's agricultural land in precise, scientific detail: "The colonial power set out to determine, for every square meter of the country's agricultural land, the owner, the cultivator, the quality of the soil, and the proper rate of tax."[73] This produced "one of the most closely mapped terrains in the world," all in the downstream shadow of the imposing Aswan Dam, built at the turn of the century and increased in height in 1933. Through the supervision of hygiene and public health, the building of model villages, the construction of networks "to channel and control the movement of commodities, Nile waters, and tourists," the surveillance of workers, and "the opening up of towns and cities to continuous inspection with wide thoroughfares, street lighting and police forces," the politics of the modern state in Egypt was produced. This was a state preeminently engaged in managing and regulating the environments in which the population lived, worked, and farmed.[74]

Many would no doubt respond that the colonial Egyptian state is far from what is meant by a green state. Certainly it is not a state that sought to "facilitate both more active and effective ecological citizenship and more enlightened environmental governance"—although it did regard itself as enlightened in the nineteenth-century meaning of the term. But if an environmental state is one where "a significant governmental focus [is] on managing environmental burdens," then colonial and postcolonial Egypt qualifies. Dryzek et al. regard the linking of environmental projects to core state imperatives of survival, domestic order, finance, accumulation, and legitimation as the main criteria for a green state.[75] Egypt's efforts to control the Nile flood, monitor its population, survey land, provide sanitation, and present an enlightened image of itself internationally are clearly all linked to essential state imperatives. If not quite a "hydraulic civilisation," Egypt can assuredly be seen as some form of environmental state, and there are continuities between these colonial practices and contemporary environmental politics.[76]

The Biopolitics of Apartheid South Africa

The second example draws on William Beinart's account of the evolution of environmentalism in South Africa in the nineteenth and twentieth centuries. His work shows how "agricultural production, environmental understanding, and the attempts to conserve natural resources were intimately linked."[77] Agricultural and rural development, encompassing such subjects as soil erosion, overstocking, husbandry and disease, and invasive species control, played a central role in producing modern environmentalism, particularly in the tropical colonies. For both British colonisers and the Union government in the Cape, issues of land degradation and foreign species proliferation were foremost concerns, and these translated into scientific reviews, popular debates, and state-driven conservation schemes on a remarkable scale. From the 1880s to the 1940s, Beinart argues, "environmental regulation became a far more central concern to the state both at local and national levels."[78]

Similar matters were rearticulated by the Nationalist apartheid government in the fifties, sixties, and seventies as Betterment, villagisation, and land reform policies.[79] While racial supremacy and the protection of the white population were increasingly paramount, environmental problems and ecological knowledge were deployed to reshape the South African countryside: both in the expansion of farmland and in the creation and intensive management of vast national parks such as Kruger. Such measures cannot be easily dismissed as preenvironmental. Beinart concludes that "at various moments in the twentieth century the South African state enacted far-reaching measures for environmental regulation, and initiated propaganda drives to encourage conservation," in the process spending millions of pounds and passing wide-ranging laws.[80] Wildlife and national parks were also crucial elements in the imagery and symbolism of the state. Beinart and Coates, for example, observe that "game animals became a recurrent motif in white South Africa's conception and projection of itself. Assorted wildlife were emblazoned on postage stamps—the springbok's head became the watermark soon after the Union in 1910 and first displaced the king's head in 1926, the year that the Kruger national park was founded."[81] The springbok and the protea are the symbols of South African rugby and cricket, respectively, and the national currency portrays the Big Five game animals: the lion, leopard, elephant, buffalo, and rhino. Thus "today's parks remain a powerful cultural statement fusing notions of nature and nation."[82]

The examples of colonial Egypt and apartheid South Africa show how a whole range of practices, discourses, technologies, and subjects were mobilised in networks and assemblages for biopolitical forms of environmental governance. These networks and assemblages were, in both of these cases, articulated and organised through the state and manifest distinctly green characteristics. These cases provide initial evidence that a methodological approach drawing upon postcolonial state theory can produce a very different understanding of politics in Africa, one better suited to showing the biopolitical implications of the ways in which environments are governed and contested.

GREEN STATE EFFECTS: A CONCEPTUAL FRAMEWORK

Green states are therefore produced as the effects of the governance of certain issues, practices, and fields in ways which explicitly invoke green, environmental, or ecological discourses. These practices have long histories but are rearticulated in new and interesting ways since the emergence of contemporary environmental movements from the 1970s and the growth of global environmental governance. Such developments are necessary for confronting the challenges of the ecological crisis, but on the other hand drawing attention to the homologies and family resemblances in power relations between contemporary green states and older colonial and racist states introduces a cautionary theme.

There are potentially many ways of organising an empirical analysis of green states in Africa, but I argue that the most parsimonious and effective way to categorise green state effects is through the governance of territories, populations, economies, and international relations. This gives rise to a set of guiding questions for the subsequent empirical analysis.

Territories

First, as Bull has noted, states govern "a particular proportion of the earth's surface."[83] Yet not all land is state territory: "Territory is land that is fixed, plotted and mapped so that sovereignty can hold sway. There is a process of territorialisation, if you will, that is necessary in order to transform land into part of a state. In this respect, we can argue that territory is the result of governmental practices."[84] Just as there are different ways of organising land and space, there are different types of territory, different territorialising processes and practices, and different state territories. We should not fall into the "territorial trap" of conflating modern state territories with all forms of territory. John Agnew warned that "even when rule is territorial and fixed, territory does not necessarily entail the practices of total mutual exclusion which the dominant understanding of the territorial state attributes to it."[85] A good place to start in mapping the production of green state effects is what Poulantzas would call the "historicity of territory."[86] Chapter 3, therefore, explores such questions as, How do African states govern land and territory through green discourses and practices? What technologies, regimes of truth, visibilities, and subjectivities are deployed, for example, in demarcating a border, zoning land use, or mapping terrain? What forms of resistance and dissent are made possible? What are the key similarities and differences produced in the forms of state territorialisation in African environmental governance? What are the reasons for these similarities and differences, and what consequences might they have for environmental politics in Africa? Such an orientation entails seeing territories and landscapes not as self-evident or natural but as effects of territorialising processes. The green state is a "political technology" for governing land, borders and territory; it takes form as "power relations written on the land."[87]

Populations

Second, Bull also observed that states govern "a particular segment of the human population."[88] But a group of people are not the same as a population or, to go even further, a population of citizens. As Kuehls observes, "People are a product of the state. They are structured, organised, and used in a particular way," and therefore "governmental processes must ensure that the people are disciplined in such a way that they can transform land into territory."[89] Similarly, Jessop notes that "actually existing societies do not pre-exist the state systems but are constituted in part through state activities."[90] One of the tasks of chapter 4 is to study, following Dean, "those practices that try to shape, sculpt, mobilize and work through the choices, desires, aspirations, needs, wants and lifestyles of individuals and groups."[91] The chapter is therefore organised around questions like, How do African states govern people and populations through green discourses and practices? What technologies, regimes of truth, visibilities, and subjectivities are deployed, for example, in the census or in tree planting, citizenship, educational and green consumption initiatives? What forms of resistance and dissent are made possible? What are the key similarities and differences produced in the forms of state biopower in African environmental governance? What are the reasons for these similarities and differences, and what consequences might they have for environmental politics in Africa?

Economies

Third, states govern, regulate, structure, and produce national economies. Referring to Foucault and Karl Polanyi, Mitchell shows how "practices of government . . . formed the economy as a field of political regulation," and dates this development not to the eighteenth and nineteenth centuries but to the mid-twentieth.[92] At this point "new ways of administering the welfare of populations, of developing the resources of colonies, organising the circulation of money, compiling and using statistics, managing large businesses and workforces, branding and marketing products, and desiring and purchasing commodities brought into being a world that for the first time could be measured and calculated as though it were a free-standing object, the economy."[93] Drawing on Bruno Latour's concept of metrology and metrological regimes, which create and stabilise objects through accepted ways of measurement, Mitchell proposes that "rather than assuming there was always an economy, then, we need to explore the rival metrological projects that brought the economy into being."[94] Chapter 5 explores these projects, including forms of commodification, measurement, standardisation, and verification, as well as the organising discourses of the green economy that give them meaning and political significance. The chapter is therefore organised around such questions as, How do African states govern economies and markets through green discourses and practices? What technologies, regimes of truth, visibilities, and subjectivities are deployed, for example, in investment programmes, regulation, innovation, and taxation? What forms of resistance and dissent are made possible? What are the key similarities and differences produced in the forms of African green economy? What are the reasons for these similarities and differences, and what consequences might they have for environmental politics in Africa?

International Relations

The above three fields of state effects have been well studied and mapped in other contexts by some of the critical theorists drawn upon here: Mitchell, Scott, Jessop, and Kuehls, for example. Scott shows how states attempt "to make a society legible" through the standardisation of names of peoples and places, property law, census surveys and registers, the design of cities, transport systems, the layout of agriculture and plantations, among others.[95] A field of governance neglected by all of these theorists, however, is the international, and this is the fourth field in which, I argue, green states are produced. As Sharma and Gupta note, "Transnational processes have clearly reshaped the presumed association between nation-states, sovereignty, and territoriality."[96]

International and transnational practices of conflict and cooperation between states and across state borders, including trade, exploration, diplomatic relations, solidarity campaigns, warfare, and negotiations, are important producers of state effects.[97] As Larner and Walters remark, in some ways nation-states can be seen as "the effects of 'international' practices."[98] Epstein asserts the strong constructivist stance that a "state is what it says it is and how it performs itself in its relations with other states."[99] States are not produced in isolation but are fundamentally relational, social entities: a state is a state because of other states. Hence chapter 6 is organised around questions like, How are the international relations of African states governed through green discourses and practices? What technologies, regimes of truth, visibilities, and subjectivities are deployed, for example, in ratings systems, diplomatic agreements and partnerships, the aid system, warfare, international regimes, and environmental institutions? What forms of resistance and dissent are made possible? What are the key similarities and differences produced in the forms of African international relations, and who are the leaders and laggards? How have common continental positions on issues like climate change been forged? What are the reasons for the similarities and differences between African states, and what consequences might they have for environmental politics in Africa?

THE POSTCOLONIAL, BIOPOLITICAL STATE IN AFRICA

This fourfold framework appears initially to exclude other key aspects of statehood, such as the law and notions of legitimacy, violence and its monopoly, administration and the broader problem of government, and the idea or myth of the state. However, in each of the four fields—territory, population, the economy, and international relations—various discourses, practices, and technologies operate to produce and regulate governable objects. Legal mechanisms, security measures, administrative structures, and legitimizing narratives can all be introduced in this manner. Therefore the four-part structure is a parsimonious, comprehensive way to frame the production of green state effects, not just in Africa but throughout global politics, and it leads to a more detailed and nuanced perspective on the implications of state forms of politics which nevertheless retains a strong critical stance.

Before considering the production of green territories in more detail in chapter 3, I want to take note of two initial implications that emerge from a biopolitical perspective on green state practices in Africa, which begins with the micropractices, assemblages, technologies, and discourses of governing in action and considers the state as an effect of these. The first is to stress the importance of international and transnational forces and relations. Colonialism, whether imperial rule as in nineteenth-century Egypt or settler societies as in apartheid South Africa, is a crucial determinant of the type of green state practices that have been embedded in Africa. This is true with respect to urban planning, conservation parks, modernist engineering, and racial classifications. Since formal independence, Africa's environmental governance continues to be powerfully shaped by the interaction between external and domestic actors.[100] Charles Tilly argued that in the European context "war

4. "Police with Sjamboks, Plein Street," Santu Mofokeng (b. 1956). © Santu Mofokeng, c. 1986 silverprint edition 5. Images courtesy Lunetta Bartz, MAKER, Johannesburg.

makes states." By contrast, I posit that transnational environmental governance and monitoring make African states. Moreover, it is in the encounter between the majority and minority worlds that core features of international politics can be discerned.[101] Some accounts of the production of green states have underemphasised the transnational and international dimensions; but it is a key claim of this book that such forces are central to the production of green states in Africa.

The second particular contribution of emphasizing the biopolitical dimension is to introduce a note of caution into the green state debate. Theorists like Eckersley and Barry have responded to those who are sceptical about the potential for a "green leviathan," yet in some manifestations of the ecological modernisation literature the assumption seems to be that a more efficient and effective state is a self-evident good. Considering the scale of threats posed by runaway climate change and the risks of unregulated financial markets and multinational capital, this assumption is plausible in many respects. Moreover, this optimism draws on a powerful tradition of Hegelian political theory which sees the state as "the ultimate attainment of the human spirit."[102] But a biopolitical perspective on the evolution of the state in Africa highlights the ways that environmental and ecological imperatives have often functioned to extend the power of state institutions and political elites. The expansion or consolidation of state practices and effects is not neutral but political, and it often comes at the expense of other groups, social orders, and power relations. The rise of what some have termed authoritarian neoliberalism in Europe raises misgivings about the role of state structures in closing down democratic spaces and stymying progressive movements.[103] In Africa many are right to be sceptical about the progressive role of the state, and the reinvention of development as state building in Africa has precipitated criticism.[104] One of the potential consequences of revived interest in the green state is the legitimation of a new environmental state-building project in Africa, one which would have political dangers and risks as well as opportunities. The biopolitical history of environmental governance warns that the future transnational green state might, in some respects, have some family resemblances to the colonial or authoritarian state.

CHAPTER 3

Green Land and State Territory

> There are rolling fields of corn and sorghum and pumpkins. There are tufts of clouds and sheets of rain. There are rivers that flow and sometimes flood and sometimes dry up. There are trees that tell us that the earth breathes. There is day and night. Sun and moon and stars. There are houses and parks, and shopping malls, and offices and factories and airports and harbours. There are roads and highways through which human energy flows.
>
> —Njabulo Ndebele, *The Cry of Winnie Mandela*

> Years ago, the open land, the farmland was a natural drain for floods. Now with development comes a road network, paving, tar. . . . That's why you get houses being flooded.
>
> —Anonymous, *South Africa Talks Climate*

In July 2010 the Royal Society for the Protection of Birds, one of the oldest conservation organisations in the United Kingdom, began a letter-writing campaign to dissuade the government of Tanzania from building a 171.5-km road through the Serengeti National Park. The road, it was claimed, would "critically affect the mammals that inhabit the park and could potentially disrupt the renowned wildebeest migration between Serengeti and Maasai Mara in Kenya."[1] The Serengeti is a United Nations Educational, Scientific and Cultural Organisation (UNESCO) World Heritage Site and one of the most famous landscapes in East Africa, an iconic vista of grassland and savannah that is beloved of environmentalists worldwide. As the Tanzanian government insisted on the sovereign right to develop its territory, pressure against the road grew from a range of international organisations, governments, NGOs, and domestic communities, including the European Commission, the Wildlife Conservation Society of Tanzania, travel companies, and the

International Union for the Conservation of Nature (IUCN). The World Bank and Germany offered to help fund an alternative southern route that would avoid impacting the migration. In December 2010 the Africa Network for Animal Welfare (ANAW) filed a case at the East African Court of Justice (EACJ) to prevent construction of the road. Despite attempts to dismiss the case by the Tanzanian government the EACJ claimed jurisdiction, and on 20 June 2014 it ruled that the road was unlawful. The court said the road would infringe on a provision of a regional treaty calling for "the promotion of sustainable utilisation of the natural resources of the partner states" because it would interrupt the wildebeest migration into Kenya.[2] After the verdict, Josphat Ngonyo, ANAW's executive director, declared, "This was not a win for ANAW, not for our lawyer, Saitabao Ole Kanchory, not for Serengeti Watch, not for our expert witness John Kuloba, but for the millions of animals in the Serengeti-mara ecosystem. It is a win for nature and God's creation. Nature has won today."[3]

This case illustrates a number of important aspects of the politics of green states in Africa. First, it is a reminder that politics means contestations, disagreements, conflicts, and clashes of interests. These occur between many social forces: in this case, ministries and individuals within the Tanzanian government, private corporations and industries on both sides of the dispute, local and transnational conservation groups, international organisations, and others. Sometimes they are legalistic or discursive; on other occasions they give rise to physical violence. In 1998, for example, a number of local people, estimated between sixteen and fifty-two, were killed by park rangers in Serengeti, leading Issa Shivji to conclude, "The beauty of Serengeti will forever carry a red blot on its face."[4] One of the key arguments of this chapter and indeed of this book is that when addressing the question, What is the green state in Africa? we should focus attention on social conflicts and political contestation rather than on innovative technologies, modernisation processes, and technocratic policy reform.

Second, this case highlights the fact that in Africa the production of the green state is closely bound up with the production of land and territory. The Serengeti road dispute is fundamentally about authority over land and the proper uses of certain types of land. Long-standing disputes between developers and preservationists frequently come to a head over national parks and protected areas, particularly when oil or other mineral resources, transport links, or food security is at stake. This is true all over the world, but it is especially visible in Africa, and it is the most important way in which green state effects in Africa have an emphasis different from those elsewhere. Sub-Saharan Africa has over eleven hundred national parks and reserves, thirty-six of which are designated as World Heritage Sites, and protected areas cover 16 percent of East and Southern Africa and 10 percent of West and Central Africa. Namibia, Zambia, Botswana, and Tanzania all have over 30 percent of their land under some form of ecological protection.[5] Symbolically, African wild spaces play a crucial role in global environmental imaginaries, functioning as a kind of Edenic, pristine wilderness despite the socially constructed nature of these spaces.[6] Symbolic and material associations between the African bush, veld, jungle, and wilderness with danger, disease, and backwardness, on the one hand, and wealth, opportunity, virgin land, and pristine haven on the other, are all deeply political. Accordingly, I address the governance and contestation of land and territory in Africa as a primary site for the production of green states.

The third insight highlighted by the Serengeti road dispute is the many actors and interests involved and the complexity of the networks implicated. The green state is not simply a homogenous and autonomous institution or a bureaucratic administration within a sovereign territory, and this fact is perhaps even clearer in Africa than elsewhere in the world. Green states are produced through international, transnational, global, and local networks and relations. The Tanzanian government sought to play the sovereignty card, asserting their right to develop their national territory. But this has been vigorously contested, with some success. NGOs and conservationists have responded by reminding the government that the Serengeti is part of mankind's "global heritage."[7] International organisations have emphasised Tanzania's legal obligations under the Convention on Biological Diversity. The EACJ proclaimed its right to hear a case brought by a Kenyan-based environmental organisation against Tanzania's sovereign right to development and ruled against the construction of the road. Local communities have intervened on both sides of the argument. And there are many perspectives within the Tanzanian state, various ministries within government, and the ruling party. The production of green state effects involves a wide range of actors and networks that extends far beyond straightforward conceptions of the state or civil society.

My core argument below is that green state effects in Africa are primarily and quintessentially bound up with the government of land and territory to a far greater extent than they are elsewhere. The motif of the road is an appropriate starting point: it is a visceral incision into a landscape, governing lived space through the movement of peoples and representational spaces through maps and imagined geographies. It is also a socially and politically ambivalent technology: associated with progress, speed, modernisation, and opportunity but also with danger, fear, hazards, and the prospect of increased environmental degradation on local and global scales.[8] The production of territory through these and other technologies, including categorisation, mapping, administering and policing of protected areas, and conservation zones, is therefore the starting point for this chapter. The next section establishes the importance of land and territory to practices of statehood before turning to a number of techniques and technologies of territorialisation. Then the chapter turns to two different types of territorialisation in Africa: exclusive and hybrid modes. These are heuristic categories rather than clearly distinguishable forms of governance in practice, and I certainly do not argue that green states in Africa are moving from exclusive to hybrid modes of territorialisation. However, some forms of conservation and land governance in both colonial and contemporary eras can be characterised as models in which land is parcelled up into mutually exclusive, bounded, homogenous territories, whereas other forms of conservation and land governance, across various time periods, involve more hybrid, overlapping, ambiguous bordering practices. Assessing the causes and consequences of these differing rationalities of land governance is a crucial first step in mapping the green state in Africa.

TERRITORY AND THE STATE

The fundamental, indeed constitutive, relationship between the state and territory is encapsulated, as noted earlier, in Weber's classic definition of the state as "a human community that (successfully) claims the monopoly of the legitimate use of physical force within a given territory."[9] Modern states since the Treaty of Westphalia in 1648 have, de jure, exclusive sovereignty within their territory; they admit no higher or competing authority over their portion of the earth's surface (see chapter 2). The familiar political maps that adorn globes, the first pages of most atlases, politics and history textbooks, and foreign offices everywhere reveal that the world is divided into neatly contiguous territories divided by infinitely thin lines representing state borders. As Agnew and Corbridge write, "The merging of the state with a clearly bounded territory is the geographical essence of the field of international relations."[10]

Territory is different from land, terrain, or soil. There is land on the moon and on Mars, but it is not territory. Columbus set foot on land in the Americas, but it became state territory only when it was claimed by the Spanish crown. The dominant mode of territory is produced by states, and states exist because of their territory. Territory is named, mapped, bordered; it is subject to the law and authority of the sovereign.[11] Stuart Elden notes that state territory is associated in European thought with the "idea of exclusive ownership of a portion of the earth's surface."[12] To Henri Lefebvre, on whom Elden and many other theorists of spatiality draw heavily, state territory is also peculiar in that it is a type of space which is abstract, even, homogenous, a tabula rasa. Such "abstract space permits continuous, rational economic calculation in the spheres of production and exchange, as well as comprehensive, encompassing control in the realm of statecraft."[13] Territorialisation is therefore a process by which uneven land or landscape is made universally codifiable, legible, and fungible and thus ownable as property.

The process by which the African landmass was territorialised illustrates these general points. Processes of European imperial territorialisation began slowly but gathered pace in the nineteenth century. Statelike entities existed in precolonial Africa, but state territory was not as hegemonic as it was becoming in sixteenth- and seventeenth-century Europe. Jeremy Black points out that in Guillaume Delisle's *Carte d'Afrique* (Amsterdam, c. 1722) (fig. 5) Africa was misleadingly divided into kingdoms with clear frontiers, thus producing a "European account of Africa in which European notions of territorialisation are employed."[14] Such a representation existed alongside parallel representations of Africa as a blank space or a void to be filled. This was most evocatively conveyed by the character Marlow in Joseph Conrad's novel *Heart of Darkness*: "When I was a little chap I had a passion for maps. . . . At that time there were many blank spaces on the earth, and when I saw one that looked particularly inviting on a map . . . I would put my finger on it and say, When I grow up I will go there."[15] Such representations, while now politically incorrect, have not disappeared: Kaplan's and Schroeder's account of the "new scramble for Africa" presents it as a rush for the "gaping heart" of the continent, for the "vast, impassable blank spot on the map" that is the Congo basin.[16]

Even if precolonial Africa did not much resemble Delisle's *Carte d'Afrique,* it was not a blank, empty space. Other forms of territory existed, produced by precolonial political formations and polities, in much the same way as medieval and early modern Europe had a variety of practices of territorialisation in

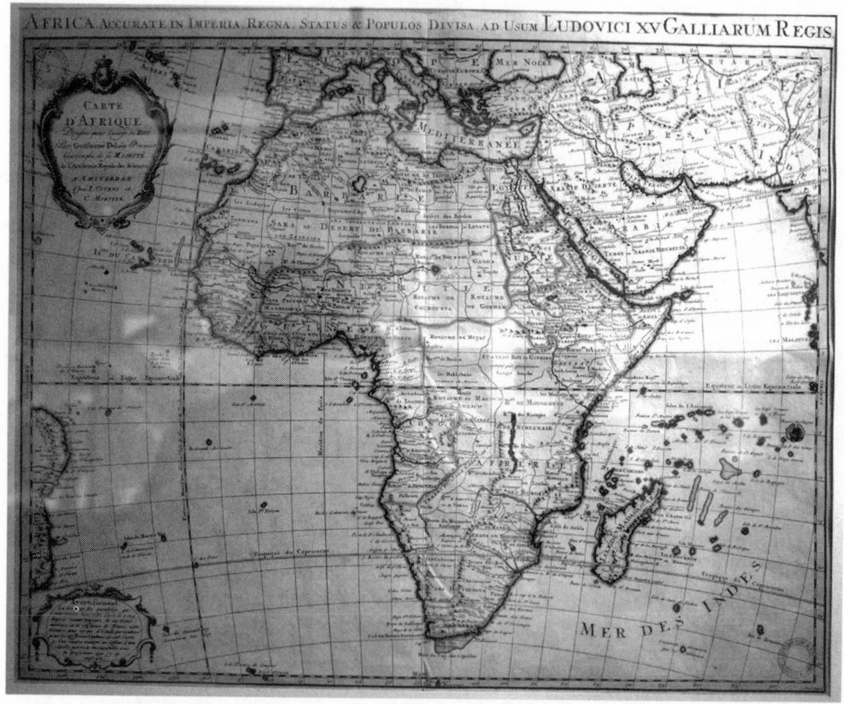

5. *Carte d'Afrique,* Guillaume Delisle (Amsterdam, c. 1722).

which sovereigns, noblemen, city guilds, villages, and the Roman Catholic Church and its various orders produced and governed territory within emerging state formations. Citing an example from what became the Zimbabwe–Mozambique border, David Hughes comments on how the nineteenth-century occupants "used land, but they seldom divided it into bounded, exclusive zones. They appear to have demarcated territory only when one polity's farmland abutted another."[17] The shift from overlapping, heterogeneous, blurred divisions of territory into the contiguous, neatly parcelled, and cartographically demarcated territories that occurred after the Berlin Conference of 1884–85 was a key turning point in the history of African territory formation, even if physical impacts on the ground did not always follow.[18] Indeed, this development helps clarify two forms of territorialisation which, although never entirely distinct, represent useful ways of thinking about how diverse forms of green state in Africa are produced.

First, more exclusive modes of territorialisation mobilise sovereign forms of power and seek to clearly demarcate distinct patches of land with distinct forms of authority and rights and obligations within them, often encapsulated in the form of property ownership. In a manner of speaking this was the aim of the Berlin Conference, which deployed ruler-straight lines to demarcate countries and their imperial possessors. As Nick Vaughan-Williams explains, drawing on William Connolly, the etymology of the word *territory* is the Latin root *terrere,* which means to frighten or terrorise, and "Connolly suggests that territory can be thought of as precisely 'land occupied and bounded by violence.'"[19] Fred Nelson writes, "The core characteristic of Africa's colonial era was the imposition of new forms of centralised political authority over access to land and resources that had previously been controlled by more localised institutions."[20] These new forms of authority were often violent, extractive, coercive, and brutal.

The second form of territorialisation is more complex, heterogeneous, and hybrid. Even colonial states in Africa were more variegated than the Westphalian ideal: imperial powers asserted sovereignty or in some cases trusteeship over their African dominions, and if the rule of the metropole applied to certain populations, usually urban ones, in other rural areas customary rule and alternative spheres of authority were encouraged or permitted. It was independence, not colonialism, which actualised the Westphalian ideal of territorially sovereign entities, and African nationalists framed liberation in terms of the assertion of national sovereignty and self-determination over a particular portion of the earth's surface. Yet despite the longevity of Africa's colonially imposed borders, postcolonial politics has often been more spatially complex, heterogeneous, and hybrid than the nationalists had hoped. African territories comprise, among other things, private property, zones for commerce or development, segregated populations, protected areas, sacred sites, world heritage locations, restricted access, common land and public thoroughfares, and borderland and transit zones.[21]

Bringing attention to these two forms of territorialisation represents an important addition and corrective to existing literatures on the green state which have hitherto displayed little interest in the politics of land, territory, borders, or even conservation.[22] If territory is a constitutive feature of the modern state, then one might assume that green states have a different relationship to the land beneath their feet than national, liberal, or welfare states. And given the importance of nature conservation and biodiversity to the environmental movement of the 1960s and 1970s and the considerable rise in protected areas in the twentieth century, one might also have expected a more central place for conservation in the discussions of green state theorists. John

Dryzek and colleagues do see the possibility of a "new state imperative: environmental conservation" for green states in the future, but they pay no attention to the existing politics of conservation even in states like the United States, let alone states like Tanzania, Botswana, and South Africa, where conservation is more deeply embedded in state politics and national identity.[23]

There are two main reasons for this absence of reflection on land, territory, and conservation. First, as noted in previous chapters, the green state literature has been shaped by sociological theories of modernisation and globalisation which have tended to stress the transformation of the nation-state into the transnational or cosmopolitan state.[24] It is often assumed, but rarely explicated in detail, that such states are postterritorial or that national borders and boundaries will play less fundamental roles than in the states of the past. Strange argued that the age of "new-medievalism" (a term first coined by Bull) was characterised by states competing for market shares in the world economy rather than "for control over territory and the wealth-creating resources within territories."[25] To Beck, transnational states are "non-territorial."[26] Indeed, for many it is precisely the irrelevance of national borders in the face of transboundary pollution, dwindling fish stocks, industrial risks and hazards, climate change, and holes in the ozone layer that necessitates transnational or cosmopolitan states. Perhaps because claims of a borderless world were associated with overblown predictions of the dwindling of nation-states and because there is little evidence that national territories and borders are becoming redundant, green state theorists and empirical studies have devoted little attention to changing practices and rationalities of land governance and territorialisation. State territory is therefore often taken as given; it is the unexamined foundation for thinking about the politics of the green state.

The second reason for the neglect of land and territory in the green state literature is that conservation has played a very different role in African state formation than in Europe and North America. In Africa, as we will see below, vast conservation parks preceded independent statehood, and protected areas became closely bound up with practices of state building, border enforcement, and the penetration of the state into rural areas. By contrast, in North America national states preexisted the creation of parks and reserves, as neatly conveyed by the aphorism "God may have created the world, but only Congress can create wilderness."[27] In Europe the model of conservation and national parks is very different again; parks there are regarded as more mixed use, inhabited, and socially produced landscapes as opposed to the vast expanses of wilderness that dominate North American or African mental imaginaries and physical landscapes. As a result, the European green state literature has focused on more urban and industrial issues such as energy policy, consumption, health, food, and transport. The argument of this chapter, contrary to most of the existing green state literature, is that the governance of land through exclusive and hybrid practices of territorialisation is a primary, quintessential element of the production of green state effects in Africa. The most important question which follows from this is, How do these practices of territorialisation produce highly disparate ways of governing land?

PRACTICES OF TERRITORIALISATION

Both exclusive and hybrid forms of territorialisation are produced through technologies, discourses, and practices of territorialisation. There are three significant practices of territorialisation: the creation or policing or contesting of borders and boundaries; the zoning or administering of space for different purposes; and the mapping or surveying of land use or land qualities.

Producing the Borderline

Borders and boundaries involve much more political work than the lines drawn on a map around a table in Berlin in 1884–85 imply. Borders and boundaries permeate society: they are found within villages and even households, agricultural land, forests, towns, cities, transport routes, and around particular zones, hubs, regions, and districts. These diverse forms of borders and boundaries can take the form of infinitely narrow lines on maps, or they can be indistinct and blurred regions negotiated through local custom and practice. They can be accepted and relatively stable and static, or constantly contested and reappropriated. They have diverse bandwidths and degrees of permeability, and a wide array of physical and conceptual manifestations, structures, and practices accompany them. They are performed and contested in a variety of ways, and Mitchell describes in some detail how national state borders are performatively produced: “By establishing a territorial boundary and exercising absolute control over movement across it, state practices define and help constitute a national entity. Setting up and policing a frontier involves a variety of fairly modern social practices—continuous barbed-wire fencing, passports, immigration laws, inspections, currency control and so on. These mundane arrangements, most of them unknown two hundred or even one hundred years ago, help manufacture an almost transcendental entity, the nation state. This entity comes to seem something much more than the sum of the everyday activities that constitute it, appearing as a structure containing and giving order and meaning to people's lives."[28] Drawing on Mitchell, Dunn provides an account of how state spaces and boundaries are performed through various rituals at national parks in Uganda and Rwanda. These include the pivoting of a tank turret every afternoon inside Uganda's Bwindi National Park; public military drills inside Uganda's Mgahinga National Park; and a visible military roadside presence at the boundaries of Rwanda's Nyungwe National Park. Through such practices, frontiers and boundaries are performatively constituted, and in turn they work to produce the modern territorial state as well as all sorts of other social entities.[29]

In addition, national borders have considerable variability and heterogeneity, especially in Africa. Whereas in other parts of the world there may be relatively uniform and consistent practices of national bordering, only a quarter of African national boundaries are actually physically inscribed or marked on the ground. Imperial border makers were often far removed from the realities of African landscapes; for example, the boundary between Nigeria and Cameroon was once thought to be marked by the river Rio del Rey, which was eventually discovered not to exist at all. Whereas some borders are heavily policed and even militarised, others are open for vast stretches to nomadic pastoralists, wildlife, and a wide range of licit and illicit social flows. Some are virtually impassable, others are zones of contact, commerce, and relatively free movement. It is evident that the writ of the state does not extend evenly across the territory of Somalia or the Democratic Republic of the Congo, nor are all borders policed in the forests of East Kivu. Moreover, the borders and boundaries that internally govern and separate the mining enclaves of Zambia, the rural regions of Tanzania and Mozambique, and the informal settlements of Nigeria and South Africa are often more significant on the ground than national frontiers. They represent spaces where state territory is not smooth and homogenous. These are features of state space and territory around the world, but they are more evident in much of Africa.[30]

Zoning African Spaces

Within these boundaries and borders a broad range of zones and categories and land types exist, and they are governed and administered in various ways. The smooth and even colouring of the political map is a powerful fiction but is only one of many fictions or territorialising practices that constitute contemporary states. How land is used, owned, ruled, and administered is a crucial element of the production of territory. For example, designating land as agricultural and then ploughing, irrigating, sowing, or grazing it is a powerful way to transform wilderness, *terra nullius,* or virgin land, into state territory.[31]

A wide spectrum of various uses, codes of conduct, regimes of law and authority, and assignations of rights shape land use and the governance of territory in Africa.[32] For example, the IUCN's Protected Areas Categories System classifies six types of land: strict nature reserves / wilderness areas; national parks; national monuments / natural landmarks; habitats / species management areas; protected landscapes / seascapes; and protected areas with sustainable use of natural resources.[33] Other categories also exist, including UNESCO World Heritage Sites, private hunting reserves, state land, community conservation areas, sacred sites, and areas of outstanding natural beauty. These protected areas exist on every continent and at sea (fig. 6), with particularly high concentrations in Africa and Latin America (fig. 7).

Within these distinct zones and spaces, spheres of authority are created and policed, standards of law or values or norms are established, and various access rights are allowed. A national park tends to have stricter rules and restrictions than a private game reserve, for example, although a private reserve

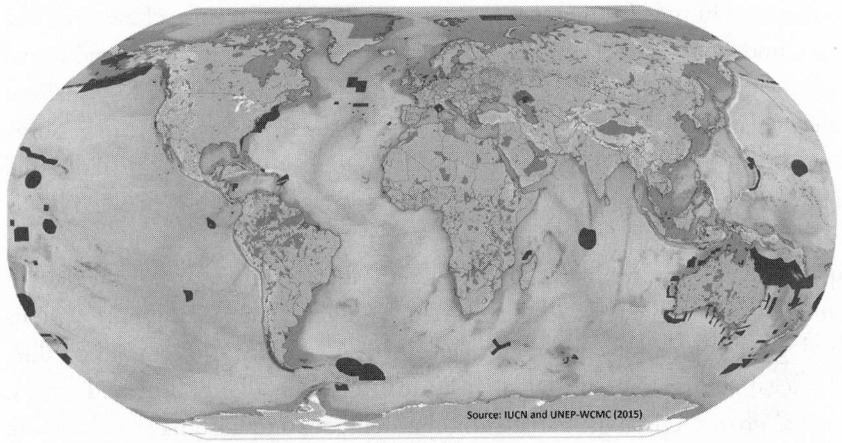

6. Spatial distribution of the world's protected areas. IUCN and UNEP-WCMC (2015)

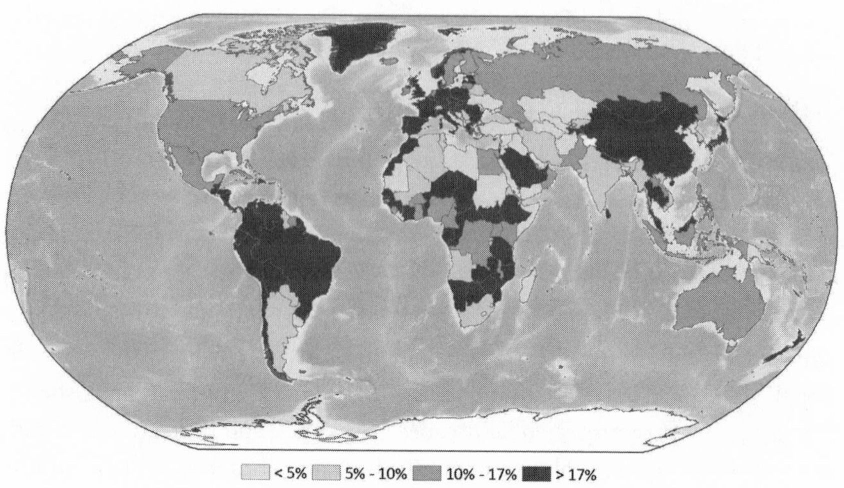

7. Percentage of terrestrial and inland water areas covered by protected areas, by country and territory. Juffe-Bignoli et al. (2014).

might have more resources available on a day-to-day basis and more intensive management of the land and biodiversity. A protected area, in contrast to a park, often comprises many zones with lots of land use types within it. For example, "a central national park or core non-use area could be surrounded by conservation areas (or corridors or buffer zones) and abutted by a traditional hunter / gatherer zone or a pastoral zone. In turn, these could be surrounded by game ranches, forest reserves, agroforests, and traditional agriculture. Still further out from the core could be zones of specialized mechanised agriculture, urban areas, and manufacturing industries. Some uses or production systems could overlap several zones, such as traditional pastoralism overlying a traditional hunter / gatherer zone, a controlled hunting zone and a game ranching zone."[34] Within each of these zones, different qualities and features of the land are established as important or incidental: the physical geography, the aesthetic landscape, the ecosystem, various biological populations and their degree of vulnerability, the economic value, the legal status, the cultural or historical meaning, symbolism and status. Sacred groves, burial grounds, and other religious sites also have a close link to the conservation of particular landscapes in Africa.[35] All of these categories have implications for the power relations, hierarchies and, inequalities that permeate communities.

The designation of land as private property is a crucial manifestation of power relations. Lund has drawn a distinction between whether land is viewed as territory or property: "As territory, space is governed, but not owned by its governing agency. As property, on the other hand, space is owned, but not governed by its owners."[36] Yet this distinction is not as clear-cut as it might seem: identification of land as property enables taxation and the monitoring of stewardship responsibilities by the state or other bodies. Similarly, establishing governance and the rule of law over a territory is a necessary step for the creation and protection of private property. To Mitchell, for example, the demarcation of private property in the Nile River Valley should be seen as "an arrangement created by the state to bring order to the system of landholding and increase its own powers over rural society."[37] These categorisations are of vital political import and are often contested. As Lund and Boone note, when land is contested, "some protagonists may view it as territorial space controlled by the central state, others as a tract of property, and yet others as an endowment attached to customary institutions that are 'guaranteed' by neo-customary entitlements for use by members of a local community."[38] Thus struggles over land are also struggles over power, authority, and legitimacy.

Mapping the Terrain

Finally, the techniques and technologies by which these borders, boundaries, and zones are mapped and made knowable are crucial territorialising practices. The very formation of colonial states in Africa was accompanied by an intense devotion of effort to properly mapping and demarcating boundaries: examples include the Sudan–Uganda Boundary Commission and the Nigeria–Cameroon Boundary Commission, both of which took place in 1912–13, and the British colonial land map in Egypt.[39] In more recent decades large-scale land registration has been implemented throughout sub-Saharan Africa, often with the support of international donors and ostensibly aimed at improving individual security of tenure in the absence of private property rights. The Africa Progress Panel in 2014 discussed land mapping and registration in Rwanda (where photomaps are used to issue land titles), Côte d'Ivoire, Benin, Burkina Faso, Tanzania, Mozambique, and Ghana.[40]

However, mapping is not simply, despite the promises of satellite-enabled geographical information systems (GIS), a quest for greater detail and ever closer verisimilitude. Rather, mapping, like all forms of representation, is an art and always makes certain things visible even as it hides others. These choices are political, or at least they can be made political when they are contested and resisted. As Jon Harley observes, "Environmentalists in the United States, for instance, at a time when acid rain or commercial destruction is threatening our forests, may be frustrated by the optical illusion of a topographical map that shows woodland only by an undifferentiated green tint to define its area."[41] Maps can crystallise the other practices of territorialisation discussed above: the production of borders and frontiers and the zoning of land usage within these borders. To map a landscape is to assert control over it and create a powerful statement of belief in mechanical replicability, objectivity, and representation. As Brockington et al. argue, mapping and classification are "not just a way of seeing the world; [they are] also a vehicle for remaking it."[42] Thus the very practical ways in which mapping and surveying are carried out, that is, which things are recorded and measured, according to what scales, and how they are represented, are crucial indicators of the ways in which green states are produced and contested.

EXCLUSIVE PRACTICES OF TERRITORIALISATION

Prevailing practices of territorialisation tend to be informed by two central and conflicting images of land in Africa. The first is that conjured up by the image of the Serengeti: a vast open space of rolling hills and savannah, wildlife, and fertility. It is this sense of space and fecundity that the proposed road discussed at the start of this chapter seems to violate. The second image, however, is that of African cities like Nairobi and Lagos and the African slum: crowded populations, teeming masses living on top of each other, resource scarcity and density of bodies. This is the apparent threat the road brings. As Richard Schroeder observes, these two conflicting images of diversity and dearth lie behind most environmental interventions in Africa, and conservation parks vividly bring them both to light.[43]

Conservation can refer to the protection of flora and fauna or of energy or of any kinds of resources and reserves. Practices of conservation are therefore widespread and diverse. Yet practices of wildlife and biodiversity conservation in Africa and around the globe have taken a relatively circumscribed number of forms. Although these have changed over time and varied between landscapes and political regimes, it is possible to identify a relatively limited number of models of wildlife conservation: these include the fortress or barriers model, community-based conservation, people and parks, peace parks, and transfrontier conservation. Here I examine several of these types, beginning with what have been pejoratively described as the fortress or barriers model, which invokes exclusive practices of territorialisation. It is not possible to simply label this an older or colonial style of conservation, although it tended to be more dominant in previous periods, as elements of it continue to inform contemporary practices of land use and governance in Africa.

Fortress Conservation

The belief that nature's greatest enemy is human civilisation has been a feature of many strands of environmentalism and conservationism. Environmentalists keen to preserve and secure what were seen as especially beautiful, valuable, or fragile pristine wildernesses were exponents of this outlook. For preservationists the solution was obvious: keep people out. Much of the history and the contemporary politics of wildlife conservation in Africa, as in North America and elsewhere, can be described as a process of making certain spaces safe for nature by excluding most types of human activity. As well as invoking the fortress metaphor, this stance is also known as "fines-and-fences."[44] The communities who live, farm, harvest, hunt, worship, and work in these lands are separated from conservation areas by fences, fined when they trespass or hunt or harvest in these areas, and in general excluded from the land. By contrast, scientists, researchers, park officials, and tourists are allowed access to the parks and even encouraged to enter them as part of the conservation project.

Much has been written about the role such protected places play in modern environmentalism, and why industrial societies have been relatively keen to protect wilderness areas. The mystique of African landscapes for European travellers, colonists, settlers, and conservationists was bound up in the idea of wilderness, a place of purity, innocence, and vitality. The allure is also that of a frontier society: a frontier that could be pushed back and tamed but that challenged and in some ways improved civilisation itself. The wildness of the frontier is seen as a proving ground of manhood, strength, and durability. This is not simply a Western, industrial attitude. In many African cultures the rites of circumcision and becoming a man take place during an extended trip into the bush. However, the phenomenon of establishing bounded, fenced, protected areas to preserve biodiversity from human degradation is a peculiarly modern and Western practice. It is one which occurs worldwide but in which African spaces play prominent roles.[45]

The Serengeti National Park, for example, was the first national park to be created in British colonial Africa, and it was a result of the lobbying of the Society for the Protection of the Fauna of the Empire. Its formation was hotly contested, both by factions and arms of the colonial state, including some Tanganyikan officials who worried that it would impede native customary rights to grazing, fuel, and hunting, and by local populations who resisted such practices of territorialisation at their point of implementation. Nevertheless, it became a model for national parks elsewhere. Communities who had lived and grazed in the Serengeti landscape for generations were forced to move outside the park boundaries. Roderick Neumann writes, "National parks were at once symbolic representations of the European vision of Africa and a demonstration of the colonial state's power to control access to land and natural resources."[46]

In the early history of the Serengeti heated debates occurred over what level and types of human activity were to be permitted within the park. For example, those Maasai who were allowed to remain within the park and continue to hunt there were allowed to use only traditional weapons and methods, that is, to remain so-called primitive. Reforms to the park's boundaries and regulations in the late 1950s reduced its size but established for the first time the unambiguous principle that human communities should be excluded from national parks. No habitation, cultivation, or hunting were to be permitted inside the boundaries. The Serengeti remains a landmark protected area, hence the outcry when the plans for the proposed road were announced. But despite the language of many conservationists, the Serengeti is not an isolated "last wilderness" in Tanzania. Including the Serengeti, Tanzania's State of the Environment report in 2006 listed 14 national parks, 28 game reserves, 38 game-controlled areas, and the Ngorogoro conservation area, which together cover over 24.5 million hectares, and 815 forest reserves covering about 15 million hectares. Once all of these are coded according to IUCN criterion an impressive 38 percent of Tanzania's land area will be under IUCN-recognised protection. The value of protected areas to Tanzania's economy, international image, land use, and settlement patterns means that green state effects here are primarily shaped by practices of conservation.[47]

Other national parks and protected areas of note exist across Africa. The Hluhluwe–Umfolozi game reserve in KwaZulu-Natal, South Africa, is a recent conjoining of the oldest game reserves in Africa. The two parks were proclaimed in 1895, the decade during which the Zulu kingdom came under direct British imperial control. As Shirley Brooks argues, this quintessentially natural, wild space has an intense political history, including the "large-scale slaughter of animals by the authorities during the anti-nagana [trypanomiasis] campaigns of the 1930s and 1940s; the removal of communities from the Corridor area between the two reserves, also in the 1940s; and a bitter history of conflict over land, particularly in the western section of the Umfolozi game reserve."[48] A large section of Umfolozi has been proclaimed a wilderness area in which no development is allowed and access is only on foot, a key legacy of the well-known conservationist and former game ranger Ian Player. The park merges the symbolism of wild Africa with the branding of the province and its cultural history as timeless Zululand. The story of the park draws upon the famous Zulu king Shaka and emphasises his keen interest in conservation and the establishment of royal hunting grounds. Brooks argues, however, that local residents distinguish between "*indawo yenkosi yokuzingela,* the royal hunting grounds, and *isiqiwu,* the fenced colonial (and postcolonial) game reserve."[49] The older meaning of the word *isiqiwu*—"beacon" or "boundary mark"—indicates that "the primary feature of the reserve, in the experience of the people who lived near it, was the fact that they were excluded from this land. Dispossession, as symbolised by the beacons, was a more obvious component than conservation."[50] The establishment of a fence around the park was bitterly resented by local communities and, combined with the forced removal of hundreds of households from the corridor between the parks, prompted widespread resistance. To Brooks, the "decreasing permeability of Hluhluwe's boundary, brought about by fencing and various other restrictions on people's access to reserve land, is a key feature of the historical geography of the reserve from 1939."[51]

Nearby is the much more well-known Kruger National Park (KNP), the oldest national park in Africa and one of the oldest in the world. Yet, like all national parks, it is not so much the preservation of a pristine wilderness as the creation of a managed territorial space. The first warden of KNP, Col. James Stephenson-Hamilton, earned the nickname Shukuza (a derivation from the Tsonga to mean "he who sweeps away") for his treatment of local communities at the turn of the century. The place of the park in South Africa's national identity is complex and sometimes uncomfortable: named after an Afrikaner hero and championed and visited by white liberals, it is an iconic national space from which many black South Africans still feel excluded.[52]

These parks and many others like them are produced through a number of practices of exclusive territorialisation. The identification, construction, and policing of boundaries is one of the most important. Thousands of miles of barbed wire and fencing have been unrolled to protect the wildlife of Africa from poachers and hunters. Border posts and armed guards watch over entry points. Mandatory passes that detail the number of guests, the length of time of the visit, the activities, and the citizenship or visa status of the visitors must be purchased. Despite an apparent emphasis on inclusion, community participation, and moving beyond the barriers in recent years, the day-to-day activities of many parks and conservation organisations still involve exclusive territorialising practices such as putting up or repairing fences, guarding wildlife, and hunting poachers. Indeed, recent worries over high levels of poaching, particularly of rhinos, have led to a revival of fortress modes of militarised conservation and shoot-to-kill antipoaching missions, with journalists alleging that places like KNP are "under siege by poachers working for criminal networks."[53] Prominent conservation organisations report on security issues and the number of kilometres of fencing set up in their parks: a quarterly report from 2014 reported that "Limpopo National Park's protection unit delivered improved successes during 2013, with the arrest of 43 poachers (up from 14 in 2012) and the confiscation of 21 rifles (up from 15 in 2012)" and predicted further successes given the "recent deployment of a new 30-man special anti-poaching unit, whose activities will be concentrated in the intensive protection zone along the park's western boundary with Kruger National Park."[54]

This model of conservation requires strict practices of zoning within the parks. Fortress conservation dictates that permanent human settlement is not permitted, and neither are farming, mining, or many other activities. Kenya has a ban even on game hunting in its national parks, enacted by presidential decree in 1977. The authority of the state can be invoked to police these rules within national parks, but many other types of territorialisation operate on a similarly exclusive model but involve private property and private security or use NGOs or nonprofit organisations to run and police particular zones or parks. Nancy Peluso has highlighted how conservation groups often "augment the financial and physical capacities of Third World states or state agencies to protect resources with 'global' value."[55] National parks in Kenya deploy automatic weapons and helicopter gunships; private military firms have been contracted by organisations such as WWF to conduct antipoaching operations in Equatorial Guinea; and defence forces have been used in Tanzania and Zimbabwe to defend their protected areas. Kenyan authorities were licensed to shoot-to-kill poachers, but park resources were also used against Somali migrants and to modernise Maasai pastoralists. The Botswana Defence Force has become a model example of the use of coordinated, militarised, top-down strategic action against poaching and in defence of wildlife.[56]

The creation and maintenance of such zones requires close mapping and constant surveillance. A closed, exclusive, fortress park requires that the flora and fauna within it form a stable enough ecosystem to be sustainable with appropriate human management; thus the scientific surveys and ecosystem assessments that identify a suitably sized area with sufficient natural habitats and resources to support the required population are a key practice of territorialisation. These are often supported or implemented by NGOs and private foundations, alongside or in place of the state. The Peace Parks Foundation (PPF), for example, supports extensive and intensive scientific research, surveys, and training and reports on increased funding for "technology applications such as drones, microchips, tracking devices and improved field communications, training and capacity building of field rangers."[57] Controversies over plans to introduce new technologies like horn dye that would render the rhinos worthless to poaching networks have spilled over into the sphere of public debate in South Africa and the Netherlands, putting large sums of funding and the legitimacy of conservation organisations at stake.

Thus parks frequently operate as states within a state: enclaves in which park authorities or international agencies determine and enforce the law, police populations, manage their natural resources, and defend their fiefdom against intruders both physically and discursively. Moreover, the practices of exclusive territorialisation associated with fortress conservation have also helped produce modern states in Africa. Conservation areas are frequently located in the most inaccessible and remote parts of the continent, for example, in mountains, deserts, swamps, and forests, places where state authority has only partially or irregularly extended. The creation and maintenance of national parks in these areas provide resources and legitimacy for state interventions, including border mapping, construction and security, the monitoring and control of population movements, and jurisdiction over taxation of farming, hunting, logging, and fishing.[58] Even in South Africa, for example, one of Africa's strongest states has found that national parks have helped to maintain and defend its borders. The country has the dubious honour of being the scene of the first conflict in which barbed-wire fences were widely used, when Gen. Walter Kitchener created lines of barbed wire and blockhouses during the Anglo-Boer War of 1898–1901 and constructed what soon came to be called concentration camps (also with barbed wire) for housing captive Afrikaner populations. Apartheid South Africa found its ability to control vast swathes of rugged land on its borders with Mozambique, Zimbabwe, and Angola through national park authorities and resources to be extremely valuable during the period of the "total onslaught" in the early 1980s. Stephen Ellis, among others, has exposed the role played by apartheid-era security forces, which included the use of parks for counterinsurgency and by covert-action units and even extensive involvement in illegal international ivory smuggling.[59] More recently, parks in East Africa have become front lines of conflict against Islamic terrorist groups like al-Shabaab.

Thus, if exclusive state territorialisation has fulfilled useful functions for transnational capitalism, as argued by Marxist geographers like David Harvey and Neil Brenner, so territorially exclusive protected areas similarly fulfill useful functions for a range of social actors and forces, including the conservation industry, NGOs, and state elites.[60] The creation of carefully policed exclusive spaces of conservation has proved to be a way of making money from ecotourism: investors want secure property rights and manageable and identifiable assets, such as the charismatic megafauna, while customers want guaranteed wildlife sightings in a wilderness environment that is not too lawless or physically dangerous. From this perspective we might be tempted to say that the quintessential green state in Africa is an authoritarian conservation state in which vast tracts of land are exclusively territorialised and secured against local populations, for the protection of biodiversity, the control of wildlife rents, and the enjoyment of foreign tourists.

Many observers and practitioners of conservation in Africa will object that the fortress model is outdated. It is certainly more easily identified in the colonial parks and those of the newly independent nation-building states, and much work has been done in recent years by park authorities, NGOs, and communities to change the image and practices of fortress conservation. But these practices of exclusive territorialisation are not simply those of a bygone era; exclusionary and militarised forms of governance are still practiced in many conservation areas, as they are on many state borders. In recent years a "back to the barriers" movement has been identified in conservation, as parks return to more exclusive and militarised practices of territorialisation after experiments with more hybrid and flexible forms.[61] Moreover, exclusive practices of territorialisation can also be identified in the governance of African land and natural resources outside protected areas, in what has been termed land grabbing or the new scramble for Africa.

Land Grabbing as Exclusive Territorialisation

Rather than make an extensive intervention into what are now very widely debated terms and research fields, I use the land-grabbing debate to make three key points. First, attempts to secure exclusive control over African agricultural land and natural resources are far from new. Second, there are many family resemblances between attempts to secure access to natural resources and conservation areas, both colonial and contemporary. Third, these practices of exclusive territorialisation by states and their allies almost always meet with resistance from communities and competing interest groups.[62]

Practices of exclusive territorialisation go well beyond conservation in Africa, and they were a fundamental feature of colonialism. For example, white settlers in places like Kenya, Rhodesia, and South Africa sought to establish exclusive control over the best farmland, often violently expropriating African communities in the process. Throughout the colonial and postcolonial periods the state and the political elites associated with it sought to bring rural areas and natural resources within the scope of exclusive modes of territorialisation. Villagisation and resettlement schemes, rural development projects, agricultural modernisation initiatives, and big hydropower and irrigation were ways in which the African state sought to make nonstate spaces legible and to secure valuable natural resources.[63]

Second, while many of these land grabs were simply about the accumulation of wealth, questions of resource conservation and the management of environmental impacts became increasingly widespread. Colonial conservation in Africa—outside of protected areas—was preoccupied with land degradation, deforestation, and soil erosion. A solution to these problems was to relocate rural residents and impose restrictions on farming and forestry. Chris de Wet suggests that around one million people were relocated in Kenya and Mozambique; at least three million in South Africa; five to thirteen million in Tanzania; and five to twelve million in Ethiopia.[64] From the 1930s to the 1970s the South African government tried to promote various soil conservation, resettlement, and betterment programmes in rural areas. Betterment planning involved the division of land into agricultural and residential land and the removal of people living on the former into the latter. It sought "a more economically rational division of land into separate arable, residential and grazing areas, together with agricultural support services."[65] Scoones writes, "The abhorrence of disorder and the apparent chaos of traditional farming systems severely upset officials who were obsessed with the aesthetics of neat and tidy straight lines."[66] Land degradation and soil erosion are not solely historic matters in South Africa. Policies to address them, such as betterment, partly explain why South Africa's current distribution of land is so profoundly unequal. Moreover, contemporary governments remain preoccupied with land degradation and continue to practice exclusive modes of territorialisation through removals of population and fencing and segregation of land.[67]

Third, these practices of exclusive territorialisation are rarely easy, straightforward, and unopposed. From the imposition of European models of statehood to the expulsion of communities from colonial and then national parkland to the exclusion of peasants from the new waves of investment in African land, such forms of territorialisation often meet with resistance ranging from armed rebellion and succession to more mundane everyday resistance, theft, corruption, evasion, and ridicule. Dunn notes how, for example, in interactions with African national parks "the basic interpretation of land is deeply contested, with locals resisting not only the state's claim to power and sovereignty, but its ability to define spatial representations as well."[68] Some forms of resistance seek to contest the boundaries, codes of conduct, and owners of the land, replacing statist or colonial exclusive territorialisations with other, similarly exclusive ones. Others manage, in certain times and places, to contest the logic of exclusive territorialisation itself.

There are a number of instances of forms of resistance that assert new and different codes and authority structures but that end up reproducing practices of exclusive territorialisation. Nationalist and anticolonial movements are the best example: foreign rule was resisted, but fundamental changes to the territorial organisation of the continent, in terms of property ownership (e.g., the Mau Mau movement in Kenya), regionalism (the Majimbo movement in Kenya), and Pan-Africanism (as advocated by leaders like Kwame Nkrumah and Julius Nyerere), were stymied by the permanence of the exclusive territorialisations produced by European colonialism. Succession movements have also sought to replace one exclusive territorialisation with another. The Nigerian civil war and the attempted secession of Biafra sought to contest the federal state's territorial claims over the southeast of the country and create a new exclusive territorial claim over the region and its natural resources. As Haynes argues, Saro-Wiwa's execution by the Nigerian regime occurred not because he led the campaign for environmental justice but because of the threat posed by ethnic regionalism to the political economy of the Nigerian federal state.[69] The secession of South Sudan in July 2011, in which the exclusive territorial control of the South's oil reserves was at the heart of the dispute, resulted in the creation of Africa's newest state.[70]

Elsewhere on the continent popular movements have contested exclusions from protected areas, tenancy evictions, genetically modified and biofuel crops, and the arrival of outsiders into existing territory. Land invasions and occupations have become familiar tactics of the rural poor in the face of land grabs by international investors, local elites, and the national state, whether officially semisanctioned, as in Zimbabwe, or criminalised and vigorously policed, as in South Africa and elsewhere on the continent.[71] Land occupation is a fascinating instance of a contestation between one exclusive territorialisation, the assertion of private ownership over land, and another, the assertion of community ownership of land. At times, however, these movements have practiced hybrid, less exclusive forms of territorialisation.

HYBRID PRACTICES OF TERRITORIALISATION

Since at least the mid-1990s a number of more flexible, overlapping, hybrid, and permeable practices of territorialisation have become more prominent, especially where people and parks has replaced fortress conservation as the defining slogan of wildlife protection. But my argument here is not that there has been a simple, one-way trend of increasingly flexible and hybrid forms of territorialisation in Africa. Rather, the exclusive and hybrid modes are ideal types: even apparently highly exclusive forms like the creation and policing of KNP always involved more contradictions, negotiations, and permeability in practice than were intended by its architects or than are sometimes conveyed by commentators. Alexander and McGregor, for example, highlight the fact that "the colonial period was not simply about the exclusion of Africans from the benefits of game."[72] However, newer practices and discourses of conservation and land management have stressed concepts like decentralisation, participation, nested sovereignty, and common property regimes. Clear, relatively impermeable borders have often been replaced by boundaries which are more ambiguous, indistinct, and overlapping. These should not be thought of as being beyond the state or as alternatives to it;

rather, in Conca's words, states are not displaced by these hybrid territorialisations "so much as they are decentred and recentered."[73]

People and Parks

In part as a result of the resistance and hostility generated towards fortress conservation among local populations, various initiatives in the 1980s and 1990s explored ways of producing mutual benefits for both people and wildlife through more inclusive and participatory conservation programmes. The people and parks movement, which can be dated, at least symbolically, from the Bali World Parks Congress of 1982, aimed to change the ways in which land use within parks was zoned and regulated and, crucially, who were regarded as legitimate participants in this land use. The movement drew upon broader trends in development discourse, including participation, partnership, and multi-stakeholder approaches, and emphasised the involvement of communities in the management and benefits of conservation. Conservation has become framed as a potential win–win opportunity for protecting nature and providing employment and empowerment to rural Africans.[74]

This new paradigm was encapsulated in Community Based Natural Resource Management (CBNRM) schemes like the Communal Areas Management Programme for Indigenous Resources (CAMPFIRE) in Zimbabwe. At least in theory, the new model involved more flexible and less hierarchical and exclusive modes of territorialisation. Land use was shared between communities for agriculture, settlement, and hunting and tourism ventures for wildlife viewing. Parks sought to remove fences where possible and create mixed-use land zones and buffer zones around the enclosures. Local communities were employed or, where possible, given a role in decision making and park management.[75]

CAMPFIRE in Zimbabwe, as Alexander and McGregor indicate, "has been hailed internationally for its participatory approach and its innovative strategies for confronting the developmental and environmental problems of some of the most marginal rural areas, by promoting local control over wildlife management and use."[76] As one of the first sustained efforts to involve local communities in conservation management, it has been adopted, copied, translated, and adapted many times. Yet it has also provoked intense resistance among some local communities, including violence, and has attracted international controversy. CAMPFIRE arose out of the recognition by conservationists within the newly independent Zimbabwean state that the manner in which hunting, wildlife management, and conservation had been practiced in Rhodesia had alienated, marginalised, and disenfranchised many rural peasants. Colonial conservation measures like the Natural Resources Act (1942) and the Native Land Husbandry Act (1952) were seen by the black majority "as a further attempt to gain control over their land and alienate it, in the guise of conservation."[77] This led to considerable hostility against conservation measures among local populations, who saw potentially dangerous, destructive, and disease-ridden wildlife being according more privileged status than humans. Indeed, the nationalist movements of the sixties and seventies actively campaigned against colonial conservation and the alienation of the land through parks. CAMPFIRE was thus intended to devolve greater responsibility for wildlife management to district councils and direct the financial benefits of conservation towards local communities. The first major CAMPFIRE project, undertaken in 1988, was driven by the Department of National Parks along with NGOs like the Zimbabwe Trust and the World Wide Fund for Nature. By 1989 eleven district councils had signed up.[78]

Although Zimbabwe's CAMPFIRE programme has been one of the most long-lasting and well-known, the spread of community conservation and decentralised natural resource management across the continent has been remarkable. Yet they have not always had the effect of empowering local communities. For example, Tanzania introduced Wildlife Management Areas after 1998 with the stated intention that "local people will have full mandate of managing and benefiting from their conservation efforts."[79] Yet Nelson and Agrawal conclude that local communities have remained somewhat marginal there, as the value of wildlife rents has prompted continued central control over the reserves. A more recent review suggests that discourses of decentralisation are now in full retreat, especially after the Wildlife Conservation Act of 2009, which strengthens central control of wildlife and gives the Wildlife Division more opportunity to intervene in the management of village lands. There is now a "reconsolidation of wealth and rent-seeking power by the state" over wildlife resources.[80]

One high-profile case in which communities have been directly involved in the comanagement of a conservation area is that of the Parfuri region of KNP, where in 1969 three thousand members of the Makuleke community had been forcibly removed from their land at gunpoint by the apartheid state. Given the ecological sensitivity of the region, the negotiations over restitution after 1994 with South African National Parks (SANP) were protracted, but in 1998 full ownership of the land passed back to the community. Ownership was, however, subject to certain limitations: "No mining or prospecting may be undertaken; no part of the land may be used for residential purposes other than those required for eco-tourism activities; no part of the land may be used for agriculture; the land will be solely used for conservation and related commercial activities; no development may take place on the land without a positive finding of an environmental impact analysis as required by law . . . and SANP is afforded a right of first refusal should the land ever be offered for sale."[81] This is frequently presented as a classic win–win case. The community had their land restored to them, but it was also preserved for conservation purposes. An alternative reading of the case is of a complex but ultimately frustrating process whereby a community found themselves cheated of the right to use the land and signed up to an agreement they didn't understand or want. Many members of the community have seen few benefits from the land since the deal was made and complain that the experts from SANP do not consult them in decision making. But it is not always easy to identify a coherent community view regarding the benefits of the deal, and the Makuleke are as divided as any social group in their perception of who has gained and who has lost from the restitution process. SANP is not entirely happy about the arrangement either, and the experiment is not seen as widely replicable. Robins and van der Waal regard the Makuleke as "border entrepreneurs" who have had a great deal of success making the most of fluid transfrontier flows: not just in their negotiations over land restitution but also in their negotiation of tribal identities and authorities over a much longer period of time in a liminal zone at the intersection of a variety of practices of territorialisation.[82]

Even where these more hybrid practices of territorialisation have failed to empower local communities, they have tended to increase the role of major international NGOs and conservation groups in the management of African wildlife. The link between conservation, territory, and the state in Africa has been changed by the quite remarkable degree of penetration of nonstate actors in the funding, management, policing, commodification, and surveillance of protected areas. Mac Chapin's controversial critique in 2004 held that NGOs were themselves territorial, dividing up spheres of the world into their private fiefdoms. "It is generally recognised," he argued, "that Conservation International has staked off Suriname and Guyana as its 'territory'; The Nature Conservancy controls the Bosawás region of Nicaragua, and Wildlife Conservation Society guards the gate to the Bolivian Chaco. Territoriality even manifests itself within organisations. Initially, WWF US had control over Tanzania but later moved aside and transferred responsibility to WWF International."[83] In Tanzania about 90 percent of conservation activities are funded by a small group of influential donor agencies and international conservation organisations.

Madagascar is another illustrative case in which donors and environmental NGOs have been involved in directly running state-owned national parks. President Marc Ravalomanana's ambitious vision to triple the amount of land under protected area status from 2003, creating a network of biodiversity corridors, parks, and marine reserves, was planned and implemented by a relatively small group of international NGOs in consultation with mining and other corporate interests. Caroline Seagle shows how Rio Tinto, for example, have made much of their commitment to green mining in Madagascar and have positioned themselves "as an environmental NGO engaged in conservation and scientific research rather than a multinational company engaged in dredge mining."[84] Despite the fall of President Ravalomanana during a political crisis in 2009 over a prospective land deal with Daewoo in which 1.3 million hectares of land was purportedly put up for sale to produce maize and palm oil for export, by December 2010 125 new protected areas and sustainable forest management sites had been created, areas which, together with the preexisting parks, covered 9.4 million hectares in total.[85]

These new practices of conservation do not so much challenge the state as relocate it within new practices of territorialisation. Such modes always exist on a spectrum of exclusive and hybrid forms. There are also continuities between elements of colonial territorialising practices and newer forms of CBNRM. For example, the appeal to local communities and traditional authorities to help manage natural resources within an overall context framed by statist and conservation imperatives recalls methods of indirect rule in British colonial Africa.[86] Such practices do not challenge the state but work to produce new types of green state effects involving a wider range of actors—NGOs, international agencies, foundations, corporate sponsors, and scientific institutes as well as local community groups—in the governance of environmental politics through land and territory.

Trans-Frontier Conservation

Another key practice of territorialisation which has the potential to challenge exclusive forms of environmental governance, particularly their bordering practices, is the proliferation of Trans-Frontier Conservation Areas

(TFCAs). The theme of the 5th World Parks Congress in 2003, held in Durban, South Africa, was Benefits Beyond Boundaries, and it encapsulated the move "beyond the fences," explicitly positioning itself in opposition to the fortress conservation and fines-and-fences practices of exclusive territorialisation. A key actor here is the PPF, a southern African NGO launched in 1997 by WWF-SA and the Rupert Nature Foundation, who have managed to attract the support of major corporations, international agencies, and African states as well as a high-profile (and oft-quoted) endorsement from Nelson Mandela. TFCAs are thus supposed to present "the ultimate form of tearing down the fences," and PPF have sought to portray a "dream of an Africa without fences."[87] Bram Büscher argues that their appeal has rested on the invocation of cutting-edge biodiversity research, which stresses the importance of interlinked ecosystems and a wide range of habitats, in combination with an explicitly liberal vision of transcending barriers, mitigating tensions and interstate conflicts, and reuniting divided communities.[88]

One of the iconic manifestations of the movement has been the Great Limpopo Trans-frontier Conservation Park at the centre of a vast TFCA, linking parks in South Africa, Zimbabwe, and Mozambique. At almost 100,000km^2 it is billed as "the world's greatest animal kingdom."[89] This, as Ramutsindela notes, was "precisely where the fence was, for the first time, literally cut in the establishment of trans-frontier parks (TFPs) in southern Africa."[90] Whereas earlier PPF parks had spanned unfenced international boundaries, such as between South Africa and Namibia, the borders between Zimbabwe, Mozambique, and South Africa were highly militarised. Hence the project secured international backing and a great deal of attention, and the World Bank offered funding to help implement it. The progress of the park has been slow, however, owing to negotiating difficulties between the three sovereign states. The Zimbabwean government is worried about the possible loss of sovereignty, and Mozambique fears economic domination by the much larger and better resourced KNP. All three states have expressed misgivings about the loss of control over their borders and the risks of illegal migration, poaching, and drug trafficking.[91]

The high-profile Great Limpopo Trans-frontier Conservation Park continues to dominate attention, but one that is even bigger is under way. The Kavango–Zambezi Trans-Frontier Conservation Area (KAZA-TFCA) is set to be the largest conservation area in the world: it "will eventually span an area of approximately 520,000 km^2 (similar in size to France)."[92] The emphasis on scale in both the Great Limpopo and the Kavango–Zambezi reveals "the bigger, the better" mind-set of the PPF. These TFCAs are a good example of what Adams and Hutton refer to as an "expansion of scale" in the planning of protected areas.[93] This has continental dimensions: the old discourse of a Cape to Cairo network has been revived as a green, continent-spanning vision of interconnected protected areas. The nascent green state in Africa is thus a potentially vast, interconnected, trans-frontier, and Pan-African conservation state.

The politics of scale here have a number of implications. The ostensible justification for these new vast areas filled with corridors and connecting areas is usually ecological and bioregional. The stated rationale for the KAZA-TFCA is to afford the elephants of Chobe and the Okavango with access to far larger areas of protected grazing. As Duffy puts it, wildlife is seen as a "'fugitive' resource: in the absence of human intervention, it moves without reference to local or national boundaries."[94] While critical reports have drawn attention to the continued problem of confusing land zoning and rampant poaching and trophy hunting in the area, NGOs such as Elephants Without Borders have praised the wildlife corridors approach being developed in the KAZA-TFCA. The group's director, Mike Chase, said, "This is the only place in the world where three parks from three different countries converge. There's no other place like it."[95]

Yet the motivation for the KAZA-TFCA is not simply ecological. At its heart it is a tourist enterprise, and a key element is the possibility of free movement for international visitors across the five states which comprise the park. A proposed "univisa" would allow tourists "freedom of movement, much like the movement and migration of non-human animal populations within the TFCAs across internationally acknowledged boundaries while, in so far as it can be monitored, restricting the freedom of movement of each country's indigenous human population. Such restrictions would also include limitations in terms of land use, circumscribing foraging areas for livestock, water management and unmonitored shopping rights in a neighbouring state."[96] This liberal vision of a borderless world in which free passage and free trade are paramount virtues was also invoked by the branding campaign for the hosts of the 2010 FIFA World Cup, "Boundless Southern Africa."[97] Yet these freedoms are not complete or absolute: they apply to certain populations engaged in certain activities at certain times and places. Other populations find their freedom and movement increasingly constrained.

For example, there are limitations on who, feasibly, can participate in park management and planning. Despite the rhetoric that TFCAs work to reconnect communities as much as animals, the larger the scale, the harder it is for local communities to take part meaningfully in park governance. These new corridors and zones connecting protected areas of continental dimensions require imperial-scale mapping and planning with the latest satellite and GIS techniques as well as computer-aided planning, biodiversity modelling, international cooperation, legal negotiations, and state-of-the-art tourist facilities. A recent PPF report highlighted how field data from the KAZA–TFCA will be available through Android and iPhone Operating System apps, which will be downloadable "and allow for users across the globe to contribute to TFCA monitoring and evaluation through crowd sourcing, also known as citizen science."[98] Most of these tools are beyond the reach of the local communities who live in or near the protected areas and who rely upon experts if they are to formally participate at all.

Other details also reveal the scalar assumptions behind the TFCA vision. Spierenburg and Wels observe that early maps of the Great Limpopo Transfrontier Park included none of the communities living there.[99] This could be interpreted as both sleight of hand to ease the sensitive political process of relocating communities as well as a reflection of a deeper assumption that scale and scientific expertise, not local community participation and knowledge, are crucial to conservation. Behind the vision of TFCA is a deep-seated assumption that small-scale farmers and local communities cannot or will not engage sufficiently in conservation and ecotourism.

The development of megaparks, whose trans-frontier nature facilitates the free movement of animals and tourists across national borders as well as landscapes, signals a new set of bordering practices through which modern conservation is reshaping the green state in Africa. These schemes seem to reshape and even challenge the traditional model of state sovereignty. Early in the development of the Great Limpopo Trans-frontier Park, Duffy wrote, "The super-park constitutes a challenge to the traditional boundaries and powers of the nation-state."[100] To Achille Mbembe, such practices of international conservation have resulted in the creation of de facto extraterritorial spaces: "Whole territories are now outside state authority."[101]

The transformations that TFCA represent, however, should not be overemphasized. In some cases they have been possible precisely because they do not challenge existing patterns of territorialisation. For example, Ramutsindela explains that "parks on the South Africa–Botswana border provided conditions under which the TFP idea could be experimented with in the region—and the continent for that matter—without difficulties, because they had always existed as a *de facto* TFP. In contrast to many colonial borders in Southern Africa, the South Africa–Botswana border along the Nossob River has been porous and people in South Africa historically managed wildlife conservation in both countries. The border is unfenced and the Nossob River does not prevent crossings by people and animals alike."[102] Indeed, as Ramutsindela suggests elsewhere, it is the privileging of the "trans-national-frontier" discourse that peace parks promote rather than the transcending of *all* fences. The PPF discourse implies that it is the colonially imposed national boundaries that lie at the root of Africa's crisis of sustainable development; conveniently ignoring the fact that most of Africa's national borders are in fact not fenced—for example, in contrast to South Africa's largely militarised frontiers, international borders and park boundaries in East Africa tend not to be fenced—and that nonnational borders and boundaries around private property, municipalities, districts, etc. also play a role in perpetuating environmental and social injustice.[103] For instance, in contrast to the Nossob river between South Africa and Namibia, the interior of both countries is densely crisscrossed by fences separating game, crops, farm animals, people, and private property. Larry Swatuk discusses how the imposition of veterinary cordon fences in Botswana have been dubbed fences of death by the international media because of their impact on San hunting routes and game migration.[104] This discursive framing allows their advocates to claim that peace parks are "a truly African solution to African problems such as (border) conflicts and underdevelopment," while not confronting some of the most profound territorialisations at work in the production of green states in Africa.[105]

Overall, therefore, we should not assume that TFCA fit easily into what Bradley Karkkainnen has called "post-sovereign" environmental management.[106] Parks do not necessarily challenge the power or sovereignty of national states, although they usually do involve bringing national conservation authorities into networks involving a diversity of other actors and authorities, what Duffy describes as "a narrow network of international NGOs, international financial institutions, global consultants on tourism / community conservation and bilateral donors."[107] Büscher and Dietz maintain that the recent history of the Great Limpopo Trans-frontier Conservation Park, despite the talk of community participation, flexibility, and partnerships, actually suggests evidence of states returning to "a formal 'government' style of governing, instead of a more 'governance mode,' dealing with multiple actors in a flexible way."[108] This entails excluding other actors and communities and rigidly defending statist prerogatives and sovereignty. In conclusion, therefore, the

TFP is not deterritorialising or postterritorial; rather it is a practice that creates new types of territory and new relationships between states, the land, and conservation. This changes the types of green state effects produced, but ensures they remain located on a spectrum between exclusive and hybrid territorialisations.

Land Politics and Hybrid Territorialisations

I turn now to the politics of land grabs and land reforms to highlight two further aspects of the production of green states through territorialising practices. The first is a wave of new forms of mapping and surveying associated with new commercial opportunities and new commodities. The second is the gradual and partial emergence of new technologies of support for rural communities struggling to cope with their environmental challenges and responsibilities. Together these produce a profoundly uneven and unequal political landscape, one in which hybrid territorialisations appear to be working in the interest of powerful commercial and political actors while entrenching rural vulnerability. The green states produced through these hybrid territorialising practices might differ considerably from older colonial and fortress conservation states, but in terms of the disempowerment of rural communities many of their effects are the same.

In the first place, the wave of investment associated with what has come to be called the new scramble for Africa or the land-grabbing phenomenon has given rise to a range of ways of bordering, demarcating, zoning, classifying, mapping, and surveying land. This new scramble involves new actors and competition for access to both new and old natural resources and growing consumer markets. The high-profile phenomenon of land grabbing refers to investments in agricultural land to grow biofuels, create carbon reserves and credits for avoided deforestation, or to feed the Middle East, Europe, North America, and Asia. The World Bank calculated that at least 45 million hectares of large-scale agricultural land deals were made in the first eleven months of 2009 alone, 70 percent of which were in sub-Saharan Africa.[109] Examples of such deals are manifold: in 2011 researchers from the Oakland Institute reported on the largest land deal in Tanzania, a purchase of over 300,000 hectares of land by the U.S.-based company Agrisol for large-scale crop cultivation, including biofuels, and beef and poultry production. In August 2012 Bangladesh signed an agreement to take out a ten-year lease on South Sudanese land to jointly produce food crops. Amanor remarks that the "increasing appropriation of customary land by commercial sectors" across the continent leads to "the conversion of large areas of customary land into freehold and leasehold sectors, estate farms, mineral concessions and conservation areas."[110]

In many cases these proposed investments have fallen through, petered out, or simply never materialised, leaving communities as well as investors to cope with the aftermath. Yet even in cases where crops do not ultimately get grown as envisioned, the representations and territorialisations of the land are fundamentally altered. A whole array of special zones, corridors, gateways, and legal and economic jurisdictions have been created as necessary conditions for this wave of new investment. An example is the Southern Agricultural Growth Corridor of Tanzania, launched by the government in 2010 with donor backing and the participation of such companies as DuPont, General Mills, Monsanto, Yara, and Syngenta. It intends "to foster inclusive, commercially successful agribusinesses that will benefit the region's small-scale farmers, and in so doing, improve food security, reduce rural poverty and ensure environmental sustainability."[111] These benefits are to be achieved through land retitling and resettlements, provision of credit and infrastructure to investors, upgrading of transport links, and connecting of producers to processors and exporters. It aims to lift two million people out of poverty by bringing 350,000 hectares of farmland into cultivation and eventually to generate US$3 billion in public and private investments. Such corridors and zones can be seen as contemporary successors to much longer histories of pilot projects, model farms and villages, special economic zones, trials, demonstrations, and experiments in African rural development.[112] Although many have failed to live up to the initial hype and attract high levels of investment, they reveal how patterns of territorialisation are changing the way states govern land and environments. The consequences for pastoralists and shifting cultivators as well as for small-scale farmers generally are potential severe.

New practices of land use accompany these economic zones, as new commodities emerge in the form of biofuels, forest carbon sinks, and ecosystem services. Payments for Ecosystems Services schemes involve paying landowners for the ecological services they provide, such as carbon sequestration, water conservation, or biodiversity protection (see chapter 5). Making these payments requires a huge extension of mapping, surveying, monitoring, and scientific technologies. As a result, trees and the soil, through such practices as REDD+ credits and biochar, are becoming commodified and reterritorialised as carbon sinks. The prospect of the rapid growth of large-scale, monocrop industrial agriculture in Africa and elsewhere in the tropics for the purposes of offsetting the industrialised world's GHG emissions has led to charges of "carbon colonialism": new practices of exclusive territorialisation which often violently marginalise or exclude local populations.[113]

The second aspect of these new territorialising practices is the gradual and partial emergence of new technologies of rural governance, through which states and other actors are seeking to extend control over new resources and markets and mitigate some of their more inequitable consequences. One example is the Food and Agriculture Organisation's (FAO) Voluntary Guidelines on the Responsible Governance of Tenure of Land, Fisheries and Forests in the Context of National Food Security, but state-led national programmes of land reform are perhaps even more consequential.[114] Land reform debates across Africa have also tended to become preoccupied with scale: volumes of land titled or transferred and extent of hectares reformed. In South Africa, for example, land reform involves three processes, restitution, redistribution, and tenure reform, and there has been much criticism of the fact that only about 8 percent of commercial farmland has been redistributed over eighteen years, woefully short of the initial target of 30 percent over five years.[115]

Yet alongside the worry over increasing the pace and scale of land reform, there is also some evidence of attempts to govern the use of land more sustainably and efficiently and to aid landowners and communities in fulfilling their environmental responsibilities.[116] Such practices are also part of the production of green state effects through new forms of territorialisation. The South African government's unease over these issues is illustrated in a report by the Department of Rural Development and Land Reform:

> Another shortcoming of the land reform process is the lack of systematic investigation into the quality of the piece of land being transferred to the beneficiaries. Components such as connectivity (road, rail), water supply, agricultural potential, mean annual rainfall, groundwater yield and groundwater quality, distance from potential markets, etc. are not fully investigated and hence is not fully understood. An attempt has been made to rectify this issue where map books have been created for the 504 land reform projects identified for recapitalisation. Each mapbook contains individual maps for each land reform project mapped according to the variables listed above. In this manner a broad overview of the actual conditions on the ground can be obtained. There should be a paradigm shift away from mere statistics

> focusing on the number of hectares transferred to a more analytical approach. Each piece of land is analysed in terms of these physical factors mentioned above and can at a glance reveal the actual quality of the piece of land. In some cases, the land being transferred to beneficiaries is good agriculturally speaking, but is located very far away from potential markets and transportation corridors.[117]

Government agencies tasked with land reform are well aware that environmental issues play a vital role in land reform processes. Favourable environmental conditions are required for beneficiaries to develop productive agriculture or profitable ecotourism initiatives. Legal responsibilities are also transferred with the land, especially when it is sensitive, vulnerable, or a biodiversity hot spot.

The risks to land reform beneficiaries stemming from these legal responsibilities and liabilities have been highlighted by the rural development consultants Phuhlisani Solutions. They reported the case of a fire which took place at a land restitution site at Covie in the Southern Cape: "The fire had been extinguished by the MTO consortium which leases adjacent plantations. Within days DWAF, the current owner of the land, received an invoice for R30,000 for fire fighting services. This was for a fire which did not actually get into the plantations. Had mature timber been destroyed damages would have been in the order of millions of rand. Clearly once the claim is settled damages from fires originating on Covie property will be referred to the new land owners and could become a significant threat to the future viability of the project."[118] Accordingly, the consultants have recommended a model for detailed environmental assessments as part of land reform procedures, including the use of aerial photographs and maps; transect walks; interviews and "ground-truthing" to access qualitative data on lived experiences; mapping "key environmental characteristics of the site and highlighting environmental opportunities (green flags) and constraints (red flags)"; "1:50,000 topocadastral maps and 1:10,000 orthophoto maps"; global positioning system and geographic information system analysis; linking photos and reports; baseline surveys; environmental impact assessments; community environmental management plans; and resource management plans.[119] However, the report concludes, "There is currently no programme run by any government department that specifically targets people obtaining rights in land under the land reform programme to make them aware of their rights, responsibilities and liabilities in terms of a wide range of environmental and natural resource legislation."[120] This is an excellent example of the production of green state effects, however tentative and partial, involving a much wider network of consultants, communities, corporations, and NGOs in attempts to govern the environmental implications of changing land use practices.

One of the most critical implications to be drawn from this discussion of practices of territorialisation and the production of green states in Africa is that straightforward accounts of the spread of neoliberal markets and the retreat or weakening of the state are misleading. The story of conservation and land reform does not fit Mbembe's argument that new territorialising practices entail "the exit of the state, its emasculation, and its replacement by fragmented forms of sovereignty."[121] Rather, when it comes to practices of conservation and land governance, as Deborah James argues in a slightly different context, "State and market intermesh and are tightly interwoven, with apparently market-oriented initiatives reliant on extensive state intervention for both design and implementation."[122] Nelson concludes that "although patterns of institutional change and governance reform are variable and non-linear in nature, the general trend within eastern and southern Africa is towards reconsolidating central authority over natural resources and consequently eroding or subverting existing local claims and rights."[123] Both exclusive and hybrid practices of territorialisation are implicated in the production of green state effects which, through wide and diverse networks of actors, are governing African territory and landscapes in new ways.

HERMAPHRODITE LANDSCAPES

The core argument of this chapter is that green state effects in Africa are primarily and quintessentially bound up with the government of land and territory to a far greater extent than green states elsewhere, and these can be conceptualised in terms of the exclusive or hybrid territorialisations produced by practices of conservation and land redistribution and the forms of resistance they have stimulated. The case of the proposed road in Serengeti and its obstruction by a regional court illustrates the challenges being made to exclusive modes of territorialisation in Africa: Tanzania's sovereign right to develop its territory was rejected by the regional and international community. In a sense, this produces what could be described as hermaphrodite landscapes, which are neither rural nor urban, national nor international, sovereign nor stateless. I close with another image associated with hermaphrodite landscapes: not a road through the wilderness, but the wild urban setting of the

African slum. Mike Davis describes slums as a "hermaphroditic landscape, a partially urbanised countryside . . . a form neither rural nor urban but a blending of the two."[124] Postcolonial African states have urbanised faster than almost anywhere else on earth, bringing with them vast new territories of periurban informal settlements (see chapter 4).[125] Hermaphrodite urban spaces offer a final illustration of the sorts of hybrid territorialisations that are reshaping green states in Africa. As Pieterse reflects, the African city prompts us to consider "the immensely complex, but also generative, dynamism of the spatial alchemy that can only be sensed there, or should I say, here."[126]

The slum is an ambiguous form of territory: it is part of the city yet liminal to it and often ignored, forgotten, and bypassed. It is an informal, temporary, heterotopic space; but slum dwellers often spend their lives there, communities form, and generations succeed one another in the same spaces. They are the dark twins of formal settlements and planned developments, without which social life could not function. Slums are poorly mapped, have limited services, transport, and facilities, and pose ever-present threats of crime and violence. It is possible nonetheless to find maps of informal

8. "Dust storms at noon on the R34 between Welkom and Hennenman, Free State," Santu Mofokeng (b. 1956). © Santu Mofokeng, 2007 silverprint edition 5. Images courtesy Lunetta Bartz, MAKER, Johannesburg.

settlements on google maps, and the local state is responsible for providing sanitation, schooling, health care, and policing. The slum has neither the civilisation of the urban nor the space and beauty of the rural. It is a transversal space, cutting across more familiar practices of exclusive territorialisation. Literatures on subaltern urbanism have drawn attention to the fundamentally ambivalent character of informal urban spaces: often unruly, emergent, and ungovernable but also policed, surveyed, governed, and integrated into statist power relations in quite intensive ways.[127] If the green African state is primarily concerned with the governance of land and territory, then the twin images which encapsulate it are the road through the Serengeti and the periurban slum. Both are central to the governance and contestation of wild African spaces.

This chapter has shown the centrality of land, borders, and processes of territorialisation to the production and contestation of green states in Africa, in marked contrast to their absence from much of the green state literature. As Lund and Boone argue, "The politics of land in Africa are integral to the larger contest to produce legitimate forms of social order."[128] Environmental politics in Africa is a politics of the land, but in ways that differ greatly from those in Europe and North America. The land has powerful economic, political, cultural, and religious functions and meanings for African states and peoples: whether as a symbol and product of liberation, an association between the bush and a precivilised state of nature, or the primary means of production for most of Africa's peasants. Tarmac is also a powerful symbolic intervention into the landscape, as the conflicts over the Serengeti road reveal. It is easy to imagine roads and conservation areas as occupying opposite ends of the environmental spectrum when it comes to land use, one encouraging increased consumption and traffic on the land, the other restricting all these things. But contemporary conservation is far more ambiguous and diverse than this, and parks and reserves function to govern movement and consumption in specific ways (often along roads within the parks). States play a crucial role in how different territorialisations, such as roads and parks and slums, govern land use, and the identity and core function of states, even green states, are still bound up with the governance of territory and borders. It is simply not true, as Strange claimed in 1996, that we have left behind a world "in which the territorial borders of states really meant something."[129]

Diverse modes of territorialisation are visible over time and across different cases. This chapter has shown that rather than a trend from exclusive to hybrid modes of territorialisation or vice versa, environmental politics in

Africa is characterised by a dynamic interplay between these forms: fragmented and heterotopic land use arrangements have prompted bureaucratic colonial and postcolonial states to codify land and impose more orderly and exclusive territorialisations. Yet in turn these actions have prompted forms of resistance from local communities and international actors which have spurred reforms leading to more hybrid and fragmented territorialisations. This dynamic is central to the politics of green states in Africa, whether they are authoritarian conservation states committed to fortress preservation or self-proclaimed boundless neoliberal states creating flexible spaces attractive to investment and facilitating the free movement of animals and tourists.

CHAPTER 4

Green Citizens and Problematic Populations

> The mimosa tree, or the umga as the amaXhosa call it, is plentiful and grows easily. It is the only tree a person can chop without the chief's permission. For all other trees, even foreign ones, one is supposed to get permission before one can chop them down.
>
> —Zakes Mda, *The Heart of Redness*

> The increasingly important question in the world is not how to feed all the people—there is plenty of food, and preventing hunger is often only a matter of adequate organisation and transport—but what to do with them. What should be done with these countless millions? With their unutilised energy? With the hidden powers they surely possess? What is their place in the family of mankind? That of fully vested members? Wronged brothers? Irritating intruders?
>
> —Ryszard Kapuściński, *The Shadow of the Sun*

In 2004 the Kenyan politician and international environmental activist Wangari Maathai was awarded the Nobel Peace Prize "for her contribution to sustainable development, democracy and peace."[1] She founded the Green Belt Movement, which helped women to restore degraded landscapes through tree planting across Africa, as well as leading high-profile international programmes like the Billion Trees Campaign in 2007. The World Bank estimates that trees planted by the Green Belt Movement in Kenya will capture 375,000 tonnes of carbon dioxide by 2017. Her story is well known, and indeed she is probably the world's most famous African environmentalist. She was honoured with numerous prizes, including the Conservation Scientist Award, the Hunger Project's Africa Prize for Leadership, and the Goldman Environmental

Prize, and UNEP listed her on their Global 500 Hall of Fame as one of one hundred "heroines of the world." She received a doctoral degree in 1971 from the University of Nairobi, becoming the first woman in East and Central Africa to gain a doctorate, and she has subsequently been awarded honorary doctoral degrees from a number of educational institutions, including Yale University. Her story fuses some of the principal themes of this chapter: individual dissidents and rural communities, education and empowerment, gender and identity, citizens and consumers, and people and trees. This chapter addresses the relationship between green African states and the people who both inhabit them and are produced by them.

Maathai, who died in 2011, was most well known for her work with the Green Belt Movement and her opposition to the authoritarian policies of the Kenyan president Daniel Arap Moi. The Green Belt Movement was started by Maathai in 1977 and focused upon tree-planting campaigns in order to both empower rural women and help conserve the environment. She attributed her interest in trees to her childhood experiences collecting wood for her mother, but she wasn't allowed to cut wood from the fig tree because it was a

9. Wangari Maathai. Photo by David Blumenkrantz.

tree of god. Much later she learnt that the roots of the fig tree helped preserve underground water reserves. After she had qualified as a veterinarian and was working in rural areas near Nairobi, she recalls seeing "rivers silted with topsoil, much of which was coming from the forest where plantations of commercial trees had replaced indigenous forest. I noticed that much of the land that had been covered by trees, bushes and grasses when I was growing up had been replaced by tea and coffee."[2] There was a moment of epiphany: "It suddenly became clear. Not only was the livestock industry threatened by a deteriorating environment, but I, my children, my students, my fellow citizens, and my entire country would pay the price. The connection between the symptoms of environmental degradation and their causes—deforestation, devegetation, unsustainable agriculture, and soil loss—was self-evident. Something had to be done."[3] The idea "just came" to her: "Why not plant trees?"[4] She worked with and through uneducated rural women. When foresters told her "You need people with diplomas to plant trees," she responded, "Anybody can dig a hole, put a tree in it, water it, and nurture it."[5] As increasing numbers of women across Kenya applied for seedlings and set up their own groups as part of the movement, "we encouraged them to plant seedlings in rows of at least a thousand trees to form green 'belts' that would restore to the earth its cloth of green."[6]

The movement's website reports that it has supported 4,034 nurseries across Kenya, and it has planted over 51 million trees since the 1970s.[7] Yet Maathai realised that there were deeper causes of environmental degradation and female disempowerment than a simple lack of trees, and she became an outspoken (and frequently persecuted and imprisoned) political campaigner. She prevented the construction of a tower block in Uhuru Park, one of Nairobi's few green spaces; fought against the dislocation of rural communities from the land and the encroachment of agriculture into the forests; and campaigned for the release of political prisoners. As Rob Nixon writes, her movement's focus on tree planting achieved "a brilliant symbolic economy, becoming an iconic act of civil disobedience as the women's efforts to help arrest soil erosion segued into a struggle against illicit deforestation perpetrated by Kenya's draconian regime."[8] A key figure in Kenya's transition to multiparty democracy, she became a member of parliament in 2002 and rose to deputy minister of the environment and natural resources under President Mwai Kibaki.

Maathai occupies a central, iconic role in the environmental movement: the outspoken, rebellious hero. She achieved impressive and demonstrable things—planting 51 million trees is by no means insignificant—and reached the corridors of power both in Kenya and internationally, while continuing to speak out against injustice. As a woman in a patriarchal political culture and an environmental campaigner before it was fashionable, especially in postcolonial Kenya where conservation was seen as a concern of whites, her outsider status and subsequent dissident cachet were assured. Her story is apposite for three reasons.

First, it emphasises the centrality of people to environmental politics in Africa. This may sound self-evident, but many accounts of conservation, climate politics, water scarcity, and agricultural innovations contain no actual people, human agency, or physical bodies. This absence is exacerbated by the familiar wilderness trope of seeing landscapes, particularly in Africa, as empty of people. Similarly, many analyses of the politics of the green state concentrate on institutions, laws, ideas, and structures but are free of actual people. Yet people are central to African environmental politics, and Maathai begins her book *The Challenge for Africa* with a story which revolves around a women ploughing a field on a hillside in Yaoundé. African environments are some of the most profoundly peopled in the world, contrary to many Western myths about African wilderness. African landscapes have been peopled longer than just about anywhere else; Africa is the origin of our species, the cradle of humankind. *Homo habilis* and *Homo ergaster* both probably emerged from Africa, and DNA testing of contemporary populations seems to indicate that all modern people are descended from African ancestors. Moreover, states have always been about the exercise of control over a particular population; indeed this is one of the constitutive characteristics of most definitions of statehood (see chapter 2). One of the most important state effects is the production of certain subjectivities: populations, citizens, gendered bodies, and rational individuals. As John Comaroff puts it, the effects of the state stretch "into the very construction of its subjects, into their bodily routines and the essence of their selfhood."[9] State effects encompass the production of populations, individuals, and subjects through green discourses and practices.

The second reason Maathai's story is useful is more explicitly political. She was ostracised, persecuted, imprisoned, and tortured by President Moi's regime for much of her political career. Her ascent to international fame and to the Kenyan parliament occurred toward the end of a long, challenging struggle to be heard and seen as a legitimate interlocutor in Kenyan politics. Her story is not, therefore, a facile account of environmental win–win solutions or of the technocratic transmission of allegedly better technologies, practices, and education. Rather, the message is that environmental innovations and reforms require political struggle and opposition to entrenched interests. It is also a story which reveals how certain types of people, citizens, populations, and subjectivities are variously constructed as problems or solutions, as good or bad. Politics, in its broadest sense, is about the enactment of subjectivities: Carl Schmitt described this as the creation of distinctions between friends and enemies, while Aimé Césaire proclaimed rather more poetically that to politicise was "to invent the souls of men."[10] Both bad and good subjectivities have been created by environmental discourses and practices, through biopolitical strategies for the management of life and species.[11]

Third, Maathai's story is pertinent because it is about trees. The Green Belt Movement sought to help restore indigenous forests through community tree-planting campaigns, nurseries, cultivation programmes, and other methods; trees were the route to social and ecological empowerment. To Nixon, "The theater of the tree afforded the social movement a rich symbolic vocabulary that helped extend the movement's civic reach. . . . To plant trees was metaphorically to cultivate democratic change; with a slight vegetative tweak, the gesture could breathe new life into the dead metaphor of grassroots democracy."[12] Trees like the baobab and the acacia are inseparable from imagined African landscapes, and imported trees like the eucalyptus, jacaranda, prickly pear, and jatropha have reshaped African vistas and economies over at least the past hundred years. Trees are intensely symbolic; they are "the green antithesis of deforestation," and they are often used explicitly or implicitly as a kind of proxy for assessing environmental quality or degradation.[13] Yet they are also economic resources, obstacles to agriculture, landmarks and boundaries, cultural symbols, artistic inspirations, social focal points and meeting places or icons for resistance, and many others things beside. Many of these characteristics come together to construct the tree planter as the epitome of the good green citizen. As one NGO working in Tanzania, Kenya, and Uganda claims, "Planting millions of trees recovers environments and changes lives."[14] The converse is also true: the tree cutter or feller has become someone to be castigated or demonised in Africa. As Ben Okri wrote in his novel *Famished Road,* "There are certain trees that seem worthless but when gone leave empty spaces through which bad winds blow. There are other trees that seem useless but when felled worse things grow in their place."[15]

Trees and people are connected within the green state through biopolitical practices of the governance of life. Trees, like humans, are organisms within ecosystems. The biopolitics of the green state in Africa is not just about the

10. Samburu boy, Maralal, Kenya. Photo by David Blumenkrantz.

production and management of human populations; it is also bound up with the management, cultivation, and modification of nonhuman populations. Biodiversity conservation is fundamentally about the ability of human managers to conserve populations of elephants, rhinos, fynbos, or the Serengeti landscape. As Bunn suggests, success in the field of wildlife population management "becomes metonymically associated with the ability to govern other populations elsewhere."[16] In the era of the Anthropocene—irrespective of whether we find this term useful or not—there is little left on the planet that we have not altered in some way, and much of the nature we see around us, whether urban tree-lined avenues and gardens or wild landscapes like the Serengeti and the Kalahari, has been shaped and impacted by human civilisation. As genetic modification becomes more pervasive, the capacity, depth, and intensity of human biopower becomes ever more profound. All of life in Africa, as elsewhere, is now fundamentally bound up with human political strategies.[17]

In exploring these issues, I structure the argument that follows around three influential problematisations of Africans and their relation with the environment, in the form of three problem-subjects and their corresponding solution-subjects. The most important problem-subjects constructed through environmental discourse and the practices of green statehood are the rural peasant, the urban consumer, and the foreign body, whereas the three solution-subjects are the educated farmer, the green consumer, and the environmental citizen. The penultimate section returns to the theme of green biopolitics in Africa and the troublesome role of the environmental dissident, rebel, or protestor, which brings us back to Wangari Maathai.

PROBLEMATISATION NUMBER ONE: OVERPOPULATION

In 2009 the population of Africa passed one billion people, and it is forecast to double by 2050. Africa has the world's highest birthrate and the highest projected population growth rate to 2050. The continent thus appears to encapsulate the familiar neo-Malthusian population bomb scenario which has been central to many environmental discourses since at least the 1970s. Malthus viewed famine as "the last and most dreadful mode by which nature represses a redundant population."[18] According to this problematisation there are simply too many people on the planet, and Africa, alongside the "teeming" populations of Asia, is seen as driving this rush toward the ecological precipice. Such global discourses have shaped the way most people, including many Africans, see the relationship between people and the environment. A survey of

South African views on climate change, for example, noted that "in all locations, people mention overpopulation as a primary and secondary cause of global warming."[19] The AfDB and WWF report on Africa's ecological footprint highlights the risks of "overshoot" and the role of rapid African population growth in fuelling "humanity's voracious demand for goods and services."[20]

There are a number of images and locales that recur in the overpopulation discourse, such as Egypt's Nile Valley. Timothy Mitchell observes that if one opens "almost any study of Egypt produced by an American or international development agency . . . you are likely to find it starting with the same simple image. The question of Egypt's economic development is almost invariably introduced as a problem of geography versus demography, pictured by describing the narrow valley of the Nile River, surrounded by desert, crowded with rapidly multiplying millions of inhabitants."[21] The fertile valleys of the Great Lakes region in east Africa are another frequently cited Malthusian nightmare. One populist interpretation of the Rwandan genocide in 1994 is that it was driven by pressures arising from one of Africa's highest population densities, exacerbated by the collapse of coffee prices in a context of political tension. Jared Diamond writes, "Rwanda represents a Malthusian catastrophe happening under our eyes, an overpopulated land that collapsed in horrible bloodshed," a land where "population growth, environmental damage, and climate change provided the dynamite for which ethnic violence was the fuse."[22] These claims, as we will see, are deeply problematic.

Debates over demography and development in Africa are complex and deeply contested. Neo-Malthusians have been opposed by those who see a marked *shortage* of bodies across many parts of the continent. To Esther Boserup and those who followed her, African economic development would come only after further sustained population growth.[23] Population densities across Africa are often lower than elsewhere: to take a few examples, in 2011 Tanzania had 52 people per square kilometre, South Africa 42, Nigeria 180, Kenya 74, and Ethiopia 89. This compares to figures of 259 for the United Kingdom, 119 for France, 34 for the United States, and 144 for China. These numbers reflect, in part, the hardship of life in many African environments: thus John Iliffe regarded "the colonisation of their immensely difficult continent" as "the African people's chief contribution to human history and one of the great adventures of man's past."[24] In Rwanda the population density actually fell from 293 people per square kilometre in 1989 to 246 in 1993.[25] Although these figures are high, accounts of the genocide which attribute it directly to a Malthusian stress on natural resources significantly underestimate the confluence of international economic stresses (falling coffee prices and structural adjustment) and a deadly power struggle within the Hutu regime and *akazu* clique surrounding President Juvenal Habyarimana. This is not to suggest either that pressure on land and resources played no part in the genocide or that some Rwandans did not use the crisis of 1994 to settle old scores with neighbours over land. But the headline attribution of the genocide by authors like Diamond to "Malthus in Africa," alongside comments like "a visitor's sense is of being surrounded by a sea of children," works to reinforce rather than challenge the unhelpful stereotypes about African overpopulation, semibarbarism and international isolation, and the absence of political agency in the causes of conflict.[26]

If the relationship between population, conflict, and development is contested, so too is the relationship between population growth and environmental degradation. Some commentators have argued that a rising population can actually contribute to environmental protection and the restoration of ecosystems. William Critchley, in his book *More People, More Trees* and the film of the same title, suggests that population growth has contributed to the regreening of parts of Kenya and Burkina Faso. He was following up on the earlier pathbreaking work of Mary Tiffen and colleagues in the Machakos District of Kenya, evocatively entitled *More People, Less Erosion.*[27] Such research demonstrates, at the very least, that global, continental, and even national population trends have to be interpreted in light of the particular geographical and environmental locations and the everyday practices of states and societies in Africa. Yet these accounts remain counterintuitive and at odds with the dominant problematisation which has prevailed in Africa over at least the past century: that overpopulation, overgrazing, and profligate tree felling, that is, inefficient farming methods, are behind desertification, soil erosion, and deforestation. At the heart of this discourse stands the problematic figure of the African peasant.

The Problematic, Prolific Peasant

For generations of colonial scientists and administrators and postcolonial bureaucrats and aid workers the inefficiency of multitudes of African peasants scratching away at the thin red soil has encapsulated the continent's ever-looming environmental tragedy. More particularly, it is the pastoralist, the nomadic grazer with his herds of cattle, the women chopping down trees for firewood, and the slash-and-burn cultivator who have tended to be seen as causing the problems which have plagued generations of environmental officials: deforestation, soil erosion, gullies and dongas, hunger, floods, and famine. In a striking formulation Kofi Annan declared in 2014, "[The] unacceptable reality is that too many African farmers still use methods handed from generation to generation, working their lands or grazing their animals much as their ancestors have done for millennia."[28]

There are many other examples of those whose racially burdened discourses blame the profligacy, laziness, greed, and ignorance of the African farmer for environmental problems. An archetypal early expression of these views can be found in the work of E. P. Stebbing in the 1930s. His work on land erosion, drought, and the spread of the Sahara in Africa was in little doubt as to the causes: overpopulation, deforestation, overgrazing, and poor land husbandry. Patterns of shifting slash-and-burn cultivation were singled out as contributing to degradation. Stebbing claimed that "many parts of Africa, with their increasing populations and flocks and the accelerated over-utilisation of the soil, are witnesses . . . to the alarming fact that this accelerated over-utilisation is producing a state of affairs which no amount of education or other palliatives will be likely to arrest in time. The world has been shocked at the appalling conditions which have been produced in the Dust Bowl of the United States and Canada, where whole populations have been migrating, within a brief period of years; a period which, in contrast to the slow extension of the Sahara, is but a grain of sand by comparison."[29] To Stebbing, the colonial state needed to intervene to prevent the encroachment of the desert, despite the fact such interventions "are likely at first to be met with much ignorant criticism and by opposition on the spot from the people whose old-time wasteful habits are being interfered with."[30] In another example, the anthropologist Audrey Richards, whose work is the foundation for Moore's and Vaughan's wonderfully nuanced restudy of northern Zambia, regarded the practice of slash-and-burn cultivation as a vestige of a tribal past, bound up with fracturing assumptions about masculinity, chiefly authority, and cultivation. In Richards's account in 1939, "The young men seize their axes, and rush whooping up the trees, squabbling as to who should take the highest trunk. . . . Each falling branch is greeted with a special triumph cry. . . . The cutter likens himself to an animal who climbs high, or to a fierce chief who mutilates his subjects, cutting off their limbs like the branches of a tree."[31] Such practices as cutting down trees were and often still are seen as quintessentially antiecological.

Ethiopia offers a powerful illustration of many of these long-standing discourses of irrational peasant farming. In addition to the prevalent view that peasants are "tradition-bound, inefficient, and incapable of improving their lot without strong guidance from above," the spectre of deforestation looms large.[32] According to widely quoted figures, 87 percent of the surface area of highland Ethiopia was "once covered with high forests," a figure which by 1900 had declined to 40 percent and by 1990 was estimated to be about 5.6 percent.[33] Even more starkly, U.S. Senator Al Gore stated in his book *Earth in the Balance* (1992) that Ethiopia's forested land had decreased from "40 to 1 percent in the last four decades," a shrinkage which, together with drought and war, had produced an "epic tragedy" that had "wreaked havoc on an ancient and once-proud nation."[34] Keller, also writing in the 1990s, expressed a view common to many analysts: that massive deforestation was part of the reason for increased frequencies of famine in the Horn of Africa.[35] These figures have been disputed by many and are as politically problematic as the Malthusian readings of the Rwandan genocide noted above, but they have been influential and significant. Not least, they were translated into a litany of initiatives to reform farming practices and educate the Ethiopian peasant. As James McCann writes, "State policy for the twentieth century undertook to transform the behaviour of local peoples to halt a process of deforestation that had never, in fact, taken place."[36]

The Educated Entrepreneurial Farmer

The corollary of the problematic peasant is the educated farmer, and "transform[ing] the behaviour of local peoples" has been one of the major practices through which green state effects have been produced in Africa. In their study of citimene cultivation in northern Zambia, Moore and Vaughan called one chapter, "Developing men: The creation of the progressive farmer," a title that perfectly conveys some of the gendered and developmental discourses surrounding the process of producing educated farmers. They note that the colonial notion of a progressive farmer "implied a rejection of 'backward' citimene methods of cultivation and a commitment to full-time, settled agriculture."[37] The promotion of progressive, enlightened practices is at the heart of this transformation from peasant to farmer, and, as David Nally points out "The promotion of agrarian capitalism was almost always couched in a rhetoric of improvement."[38]

Such schemes have adopted a variety of means, have been employed by a range of actors, and have aimed at a diversity of ends. These range from encouraging smallholders to micro-dose crops with fertiliser and plant indigenous trees to the "sustainable intensification" of commercial export-orientated agriculture. But in all cases there is a central role for the empowered African farmer (rarely a pastoralist), assisted by an array of supporting cast members: scientists, bureaucrats, development experts, aid workers, accountants and financiers, veterinarians, and traders. This refashioning of the African farmer lies behind calls to "build human capacity, stimulate entrepreneurship and improve the governance of innovation."[39]

Most rural development throughout the twentieth century was top down and state directed, taking the form of what Foucault would refer to as pastoral and disciplinary forms of power. Pastoral power aimed at the good of the flock, and the good shepherd, that is, the state, sought to improve the practice of each and all (*omnes et singulatim*) through the guidance and shaping of conduct. Disciplinary power worked through institutions such as food-for-work programmes, compulsory terracing, bunding, and tree planting to reform conduct and mentalities through repeated and regulated practices. The production of what Peluso and Vandergeest call "political forests" in place of the jungle, through techniques of scientific forest management, has been closely bound up with the production of nation-states and the mobilisation of political violence against insurgencies and enemies of the state.[40] Again, the best examples of some of these forms of rural intervention come from Ethiopia.

In the 1950s an FAO advisor to the government on forestry, W. C. Bosshard, recommended a massive programme of afforestation, involving "the co-operation of the nation as a whole," even though he warned that with the "help of all the people" it would take one hundred years to reforest 25 percent of the Ethiopian highlands.[41] Not until later in the century could this vision be put into practice. Following the famine of the early 1970s, which led to the fall of the emperor Haile Selassie in 1974, the communist Derg regime began wide-ranging programmes of rural development. Mass public works campaigns that reached their peak during the 1980s involved tree planting, hillside enclosures, terracing, bunding, and road building. These were financed through international aid, and the Rehabilitation of Forest, Grazing and Agricultural Lands Project (Project 2488), funded through U.S. food aid, was at the time the largest food-for-work programme in Africa and the second largest in the world. At their peak they employed between 1.5 and 2 million peasants annually.[42]

Such top-down attempts at rural governance are not merely historic. Ethiopia has continued its adherence to agricultural modernisation, more recently through a focus on "model farmers" who will drive "agricultural development-led industrialisation."[43] Those designated as model farmers receive massive state assistance for their farms in return for two forms of conduct:

> The first is socio-economic: "gaining wealth" by "developing well his land" by "working hard" and by "learning new technologies" and "putting them into practice." . . . Model farmers must set an example socially, in the widest sense, in terms of moral rectitude (starting with sobriety), sending all their children to school, keeping an orderly house, and following rules of hygiene. . . . The second criterion is exclusively political. The model farmer must above all be a dedicated militant of the ruling party. He has to carry out his duties "as a vanguard," keen "to improve his political efficiency," active and at ease in the "political institutions," committed "to change the farmers around him," notably because he is willing "to administer [them] politically," by organising their participation in "revolutionary activities of communal works."[44]

In 2010–11 these communal works included tree planting which required sixty uninterrupted days of reforestation work and the cultivation of three hundred indigenous tree seedlings per year. Ethiopia also has plans to replant a further 15 million hectares of degraded land by 2030.

Both historic and contemporary manifestations of these state effects have produced widespread resistance from peasant populations, who resent heavy-handed governmental interference and recognise the ecological and agricultural illiteracy of many of their rulers. Resistance took the form of "the illegal felling of trees, the grazing of livestock in closed areas, the uprooting of tree seedlings in forest schemes, and the invasion of national parks."[45] Rahmato estimates that after the collapse of the Derg regime, "up to two-thirds of the forests planted under Project 2488 may have been 'harvested' illegally in 1990 and 1991."[46]

Ethiopia is perhaps the best example of top-down pastoral and disciplinary rural development in twentieth-century Africa, but it is not the only example nor have these programmes ended. In 2006, the National Strategy for Urgent Action on Land Degradation and Water Catchments in Tanzania identified problems like overgrazing and deforestation due to firewood collection and charcoal production: it prompted a range of responses, among them "the relocation of pastoralists and tree-planting."[47] The Africa Talks Climate survey found considerable backing for governments to spearhead tree planting and to "educate people about the importance of trees"; and "tree planting is by far the most common environmental activity mentioned by local government officials" across the continent.[48] Indeed, the survey advised that the primary framing which resonated with many African populations when communicating climate change was "the importance of trees," while warning that such an emphasis "could provide a false sense that all climatic problems, such as drought and desertification, may be solved at a local level through tree-planting."[49]

Africa is regarded as a leader in restoring the world's degraded land through tree planting, and at a New York climate summit in 2014 a number of African countries made high-profile commitments to restore deforested landscapes, including Ethiopia (15 million hectares), Uganda (2.5 million hectares), and the Democratic Republic of the Congo (8 million hectares).[50] Another prominent initiative is the Great Green Wall in the Sahel. It was formally launched in September 2011 with a €1.75-million grant from the African Union (AU) and supported by the EU, FAO, and the Global Mechanism of the UN Convention to Combat Desertification. The 15km-wide and 7,100km-long tree belt spans Algeria, Burkina Faso, Chad, Djibouti, Egypt, Ethiopia, the Gambia, Mali, Mauritania, Niger, Nigeria, Senegal and the Sudan and is endorsed by regional and international organisations. It has evolved from an ambitious plan to plant a line of trees across the continent to "a mosaic of interventions addressing the challenges facing the people in the Sahel and Sahara," including rural development and infrastructure, terracing, and tree planting.[51] In October 2013 the Global Environment Facility announced it has committed US$4.6 million to one component entitled "Building Resilience through Innovation and Knowledge Services" to promote sustainable land and water management in key landscapes and climate-vulnerable areas of West Africa and the Sahel.[52] So far these projects, most of which remain in the planning stage and involve interminable vision documents, strategies, and workshops, appear remarkably reminiscent of the many decades of top-down rural development which precede them.

There are also many bottom-up development initiatives which have sought to build upon existing practices of communal and peasant tree planting. Machakos District in Kenya has become emblematic of the achievements made possible by giving technical resources to existing tree-planting practices, thanks to its profile in the reports *More People, Less Erosion* in 1994 and the follow-up, *More People, More Trees,* in 2010. The follow-up work also discusses the successes of farmer-led tree planting in Burkina Faso and the widely reported and notable recovery of dryland ecology in Niger. Yet even such apparently successful regreening programmes are often not the restoration of past indigenous forests but the introduction of new plantations, tree farms, and foreign species. Critchley asks whether trees are "migrating, metaphorically speaking, from forests to fields?"[53] This shift from tree planting as a way to reforest Africa's dry lands with native species to on-farm agroforestry as a commercial interest is revealing, and it hints at a broader, historical process beneath these programmes of rural development and tree planting, namely, the transformation of subsistence peasant cultivators into commercial agriculturalists.

The construction of the entrepreneurial farmer as the solution to sustainable rural development is exemplified by the 2003–4 budget speech of the provincial agriculture minister in South Africa's Eastern Cape, Max Mamase. He identified two categories of farmers: "The so-called 'resource limited farmers' who are presented as an environmental threat and described as targets of poverty alleviation programmes, and the commercial farmers, who were presented as vital cogs in the wheel of growth-orientated development."[54] The production of the commercial farmer stands on the horizon of most of these attempts to educate and reform the conduct of the problematic African peasant. These new imagined farmers, "typically specialised in the production of higher-value export crops using 'modern' inputs and techniques on government managed schemes," serve as "a vanguard of technical modernisation and agricultural productivity growth, as exemplars of cultural modernity, and as a force for civic responsibility and social stability."[55]

Two examples from South Africa are revealing, not least for the terminology employed. During the FIFA World Cup in 2010, the city of Durban launched a "Treepreneur" programme in which community members would grow trees and plants at home which could be traded for credit notes redeemable at "Tree Stores" for goods such as food and clothing and services such as school fees and driving lessons. Offsetting the GHG emissions produced by the hosting of the football tournament entailed employing 101 local people as workers in invasive alien plant clearing, ecosystem restoration, fire protection and as community facilitators supporting the 160 Treepreneurs.[56] A second project, the Mapfura-Makhura Incubator for biofuel production, is discussed by Agnes Musyoki as a case study of the greening of the rural economy in Limpopo province. It involves support for "subsistence farmers or unemployed people, including youth and women . . . in becoming men and women entrepreneurs"; thus "local farmers are transitioning to growing soya and sunflower for biofuel production and are referred to in the project as 'incubatees / farmers.'"[57] Organisers have "managed to recruit 150 incubatees/farmers into its incubation programme and so far 51 (out of 150) farmers have successfully completed three years of the incubation (training and support) process, while 124 (out of 150) are considered SMMEs [small, medium, and micro enterprises]."[58] Apart from the rather unfortunate terminology of "incubatees/farmers" (which positions rural bodies as the quasi-willing hosts of new biofuel production systems to be painfully birthed in future trauma), such support has attractive features and is doubtless welcomed by many impoverished rural peasants. The point here is simply that such enterprises are ambitious, entail the complex and political reproduction of bodies, social relations, and landscapes in Africa, and as such will produce new relations of wealth, power, and exploitation. As Goran Hyden conveyed it, development, or "the road to modern society," has only ever "been completed at the expense of the peasantry."[59] Reforming the conduct of rural Africans is a central part of broader historical processes of replacing peasants with educated farmers, enlightened tree planters, and commercial entrepreneurs (or Treepreneurs), through which the green state in Africa has been produced over decades and even centuries.

PROBLEMATISATION NUMBER TWO: OVERCONSUMPTION

The transformation of profligate peasants into educated farmers and tree planters has been the primary way in which green states have worked to construct individuals and populations in rural Africa. Yet overconsumption is an alternative problematisation that is likely to have increasing salience in the twenty-first century. It has traditionally been central to Western environmental movements but is not usually regarded as pressing in Africa. Overconsumption encompasses a range of problems: "For some, the concern is consumerism, the crass elevation of material acquisition to the status of a dominant social paradigm. For others it is commodification, the substitution of marketable goods and services for personal relationships, self-provisioning, culture, artistic expression, and other sources of human well-being. For still others it is overconsumption, in the popularly understood sense of using more than is necessary."[60] The predominant popular association is with rich westerners eating themselves into early graves, and one prominent report proclaimed that "a billion people are substantially over-consuming, spawning a new public health epidemic involving chronic conditions such as type 2 diabetes and cardiovascular disease."[61] Such matters seem far removed from the dominant perception of Africa, which tends to focus on the malnourished and impoverished. Nevertheless, although the politics of consumption plays out quite differently, it is central to emerging practices of green statehood in Africa.

As one of the world's poorest regions Africa has usually been conceptualised as suffering from a lack of consumption: shortages of food and water, hunger, and famine, lack of jobs, poorly developed internal and regional markets, and so on. For example, the 2013 report on the Millennium Development Goals in Africa observes that "the proportion of people living in extreme poverty (on less than $1.25 a day) in Southern, East, Central and West Africa as a group fell from 56.5 percent in 1990 to 48.5 per cent in 2010; about 20.25 percentage points off the 2015 target, compared with just 4.1 points for South Asia. However, more people are joining the ranks of extreme poverty than exiting—some 124 million people fell into extreme poverty over 1990–2010."[62] Although the dominant historical memory of famine in Africa remains associated with Ethiopia in 1984–85 and Somalia in 1992, famines and chronic hunger have not been eliminated from Africa in the twenty-first century. Since the millennium there have been serious famines (although the terminology is disputed) in Ethiopia (1999–2000), Malawi (2001–2), Niger (2004–5), and the Horn of Africa in 2010–12. At the continental level, most African countries endured "serious to alarming hunger" over 1990–2012, some 46 percent of Africa's workers earn less than $1.25 per day, and Africa's share of global trade remains marginal. In the light of these figures, which inevitably conjure up images of starving mothers and stunted babies with distended bellies, it seems almost perverse to see overconsumption as an African problem.[63]

Yet considering consumption critically immediately requires an assessment of who is consuming what. As soon as one gets beyond the stock images of starving African babies and looks at the diversity of African social relations, a number of ways in which overconsumption is problematised in Africa become clearer. To take one simple and strikingly visual example, Africa's leaders have often been associated with physical size and corpulence, leading Bayart to deploy the phrase "the politics of the belly" as a metaphor for African political culture. He notes the proliferation of phrases associated with eating, sitting at the table, appetite, and gorging to refer to a politics of personal accumulation and acquisition in Africa: "A system of power-through-eating."[64] He stresses, however, that "not everyone 'eats' equally."[65] A concern with overconsumption can thus very literally involve developmental agendas centred on new afflictions of affluence such as diabetes, obesity, and "double-burden households," that is, households that contain both an underweight and an overweight member, as well as more metaphorical and symbolic concerns with corruption, nepotism, and personal enrichment.[66]

Many of these issues are framed as problems caused by globalisation: the arrival of Western foods and cultures in Africa, new sources of wealth and enrichment for a small minority, and the increasing speed of urbanisation on the continent. The growth of sprawling urban cities and slums filled with fast-food vendors and outlets, alcohol and drugs, waste and refuse and pollution, and swelling numbers of hungry, greedy inhabitants stands as the archetypal form of the problem of overconsumption. This image is very different from that of the starving rural peasant or of the deforested, eroded land, but it is an increasingly significant environmental problematisation which constructs certain urban populations as troublesome and casts responsible individual consumers as the solution.

The Unruly Urban Masses

Over half the world's population now live in cities, and Africa has the fastest rate of urbanisation of all the world's regions. By 2050 Africa will have a higher number of people living in cities than Europe, Latin America, and North America. Lagos, Johannesburg, Accra, Cairo, Nairobi, and Abidjan are continental melting pots and present a compelling vision of Africa's future. Even in Tanzania, usually imagined as a quintessentially rural African country, the State of the Environment report noted that "the urban population of Tanzania as a whole increased from 787,000 in 1967 to 7.9 million in 2002, an increase of over ten times during the period of 35 years."[67] In West Africa, where urbanisation has been historically far more advanced, the urban population has "increased 10 fold between 1950 and 1990 (and 20 fold between 1950 and 2010) . . . the number of urban centres with populations above 10,000 has grown continuously, from 125 in 1950 to over 1000 today," and "the average distance between urban centres of over 10,000 inhabitants has declined from 111 km to 33 km."[68]

The African city presents a number of very obvious environmental issues and challenges to those who live there, including overcrowding, traffic congestion, air pollution, dirty water, poor sanitation, noise, disease, and crime. With their tens of millions of people living in often unregulated and unserviced slums, African cities have some of the highest levels of inequality in the world. In apartheid South Africa, Nomavenda Mathiane reported that "in squatter areas there are often no toilets and no running water, let alone refuse removal services. And most townships are as bare as deserts. There are no trees to beautify the environment, give shade and help prevent soil erosion."[69] The causes of these problems are manifold, encompassing the overt racism of the apartheid regime in South Africa, the colonial legacy of urban planning, bureaucratic inefficiencies, patrimonial politics, and rapacious capitalism. Tanzania's State of the Environment report states more bluntly that there is "a clear cause-and-effect relationship between urbanisation and environmental degradation," and it is this framing which has dominated discourses about overconsumption in Africa.[70] It is easy to see how the manifestation of these problems crystallises in the figure of the urban African consumer. The behaviour of urban populations appears almost self-evidently problematic: Why do they toss their rubbish and human waste into the street? Why do they insist on burning charcoal when "green stoves" are available? Why are tyres burnt in the streets and buses torched by angry youths? Why are toilets destroyed or defaced? To some weary environmentalists the problem is, quite simply, that Africans do not care about the environment.

11. "Old Man, Dukathole," Santu Mofokeng (b. 1956). © Santu Mofokeng, c. 1988 silverprint edition 5. Images courtesy Lunetta Bartz, MAKER, Johannesburg.

Worry over urban consumption and waste has always been present: colonial regimes were haunted by the presence of rural Africans in so-called civilised cities. The South African Natives (Urban Areas) Act of 1923 regarded African populations as "temporary sojourners" in the city.[71] Yet these concerns have increased as urbanisation has skyrocketed in recent decades. As economic growth rates remain high for many African countries and elites get wealthier, public and political disquiet at the habits of both wealthy consumers and the urban poor in cities like Accra, Abuja, Nairobi, Addis Ababa, and Johannesburg is likely to rise. This is particularly the case in South Africa, where consumption is a common topic among politicians and the populace. The reason is not surprising: South Africa is one of the wealthiest but also most unequal countries in Africa. On the drive from Cape Town or Johannesburg international airports to the city a visitor is immediately confronted by the discrepancy between fabulous wealth alongside urban squalor. Moreover, a number of high-profile cases of corruption and greed among political and corporate elites has been explicitly contrasted with the purity of the antiapartheid struggle, leading many to ask, Was this what it was all for? This sentiment was articulated by President Thabo Mbeki in 2006 when he "excoriated the new nation—including the black majority—for 'having absorbed the value system of the capitalist market, [and having] come to the conclusion that for them, personal success and fulfilment meant personal enrichment at all costs, and the most theatrical and striking public display of that wealth.'"[72] In a society with strong traditions of Calvinist puritanism, a wilderness ethic, and the self-denial of the political struggle, the ostentatious consumption of the new elites typified by footballers, music stars, television celebrities, and empowered black businessmen has provoked widespread self-examination about the relationship between wealth and social values.

The Green Consumer

The solution to the wastefulness and profligacy of unruly urban populations, whether by the lumpen poor or the consuming rich, is discursively framed as the green consumer. The green consumer is constructed as a gendered subject who responds rationally to price signals in order to achieve economic efficiency rather than waste as well as performing her green values and identity through consuming environmentally friendly products. Such efforts cannot be dismissed as merely superficial: indeed, the production of individuals as rational, self-interested economic calculators has been one of the most far-reaching achievements of modern capitalism. As Foucault's work has shown, neoliberal rationalities of government have been devoted to the production of an "eminently governable" *Homo oeconomicus*.[73] To John and Jean Comaroff, consumption has become "the prime medium for producing selves and identities since the late 20th century."[74]

Defining people as individuals and focusing on their private acts of consumption are therefore the first steps in producing green consumers. The fact that "we heat our homes, we cool our homes, we buy food to consume in our homes" means that these are all realms amenable to governmental action.[75] Decisions about water, electricity, and housing bills have environmental implications and are often associated with female responsibilities. As MacGregor points out, "The feminization of the private sphere, and of the responsibility for household management in most cultures, means that making it a site for environmental action poses particular threats for women and for feminist politics."[76] Moreover, attempts to govern these spheres have long, contested histories. During the 1990s and 2000s cost-recovery policies in many of these sectors, promoted across Africa by neoliberal governments and the World Bank, led to the installation of meters, cutoffs of water and electricity, and housing evictions when consumer debts began to mount. Goldman notes that in 1990 fewer than 50 million people received their water from private water companies whereas by 2000 the number was more than 460 million, all of whom were reliant on a few global water firms, and the growth markets were all in the global South.[77] Such concentration was primarily justified in terms of the economic sustainability of service provision by struggling metropolitan authorities, but in many cases it was also accompanied by implicit or explicit intimations that the profligacy and waste of the poor in consuming these resources needed to be curbed. For example, in 2013 the executive secretary of the Energy Commission in Ghana, Alfred Ofosu, declared he was "pleading with Ghanaians not to waste electricity" after a 78.9 percent increment in electricity and 52 percent increase in water tariffs.[78] It is a common claim that in the absence of pricing such resources, they will not be valued or used responsibly. The installation of water meters and enforcing of cutoffs thus became powerful tools in the creation of responsible, prudent household consumers, who manage their budgets and control their expenditure. Yet such technologies are far from smooth or straightforward: the scale of opposition they have produced has led in many cases to the stalling or renegotiation of privatisation contracts. Goldman asserts that an astonishing 80 percent of the water privatisations in Africa had either been nullified or were under serious renegotiation by 2006.[79]

In addition to incentives and measurement technologies to reduce consumption in the areas of water, electricity, heating, and travel, there has been some growth in nonessential or luxury markets for green products in Africa, although not to the same extent as in Europe or North America. One study observes that "a wide range of green products including organic foods, recyclable paper, eco-light bulbs, eco brooms, environmentally designed tyres and eco-friendly detergents amongst others are now available in Mauritius."[80] A number of applicants across the continent have received financial support from Consumers International and their Green Action Fund (partly funded by the Swedish Society for Nature Conservation) for advocating green consumption. Twenty African entrepreneurs and start-up enterprises were recognised for their social and environmental innovation in 2013 in the SEED Awards for promoting entrepreneurship for sustainable development, which had thirty-four winners worldwide, including in Ethiopia, Morocco, Mozambique, Namibia, South Africa, Tanzania, and Uganda. In Uganda, for example, BanaPads Social Enterprise produces comfortable sanitary pads from natural agricultural waste materials. They are apparently low-cost, fully biodegradable, safe and hygienic, and made locally according to international standards.[81]

An even more explicitly environmental technology for focusing governmental attention on individual or household consumption is the concept of the ecological or carbon footprint. This involves measuring the outputs and costs associated with a particular lifestyle and comparing it to local, regional, national, or international averages. Such analysis produced the frequently reported statistic that if everyone lived like the average American we would need the resources of five planets to sustain us; currently, "humanity uses the equivalent of 1.5 planets to provide the resources we use and absorb our waste."[82] While such statistics are available for variously scaled communities, the language and technologies associated with footprinting indelibly link it with individual people and their bodies. As Middlemiss notes, "[The] eco-footprint implicitly judges the individual or consumer (rather than other agents), and her/his success or failure in meeting responsibilities."[83] Thus in the Western world people have become increasingly familiar with technologies to measure and reduce their footprints and offset their flights and holidays. According to Paterson and Stripple, "Carbon footprinting has become perhaps the elemental form of practice as individuals self-govern in relation to climate change."[84]

This technique has been most widespread in highlighting the massive overconsumption of Western countries, but it is beginning to be used as a tool for development. A report by the AfDB and WWF prior to Rio+20 in 2012 observed, "The ecological footprint of all African countries increased by 240 per cent between 1961 and 2008 as a result of growing populations as well as increased per capita consumption in a minority of countries. The average per capita footprint in Africa in 2008 is now rapidly approaching the available per capita biocapacity within Africa's borders of 1.5 gha [global hectares]."[85] The report compares countries according to their per capita ecological footprint to determine which are living beyond their means. It records that "Mauritius has the highest per capita footprint at 4.6 gha and, together with Libya, Mauritania and Botswana, is one of four countries with an average per capita Ecological Footprint greater than the global average. Ten of the 45 countries [compared] have an Ecological Footprint greater than the global per capita available biocapacity of 1.8 gha. In 2008, Eritrea had the lowest per capita footprint at 0.7 gha."[86] In addition, the account notes that the continent's carbon footprint per capita has risen by 122 percent between 1961 and 2008, and carbon accounts for over 50 percent of the ecological footprint of countries like Libya and South Africa.[87] It is predicted that consumption of electricity will "increase more than six-fold over the next decades with more than 80 per cent of the new demand in urban areas."[88]

The report also provides data correlating countries' ecological footprints with their Human Development Index (HDI) scores to determine whether progress on human development is at the expense of the ecosystem. The overall message is that while "average per capita footprint on Africa has actually declined by about 5 per cent" between 1961 and 2008, the huge population increases have caused the overall ecological footprint of the continent to rise massively.[89] By 2015 it was confirmed that Africa as a whole was in biocapacity deficit in that its footprint exceeded the resources available within its borders.[90] The language of Malthusian population crisis and overshoot and collapse pervades these reports and indicates a slow but rising preoccupation with the ecological impacts of consumption in Africa. The implication is that states need to take action to ensure the sustainability of their patterns of production and consumption. Consumers (often female) must be made aware of their responsibility in reducing waste and buying green, such "responsibilisation" will be increasingly central to African environmental governance in the future.

Some African governments have already begun to internalise these assumptions. The South African Climate Change Strategy of 2011 stakes out a proactive position on producing green consumers:

> Developing climate resilience requires all of us to change our behaviour and become conscious of our individual carbon footprints. A nuanced approach to communication will be followed, recognising that a communication strategy aimed at individuals and communities with the largest carbon footprints (the urban wealthy) needs to be very different from a communication strategy aimed at the individuals and communities most vulnerable to climate change impacts (the rural poor). It is also recognised that people will only make climate-friendly decisions if they have convenient, reliable and safe climate-friendly alternatives and if they know about these options.[91]

The plans also include mainstreaming "climate change knowledge into education and training curricula" and providing climate change education as "part of the broader framework of education for sustainable development," to "equip South African citizens to re-orient society towards social, economic and ecological sustainability."[92] The neoliberal implications of such an outlook, reliant upon the "responsibilisation" of consumers, become clearer in the conclusion of the strategy, which proclaims that its ultimate success "will depend on decisions by individual citizens to embrace climate-friendly lifestyles and habits."[93]

As part of a broader strategy on addressing environmental impacts, one that does not presume all change must be top-down and state-led, such an attitude seems laudable. Yet the actual mechanisms of change deployed by governments to produce green consumers often seem hopelessly inadequate to the task and a neglect of public responsibility. In South Africa one of the legacy projects of the Johannesburg World Summit on Sustainable Development (2002) was Indalo Yethu, an "endorsement brand promoting greening and eco-friendly practices as a way of life." This enterprise was a state-supported partnership intended to enhance and encourage green products and services, promote excellence, and facilitate wider participation in the green economy. The Indalo Yethu Trust was intended to generate sufficient income through eco-endorsement to fund its operations, but in 2012 it was announced that the project was being wound up due to lack of money.[94] In such a context it is tempting for politicians to blame individual consumers for their lack of green thinking instead of building political coalitions behind transformational or even revolutionary green economy strategies (see chapter 5).

An even more problematic implication of many of these green consumption discourses and practices has to do with the type of subjects produced:

individualised, gendered, rational, and utility maximising. The problems caused by the reliance on such subjects in the absence of proper standards and regulations for employment, land use planning, and environmental health can be seen in the waste disposal and recycling sector. The 2010 social attitudes survey reported that, when asked about an environmental issue that is most worrying in South Africa, 20.3 percent of respondents cited unclean water, followed by littering (17.6 percent), unclean air (16.1 percent), and the wasting of water (14.1 percent).[95] The *Africa Talks Climate* survey revealed that many South Africans, above all those in townships and informal settlements, feel that "the government could do more to provide decent housing and to organise adequate litter collection and recycling facilities."[96] In addition, there is a strong sense that individuals also have to take responsibility; the survey noted that "recycling is unanimously seen as the one action that South Africans as individuals can take against climate change," reflecting decades of school and community campaigns urging individuals to recycle their cans and bottles.[97] One of the first of these campaigns "led to the establishment of Keep South Africa Tidy (renamed Keep South Africa Beautiful) in 1971," and similar efforts can be found in most other African countries.[98] Recycling of cans and bottles can seem woefully inadequate when considered against the scale of Africa's environmental challenges—climate change, rampant oil and gas exploration, biodiversity loss, pollution, soil erosion, and deforestation—but this is to miss the real import of such initiatives: they are about producing rational individuals who regard the private (feminised) sphere of consumption as the primary site of green politics. The "social shadows" produced by these policies, including risks to health and safety, precarious employment, and dumping of waste in the global South, are discussed by Dauvergne and LeBaron in their study of waste pickers and dumps in South Africa, Egypt, and elsewhere.[99] Such modes of subject production are central to the assembly of green state effects in Africa today, and they have crucial political consequences.

PROBLEMATISATION NUMBER THREE: FOREIGN BODIES

The third and final problematisation relates to matter out of place. It encompasses what could be referred to as anomie, the general feeling that the speed of social and technological change has accelerated, destabilising the familiar, normal, and natural. Such anxiety about a state of flux in the world and the concomitant breakdown of boundaries, be they national, ecological, natural, sexual, gendered, gastronomic, religious, or cultural, links to environmental concerns as both a cause and a consequence. Hyperglobalisation is perceived as driving environmental degradation, and the unfolding of ecological catastrophe is equally seen as a contributing factor to the unravelling of social and cultural norms. Richard Grove writes that in an earlier era "anxieties about environmental change, climatic change and extinctions and even the fear of famine, all of which helped to motivate early environmentalism, mirrored anxiety about social form (especially where the fragile identity of the European colonist was called into question) and motivated social reform."[100]

Genetic modification, HIV / AIDS and disease, immigration, alternative sexualities, and invasive alien plants are not conventionally regarded as environmental issues, and certainly they are not *only* environmental issues. However, they link to a recurring ecological question about what is natural and wholesome, summarized in Aldo Leopold's famous dictum: "[A] thing is right when it tends to preserve the integrity, stability and beauty of the biotic community. It is wrong when it tends otherwise."[101] Leopold's deep ecology can be read as an appeal to localism, community, humility, and a reverence for natural beauty; but it has also been mobilised by a politics of exclusion, hostility, and fascism. Environmentalists in the United States, for example, have sometimes ended up aligning with right-wing groups opposing immigration and reifying the national body, character, and environment.[102] The primary problematisation constructed through this anxiety is the invading alien or foreign body.

The Invading Alien

The object of anxiety over the invading alien can vary considerably: from nonindigenous plants, to cancers or perceived foreign genetic material, to different human ethnicities, cultures, and practices. The threat of disease is one of the most obvious manifestations of the danger posed by a foreign body to natural stability and health. Such a perspective resonates in Africa, where the history and demography of the continent can be told in terms of the human struggles against prevalent, debilitating diseases: Ebola, malaria, sleeping sickness, polio, leprosy, and typhoid, among others. In more recent years the threat of HIV/AIDS has become inextricably connected to the African condition—at one point two-thirds of the global HIV-positive population was in Africa—and this disease is an almost quintessential example of fears of perversion and foreign penetration. These connotations are due not only to the initial links, in public discourse, with dark tales of the origin of the disease in cross-species encounters in the African jungle and then to its representation as a homosexual plague, but also to the way the disease attacks the body's immune system, leaving sufferers in a state of drawn-out near-death, a zombie or ghostlike existence. This interpretation was exacerbated as analysts proclaimed the threat the illness posed to the coherence and sustenance of the nation itself, to its economy and military security, by the scale of the infections. High rates of infection were associated with migrant labour, especially among miners and military personnel, as well as to the presence of vulnerable, precarious workforces, the sex industry, and patriarchal power relations. In Uganda, Colin McInnes notes, the first major epidemic of HIV / AIDS "coincided with the invasion of that country, while there appeared to be a strong link between the deployment of peacekeepers in Cambodia in the early 1990s and the spread of the disease there."[103] Politically, in South Africa and elsewhere, the disease became the battleground for a cantankerous public debate about science and knowledge, the "African renaissance" and African solutions to African problems, Western imperialism, and the politics of drug companies versus natural remedies such as good nutrition and garlic. Continuing associations of HIV / AIDS with homosexuality have contributed to the paranoid vilification of same-sex relations across much of the African continent.[104]

Environmental campaigners in Africa have been largely silent on issues like HIV / AIDS and homosexuality, but a parallel connection to deep-seated convictions about what is natural and healthy can be found in anti–genetic modification campaigns. The development and transmission of GMOs has proved highly controversial, and even in South Africa, where the technology is the most advanced on the continent, almost two-fifths (38 percent) of the population thought that genetic modification was either extremely dangerous or very dangerous to the environment.[105] The most conspicuous instance of this fear occurred during the drought and food shortages of 2002, when the United States sent food aid to southern Africa comprised of genetically modified material. Many of the recipients refused to accept it, "partly as a health precaution and partly on the grounds that it could contaminate their own crops, thus hurting potential future exports to Europe."[106] In Zambia, Home Affairs Minister Luckson Mapushi asserted that the GM maize was poisonous. At a conference on food security in Lilongwe in December 2002, social activists from ten African countries argued that "the decision to accept GM food aid would put in jeopardy the lives of 'future generations of people, plants and animals.' "[107] Zambia eventually accepted the GM grain in milled form but "only for the 130,000 Angolan refugees in camps within its borders," not for the general population.[108]

Opposition to GMO technology has many other dimensions, not least resistance to agroindustrial corporatisation and privatisation, but the Zambian example does show the presence of a stark biopolitical logic: drawing a line between what is acceptable for a certain population but unacceptable for others. Such divisions are routinely made by nationalist and ethnic forms of politics, and they are also part of the production of green citizens in Africa. This can also be illustrated in policies to restrict the incursions of foreign or invasive plant and animal species. In 2004 the IUCN "identified 81 IAS in South Africa, 49 in Mauritius, 44 in Swaziland, 37 in Algeria and Madagascar, 35 in Kenya, 28 in Egypt, 26 in Ghana and Zimbabwe, and 22 in Ethiopia."[109] Farmers in Ethiopia have remarked upon the exponential rise in foreign eucalyptus trees at the expense of indigenous species like junipers, olives, and acacias. The introduction of the Nile perch into Lake Victoria is an oft-cited case of the disastrous destabilisation of an ecosystem, made famous worldwide through the vividly titled film *Darwin's Nightmare* (2004). The evocatively named Devil weed (*Chromolaena odorata*) is a flowering shrub native to North America that, since being introduced to Côte d'Ivoire, has proved virulent in disturbed ecosystems and has contributed to flash fires across west and southern Africa.[110]

South Africa provides one of the best studied and perhaps most dramatic manifestations of the concern with IAS, with particular threats identified from black wattle trees, various species of carp and trout, and other pests. Trees remain the iconic concern, however. Closed indigenous forests cover less than 1 percent of the land and extensive plantations of Australian trees like acacia, eucalyptus and hakea were established in the twentieth century. After 1994, however, the dominant discourse of environmental conservation shifted towards water conservation rather than reforestation, and alien trees that absorbed large quantities of water suddenly became the problem. Bennett reports that "Australian trees are hunted down and exterminated by government employees funded by Working for Water," and "popular discussions of Australian trees in newspapers sometimes display a powerful combination of ecological nationalism and xenophobia."[111]

This issue has been most vividly covered by the Comaroffs in an article from 2001. By exploring public discourses in response to a destructive fire on Table Mountain in 2000, they observe how IAS like the Australian acacia became defined as a problem because of their fast growth and high water usage. The Comaroffs saw such a discourse as intersecting with the rise of xenophobic attitudes towards and attacks on foreigners in South Africa. The vulnerability of national icons such as Table Mountain and the supposedly indigenous *fynbos* plants, which produce South Africa's national flower, the protea, to these "alien interlopers" seemed to parallel postapartheid angst about the cohesion of the national body.[112] Moreover, "when the fire was followed some two weeks later by ruinous floods to the north . . . it was not altogether surprising to read that 'huge forests of alien trees' were being held by experts to have 'caused all the trouble' in the water-logged Mpumalanga province."[113] Political fervour reached such a point that President Mbeki, at a Cape Town symposium held to discuss international cooperation in the control of IAS a month after the blaze, declared that alien plants "stand in the way of the African renaissance."[114] Such a preoccupation with "weeds" is not new, as Neely points out, and neither is the inherent tendency for political communities to radically "Other" those outside their boundaries.[115] However, these discourses do highlight the tendency of the biopolitics of the green state to become quite defensive and violent.

In South Africa there have been widespread, often very violent attacks on African immigrants, especially in the townships but also by police in city centres. In May 2008 a series of horrific xenophobic attacks left sixty-two people dead, hundreds injured, and thousands displaced. These incidents, typically directed against Somali shopkeepers but also targeting other African immigrants, have invoked perceived threats not only to jobs and incomes but also to the sanctity of the national body and cultural traditions. The Comaroffs suggest that these migrants are popularly held to be "economic vultures" who usurp jobs and "foster crime, prostitution and disease. . . . these doppelganger anti-citizens are accused—in uncanny analogy with non-indigenous flora—of spreading wildly out of control."[116]

It is therefore crucial to address the role of environmental discourses and practices in potentially reinforcing some of the exclusive and even violent politics that are promoted through notions of autochthony and belonging. References to autochthons—Stephen Jackson explains that the word means " 'from the soil itself' and implies intimate, aboriginal connection with territory: indeed, it is sometimes rendered as 'sons of the soil' "—have increased in political salience in many African countries in recent years.[117] Mahmood Mamdani's study of the Rwandan genocide argued that it was not viewed as an ethnic conflict against a hated neighbour but racial cleansing against an alien invader who needed to be banished or exterminated.[118] Invocations of such identities as "sons of the soil" and "strangers" often invoke cultural belonging and centre on rights to employment and land, but they can also connote environmental stability. Tanzania's State of the Environment report, for example, is not atypical in noting, "The influx of refugees has . . . posed a serious stress to the environment and in some areas to catastrophic environmental degradation."[119] Dan Brockington's book on the creation of the Mokomazi game reserve also mentions the reliance of both the Tanzanian government and international conservation organisations on the claim that the pastoralists who were to be evicted were "not indigenous to the area."[120]

A different manifestation of the unease over migration in African environmental politics is discernible in a case of a proposed land deal in western Tanzania. The case centres on the development of a large agricultural enterprise on land that the developers, AgriSol Energy, describe as three "abandoned refugee camps" at Lugufu, Katumba, and Mishamo in the Great Lakes region. These camps were established in the 1970s for Burundians fleeing the civil war in their country. Currently "there are more than 72,539 registered residents of Burundian origin in the Katumba settlement" and another 90,000 or so at Mishamo.[121] These villages are no longer refugee camps, despite their legal status as temporary; communities have built lives, farms, and businesses in the area. In 2008, following a declaration by the UN High Commission for Refugees that Burundi was safe to return to, the Tanzanian government gave the refugees the option to stay in Tanzania and apply for naturalisation and eventually citizenship. Yet "according to the Tanzanian government's stipulations, the newly naturalised residents in Katumba do not enjoy full rights as Tanzanians, including freedom of movement and the right to be employed in the country, until they have been relocated from the settlement and integrated into the Tanzanian society."[122] In 2011 they were explicitly ordered not to "cultivate perennial crops such as cassava, trees, or build new homes or businesses."[123] When villagers complained and demanded compensation for the enforced resettlement, "the argument against their inquiry amounted to 'Katumba is not your land for you to start asking questions.'"[124] Moreover, many of those involved resist the label refugee, as they fear ostracisation or attacks by the Tanzanian population because of the word's negative associations. According to a report by the Centre for the Study of Forced Migration and International Refugee Rights Initiative, many in Tanzania argue that "Burundians are people who are combative, prone to revenge and hate and that giving them naturalisation could destabilise Tanzania."[125] A campaign in 2013 to repatriate nearly seven thousand so-called aliens from Tanzania has been criticised over the language and framings employed and particularly the implied link between foreigners and crime in the country. The campaign took place in the context of heated debates over the availability of land, foreign land grabs, and biofuel plantations, and the language employed by the government spokesperson, Asa Mwambene, was intriguingly horticultural: "What we are trying to do is to weed out illegal immigrants."[126]

The fixation on identity, belonging, mobility, and immigration has become bound together in a concern with the increasing potential for vast waves of climate change migration in the future. As the authors of the *Africa Talks Climate* survey observed, "Many people in rural areas speak of migration as the only viable option to respond to their changing climate. Some people say that they have left rural areas because their livelihoods have become unsustainable. Others say that if the situation worsens they too will have to migrate."[127] Norman Myers has estimated that "by 2050 200 million people will migrate due to climate change," but both the category and the prediction are highly disputed.[128] Despite—or perhaps because of—the uncertainty, the figure of the climate migrant is a problem in two ways. First, such migrants represent the increasing risks and perils of climate change: the assumption is that mass movements of people, above all, the poor and foreign, will be a clear prelude to the coming climate apocalypse. Second, as in the case of broader discourses of migration, they frequently are held to presage economic and ecological instability, cultural tension, religious conflict, and security threats. Thus "the figure of the climate-change migrant expresses a set of 'white' anxieties to do with an impending loss of control and disorder, and the dissolution of boundaries."[129]

Baldwin draws attention to the racialisation and feminisation of the climate change migrant: "It is frequently pictured as a figure originating in the Global South; usually though not always from Africa, South Asia or Latin America; usually characterised by its forced mobility; and usually depicted as brown and/or feminised."[130] Race is thus a powerful, underrecognised element of many environmental problematisations. The racialisation of environmentalism takes two main forms. First, as the discussion above implies, the figure of the climate change migrant is racialised. So too are the African and Asian bodies that drive contemporary worry over Malthusian population growth and urban consumption and overconsumption. Second, environmental conservation is often portrayed as a white issue imported into Africa and other developing countries by European settlers and international NGOs. Colonial conservation and the prominence of international institutions and NGOs in championing environmental discourses have led green politics to be associated with white skin in many African countries. To Thembela Kepe, "African conservation policy, including in South Africa, simply cannot escape questions about environmental racialisation."[131] Race, along with gender, sexuality, belonging, identity, and community, are all subsumed in a complex set of problematisations which position the foreign body or invading alien as a major threat to Africa's nature. Green state effects are produced by the practices of environmental citizenship which arise in reaction to these threats.

The Environmental Citizen

The typical response to the invading foreign body is a reassertion of the norm and the natural, which can be epitomized in the figure of the environmental or green citizen. This dimension is largely missing from the substantial literature on environmental and ecological citizenship. As Andrew Baldwin observes, "As a category of political being, the citizen does not simply emerge internal to its own history or self-conceptualisation. It emerges, and its meaning is constituted, in relation to some form of colonial Other."[132] The environmental citizen must be understood in relation to those troubling environmental subjects—the foreign bodies—which stand across the border.

The environmental citizen is a figure which goes beyond the eco-rational consumer discussed above. Such citizens take pride in their country and in the flora and fauna indigenous to that country, and they can be relied upon to do their part to expunge invading plant and animal species. They are the good gardener, weeding, pruning, maintaining the environment in its optimum state. These civic roles can take more liberal or republican forms, either by articulating individual preferences and voting or by the compulsory "civic sustainability service" called for by John Barry. A striking example of the latter is Rwanda's requirement that citizens participate in public works programmes, often involving agricultural labour or picking up litter and plastic bags (which are now banned).[133] This more disciplinary or pastoral model of producing green citizens is at the other end of a continuum from programmes which steer subjects into appropriate and responsible behaviour. As Jean-Jacques Rousseau noted, "It is not enough to say to the citizens, be good; it is necessary to teach them to be so."[134]

The most powerful technique for producing good environmental citizens is environmental education. Environmental education programmes have been rolled out across Africa by governments, NGOs, and international institutions, particularly since the 1990s and the rise of the discourse of sustainable development, with its emphasis on public involvement, information, and participation in environmental policy. The first chair of environmental education in Africa was occupied by Eureta Janse van Rensburg at Rhodes University in South Africa in 1991, and the first environmental education postgraduate degree was established in 1990. In 1994 the United States Agency for International Development (USAID) studied the impacts of commitments to introduce environmental education in Gambia, Guinea, Madagascar, Namibia, and Uganda. The agency "found a wide array of environmental education activities in place throughout all five countries" and "concluded that the initial groundwork had been laid for environmental education programs that would support larger national and regional sustainability objectives."[135] One notable project, the Southern African Development Community (SADC) Regional Environmental Education Programme, is funded by SADC and the Danish and Swedish governments and is managed by the Wildlife and Environment Society of South Africa. It has run across the fifteen SADC countries since 1997 and focuses on policy, training, networking, and the development of education materials. Environmental education programmes were running with various degrees of effectiveness through the 1990s in Ethiopia, Kenya, Uganda, Tanzania, Malawi, Zimbabwe, Zambia, Mozambique, Namibia, and Botswana, and civic and environmental education seminars are a core element of the work of the Green Belt Movement.[136]

Many problems and weaknesses have been identified in the design and implementation of environmental education in Africa, including lack of resources, poor implementation, a preservationist mentality, and the predominance of English as a language of instruction and conceptualisation. The USAID review noted "a lack of knowledge about the need to coordinate efforts, strategise for the future, and 'go to scale,'" "[little] momentum to translate policy into reality on the ground," and "few informal interventions such as communication campaigns or the use of indigenous people's communication channels to impart environmental messages."[137] In Tanzania, for example, the National Environmental Management Act of 1983 declares that the government "must stimulate public and private participation in natural resource management programs and promote general environmental education programs to create enlightened public opinion regarding the environment," but civil society voices have questioned the degree to which these aims have been implemented.[138] Notwithstanding these caveats, environmental education has been proliferating across the continent in recent years and is likely to expand further with the inclusion of education for sustainable development as target 4.7 of the post-2015 Sustainable Development Goals (SDGs).

In South Africa the incoming African National Congress (ANC) government in 1994 made environmental education a priority. They sought to build upon earlier initiatives such as the National Environmental Awareness Campaign, founded by Japhta Lekgetho in Soweto in 1977, and an environmental education conference in April 1982 at Treverton College in the Natal Midlands, while going well beyond the racial foundations and patronising tones of the apartheid regime's approach to environmental participation. The ANC's programme for government, the Reconstruction and Development Programme, eloquently called for "environmental education programmes to rekindle our people's love for the land, to increase environmental consciousness amongst our youth, to coordinate environmental education with education policy at all levels, and to empower communities to act on environmental issues and to promote an environmental ethic."[139] Accordingly, during the 1990s there was an array of policies to promote environmental education. In 1995 the Department of Education and the Department of Labour published a report stating the importance of environmental education as a "vital element" in "order to create environmentally literate and active citizens and ensure that all South Africans, present and future, enjoy a decent quality of life through the sustainable use of resources."[140]

A crucial dimension of environmental education is an emphasis on creating active citizens who will participate in the broader life of their community. The environmental citizen is not limited to the individual, eco-rational consumer, but is someone who acts within society and speaks out politically. This discourse is best embodied by the membership of environmental groups, community based organisations (CBOs), and NGOs. Across Africa there are innumerable instances of such groups whose everyday activities, from tree planting in Niger to youth recycling in Nairobi, are enactments of environmental citizenship. Brockington and Scholfield identify 281 conservation NGOs working in sub-Saharan Africa, while recognising that they could not possibly include all of the diverse smaller organisations in South Africa and that they have doubtless missed many French- and Portuguese-speaking organisations. They also suggest that this sector is experiencing more or less continual growth, in no small part due to levels of environmental education.[141] In her history of the Wildlife Clubs of Kenya McDuff describes the group as "the largest grassroots environmental education organisation for youth in Africa."[142] She writes that, since the formation of these clubs in 1968, the model has spread prolifically to the point where "wildlife clubs are found in at least 17 Anglophone countries and 10 Francophone countries in Africa."[143]

South Africa has the most well-established and well-resourced environmental NGO sector on the continent, one with a long history that substantially predates modern environmentalism. NGOs such as the Habitat Council, the National Veld Trust, and Keep South Africa Tidy received annual grants from the apartheid government. There is also a range of locally based environmental groups, among them the Kleinmond Ecological Society, the St Francis Bay–Kromme Trust, the Save Gordons Bay Society, and the Save the Garden Route Committee. Over the long term, however, organisations like the Wildlife Society (founded 1926), the Southern African Nature Foundation (founded 1968), and the Endangered Wildlife Trust (founded 1973) have dominated nongovernmental wildlife conservation activities in the country; along with IUCN-SA, WWF-SA, and the PPF, they are the contemporary NGO wing of a sizable industry which spans state institutions like SANP and private ranches and game reserves. These groups often have wealthy corporate sponsors, close links with scientific and research institutions, and large supporter networks. Their members tend to be white, relatively well-off, and relatively passive politically. Yet their numbers are noteworthy: Birdlife South Africa are reported to have some eight thousand members across forty branches; the Endangered Wildlife Trust have six thousand members; and the Wildlife and Environment Society of South Africa have twenty thousand members.[144]

The environmental movement worldwide has typically relied upon such movements, groups, and values amongst the broader population to produce ecological reforms and transitions to more sustainable pathways. In the view of Dryzek and his colleagues, emerging green states can only be produced by interaction between such social movements and elites.[145] Politicians sometimes use the absence of mass protest as an excuse not to press forward with potentially unpopular environmental reforms. According to Cock, during a meeting in South Africa in 2008 "an official from the government department of environmental affairs stood up before a group of environmentalists and NGO representatives and said: 'Where is the environmental movement? Where are the placards? We can't change things without the pressure of citizens.'"[146]

Environmental movements, however, can sometimes be bound up with broader reactionary discourses of belonging, autochthony, and naturalness. Even education policies are far from neutral and apolitical. Sustainable development programmes are often conceived, in the words of Mark Duffield, as "an educative trusteeship that aims to change behaviour and social organisation according to a curriculum decided elsewhere," over "an otherwise superfluous and possibly dangerous population."[147] For example, Cloete notes how the dominance of the English language in environmental education programmes occurs "at the expense of local indigenous communities' knowledge systems about and local languages' evolution within the environment."[148] In her assessment of environmental education policies in South Africa, "there is, in effect, almost no space for learners to 'name their realities' and reveal their (often untranslatable) indigenous knowledge in a language other than English."[149] Maathai regarded her education as, at least in part, a form of colonial indoctrination and the deliberate trivialisation of her indigenous culture.

Moreover, education plays a role not only in the creation of good environmental citizens who have the ability to make informed, rational decisions about their consumption practices or waste disposal habits, but also citizens who display "loyalty to the state and patriotic thinking."[150] The landscape and iconic flora and fauna are often invoked in nationalist discourse: Deputy Prime Minister Jan Smuts, in an address to the South African parliament in 1934 linking patriotism, love of the land, and conservationism, declared, "Erosion is the biggest problem confronting the country, bigger than any politics."[151] This is an important reminder that there is a strand of environmentalism in which the ultimate responsibility for caring for an environment lies with those who live there.[152] The role of those who are just passing through—the noncitizen, the other—is not always as clear.

GREEN BIOPOLITICS IN AFRICA

It is through these three problematisations that green subject–producing practices can be understood in Africa. The problematic peasant and the educated entrepreneurial farmer are the primary ways in which green state practices have been produced through particular types of subjectivity in Africa. These have dominated historically and geographically across much of rural Africa where environmental and conservation initiatives have tended to be focused. Yet, the figure of the green consumer is also of increasing salience, particularly in response to the growth of Africa's cities and middle classes and their environmental problems. The third trope is the problematic foreign body, which demands a reassertion of the rooted environmental citizen. The importance of discourses and practices of belonging and community, of the land and the past, of the future and what is natural cut across all forms of environmental subject production and highlight some of the most politically worrying implications of some aspects of African environmentalism.

It is here that the conceptual utility of referring to African biopolitics, instead of just African environmentalism, becomes clear. Environmentalism is frequently imagined as either politically progressive or technical and depoliticised, whereas the concept of biopolitics—the governance and administration of life—immediately begins to raise some more troubling issues.[153] The construction of bodies and populations as problematic or dangerous often leads to intensive and pervasive mechanisms of surveillance, policing, and disciplining, actions which forcefully produce and impose new subjectivities. Africa has often been a laboratory for the extension and testing of biopolitical modes of governance which have subsequently become more widespread globally.[154] Conservation biology and crop science can both be conceptualised as discourses and practices of making live and letting die, processes through which biopower is extended beyond human populations.

It is not plausible to suggest, however, that the state is increasingly hegemonic, monolithic, or necessarily successful in the production of green subjects. Moreover, one of the inherent attributes of this manufacture of difference is the creation of spaces for disagreement and antagonism. If the biopolitical techniques of colonial powers, Christian missionaries, and nationalist states were resisted in Africa—and they were, often violently—then environmental practices are also resisted through alternative practices and discourses which produce unruly subjects. As Judith Butler observes, "Just as bodily surfaces are enacted as the natural, so these surfaces can become the site of a dissonant and denaturalised performance that reveals the performative status of the natural itself."[155] It is perhaps one of the core features of environmental thought and practice that it retains a kind of dissidence, rebelliousness, and radicalism.

The Troublesome Dissident

Wangari Maathai, a Nobel prize winner, MP, and deputy minister, may appear to be a well-integrated, even mainstream figure. Her female tree-planting groups in rural communities are remarkably easy for international organisations to invoke and buy into and may have served to reproduce and enact many of the core problematisations discussed above. The Green Belt Movement even worked with the Kenyan military on tree-planting programmes. For most of her life as an activist, however, she was a thorn in the side of the Kenyan political elite. She recalled that in the 1980s "the regime labelled me 'disobedient,' and sought to curtail my activities and my voice."[156] After the election of 2007 she received death threats, apparently for criticising Kibaki's position. Her brand of green politics includes a strident condemnation of colonial violence, elite power, gendered inequality, and the naivety of faith in consumption, growth, and innovation. Thus she is an excellent leitmotif for the environmental dissident, a troublesome figure who questions accepted norms and values and poses challenges to established ways of doing things.[157]

John Barry writes, "To be a dissident and 'dissent' is to stand within one's society and political structure but not be of that society and political order in the sense of being reconciled and content with it. . . . *To be a green dissident then is to never be satisfied.*"[158] Dissidents and the social movements they produce or represent are crucial forces in the production and shaping of green states, and I have argued here that the converse is also true. As Dryzek and his colleagues note, "States and social movements cannot escape one another. The outcomes of their interaction give shape to the political world."[159] Each of the four empirical chapters of this book discusses forms of environmental dissent and resistance ranging from land occupations to Niger Delta militants and community struggles against urban pollution and rural dispossession. Some have taken very localised forms and have drawn upon religious and traditional authorities, such as Terence Ranger's discussion of the rise of various ecological movements which swept southern Zimbabwe in the 1990s. Others have gained international backing through networks like FoEI, and some, like Maathai, received international recognition for their work. The South Durban environmental activist Des D'Sa won the Goldman Environmental Prize in 2014, after being firebombed at home during a campaign he waged against a toxic waste dump in 2010. In May 2015 one of the winners of the Goldman Environmental Prize was Kenya's Phyllis Omido, who has campaigned against her employers' running a poisonous lead smelter in Mombasa. After she received death threats and experienced an attempted kidnapping of herself and her son, Kenyan politicians have finally begun to investigate the allegations of blood poisoning in the community surrounding the smelter.[160]

12. Caricature of Wangari Maathai. gadocartoons.com.

Other forms of dissenting practice can be found within green political parties. Green parties have been relatively rare in Africa but are currently active in a small number of states as well as within the African Greens Federation, which organises events on a continental level from a secretariat in Burkina Faso. The Global Green Congress in Dakar in March and April 2012 was attended by six hundred Greens from seventy-six countries. It was addressed by Haidar El Ali, the president of the Senegalese green federation, who drew inspiration from the election of Macky Sall in April 2012 and said that "Africa is becoming an engine for democracy, both sustainable and green."[161]

The rise of African green parties is noteworthy. The Mazingira Green Party of Kenya was formerly known as the Liberal Party of Kenya, under whose banner Maathai won election in 2002. The party won seats in 2007 and 2012. In Mauritius the Verts Fraternels have been a green political party since 1989. Under the charismatic leadership of Silvio Michel it has campaigned actively on issues like reparations for the descendants of slaves on the island and held a hunger strike in 2013. The Partido Nacional Ecológico de

13. Global Green Congress, Dakar 2012. © Global Greens / European Green Party.

Angola are part of the Aliança Democrática and have close links to Portugal's Partido da Terra (Earth Party). In 2003 the Green Party of Benin was able to send three deputies to parliament. The Rassemblement des Ecologistes du Burkina Faso is led by Ram Ouédraogo, who has stood for presidential election since the 1990s and served in the government as minister of state for national reconciliation from 1999 to 2002. The Green Party of Egypt was founded by the former diplomat Hassan Ragab in 1990 and receives a small amount of funding from the government; they claim to have forty thousand members and offices in twelve of the twenty-four governorates. Le Parti Écologiste Congolais was formed in 2008 by Environment Minister Didace Pembe Bokiaga. The Green Party of Mozambique won almost twenty thousand votes in the 2009 elections, putting it in sixth place, but it won no seats. The Ecological Party of Uganda, under the leadership of Robinah Nanyunja, aimed to field ten candidates for parliament and twenty local councillors at the 2016 elections. There are also small green parties in Burundi, Rwanda, Guinea, Madagascar (where President Albert Zafy in the early 1990s was seen by some as an environmentalist head of state with political origins in green movements), Mali, Morocco, Niger, Somalia, Tunisia, and Côte d'Ivoire. A number of very small green parties have contested various levels of elections in South Africa, including Ecopeace and the Green Party of South Africa. The circumstances of these small parties are often far from auspicious: the Rwandan Green Party has experienced political harassment and attempts to prevent it from contesting elections, and, according to journalists, "Their meetings have been violently broken up or blocked by police and their leader has had anonymous death threats."[162] During the 2010 election campaign the party's vice president, André Kagwa Rwisereka, was found beheaded.

It may seem surprising to invoke political parties as forces of disruption and dissent, especially in African democracies where many parties have smoothly inserted themselves within a neopatrimonial structure of rents and clients and ethnic factions and elite reproduction.[163] Moreover, the practices and discourses of many of these green political parties can reinforce processes of green subject formation along the lines of educating farmers, planting trees, encouraging green consumption, and performing green patriotism. But the formation of political parties around green ideology—notwithstanding the problems associated with such a move—is one way of seeking to contest some of the hitherto predominant problematisations that have dominated African environmental politics. The green activist and dissident—in the mould of Wangari Maathai—is a very different character from the educated farmer, green consumer, and environmental citizen. Maathai may have planted trees, but it was her intransigence and obstinacy on issues related to corruption, human rights and gendered inequality that changed Kenya's political landscape. She was a radical who was prepared to enter Kenya's political system. Such forms of activism can be crucial sources of resistance to the dominant practices of green subject production through educated farmers, green consumers and environmental citizens, and they are also a reminder that green state effects are produced by real people, people who exercise political agency in order to reshape the states in which they live.

CONTESTING THE PRODUCTION OF BIOPOLITICAL SUBJECTIVITIES

Igoe and Kelsall recall an aside uttered by an NGO leader in Cape Verde, who explained that Western donors wanted to fund the people directly. But, he added, "the people do not exist."[164] This insight has underpinned the analysis in this chapter. The people—individuals, subjects, citizens, populations—must be constructed. This chapter has explored the politics (or biopolitics) of the construction of individuals, populations, citizens, and subjects through environmental discourses and practices in Africa. In identifying and discussing these techniques, I have been influenced by the sort of analysis developed by Arun Agrawal in India, where he showed how "modern forms of power and regulation achieve their full effects not by forcing people toward state-mandated goals but by turning them into accomplices. The very individuality that is supposed to be constrained by the exercise of power may actually be its effect."[165] An important insight of such analyses is that it makes little sense to suggest that these processes of subject formation are bad or repressive. Indeed, they directly contrast with the argument for a human nature that is repressed or perverted by power relations: power relations and practices of governance and resistance are the ways in which subjects are produced. From an environmental point of view, therefore, these practices of producing educated farmers, green consumers, and environmental citizens "could be one of the conditions for the subsequent emergence of radically different green subjectivities."[166] By starting and ending with Wangari Maathai and green dissenters this chapter has emphasised some of the most vibrant and creative aspects of the production of subjectivities within environmental governance.

Yet the broader message has been more cautionary. Simply proposing more environmental education or spreading environmental values or green consumption practices is not enough to produce green state effects that might have more radically progressive or transgressive potential.[167] Indeed, some of the impacts of these processes of environmental subject formation are politically troubling, especially when predicated on values of rootedness, belonging, and invocations of what is natural. One of the risks of techniques for the production of educated farmers, green consumers, and environmental citizens is the reification of a particular essentialist, regionalist, or located politics, which thrives on notions of what is natural and belongs to one place. Green biopolitics in Africa, I have argued, could be characterised in terms of the production of multiple heterogeneous populations. The creation of difference allows for considerable interplay of politics and dissent, but it also facilitates the birth of some potentially violent and exclusionary political forces. It is not too much of a stretch to link programmes of tree planting to these discourses of autochthony and belonging; trees are rooted in the soil and can easily stand for "the embodiment of ethnic authenticity."[168]

In responding to such problematisations, critical environmental and postcolonial theorists have sought to contest "the cultural production of colonised people."[169] This can be done in all sorts of ways, and I have discussed here how protest and dissent are also central to the biopolitics of African environmentalism. To conclude, I want to consider two contestations from the realm of the arts and culture. The first is the South African sci-fi film *District 9*, in which an extraplanetary spacecraft which arrived over Johannesburg in 1982 turns out to be populated by weak, malnourished insectoid bodies called prawns. The aliens are interned in a camp called District 9, sustained with cat food, policed by a powerful multinational corporation, and exploited by Nigerian gangsters. The film is full of ambiguous foreign bodies (cannibalistic Nigerians, robotic weapons, and the prawns themselves) and anxiety about the transgression of frontiers. When the white antihero, the bureaucrat Wikus van de Merwe, becomes infected with "alien fluid" and begins to violently mutate into a prawn, the change is portrayed as a degrading transformation which "enacts the horror of the collapse of obsessively maintained borders."[170] This metamorphosis does enable Wikus to "change sides" and begin to reject his racist attitudes, but he and the audience are left hoping for a future in which he can be transformed back into a human and the disturbing prawns will "really and finally disappear."[171] As Veracini notes, "*District 9* tells the story of a white guy who ends up spatially constrained, alone and stranded, surrounded by aliens, living like one of them, turning into one of them, abandoned by family and betrayed by corporate capital after a lifetime of service. We should not ignore the significance of his personal development, but as far as nightmares go, this is the most (settler, white) South African nightmare one can tell."[172] As such, this film has clear echoes of Stephen Jackson's reflections on the politics of autochthony in the DRC, where the "discourse is obsessed with a purity that can never be achieved, and as a result it is deeply unsettled by the thought of creeping impurity."[173]

The second example of cultural contestation, bringing together themes of race, protest, and environmentalism, is beautifully conveyed in all its ambiguity through a stand-up routine by the South African comedian Loyiso Gola. "White people don't march for sh*t. You guys just send an email. (*Mimes typing*). 'I am upset,' enter; cc. Mary. And when you do march, you march over the dumbest sh*t. (*Mimes a march*) 'Don't cut the trees, Don't cut the trees!' 'Save the panda bear!' I'll tell you now, there's no black person in this room that will march for a f*ck'n panda bear. Imagine Julius [Malema] trying to mobilise the youth for a f*ck'n panda bear. (*Mimics Malema*) 'But comrades we must be sure that we are only marching for the black part of the panda bear. The white part of the panda bear cannot be trusted.' "[174]

Both Gola's jokes and *District 9*'s violence are subversive in powerful ways, and both prompt us to reflect upon the role and place of other bodies in environmental politics. They show how environmental themes can be connected to popular discourses and the language of ordinary people. As the photographer Santu Mofokeng (whose images are reproduced throughout this book) remarks, "I just can't find words violent enough to show that climate change debates fly above the concerns of ordinary people. People who live on the land and walk on the ground. The very people who stand to benefit most from green technologies; the 'boers,' the benighted peasants and the redundant or excess peoples who live on the margins of our society."[175] How marginalised, redundant, alienated populations are brought within the discourses and practices of environmental governance is a central element of investigating green states in Africa, as is the subversion of dominant forms of subject production. Fundamentally, the African green state is produced as an effect of the constitution of the bodies and populations—the life—of those within its ambits.

CHAPTER 5

Green Economies and Environmental Markets

> We need an energy revolution on the scale that the industrial revolution was—where we seriously reconfigure our economies, where we maximize all the renewable energy potential—we can do it in a way that also is sensitive to economic development, and we can have a double win for the climate and the environment on the one hand, as well as job creation and addressing poverty and development on the other.
>
> —Kumi Naidoo, *On the Climate Struggle*

> Mehring read in the paper how hippos were aborting their foetuses in dried up pools. It was the fourth (fifth?) year of drought. Of course, it didn't affect him: the river, if reduced in volume, was perpetual, fed by an underground source. The farm didn't depend on surface water. He didn't depend on the farm. He would have to buy a considerable amount of supplementary feed for the cattle, but that could go down as a tax loss.
>
> —Nadine Gordimer, *The Conservationist*

Near the end of Charles van Onselen's magisterial social history of Kas Maine, a South African sharecropper, we find lines which seem to encapsulate Maine's worldview: "As you know, everyone, black or white, has a gift. Some men are gifted livestock farmers. In my case it is tilling the land. My survival depends on that. . . . If you plant beans in October, you could be harvesting them by February."[1] Van Onselen reflects on these words, spoken by a patriarch in his nineties after a lifetime in the fields, with barely concealed awe: "Even at ninety-one there was always just one more season, just one more plan, just one more way of cheating adversity."[2] Struggles to make a living from the soil, to make progress, and to accumulate wealth are bound up with the politics of the green state in Africa, and if the previous chapter focused on the ways in which farmers like Kas Maine are produced as environmental subjects, here I consider how wider economies and markets are produced through green discourses and practices. This can involve revolutionary attempts to structurally transform national and transnational economies, but even as these practices work to produce the national economy as a key green state effect they are redefining the relations between people and the land (see chapters 3 and 4). The increasing prominence of national green economy strategies across Africa reflects the importance of discourses of economic transition and transformation to the production of green state effects, in Africa as elsewhere in the world.

I start with one of the most salient examples. For several years South Africa has been scheduled to introduce a new national carbon tax.[3] Financial instruments like taxes and tradable permits are typical ways for states to govern and regulate the economy, and this proposal, the first in Africa and one of the first in the global South, is a straightforward measure to internalise environmental costs and penalise polluters. The stated intention is to incentivise more environmentally responsible behaviour. The National Treasury's Carbon Tax Discussion Paper, released in May 2013, confirms that "the primary objective of implementing carbon taxes is to change future behaviour, rather than to raise revenue."[4]

This example highlights three features of the way in which environmental discourses are used to produce and govern economies in Africa. First, proposals for measures like a carbon tax entail winners and losers: they are deeply political interventions. South Africa has one of the highest rates of per capita carbon emissions in the world, largely a product of an intensively coal-based economy, and the fossil fuel industry, manufacturing firms and workers, transport sectors, and many others have expressed their concerns about the potential impacts of this new tax on growth, jobs, and profits. Others worry that costs will be passed straight onto hard-pressed consumers. Some have suggested that "the higher cost of investment in new and more energy-efficient technologies could reduce the size of the economy by around one per cent by 2025."[5] In response, the proposed regulations, which have been repeatedly revised, renegotiated, and contested, make a number of compromises: the initial rate of the tax will be low, amounting to 120 rand (R) per ton of carbon dioxide equivalent (CO_2e), but with the prospect of subsequent increases; there will be a tax-free threshold and a range of additional forms of relief, meaning the effective tax rate will range between R6 and R48 per ton of CO_2e; and certain sectors of the economy may be exempted altogether. These concessions are seen by many environmentalists as emasculating the policy, which will result in it having a negligible effect in transforming the country's development pathway to a low-carbon trajectory.

Second, although the carbon tax is a national policy tool introduced by a national government, global and local dimensions are at play. South Africa has proudly emphasised its desire to be seen as a global leader on climate change and indeed on sustainable development more broadly. It hosted the Johannesburg World Summit on Sustainable Development in 2002 and the Durban COP17 climate change conference in 2011; prior to the Copenhagen COP15 conference in 2009 it made a high-profile commitment to reduce CO_2 emissions 34 percent and 42 percent below business-as-usual emissions growth by 2020 and 2025, respectively, if additional financing was made available. South Africa has made international commitments to promoting a green economy and stimulating green jobs, and investments in renewable energy ($16 billion of committed investments in wind and solar by mid-2015) and the proposed carbon tax are important elements of this. As such, they represent a powerful discourse of green growth, one in which environmental investments and green financial stimulus packages are being promoted as a response to the financial and economic crises since 2007. In this respect South Africa is emblematic of wider trends across the continent and beyond. In June 2013 UN Secretary-General Ban Ki-moon said, "Investors and entrepreneurs in Africa and beyond can help realize Africa's enormous potential for green growth."[6]

There are also, however, highly significant local dimensions of South African energy and development politics raised by the carbon tax debate. The primary energy generator in South Africa is the parastatal Eskom, and South Africa's macroeconomic growth path has long been based on the provision of cheap electricity to dirty industries like mining and steel and aluminium manufacturing. The mining, electricity, and manufacturing companies are thus intertwined and are closely linked to state elites, forming what has been described as the minerals-energy complex (MEC). Ben Fine describes how this state of affairs emerged in the 1870s and flourished during the interwar and immediate post–World War II periods, when "state corporations in electricity, steel, transport and so on, represented an accommodation across the economic power of the mining conglomerates and the political power of the Afrikaners, an uneasy compromise of evolving fractions of classes and their interests forged through both state and market."[7] While some elements of the state bureaucracy and the political class are doubtless committed to greening the economy through measures like a carbon tax, other powerful vested interests within the MEC are committed to preventing, delaying, or altering the course of such change. South Africa is building two of the largest new coal-fired power stations in the world, located at Kusile and Medupi and funded with controversial World Bank loans, and is thus "locked into coal-fired electricity until at least 2020."[8] Just as the sharecropper Kas Maine struggled in the fields for survival and prosperity in the context of national and global structural changes such as the Great Depression, currency fluctuations, and the rise of apartheid, so programmes to green the South African economy occur in larger structural contexts. Complex lines of alliance and networks of power cut across the state, capital, workers, political parties, and international agencies, coproducing green states and green economies as complex assemblages which structure environmental politics in crucial ways.

Third, the introduction of the carbon tax in South Africa is an excellent reminder of the degree to which economies and markets are political and social creations. The tendency of economists, politicians, and publics to reify the free market means it is seen as an autonomous or preexisting reality which can be freed or, conversely, distorted. But markets are produced through political measures such as enforcing private property rights, creating scarce commodities, introducing new taxes, changing landownership regulations, and building infrastructures like roads, ports, power lines, factories, settlements, and irrigation systems. Nally shows how the creation of so-called free markets in food supply in nineteenth-century Europe required "the active collusion of state forces."[9] This comprised, among other things, the dismantling of "anti-scarcity systems" and legislative and policing measures: "In other words, free markets emerge from the intimate connections forged between the state and capital."[10] The position I take here therefore echoes Thomas Lemke: "The market does not amount to a natural economic reality, with intrinsic laws that the art of government must bear in mind and respect; instead, the market can be constituted and kept alive only by dint of political interventions."[11]

The political nature of markets and economies as products of particular interventions has been made more explicit following the global financial and economic crises of 2007, which, it is claimed, involved "unprecedented public interventions into economic life."[12] Yet these crises merely made more visible the historical processes through which economies and markets are politically produced. That said, the financial crises, together with a growing sense of a climate and broader environmental crisis, did strengthen global public and governmental enthusiasm for a new green economy. According to UNEP's definition, a green economy is one that results in "improved human well-being and social equity, while significantly reducing environmental risks and ecological scarcities."[13] This chapter is not about how to define these terms more precisely or to determine which policies are most likely to achieve UNEP's vision. Rather, it is an assessment of the ways in which the green economy discourse has been mobilised in Africa and of the political consequences of some of these mobilisations.

The next section introduces the relationship between environmental politics and green economies and markets, while the subsequent section locates these within a longer-term history of the creation of African economies. I then identify four contemporary global discourses of the green economy—resilience, growth, transformation, and revolution—and offer a number of illustrations of these discourses from strategies across Africa. I argue that green growth is currently dominant globally and is working to legitimise a new era of big infrastructure development and modernisation in African agriculture and natural resource sectors, but that it is also possible to see evidence of discourses of resilience, transformation, and even revolution. Given the failure of green growth, resilience, and transformational discourses to radically change the lives of the most marginalised African populations for the better, the appeal of revolutionary discourses—even when they include violence—is increasing, and this constitutes one of the most important political sites of contestation in the production of green state effects in Africa.

CREATING ENVIRONMENTAL MARKETS

Natural resources have always been central to the functioning of markets. The earliest human economic exchanges were of animals, crops, timber, minerals, and countless other things, and the use and conservation of these renewable and nonrenewable resources have been intimately tied up with the rise of modern environmentalism. Ideas such as maximum sustainable yield, sustainable harvesting, and the wise use movement have been central forerunners of, or branches of, contemporary environmental movements, especially in the United States.[14] The relationship between natural resources, markets, and environmentalism prompts the questions, Through what techniques and processes do environments become resources? and, What political structures, institutions, and interventions are seen as legitimate for their sustainable management?

In order to function within a market, items have to become commodities, that is, they have to become commodified. This involves a variety of processes: standardisation (e.g., weights and measures), transfer and exchange (e.g., packaging, shipping, currencies, tariffs), and verification (e.g., proof of ownership, trade-marking, copyrighting, branding).[15] The operation of these processes with respect to new environmental commodities such as carbon credits and ecosystem services will be explored below. However, the production of national economies involves a different, or at least additional, set of processes which emerged at a specific historical juncture. For theorists like Polanyi and Foucault it was in the eighteenth and nineteenth centuries that the economy was imagined and produced through such practices and technologies as statistics, mass taxation, national planning documents, poor relief, and ensuring food supplies. Yet, as Timothy Mitchell notes, many of the theorists of moral and political economy in the nineteenth century were not really writing about the economy as we understand it today. Rather, they were thinking about thrift and personal consumption (or morality) and the politics of managing the population and its resources (or government). Mitchell sees the birth of the modern conception of the national economy happening in the interwar period, during the Great Depression, and during and after World War II.[16] The corollary of these crises and collapses, as Mitchell sees it, is the massive Keynesian public investments of the 1930s–60s, which literally built modern national economies. Using Egypt as an example, he draws attention to the construction of the second Aswan dam between 1964 and 1970 as well as to industrial agriculture and Nasser's land reform programme. To Mitchell, "This ability to rearrange the natural and social environment became a means to demonstrate the strength of the modern state as a techno-economic power."[17]

New Environmental Markets

If Mitchell's dating of the creation of modern national economies to the middle of the twentieth century is rather later than is often posited, the emergence of a truly global economy is usually dated to the post-1970 period and the era of globalisation. These debates over timing notwithstanding, the key claim here is that the early twenty-first century is characterised by another period of crisis and the concomitant creation of new bioeconomies through technologies associated with ecological economics, the biosciences, carbon accounting, and so on.[18] The (re)emergence of the notion of a green economy is therefore a crucial contemporary site of the production of new markets and economies and of new forms of state regulation and governance of these markets and economies.

How has the creation of new markets been reconciled with traditional environmental issues like limits to growth, ecological balance, and low consumption? It is certainly true that many environmentalists have long lamented the neglect of ecological values, the commodification of life-worlds, the dominance of instrumental rationality, and the greed for growth. Yet the degradation of natural resources, that is, inputs and sinks, is an easily identifiable problem for orthodox economists. They have responded to increasing evidence of air and water pollution, species depletion, and resource exhaustion by arguing that many natural resources, among them clear air, water, the sustainability of fish stocks into the future, are exploited because they are not valued. Moreover, the negative costs of production processes, for example, the emission of wastes into the soil, oceans, and rivers and the atmosphere, are externalised, or passed onto others, rather than being accounted for. Thus even a World Bank economist could write in 1995 that "markets are almost invariably deficient as distributive mechanisms when natural resources are concerned."[19] The economist Nicholas Stern argued that climate change "is the greatest and widest-ranging market failure ever seen," as the costs of emitting GHGs are not accounted for.[20] The solution, in the view of environmental economists, is to internalise these externalities. A carbon tax is a straightforward way of doing so: now that scientists can show that carbon dioxide emissions contribute to climate change through the greenhouse effect, emitters of carbon dioxide can legitimately be charged in order to help cover the costs incurred by others as a result of changing temperatures.

The internalisation of environmental externalities has been central to attempts by political scientists and sociologists to theorise the positive relationship between economic instruments and environmental protection through the concept of ecological modernisation (see chapters 1 and 2). Ecological modernisation theorists have argued not only that capitalism is sufficiently flexible to permit movement in the direction of "sustainable capitalism," but also that the "imperative of competition among capitals can—under certain political conditions—be harnessed to achieve pollution-prevention eco-efficiencies within the production process, and ultimately within consumption processes as well."[21] The central claim here is the possibility of achieving "the decoupling or delinking of material flows from economic flows."[22] Decoupling can be absolute—net economic growth without net environmental degradation—or relative—lower rates of environmental degradation per unit of economic growth—but the central idea is that previously antithetical impulses of economic growth and environmental protection can be reconciled in a vision of green growth or sustainable development.

A whole array of policies, technologies, practices, and institutions have emerged from the discourses of environmental economics and ecological modernisation. Emissions trading, such as in the creation of carbon markets, is a good example of the adoption of market mechanisms to internalise environmental externalities. Markets like the EU Emissions Trading Scheme (EU ETS), for example, work by granting or auctioning a permit to countries or to companies to emit a certain volume of carbon dioxide or other pollutants. If they emit less than their permit they can sell the excess on the carbon market. If they emit more, they need to buy extra credits to cover their emissions. The intention is that the invisible hand of the market will locate the most efficient, cost-effective places to cut carbon emissions and the correct price for doing so.[23]

A carbon market exemplifies how states and other sociopolitical actors, such as NGOs, consumers, and corporations, actively produce markets: a commodity, for instance, a ton of carbon dioxide (tCO_2), must be created, standardised, exchanged, and verified. Other GHGs can also be "carbonified," that is, expressed as CO_2e. In the case of the EU ETS, the overall number of permits in the system must also be adjusted in order to bring emissions into line with the agreed safe level for controlling climate change. This adjustment is what is supposed to control the cost of a carbon credit. Despite a crisis in 2006, when the price collapsed owing to a lack of restriction on supply, the EU ETS, in the view of Newell and Paterson, "has become a success—in political terms at least—because it satisfies one of the key questions raised by the imperative of climate capitalism; it has created a cycle of economic growth which can (in principle) promote decarbonisation, and can generate a whole constituency of interests in maintaining, even ratcheting up the system."[24] The key point here is the creation of new sets of subjects with rational economic interests in apparently greener goals, such as reducing carbon emissions. Financial traders, green investors, manufacturers of renewable technologies, and insurance firms all now (supposedly) have a financial stake in protecting the climate.

Two other technologies, the Clean Development Mechanism (CDM) and Payments for Ecosystem Services (PES), are relevant to the emergence of green economies in Africa. The CDM was created under the Kyoto Protocol to generate carbon credits from developing countries for purchase by industries in the developed world to offset their carbon emissions. Typically this has worked through end-of-pipe measures like pollution controls on dirty factories, and indeed the Abu Qir factory in Egypt, Africa's largest fertiliser factory, generates more carbon offsets than the rest of the continent combined. Other credits are produced through the provision of renewable energy and heat insulation to poor households, for example, and are described as gold standard in terms of their more developmental and social benefits. The first CDM project in South Africa, in Kuyasa, a Cape Town township, implemented low-cost urban housing energy upgrades in the form of solar water heaters to generate gold standard credits.[25] In February 2012 the UNFCCC registered a Gold Standard Programme of Activities for a cooking stove technology that aims to disseminate up to one hundred thousand cookstoves in Nigeria within the next five years, thereby saving up to 250,000 tCO2e annually.[26] Yet these developmental credits are the exception rather than the rule, and large industrial offsets have tended to dominate the CDM. By 2010 India, Brazil, and China accounted for 60 percent of CDM projects and over 70 percent of the credits, while the entire continent of Africa had just 1.86 percent of projects, mostly in South Africa and the Maghreb.[27]

Although CDM has largely been a disappointment for Africa, there is increasing interest in the credits available through REDD+ by maintaining Africa's vast forests as carbon sinks. To Gomera et al., REDD+ "represents an opportunity to introduce payments for global ecosystems services on a massive scale" for many African states.[28] Such PES schemes go well beyond carbon, GHGs, and climate change. They are an attempt to create commodities out of all the things that the environment does which are valued by human society but are not explicitly priced: for instance, the role of forests in providing oxygen in the air, pollination of crops by insects, and the purification of water by wetlands. UNEP have calculated, for example, that the contribution of insect pollinators to agricultural output is approximately $190 billion per year.[29] The economic rationale is that only by properly valuing and pricing these services can their protection be assured: if we knew and valued the full economic contribution made by a coral reef, for example, then the economics of dynamite fishing could be reevaluated. A South African document on the green economy advocated the use of ecosystem service valuing because "decision-makers with access to information on ecosystem service values are better placed to make more efficient, cost-effective and fair choices, and to justify their reasons for taking action and for choosing between options."[30] Yet such interventions in the valuing of natural resources have huge implications for local communities and their relationships with forests, rivers, and the land. For these reasons REDD+ has attracted widespread criticisms over the risks of excluding communities from forests and replacing old-growth biodiversity hotspots with carbon-intensive agroindustrial plantations. Through new practices of surveillance and mapping, new forms of exclusive territorialisation are produced (see chapter 3). To Büscher and Fletcher, these new forms of commodification can be understood as a new phase of capital accumulation through the incorporation of conservation mechanisms on a global scale.[31]

Governing the Market

In light of these ways in which markets are politically produced and governed, it is a mischaracterisation to suggest that environmental economists believe in full-throttle laissez-faire economics, deregulation, and the minimal state. Instead, environmental economics requires a vast array of enforceable mechanisms, institutions, regulations, and scientific assessments. The market does not exist before or outside politics; environments must be meticulously created, regulated, monitored, corrected, and communicated. The crucial political choice is not between state-centric and market-centric approaches, but about the balance between diverse types of governance and regulatory structure and the mechanisms for determining social, political, and economic prices.

Environmental thinkers and activists adopt a great variety of positions on the politics of governing markets. Some are convinced by the environmental economists and seek to internalise or commodify as many environmental goods and services as possible, provide all available information, and then let the invisible hand do its work. A more political strategy of social regulation is advocated by Peter Newell and Matthew Paterson, who have argued that, given the current capitalist system, the urgency of the climate challenge requires working tactically through financial and market instruments to achieve the necessary socioeconomic change. They envision a plausible future for "climate capitalism," one which would be "a model which squares capitalism's need for continual economic growth with substantial shifts away from carbon-based industrial development."[32] Others remain unconvinced by the prospect of decoupling economic growth and the market system from ecological degradation and see continual growth as leading inexorably towards disaster on a finite planet; at the mercy of the treadmill of production and the second contradiction of capitalism. Some object in principle to the logic of commodification, holding that monetary or exchange value does not capture the true value of intangible goods like a walk in the forest or the sound of birdsong. Others note the potential for fraud in the measurement and verification of carbon credits, especially where a small group of companies act as consultants, accountants, and verifiers for themselves and each other, or the dangers of mechanisms like the CDM leading to carbon colonialism in the global South.[33]

Crucially, however, a shared feature of most positions on environmental economics is the need for more and better planning. There has been a sea change from the way in which planning was regarded as a dirty word in the 1980s and 1990s: the rise of bioeconomies in carbon emissions and ecosystems services in the twenty-first century has brought social planning and regulation back into political practice. This should not be too surprising. To economists like Karl Mannheim, writing in the first half of the twentieth century "Governmental planning was associated with progress, rational and collective control, improved economic efficiency, equity and democracy."[34] From the 1960s to the early 1980s, as Mol and Buttel write, "The state rapidly expanded the span of its activities and powers in environmental protection and occupied a 'comfortable' and unquestioned position in dealing with environmental problems."[35] Most environmentally-minded commentators called for "more rather than less state activity intervention in the economic processes of investment, production, and even consumption."[36]

There has, however, been a change in assumptions about how planning will be implemented and by whom. Meadowcroft sees "the emergence of explicit forms of cooperation among various configurations of government agencies, private business interests, and environment and / or development-related non-governmental organisations."[37] An example here is the proliferation of semivoluntary instruments such as fair trade standards and corporate social and environmental responsibility (CSR) charters. The term "semivoluntary" is applicable, as Blowfield and Frynas note: "Many 'voluntary' initiatives also have a 'mandatory' aspect, and there are already many intersections between CSR and the law, including actual new legislation (as passed by Ghana to require logging companies to secure a Social Responsibility Agreement with customary landowners) as well as legal aspects to some CSR initiatives (as when a code of conduct by a multinational firm is incorporated into a contract with a supplier, becoming legally binding)."[38] Some codes are almost entirely voluntary, but others become increasingly necessary thanks to the structural logic of the market (such as for organic food producers to be accredited with one of the formal trademarks), and some, like the Ghanaian case for logging companies noted above, have become legally mandatory. Falkner writes that states still "exercise considerable influence over such private forms of governance in that they tolerate, and even encourage, their creation and maintenance by the private sector."[39] Activist groups, state bureaucracies, scientists, and private actors design, collaborate with, and contest these mechanisms for governing markets. Meadowcroft concludes that "as the decades have advanced, the state has been forced to accept that an ever more profound transformation of economic activity and of political and legal obligations will be required if environmental problems are to be managed."[40]

CREATING AFRICAN ECONOMIES

The prospect of an "ever more profound transformation" has a special relevance for economies in Africa, a continent still synonymous to many in the West with images of child mortality, famine and hunger, stagnant and old-fashioned economies, aid dependence, burgeoning slums, and underemployed masses. Some of these images are unfair. As noted earlier, many of the fastest growing economies in the first decade of the new millennium were in Africa. Ethiopia, a byword for famine and infant emaciation in the 1980s, is experiencing robust and energetic growth, and Rwanda's future seems brighter than its past. Yet it is also true that some of the poorest economies in the world are in Africa, and the gap between African economies and the rest of the world seems to be widening, not closing. Heather Deegan notes, for example, that in 1980 Africa had 3.7 percent of global exports and 3.1 percent of global imports, whereas in 2006 it had 1.8 percent and 1.5 percent, respectively.[41] The failure to achieve the Millennium Development Goals across much of Africa, despite their partial and somewhat arbitrary nature, is shorthand for the continued existence of extreme poverty and deprivation to a degree unlike anywhere else in the world.

To frame things very broadly indeed, there are two accounts of why Africa remains so poor, and the political creation and governance of markets are central to both. The first story locates the causes of African underdevelopment outside the continent. Colonialism and neocolonialism have inserted African countries within the global economy in certain ways: as sources of natural resources and cheap labour in the form of slaves and, in more recent times, indentured cash-croppers. Exploitation and the violent extraction of wealth were the central features of imperial relations.[42] Many of the world's largest multinational corporations boomed through their access to African resources: to name a few, the Lever Brothers (later Unilever) in the palm oil business in Nigeria and Congo; Firestone manufacturing its tyres from rubber trees in Liberia; and Cadbury on the cocoa plantations of West Africa. Although the account of the dependency theorists has sometimes proved cumbersome in dealing with local particularities and has underestimated the degree of African agency in strategies of extraversion, it is inescapably true that often the degree of Africa's penetration by global economic markets, not its isolation or marginalisation, has driven its deprivation.

The second, more dominant account focuses on causes internal to the African state and African societies. This outlook is characteristic of liberal and neoliberal views of the world, in which different countries might take diverse routes to modernity but the basic trajectory is the same: traditional societies, preconditions for takeoff, takeoff, drive to maturity, and then the age of high mass consumption. The obstacles to this process in Africa are manifold, according to neoliberal theorists, but they are primarily located within the national economy: a lack of natural resources or a coastline; a peasant-based agrarian economy; an overblown, corrupt, and inefficient state; and poorly directed economic and fiscal policies. Such obstacles present the ecological modernisers with a major reason for their lack of faith in the developing world: Mol and Buttel observe, "The nation-states of the South are confronted with actors—particularly various fractions of capital, but also party, bureaucratic and other elites—who can undermine particularly forcefully the environmental tasks, priority-setting activities, fiscal allocations, and goals of environmental regulatory agencies."[43] The political creation of proper markets, proper infrastructure, and proper institutions is the familiar prescription here, a cause which has underpinned modernising development for at least the past fifty years.

One of the most far-reaching manifestations of this strategy in the last century was through SAPs as a condition of access to World Bank and IMF lending. Yet despite being conventionally seen as a policy of rolling back the state in all areas of social and political life, one of the ironies here was that the agent of these reforms was to be the African state, and the reward for instituting them was financial aid to the state. SAPs were also responsible for expanding and remoulding some parts of the state: they required a great deal of intensive monitoring and auditing of African budgets and economies, for example. Clapham reports that in Kenya "the number of conditionalities attached to World Bank loans had by 1991 reached 150, many of them not precisely quantified and virtually impossible to monitor."[44] This conditionality required the building of capacity and data, especially within finance ministries, and a general expansion of fiscal capabilities. Clapham concludes that a better way to view structural adjustment might be as an attempt "to bring economic management back within the realm of government," as part of the struggle against neopatrimonialism and informal and black markets.[45]

Structural adjustment is also a good example of the fact that attempts to manage and modify markets and economies in various ways are highly political, and they result in winners and losers. In many cases SAPs caused a great deal of harm to the poorest African populations. Health and education budgets were slashed, state capacity outside the finance ministry crumbled, social safety nets were torn away. The consequences for African environments were also severe: support for farming, environmental departments, and rural development was decimated, regulatory functions effectively ceased in many areas, and IFIs required economic growth based on areas of "comparative advantage," which usually meant expanding primary resource exports. McMichael reports that "between 1980 and 2006, public expenditure on agriculture in the Global South fell 50 percent from US$7.6 to $3.9 billion."[46] The slashing of food subsidies not only caused political disturbances but also exacerbated environmental degradation as impoverished rural populations found their farms were economically unsustainable and accordingly—in some cases—turned to foraging, deforestation, and informal or illegal trade. Elites began hoarding food and speculating on financial markets on spectacular scales. As McCarthy and Prudham contend, "assaults on Keynesian-era environmental regulation have been as central to neoliberalism as assaults on labor and social entitlement programs that have received far more critical attention."[47]

Just as SAPs fostered resentment and produced antireform coalitions in many African states, Resnick et al. submit that the challenges to entrenched interests posed by green economy programmes may generate opposition.[48] They may have far-reaching effects and produce both winners and losers. Although the scale and impact of green economy initiatives is still in doubt, as we will see, the rhetoric they employ is not. UNEP demands that the green economy will "fundamentally shift the trajectory of human civilisation."[49] The green economy is one aspect of the new enthusiasm for massive governmental interventions in transforming economies, which has produced wide-ranging green state effects in Africa.

FOUR GLOBAL GREEN ECONOMY DISCOURSES

One of the themes of the Rio+20 Conference on Sustainable Development in June 2012 was the green economy, which was presented as the latest big idea in international environmental politics. While the official outcome text cautiously promoted it as "one of the important tools available for achieving sustainable development," others asserted, "What is needed is the same kind of initiative as shown by Roosevelt's New Deal in the 1930s" and proclaimed a Global Green New Deal as the next stage of human progress, akin to the industrial revolution.[50] Yet, like many apparently innovative big ideas, the concept of the green economy is not really that new. Moreover, the apparent consensus on its importance in recent years masks four alternative, sometimes competing discourses on the relationship between the economy and the environment. These four global discourses provide a framework for the subsequent analysis of the green economy in Africa and the production of green state effects.

The concept of a green economy was reinvigorated in public policy discussions after 2008, when UNEP launched their Green Economy Initiative and other international institutions such as the OECD and the World Bank enthusiastically promoted the idea. But as World Bank economists have pointed out, proposals on how to make the economy greener can be found in economics "textbooks going back at least to the 1950s . . . with environmental taxation, norms, and regulations being the main tools of a green growth strategy."[51] Interest in environmental economics burgeoned in the 1980s, alongside the idea of sustainable development, and the work of researchers like David Pearce and his coauthors—for example, their report for the UK government, *Blueprint for a Green Economy,* in 1989—attracted widespread attention. The central idea was that a green economy would be one in which environmental externalities would be fully accounted for. If the environment continued to be treated as a free resource, then, as noted above, it would inevitably be depleted and polluted. To Pearce, "sustainability" meant "sustaining the overall stock of natural resources so that they are available for the future, as well as for the present."[52] In 2012 two of Pearce's original coauthors, Edward Barbier and Anil Markandya, published *A New Blueprint for a Green Economy,* in which they affirm that the message of 1989 is still relevant, and the threefold challenges of valuing the environment, accounting for the environment, and incentivising environmental improvements are more urgent than ever. As Barbier explains, "We use our natural capital, including ecosystems, because it is valuable, but we are losing natural capital because it is free."[53]

If the arguments of the environmental economists have changed little since the 1980s, the political and economic context of the early twenty-first century is somewhat altered. Two crises are crucial to understanding why the idea of the green economy has returned to prominence: the climate crisis and the financial crisis. During the 2000s the Kyoto Protocol came into force and climate change was discussed at the UN Security Council. Nicholas Stern made the economic case for climate mitigation and adaptation in as clear and compelling a manner as is possible: action later will be more costly than action now. The detrimental impacts of climate change on temperatures, rainfall, diseases, flooding, grazing patterns, and crop production in Africa have contributed to heightened fears among African politicians, activists, and citizens, even if scientific discussion of climate change has been slow to permeate popular discourse.[54]

Enthusiasm for a green economy would not have arisen, however, were it not for the interlocking financial and economic crises which began in 2007 and 2008 and which rocked, first, the U.S. and European economies and then those of the rest of the world. UNEP's key report on the Global Green New Deal begins by noting that "the world today finds itself in the worst financial and economic crisis in generations."[55] Their diagnosis of the interconnected financial, economic, social, and environmental crises became even more explicit in a later publication: "The causes of these crises vary, but at a fundamental level they all share a common feature: the gross misallocation of capital. During the last two decades, much capital was poured into property, fossil fuels and structured financial assets with embedded derivatives. However, relatively little in comparison was invested in renewable energy, energy efficiency, public transportation, sustainable agriculture, ecosystem and biodiversity protection, and land and water conservation."[56] To the UNEP authors the solution is clear: greater public regulation of the economy. "To reverse such misallocation requires better public policies, including pricing and regulatory measures, to change the perverse incentives that drive this capital misallocation and ignore social and environmental externalities."[57] Together, climatic and financial crises have relegitimated demands for a new, cleaner, greener economy.

This discursive consensus about the need for a green economy is possible only because the content of the idea is usefully vague, much like the older concept of sustainable development.[58] However, studies which reproduce this artificial unity risk losing their critical purchase. Rather, it is important to show how the content and aspirations of the green economy often vary strikingly when deployed by different actors and institutions. Kyla Tienhaara, for example, distinguishes between the Green New Deal, Green Stimulus, and Green Economy variants.[59] Bär et al. identify three main strands of the green economy: the greening of the existing economy; green development; and sustainable development.[60] These terms tend to be deployed by different actors in different ways at different times, though, and hence it is more useful to disaggregate four discourses of the green economy that often overlap in practice but that represent clearly identifiable competing priorities. Hence I distinguish between the discourses of green revolution, green transformation, green growth, and green resilience.[61]

Green Revolution

Many environmentalists in the 1960s and 1970s used the term "green revolution" to describe fundamental transformations of economic, social, and political relationships to bring them in line with natural limits and ecological virtues. Many deep ecologists, ecosocialists, ecofeminists, indigenous peoples, and others feel that a radical revolution in society is necessary to repair our relationships with the natural world and each other. The limits to growth proclaimed by environmentalists in the seventies have inspired a range of alternatives such as "degrowth," steady-state economics, and prosperity without growth. For such voices, green development "means that natural resources are used in such a way as to enable us to live in harmony with the environment and with each other far into the future."[62] The idea that the economic system requires greening in order to resolve its contradictions and end the systematic exploitation of nature has been a central tenet of these traditions.

A fundamentally different economic system is needed, from this point of view, to produce genuinely sustainable human development and a more just system of social and environmental relations. This is not seen simply as a required shift but as a positive, progressive opportunity to form a better society. To Barry, "Removing the imperative for orthodox economic growth would create *more not less* options for human flourishing."[63] A green economy is therefore something completely unlike our current economy in terms of what we eat and how it is produced, the energy we use, our transport systems, how we relate to each other, and relations among genders, indigenous communities, classes, youth, and the natural world. A transition to a green economy would accordingly revolutionise many aspects of contemporary society, including patriarchy, race relations, the state and the state system, capitalism, and the aspects of Enlightenment thought that portray nature and society as separate and distinct.

Unsurprisingly, this vision has often been marginalised in mainstream discussions of the green economy, and it can be hard to see examples of such a discourse in practice outside of small, communal ecovillages and retreats. Yet radical voices and proposals have been heard in recent years. These are perhaps best encapsulated in calls made at Copenhagen, Rio+20, and elsewhere by many Latin American states (led by Bolivia) for the international community to respect the rights of Mother Earth and to aim for *buen vivir,* or the good life, rather than endless economic growth. The head of the Sustainable Development Commission in the United Kingdom, Tim Jackson, published a well-received book entitled *Prosperity Without Growth* that contained some far-reaching proposals, at least in terms of how to imagine human prosperity in the context of fixed ecological limits and a postgrowth economy. Dismissing these radical discourses as being "of little strategic value" is problematic and risks neglecting the revolutionary potential at the heart of the notion of a green economy.[64]

Green Transformation

The second discourse of the green economy is best exemplified by the Brundtland Report's vision of sustainable development as a realignment of prevailing growth models and development paths. This notion envisages a transformation in current socioeconomic and political systems even as their basic elements and assumptions remain the same. Thus economic growth remains the driver of progress, the environment is a resource for human development, and states and the state system are the regulators and guarantors of development.

Transformation—often understood as the creation of millions of new green jobs—is accordingly seen as being possible within the current global system, that is, a capitalist society of states, and achievable through existing institutions. Typical policies include Keynesian strategies of public investments and fiscal stimulus, mobilised for green ends: clean air and water and food, safe and efficient public transport, tree-planting campaigns, and so on. In this way of thinking, the green economy explicitly invokes the historical precedent of Roosevelt's New Deal, which included a public works programme called the Civilian Conservation Corps that employed more than three million young men between 1933 and 1942 to plant approximately two billion trees and develop eight hundred new state parks into order to simultaneously tackle widespread unemployment and land degradation. Thus a Global Green New Deal would include, in Barbier's view, green stimulus policies such as "support for renewable energy, carbon capture and sequestration, energy efficiency, public transport and rail, and improving electrical grid transmission."[65] The International Labour Organisation (ILO) has suggested that "a greener economy could lead to net gains of up to 60 million jobs."[66]

There are similarities between green transformation and green growth (see below), which also advocates the use of targeted investments in high-tech industries and green jobs, but the discourse of green transformation has two distinguishing elements. First is its explicit focus on social justice, equity, and redistribution, including intergenerationally: in other words, growth is seen as a means rather than an end. Thus relations between rich and poor and the global North and South require transformation; UNEP urge that a "pro-poor orientation must be superimposed on any green economy initiative."[67] The second feature is the explicitly political acknowledgment that such a strategy will be tough and will entail costs as well as benefits. As the Brundtland Report noted with respect to sustainable development, "There are usually winners and losers."[68] A UN Conference on Trade and Development (UNCTAD) report points out, in an expressive phrase echoing Joseph Schumpeter, that structural transformation implies "a continual process of creative destruction, as some activities wither away whilst others mushroom."[69]

Green Growth

The third discourse is that of green growth, in which green markets represent an opportunity for further capital accumulation. As the World Bank report *Inclusive Green Growth* contends, "[The] current system is inefficient, thereby offering opportunities for cleaner (and not necessarily slower) growth."[70] In the context of financial crisis and widespread recession, new markets, sources of wealth, and areas for innovation are required, as are new sources of employment. Given the rapid rises in the price of raw materials and natural resources on the world market during the first decade of the twenty-first century, including oil, gas, foodstuffs, and land, as well as widely predicted shortages in resources like freshwater, many businesses have sensed there is money to be made in going green. Rising world populations and rapidly growing economies in Asia, Latin America, and Africa present new markets, and even in older markets the niches for organic and green products are becoming increasingly attractive commercially. Carbon markets create new opportunities for financial speculation, and developers of new energy technologies seem to be perpetually on the cusp of the next big breakthrough that will take humanity into the next stage of its development: postfossil fuels.[71] From this perspective the green economy is a good place to bet on future growth, profits, jobs, and markets.

Many publications blur the lines between green transformation and green growth, as economic growth is also central to the language of transformation, and growth can involve seismic shifts and forms of creative destruction. But the idea of green growth is explicitly growth-centred; capital accumulation appears as an end rather than as a means. This discourse is also far less political than that of transformation—exponents may, when pressed, articulate a win-win or trickle-down narrative—and there is barely even any lip service paid to inequality. Whereas the Brundtland Report and most UNEP publications are clear that the model of growth itself needs to be transformed, World Bank economists have explicitly defended the gains from economic growth in recent decades, and they call for more of the same driven by new green sectors. Rather than focusing on limits and scarcity, as most environmental texts do, green growth advocates highlight new markets, new services, and new forms of consumption. As Paterson notes, there is a shift going on here which reflects a broader trend in environmental governance away from "regulatory mechanisms designed to restrict certain forms of economic activity and toward the promotion of a particular path of growth."[72]

Green Resilience

The fourth discourse is essentially reactionary, defensive, and cautious. It can be seen as an attempt to protect the status quo, although, in the face of the two crises discussed above, financial and environmental, achieving resilience is no small task. At some point peak oil and decarbonisation will require a transition to electric cars or mass transit systems. Changing climates will require climate-smart agriculture, new crops, and techniques, and diversification of landholdings in order to protect farmers from these changes. Communities will need to think about how they source their food and water and reconsider their dependence on external sources of energy and raw materials. The notion of resilience, therefore, has progressive and transformational potential—and indeed was developed by political ecologists in contrast to the limitations of vulnerability approaches—but its dominant contemporary articulation usually appears as a conservative defence of the status quo.[73]

Varied technologies, techniques, and programmes can be interpreted as manifestations of green resilience: these include climate adaptation, flood defences, insurance, risk indexing, disaster relief plans, and attempts to build self-sufficient local economies. As well as vulnerability to direct environmental changes, disasters, or scarcity, a risk is posed by the political and economic requirements of responding to environmental challenges. Many countries and markets are worried about the threat of new forms of economic protectionism, the loss of comparative advantage in sectors or markets as technology changes, and new forms of governance and regulation. In this respect, the South African Industrial Policy Action Plan points out that there is a "growing threat of increasing 'eco-protectionism' from advanced industrial countries in the form of tariff and non-tariff measures such as carbon taxes and restrictive standards."[74]

The dominant note of caution within green resilience discourse sets it off from the more optimistic language of green growth, transformation, and revolution. Such wariness is also a reminder that despite the current enthusiasm and prominence of the green economy concept, many still regard it with scepticism and trepidation. Many developing states, especially in Africa, have misgivings about the implications of the green economy. These surfaced during the negotiations prior to the Rio+20 conference, during which it was notable that many G77 countries, including China, resisted an overemphasis of the concept. Their reasons for doing so included the threat of ecotariffs on exports from the global South and an overly homogenous formulation of the green economy which neglected the principle of common but differentiated responsibilities and the continuing priorities in the global South for poverty alleviation and meeting of basic needs. Negotiators from developing countries were adamant that the green economy be viewed through the prism of the 1992 Rio Declaration and the sustainable development framing: a one-size-fits-all approach, they maintained, was unworkable.[75] Moreover, there is still an influential body of opinion and political weight that views anything green as anathema because it is perceived as a threat to growth and innovation, particularly within the United States but also in some developing countries.

THE GREEN ECONOMY IN AFRICA

Despite the fact that the greatest emphasis on the green economy until now has come from the industrialised world of Europe, North America, Japan, and South Korea, I argue here that it is increasingly politically salient for the poorest continent in the world. At the thirteenth session of the African Ministerial Conference on the Environment in June 2010, African ministers of environment adopted the Bamako Declaration on the Environment for Sustainable Development. Here they recognised "the need to take advantage of the opportunities provided by a growth and development trajectory that embraced the green economy model."[76] The 11th annual Africa Environment Day was convened in Tunis on 3 March 2013 under the theme Partnership for Africa's Transition to Green Economy in Support of African Renaissance. The participants expressed their enthusiasm over the role of the green economy in achieving a sustainable future on the continent and for the potential to leapfrog pathways of development witnessed elsewhere in the world.

These high-level continental positions and statements have been reproduced within a range of pronouncements and declarations of support from national governments. In May 2010 the South African government hosted a Green Economy Summit, and in November 2011 Economic Development Minister Ebrahim Patel revealed the details of a new green economic accord which aimed to create three hundred thousand green jobs in the next ten years. In 2011 the Ethiopian government announced a strategy for developing a climate-resilient green economy by 2025. Paul Kagame's government in Rwanda announced a National Strategy for Climate Change and Low-Carbon Development in 2011. In 2008 Mauritius announced the Maurice Ile Durable concept as the new long-term vision for making Mauritius a sustainable island.[77] Many other statements endorsing the green economy can be found, some of which are briefly profiled here:

- In August 2013 Joe Oteng-Agyei, the minister of environment, science, technology, and innovation in Ghana, reiterated his commitment to implementing green economy policies, including the declaration of "different energy-related targets, most notably increasing the share of renewable in the energy mix and increasing energy access."
- Mozambique announced a new Green Economy Roadmap at the UN Conference on Sustainable Development in Rio de Janeiro in

2012, supported by WWF, and its national action plan for green growth was developed with the support of the AfDB and approved in September 2013.

- Labour and Social Welfare Minister Doreen Sioka of Namibia declared in April 2013 that "the green economy is an area where future economic growth and employment creation are possible as far as Namibia is concerned."
- Commerce, Trade, and Industry Minister Emmanuel Chenda of Zambia stated in June 2013 that his country "will pursue green productivity in accelerating its development to ensure reasonable economic growth while developing capacity for lasting environment protection."
- Minister of Environment and Climate Change Management Halima Daudi of Malawi declared in 2013, "All of us in the SADC region need to work together in implementing green economy through our national development strategies" and to promote green investment.
- In November 2014 UNEP reported that a transition to a green economy in Senegal could lift an estimated half a million people out of poverty and create thirty thousand new jobs. Abdoulaye Balde, minister of environment and sustainable development in Senegal, said that a green economy transition could "support Senegal's development process, without jeopardizing our future growth."
- Minister of Environment and Natural Resources Management Francis Nhema of Zimbabwe wrote in 2012, "[The] Green Economy touches almost every aspect of our lives and concerns our development. I therefore urge all Zimbabweans to invest in renewable energy such as solar, which can also make indirect contributions to alleviating poverty by providing energy for cooking, lighting in homes and schools."
- In May 2013 Environment Secretary Alice Kaudia of the Kenyan Ministry of Environment and Mineral Resources said, "We have an inclusive green growth program whose implementation is progressing without hiccups. Green economy is at the heart of new administration policy agenda in line with vision 2030."[78]

Such statements can be easily dismissed as overblown rhetoric, greenwash, or jumping on the bandwagon. Indeed, in many cases there is probably a great deal of this. But they do confirm that the concept of a green economy is being explicitly articulated by ministers in press statements and national strategies. This is happening because they are aware that the green economy is highly relevant to African states owing to the importance of natural resources, agriculture, conservation, and large energy infrastructure to their economies.

Natural resource extraction, particularly oil, gas, and minerals, have been at the heart of the high African economic growth rates over the past decade. The extraction of these nonrenewable resources raises a number of environmental issues, among them the depletion of the resources, their local and global environmental impacts, and their relationship to global consumption patterns. With the example of the ecological and social devastation of the Niger Delta standing as a warning (see chapter 6), the discovery and extraction of substantial oil and gas reserves elsewhere on the continent, notably in Uganda, Sudan, and Ghana, are proceeding apace while activists and some politicians discuss the "resource curse" and the possibility of emulating "Norway not Nigeria." Major multinational mining companies are therefore seeking to legitimise and brand their operations by talking of green mining and CSR. Partly in response to community protests against the impacts of ilmenite mining in Madagascar, Rio Tinto have promoted tree-planting programmes, conservation projects, and even so-called cultural heritage offsets by building new museums when ancestral land and shrines are damaged. As a result, they received an award from Nedbank in 2009 for their commitment to sustainable development. The paradoxes and contradictions of these attempts to greenwash environmentally degrading activities could be dismissed as purely superficial; but on the other hand the enthusiastic participation of major extractive companies in conservation and the sponsoring of climate conferences, as in COP19 in Warsaw in 2013, is profoundly shaping the production of Africa's green state effects.[79]

The renewable energy plants which are burgeoning across the continent are an apparently very different form of investment and infrastructural development. Between 2011 and 2012 the AfDB increased its investment in clean energy in Africa by 92 percent, to $1.475 billion, backing the Moroccan Integrated Solar and Wind Energy Programs and the Geothermal Development Project in Kenya. The Mediterranean Solar Plan aims to become a global powerhouse for green energy and, despite the problems associated with Desertec and the disputed status of the Western Sahara region, Morocco is going ahead with an AfDB-funded concentrated solar power plant at the

Ouarzazate solar complex. The Lake Turkana Wind Power Project will be sub-Saharan Africa's largest windfarm and the largest single private investment in Kenya's history, which will enable Kenya to generate over half of its electricity through renewable energy by 2016. Algeria is planning to invest $60 billion in renewable energy by 2030, and Ghana is set to begin construction on the Nzema solar photovoltaic plant, which would be Africa's largest and the fourth largest of its kind in the world. South Africa's Renewable Energy Independent Power Producer Procurement Programme (RE IPPPP) has been widely praised for kick-starting the renewable energy industry in the country, and wind and solar energy now produce 5.2 gigawatts of South Africa's electricity supply.[80]

Another manifestation of the zeal surrounding big infrastructural development is the return of big dam construction. While the social effects of dams are well known, the prospect of relatively cheap low-carbon electricity on a massive scale from hydropower is proving attractive to African states and to lenders like the World Bank, India, Brazil, and China. On 18 May 2013 the government of the DRC announced that it was initiating the world's largest hydro plant on the Congo River's Inga Falls. Here the world's second largest river drops one hundred meters within a fifteen-kilometer stretch, and the proposed first phase of the dam will generate 4,800 megawatts (MW), more power than Africa's current largest hydroelectric dam, the High Aswan on the Nile. Applications from engineering firms to begin construction were sent out in September 2015, leading to hopes that the troubled project would eventually start to become a reality. This phase is scheduled to cost at least $8.5 billion, but the eventual aim is even grander. According to the DRC's water and electricity minister, Bruno Kapandji Kalala, when completed it will cost around $50 billion and will be almost ten times larger, making it twice the size of the current largest dam in the world, China's Three Gorges.[81]

Inga Falls is only one of a raft of new dams being proposed or constructed across Africa, all justified through discourses of the green economy, mass electrification, and low-carbon development. Ethiopia is building the controversial 6,000MW Grand Renaissance dam on the Blue Nile near the border with Sudan as well as the 1,800MW Gibe III dam on the River Omo, one of five new dams on this river. The 1,250MW Merowe dam on the Nile in Sudan was recently constructed. Smaller examples include the 250MW Bujagali dam on the Nile in Uganda; the 300MW dam in Tekeze canyon at the headwaters of the Nile in Ethiopia, one of Africa's highest at 185 meters; and the 120MW Djibloho dam on the Wele River, which now supplies 90 percent of the electricity in Equatorial Guinea. In West Africa, Guinea has plans to dam the River Niger upstream of the river's inner delta; in southern Africa, work started in 2013 on damming the Batoka Gorge for a 1,600MW scheme downstream of Victoria Falls on the Zambezi River, and China's Export-Import Bank has agreed to help fund the 1,500MW Mphanda Nkuwa dam further downstream on the Zambezi in Mozambique. An agreement signed in August 2011 by the Lesotho and South African governments to build the Polihali dam has initiated the second phase of the controversial Lesotho Highlands Water Project (LHWP), whose earlier dams, Katse and Mohale, have been subject to criticisms ranging from the mass displacement of villagers to ecological damage and financial scandal. The second phase of the LHWP will be the largest water infrastructure project on the African continent and, when completed, will transfer over seventy cubic metres of water per second to South Africa.[82]

Similar grandiose visions and modernist megaprojects can be seen in the agricultural sector. These are not new but have instead returned to prominence: in the 1980s the World Bank backed a concerted Green Revolution strategy in Nigeria, as well as elsewhere, characterized by large-scale mechanized farming and cheap credit for fertiliser and insecticide. The current incarnation of the green economy in Africa remains closely bound to crops and the soil: agriculture accounts for 65 percent of full-time employment in Africa, 25–30 percent of GDP, and over half of export earnings. The transformation and (re)modernisation of this sector are proposed in a number of prominent agreements: the Alliance for a Green Revolution in Africa, part of the Bill and Melinda Gates Foundation; the New Alliance for Food Security and Nutrition, launched by Barack Obama and USAID in 2012; and the AU's Comprehensive Africa Agriculture Development Programme (CAADP) are three examples which have been at the forefront of calls for a reinvigoration of African agriculture based around increasing smallholder farmers' access to fertilizers, high-yield seeds, and irrigation. CAADP seeks to increase foreign and domestic investment in agriculture to drive growth by increasing research collaboration, promoting infrastructural development, and modernising farming. By May 2011 twenty-six states had pledged to raise agriculture's share of their national budget to 10 percent, in contrast to a typical spend of only 5 percent between 1980 and 2005 (and a parallel collapse of international donor support for the sector). The Abuja Declaration on Fertiliser for an African Green Revolution (2006) supported an increase from eight to fifty kilograms of fertiliser per hectare between 2006 and 2015, although many environmentalists are worried about the effects of intensive fertiliser and pesticide use on ecosystems. The World Bank is promoting "climate-smart agriculture" as a means to fix carbon via developing commercial plantations, and it regards Africa as "the big prize." The bank's BioCarbon Fund is financing the Kenya Agricultural Carbon Project, which covers 40,000 hectares of farmland in a densely populated region of the country and is projected to capture sixty thousand tons of carbon dioxide a year and increase annual farm incomes by $200 to $400 per hectare.[83]

These examples seem to indicate that the "age of infrastructure" is back in African development.[84] Environmentalists are frustrated that the language of the green economy is being used to legitimate extractive industries, big dam construction, and industrial farming models. The green economy many environmentalists desired or envisaged is not to be found in such enterprises. Moreover, many elements which would normally be assumed to be central to environmental governance, including stringent regulation and precaution, impact assessments, pollution fines, legal accountability, and public consultation and participation are often nonstarters in many African countries. Budgets for environmental innovations and investments are still low, and in many countries environmental issues remain well down on the political agenda. Monitoring and enforcing environmental laws across the continent are uneven at best, and it is rare for environmental impact assessments (EIA) to pose any serious obstacles to development as usual. In Tanzania a report noted that "the option of stopping projects is hardly considered."[85] Research by the Oakland Institute into land investment deals in Ethiopia, Mali, and Sierra Leone found that they often lacked even a superficial engagement with the EIA process. In Ethiopia, for example, "despite assurances that EIAs are performed, no government official could produce a completed EIA, no investor had evidence of a completed one, and no community had ever seen one."[86] The land investments in Mali were in an area designated as a Wetland of International Importance under the Ramsar Convention but seem to have been implemented without environmental and social impact assessments. Even in South Africa, one of the most enthusiastic advocates of a green economy, national and municipal priorities lie elsewhere. As one official reported, "The real budget of municipalities lies in departments other than the marginal and poorly funded environment departments."[87] The expansion of the coal industry and plans to frack the Karoo, revive the nuclear industry, and begin mining in designated conservation areas all sit uneasily alongside South Africa's rhetorical enthusiasm for the green economy. As such, my argument in this chapter is not that Africa is undergoing a transition to a green economy as it is conventionally understood. On the other hand, the concept is being deployed by states in a number of ways.

Green Resilience and Surviving Environmental Shocks in Africa

The primary reason the idea of the green economy has so easily taken root in Africa is closely related to the power of the discourse of green resilience. African economies are already green in the sense of having many learnt and socially embedded practices to deal with environmental risks. In the foreword to the Africa Progress Panel Report of 2014 Annan declared, "Our smallholder farmers, most of them women, have repeatedly proven how innovative and resilient they can be."[88] However, this resilience is often tested: by the rapidity and scale of the already observable changes in climate; by the extent of processes of industrialisation and extraction; and by the pace of urbanisation and rural migration. As a result, many large-scale green economy programmes emphasise building and bolstering local resilience. Many governmental interventions have also occurred in response to disasters: in the South African city of Durban "one of the triggers for getting support for the work of climate adaptation innovators in the City was a big sea event along the Durban coast in 2007, rain storms that damaged properties in 2008 and two tornados that wrecked two informal settlements."[89] As researchers observed, "When the politicians saw the extent of the storm damage, they recognised that the Integrated Coastal Management Act, long in the wings, was needed urgently and it got pushed through the system."[90]

As well as legislative responses, measures to promote green resilience include climate-proofing crops, disaster response departments and planning, soil conservation measures, weather-indexed crop insurance, employment guarantees, early warning systems, controversial resettlement plans, food-for-work, safety nets and loans, and many others. A World Bank programme launched in 2009 entitled *Making Development Climate Resilient in Sub-Saharan Africa* sought to provide developmental assistance to African states, including "making adaptation and climate risk management a core developmental component," financing, and helping develop knowledge and capacity in "weather forecasting, water resources monitoring, land use information, improving disaster preparedness, investing in appropriate technology development, and strengthening capacity for planning and coordination, participation and consultation."[91]

Ethiopia's Climate-Resilient Green Economic Strategy was launched in 2011 and aims for zero net GHG emissions; for reduced vulnerability to risks associated with climate change; and for the country to become a "green economy frontrunner" by investing in low-carbon infrastructure. Ethiopia continues to be associated with famine and drought in many Western minds and newspapers since the catastrophic famines of the 1970s and 1980s and the more recent periods of severe hunger in 1999–2000 and 2002–3. Yet Ethiopia has been one of the fastest-growing economies of the 2000s, averaging 10.7 percent per year. In 2012 it was the twelfth fastest-growing economy in the world, and the green economy discourse is one element of a broader strategy to reposition the country in both cultural and economic global political imaginaries. The central thrust of the Climate-Resilient Green Economic Strategy is a massive increase in hydropower generation through dam construction, with a projected growth in electricity capacity from seven to eighty terawatt hours by 2030, of which 90 percent will be generated by hydropower.[92]

A number of other programmes are designed to increase resilience, for instance, through microinsurance. UNEP note that "enabling the poor to access microinsurance coverage against natural disasters and catastrophes is important for protecting livelihood assets from external shocks due to changing and unpredictable weather patterns."[93] Nicole Petersen's research focuses on a trial of index insurance for small-scale farmers in Ethiopia. Payments are made to farmers when rainfall levels fall below a certain level, helping them survive dry seasons. This has advantages over traditional insurance, as premiums are lower in that only one variable, low rainfall, is insured against and measurement is easier because rainfall rates can be recorded accurately at the local meteorological station. In addition, it removes the risk of moral hazard, as it is not crop loss that is directly insured against but the rains, something the farmer has no control over. In combination with larger, more established supports, such as the government-run, USAID-funded Productive Safety Net Programme, through which residents of the community work as labourers, vulnerable small-scale farmers are able to survive irregular weather patterns and other periods of dearth. For reasons like this microinsurance, along with other techniques like microcredit and microfinance, has been portrayed "as the new green revolution."[94]

Even such potentially positive interventions, however, have a number of unintended or undesirable consequences. As Petersen's study shows, the provision of crop insurance to smallholder farmers can be viewed by the private sector as a way of accessing a previously untapped market: "Insurers involved in the Ethiopia index insurance anticipate offering health and automobile insurance to the participants and banks envision larger loans to increasingly wealthy farmers in Malawi," creating a "culture of insurance" and further entrenching the monetisation and financialisation of rural agriculture.[95] Low rainfall is not the only risk farmers will be encouraged to insure themselves against. Given the role of irresponsible lending and the deceptive marketing of financial products, including insurance, in the financial crisis, it would be wise not to be too sanguine about the developmental contribution of increased levels of personal debt. Moreover, Ethiopia's overall climate resilience strategy is largely top down and driven by an autocratic political structure, meaning that it should be seen in a longer history of state-led, hierarchical, often coercive modernisation projects.[96]

Overall, green resilience strategies in Africa are widespread and include everyday communal coping mechanisms as well as donor interventions and state support. It is likely, however, given the scale of forecast environmental changes over the coming decades, that existing measures will be insufficient to make African economies genuinely climate-proof. More funding and investment in climate adaptation are undoubtedly needed. The Climate Adaptation Fund created through the UNFCCC process is designed for this purpose, but rather than the $100 billion per year needed for climate adaptation, its website reveals that it has thus far only "dedicated US$ 318 million to increase climate resilience in 44 countries around the world" over a three-year period.[97] Moreover, the green resilience discourse is fundamentally orientated toward protecting the status quo. It lacks the power either to capture imaginations or to offer a positive vision of the future, a drawback in a continent where there is much evidently wrong with the status quo.

The Green Economy as a Driver of African Growth

The green growth discourse, by contrast, holds out the promise that environmental investment could make the future much better than the present, at least for those in position to benefit from modernisation and accumulation. Several African countries view the green economy as the source of sustained economic growth in the medium-term: Kenya's green economy report states, "Under a green economy scenario, real per capita income in Kenya is expected to nearly double by 2030, outpacing income growth under business-as-usual (BAU) scenario."[98] Commercial agriculture is the key sector for green growth across most of sub-Saharan Africa, both for agroindustrial technologies in food crops and the bioeconomy of ecosystem services, carbon credits, and REDD+. Agricultural expansion in Malawi was a major driver of GDP growth rates, which increased from 6.7 percent in 2006 to 9.6 percent in 2008, for example. Although biofuel plantations have not turned out to be the lucrative driver of growth many hoped for, Hall observes that "the widespread uptake of jatropha and sugarcane (for ethanol) has been seen across the region, in Tanzania, Zimbabwe, Zambia, Angola, Madagascar and South Africa."[99] Resnick et al. report that there are currently more than thirty biofuel projects under way in Mozambique with a total investment of over $100 million.[100]

New sources of climate finance are being positioned as resources for growth in many countries: the DRC has been awarded a $21.5-million grant from the AfDB's Climate Investment Funds to assist with forest governance. In Tanzania a REDD Framework was drawn up in 2009, and bilateral Norwegian funding from 2009 to 2014 was allocated for the development of forestry institutions, research, and pilots. The potential financial rewards, given the extent of Tanzania's forests, are predicted to be substantial: donor officials "estimate that payments could amount to USD 300 million annually at the upper end of the range."[101] A World Bank report calculates that "the asset value of carbon sequestration services provided by Tanzania's standing forests is estimated to be between US$700 and US$1,500 per hectare; for the 33.5 million ha forest estate as a whole, this translates to a minimum asset value of US$24 billion."[102] Yet the recent history of biofuel developments, tree plantations, and the extension of state and investor property over so-called virgin land in Tanzania is full of cautionary tales: violent expulsions, collapsed projects, and local and regional food insecurity.

Besides agriculture, Africa is positioned as a growing market for renewable energy technologies. In August 2013, for example, it was announced that the continent is likely to become the world's largest market for solar lanterns by 2015: "Market growth for clean, off-grid lighting has consistently beaten expectations, growing 300 percent in the past three years" and attracting big multinational investors like Schneider Electric, TOTAL, Panasonic, and Energizer.[103] South Africa is best placed to take advantage of these green growth opportunities. The Development Bank of South Africa (DBSA), for example, notes that "South Africa is well positioned, based on the strength of its existing institutional platforms, to support, invest in and implement climate interventions across the Southern African Development Community (SADC) region."[104] South Africa responded to the world financial and economic crisis by launching a $7.5-billion stimulus package, of which about 11 percent, or $0.8 billion, was allocated to environment-related themes such as railways, energy-efficient buildings, and water and waste management. The Green Economy Accord launched in 2011 established four principles for the Green Economy, opportunity, innovation, responsibility, and partnership, conveying the vision of green investment and entrepreneurship as a driver of growth. Projects include the installing of one million solar water heaters, the manufacture of renewable energy plants, energy efficiency, waste disposal and recycling, the retrofitting of buildings with low-energy fittings, and expanding the biofuel industry. Minister Patel claimed that as part of South Africa's New Growth Path, "The green economy can create a large number of jobs, provide a spur for industrialisation and help to create a sustainable future for this and the next generations."[105]

South Africa's renewable energy feed-in tariffs have evolved into the RE IPPPP, through which independent power producers can bid for contracts to generate renewable electricity for the national grid. These developments have been widely lauded and have attracted a great deal of attention nationally and internationally. Over four rounds of bidding, a total of $16 billion of investments have been secured, involving national and international companies that are also committed to provide community benefits and Black Economic Empowerment components. Over the course of the competitive rounds the price of renewables has dropped dramatically, to the point where both wind and solar are cheaper than new-build, coal-generated electricity. Tensions and problems have emerged however: the sector is increasingly dominated by a few large foreign investors; the deliverability and political implications of the local community benefits remain uncertain; the capacity of the grid and of the public electricity utility, Eskom, to keep the lights on has been tested during load shedding and essential maintenance; and the financialisation and on-selling of the investments means the complexity of the risks involved is increasing.[106]

The South African RE IPPPP is a good example of the green growth discourse in action: renewable energy is primarily seen as a potentially profitable new growth industry in South Africa. Yet this outlook does not represent a structural transformation of the energy sector, which continues to be dominated by the MEC. Current plans are to procure more than 9,000MW of new electricity from coal, gas, regional hydro, and cogeneration at industrial plants by 2025 as well as increased supplies (potentially 9,600MW) of nuclear power. The large coal power plants at Medupi and Kusile are under way, and a new, third plant known as Coal-3 has been approved. The vast sums of money, "tenderpreneurs," and political careers which have been built on the back of the MEC mean that meaningful transformation of South Africa's high-carbon development strategy appears almost impossible in the medium term.[107]

South Africa is perhaps the clearest example in which green growth discourse is being strategically employed to brand the country internationally. This positioning is partly a diplomatic and foreign policy one, but it is also economic. In a competitive global economy, so-called competition states must market themselves effectively in order to maximise their assets and attract investment and tourism. South Africans' marketing and branding of the country's environmental resources and landscapes have been effectively deployed at key moments, for instance at the Johannesburg World Summit on Sustainable Development in 2002, the FIFA World Cup in 2010, and the Durban climate conference in 2011 (see chapter 6). This trend is most identifiable in South Africa, but the green growth discourses of Tanzania, Ethiopia, Rwanda, Mozambique, and many other countries share many similar features. Familiar images in glossy adverts and business magazines publicising protected areas, wind farms, solar energy, fields of lush green crops, and new dams and roads, have become familiar elements of the optimistic modernisation narrative that the green economy will be one of the drivers of rising African economies in the twenty-first century. In the words of Rob Davies, the South African minister of trade and industry, "The next industrial, technological revolution is green industrialisation. The last one was ICT [information and communication technology] and South Africa and Africa largely related to that as service providers for somebody else's product and technology."[108] The implication, perhaps more hope than judgment, is that green growth will be different.

Transforming African Economies Through Sustainable Development

In the "African Consensus Statement to Rio+20" the emphasis was on the green economy "as a tool for achieving sustainable development."[109] African countries have made it clearer than any other international grouping that the green economy must be seen as a means to sustainable development, and this requires tackling poverty and broader socioeconomic transformation. In practice, however, it is often difficult to disentangle the discourse of green growth from that of sustainable development or green transformation. All the national strategies produced by countries like Ethiopia, Rwanda, Mozambique, Tanzania, South Africa, and others imply that they are committed to sustainable development and green transformation and that green growth is a means to an end. For example, Jones and Carabine conclude that Ethiopia's Climate-Resilient Green Economy strategy "represents one of the most far-reaching climate and development plans in any developing country context, let alone for Africa: one that deserves the label 'transformational' in terms of the scale of change and institutional reform outlined."[110]

Another instance of transformational elements within a broader green growth plan comes from South Africa. The DBSA proclaimed that "greening the South African economy represents a critical lever for bringing about the structural transformation needed for a more equitable and inclusive economy. Coordinated activity is required to achieve the envisaged economic shifts to transition the country to a low-carbon and greener economy, with the ultimate objective of a carbon-neutral economy by 2050."[111] The commitment to create three hundred thousand new green jobs, for example, resonates in an economy where only two-fifths of adults are in full employment. Although South Africa is classed by the World Bank as an upper-middle-income country, it also has the features of what ex-President Mbeki described in 2003 as a dual economy: "one is modern and relatively well developed. The other is characterised by underdevelopment and an entrenched crisis of poverty."[112] While his narrative has been critiqued for underemphasising the relationship between formal and informal sectors and the systematic production of precarious livelihoods through neoliberal development, the broader point is that any plausible development strategy must address job creation and structural transformation. Thus public works programmes like Working for Water, Working for Woodlands, Working for Wetlands, and Working on Fire have been labelled as models of a green economy approach. The largest of these, Working for Water, employs approximately twenty to twenty-five thousand people per year from the most remote rural areas, of whom 52 percent are women, to clear alien trees and plant species. It aims to recruit from the most vulnerable groups in society, and its goal is to have an employee aggregation with 60 percent women, 20 percent youth, and 5 percent disabled. The stated focus is "on job creation in support of an important ecosystem service."[113]

Another example of transformational aspirations and rhetoric comes from Rwanda's National Strategy for Climate Change and Low-Carbon Development, which envisages that by 2050 "development will be achieved with

14. "Wine-route—RDP houses on the N7, Western Cape," Santu Mofokeng (b. 1956). © Santu Mofokeng, 2002 silverprint edition 5. Images courtesy Lunetta Bartz, MAKER, Johannesburg.

low-carbon domestic energy resources and practices, reducing Rwanda's contribution to climate change while allowing it to be independent of imported oil for power generation."[114] Current predictions are that Rwanda's population will more than double by 2050; it is vulnerable to climate change, as it is strongly reliant on rain-fed agriculture; and it is 100 percent reliant on oil imports and therefore vulnerable to price increases and fluctuations. The strategy aims to fix the country's growth trajectory in the direction of low-carbon development by ensuring energy security through a low-carbon energy grid and roll out of small-scale energy access in rural areas; improving sustainable land use management, integrating water resource management, and adopting climate compatible mining; the sustainable intensification of small-scale farming and diversification of agricultural markets; and instituting resilience in transport systems, urban planning, and disaster management. The plan focuses on a number of so-called big wins in the sectors of agriculture, energy, and transport, where reforms can enable low-carbon development. For example, imported inorganic fertilisers produce a high proportion of Rwanda's GHG emissions through soil nitrous oxide emissions but also through the fertiliser manufacturing process and transportation. The architects of the strategy propose to reduce demand by applying "an integrated approach to soil fertility and nutrient management, which employs agroecology, resource recovery and reuse, and fertiliser enriched composts."[115]

State-led innovation can also be seen in Uganda, which is now one of the largest producers of organic vegetables in the world. The development of an organic sector began in 1994, when a few commercial companies began to invest, and by 2003 the ILO described it as "a general movement towards developing sustainable agriculture as a means of improving people's livelihoods." At that point the area of Uganda's land under organic agriculture production was the world's thirteenth largest and the largest in Africa. In July 2009 the government released a Draft Uganda Organic Agriculture Policy, and both the Uganda Export Promotion Board and the Uganda National Bureau of Standards play a proactive role in promoting organic exports and developing organic standards. In 2011 the country had 226,954 hectares under organic agricultural management, and 187,893 certified organic farmers. The country uses among the world's lowest amounts of artificial fertilisers, less than 2 percent of the already very low continent-wide average of 9kg/ha in sub-Saharan Africa. This example stands somewhat at odds to the prevailing emphasis on GMO technology, intensive modern agriculture, and high fertiliser and pesticide use promoted through much international funding. Notably, the Africa Progress Report of 2014 does not contain a single mention of organic farming in over 180 pages of analysis on the need for green and blue revolutions in Africa.[116]

Many green economy interventions are designed to bring about social benefits as well as economic growth. The World Bank's Lighting Africa initiative has twin aims of driving economic growth while tackling poverty and social exclusion: it aims to catalyse and accelerate "the development of sustainable markets for affordable, modern off-grid lighting solutions for low-income households and micro-enterprises across the continent."[117] Another so-called win-win enterprise, the Kibera Community Youth Program in Kenya, "involves Nairobi's unemployed youth in the assembly of small and affordable solar panels that can be used to charge radios and mobile phones in both the slum of Kibera and elsewhere in Kenya."[118] These efforts have an economic benefit in terms of training and employment, but their primary focus is social change. While they often work through international agencies, foreign donors, and local NGOs, they require state permission, facilitation, infrastructure, and support. In so doing they can help extend state governance into new geographical, social, and economic areas. These green transformation discourses legitimate new practices that contribute to producing new green state effects across Africa.

Revolutionising Green Economies in Africa

Finally, I want to return to some of the more radical visions of environmentalists and social justice activists who believe that a truly green economy, one in which human needs are met in balance with natural ecosystems, will require a fundamental revamping of the social, political, and economic system. As might be expected, there are very few manifestations of this discourse within the mainstream discussion of a green economy, and there are no African states in which it is possible to identify a revolutionary economic and ecological development path.

Yet an absence of state commitments does not mean a lack of radical activist and social movement pressure. In recent years many of these have coalesced around campaigns on food and land: in a continent where agriculture accounts for 65 percent of full-time employment, any real engagement with the prospect of a green economy—what UNEP would term "low carbon, resource efficient, and socially inclusive"—must confront the radically unequal legacy of settler colonialism in countries like Kenya, Zimbabwe, and South Africa as well as the gendered, ethnic, class, and age-related inequalities in land distribution. One instance of radical voices proposing a foundational shift in patterns of land control and food production came in February 2007, when delegates and activists from more than eighty countries assembled under the banner of food sovereignty at Sélingué, Mali, for the Nyéléni Forum for Food Sovereignty. They submitted ideas for making profound changes in the global food system, including shortening the chain between producers and consumers, removing agriculture from the World Trade Organisation, the prioritisation of indigenous knowledge and agroecological production methods, and resisting the privatisation of the commons and the encroachment of intellectual property rights. They called for "a food system that puts those who produce, distribute, and consume food at the heart of food systems and policies rather than the demands of markets and corporations."[119] I interpret such statements as a manifestation of the green revolution discourse, despite the reluctance of activists to use this term because of its associations with agroindustrial modernisation and genetic modification.

While most African states, in contrast to Latin American ones, have avoided revolutionary discourses, one case of state-led revolutionary economic intervention is notable in the context of campaigns on land and food in Africa. The Zimbabwean fast-track land reform process initiated by President Robert Mugabe in 2000 has become a reference point for both mainstream and radical commentators, the former seeing it as an embodiment of the dangers of unilateral state action and revolutionary rhetoric, and the latter seeing it as a flawed but nevertheless praiseworthy attempt to reverse inequitable historic land use patterns. The fact that the Zimbabwean case is rarely referred to in the context of green economy discussions is itself revealing and demonstrates the dominance of the discourses of green resilience and green growth in Africa. From these perspectives, the Zimbabwean story of financial collapse, economic implosion, and chronic food shortages is the antithesis of a model green economy. But the experience there does bring into stark focus one central feature of the green economy debate: the role of the state in steering, guiding, or forcing a radical shift in how agricultural production is organised.

The process of fast-track land reform in Zimbabwe was intended to revolutionise the structure of the economy and its racial profile, redistributing land from a small number of white farmers to a large number of black farmers. Initially, the Zimbabwe African National Union–Patriotic Front (ZANU–PF) government hoped to accomplish this through a "willing-buyer, willing-seller" market-led model, by which the state would buy available land at the market rate and redistribute it to black smallholders. The process stalled, however, and after the UK Labour government under Prime Minister Tony Blair refused to provide funds, Mugabe embarked on fast-track reforms in 2000 in which land was unilaterally expropriated and handed to settlers. Realising the government would support them, groups of rural landless people and war veterans began to invade farms and conservation areas, displacing farmers and squatting on the land. There were, indisputably, widespread abuses and a great deal of violence, not only against white farmers but also against many black labourers and rural populations in places like Matabeleland. As is also well known, the threat of compulsory expropriation, together with Mugabe's increasingly erratic fiscal policies and political instability, led to an economic crisis during which inflation reached 231 million percent in the summer of 2008.[120]

Notwithstanding these deeply flawed aspects of the land redistribution process, it has produced a dramatic shift in Zimbabwe's agrarian structure. Not all of the farm seizures can be interpreted as the result of political cronyism or as having led to agricultural collapse. Research by Ian Scoones and colleagues has shown that in 1980 the sector was dominated by large commercial agribusiness, six thousand mainly white farmers on over fifteen million hectares of land, whereas after a decade plus of land reform the sector is now predominantly small-scale black farming, with only five million hectares of large commercial farms remaining. Contrary to prevalent myths, the beneficiaries have not only been political allies and war veterans; almost half those who gained property in Masvingo Province, for example, were rural farmers from other areas. The broader popularity and legitimacy of land reform within Zimbabwe, in combination with the opposition's weaknesses and Mugabe's manipulation and intimidation, help to explain ZANU–PF's convincing victory in the elections of 2013.[121] This is not to claim that land reform in Zimbabwe should be interpreted as putting UNEP's green economy into practice. Rather, the point is that in terms of state interventions into the agricultural and land-based production systems of southern Africa, Zimbabwe represents the closest to what might be termed a revolutionary economic policy, with all the dangers and risks inherent in such a course of action.

This example has been widely discussed in Africa, where verdicts are more nuanced than many international perspectives on Mugabe's policies. Comparing land reform in Namibia, Zimbabwe, and South Africa, Aliber and Cousins conclude that "only in Zimbabwe, where the scale of land redistribution has been much larger than in South Africa and Namibia, has the 'dualistic' structure inherited from the past been radically transformed."[122] As General Secretary Zwelinzima Vavi of the Congress of South African Trade Unions pointed out in South Africa, "In 2014, we will be 20 years into (our) democracy and if we . . . have not redistributed the land by then, we will find ourselves in a Zimbabwean situation."[123] In May 2013 an opposition MP, Pieter Groenewald, warned the government during a budget debate in parliament that "whipping up emotions" about land reform threatens to create a "Zimbabwe situation." Gugile Nkwinti, minister in the Department of Rural Development and Land Reform, responded by calling the comparison with Mugabe an honour. Nkwinti observed that President Mugabe "is reversing what the British did to the people of Zimbabwe." When this statement was greeted with loud cries and heckling from opposition benches, he asked, "Would you have been happier if he [Groenewald] had said, we were like the British colonialists who killed South Africans to take our land? Would that have been an honour?"[124]

One reason for the attractiveness of the Zimbabwean experience is the enduring poverty of many parts of Africa, above all in rural areas. Even where GDP growth rates are high and money is being made from oil, gas, and commercial farming across the continent, poverty remains widespread and is often barely dented by governmental interventions. In the Eastern Cape in South Africa, to cite one instance, poverty levels have deepened since the end of apartheid, and roughly half the rural population remain under the poverty line. South Africa, as I have noted, has a starkly divided, unequal economy, but the divisions between formal and informal economic sectors exist elsewhere on the continent as well.[125] For many stuck in the informal sectors or in grinding poverty nothing less than seismic structural changes to the economy—even revolution, perhaps—seem necessary. The centrality of issues of landownership, food production, and the control of natural resources means that such struggles should be more prominent in discussions about the green economy in Africa. They are also a reminder that the core idea of a green economy—one that is low carbon, resource efficient, and socially inclusive and in which relations between human societies and the rest of the natural world are reshaped—is a radical, indeed a revolutionary, idea.

GREEN STATES AND THE TRANSFORMATION OF AFRICAN ECONOMIES

Despite my focus here on economic strategies, development plans, and big infrastructural projects, the daily work of trying to extract a living from the land is still central to many African livelihoods, just as it was for Kas Maine. According to the FAO, agriculture still accounts for 58 percent of Africa's economically active population, and in countries such as Burkina Faso, Guinea, Mozambique, Niger, and Rwanda it is over 80 percent. Van Onselen begins his book with a reflection: "Those intent on building our future around industry may do well to pause and reflect on the fact that we live in times when the field has barely given way to the factory, the peasant to the proletarian, and the patriarch to his family."[126] This chapter has shown how both agriculture and industry, the land and the factory are bound together in new discourses of the green economy, which together are producing green state effects in Africa. Whereas most academic and popular discussion of the green economy has focused on industrialised countries in Europe and North America, I have sought to show that environmental sectors and discourses play central roles in creating and regulating African economies.

Moreover, in Africa as elsewhere the state is far from absent in the production of certain types of environmental markets and the bioeconomy. The creation of markets in carbon credits and ecosystem services and the stimulation of economies through agricultural investment and employment programmes are central ways in which state institutions are seeking to relegitimate their role in local, national, and global economies. Renewed demands for entrepreneurial or developmental states which can forge new green economy pathways are being heard from policy makers, activists, and academics. As UNEP's Global Green New Deal makes clear, the green economy is necessary precisely "because the unregulated market cannot resurrect itself on its own from a failure of a historical proportion without significant and coordinated government interventions."[127] Similarly, the UNCTAD Economic Development in Africa Report 2012 argues that "achieving sustainable development in Africa requires deliberate, concerted and proactive measures to promote structural transformation and the relative decoupling of natural resource use and environmental impact from the growth process."[128] The report goes on to note that in Africa "a major negative side effect of the structural adjustment phase was the erosion of State capacities. Building up developmental States' capabilities to formulate and implement structural transformation policies will thus be an important challenge."[129] Such interventions are far from neutral, or win-win, solutions: they all involve winners and losers, and the balance of evidence across the continent suggests, unsurprisingly, that those best positioned to take advantage in the medium to long term from green economy and green growth programmes are those who are already privileged and wealthy.

Given this reality, few believe that the contemporary incarnation of the green economy will be able to deliver profound economic shifts in Africa. At best, limited green transformation may be achieved or green growth might create a few more jobs and some trickle-down benefits. Green resilience policies may, just may, help African countries to weather coming storms of climate, population growth, and global financial instability. Meanwhile, the appeal of revolutionary rhetoric and the prospect of far-reaching state intervention in the economy—as in Zimbabwe, with all the flaws and risks that land reform entailed there—will continue to be attractive to the continent's most marginalised sectors. The green economy is therefore at the heart of the politics of development in Africa, and the interplay between its competing discourses helps explain the political stakes at work in different visions of how to produce, regulate, and steer the continent's economies and markets.

CHAPTER 6

Green African States and International Relations

Everyone in America or Europe enjoying cheap oil or thinking that oil is expensive, needs to come down to Nigeria and see the situation of the communities in the oilfields who have been subsidising with their blood and lives and livelihoods the production of petroleum and the massive criminal profits of the oil corporations. They should think that every pint of oil may well be equated to a pint of blood in the Niger Delta.

—Nnimmo Bassey, *Crude Justice and Ecocide in the Niger Delta*

It is not just playing with metaphors to say that we are fighting to free the land, the sky, the waters as well as the people. Apartheid not only degrades the inhabitants of our country, it degrades the earth, the air and the streams. When we say "Mayibuye i Afrika" (Come back Africa), we are calling for the return of legal title, but also for restoration of the land, the forest and the atmosphere: the greening of our country is basic to its healing. There is a lot of healing to be done in South Africa.

—Albie Sachs, *The Right to Beauty*

On 5 August 2013 Friends of the Earth International began an international campaign calling upon Shell to clean up its operations in the heavily polluted Niger Delta region of Nigeria. The date is significant: it was two years to the day since UNEP had issued a report on the region which found environmental issues ranging from "serious threats to human health from contaminated drinking water to concerns over the viability and productivity of ecosystems."[1] The UNEP review followed decades of activism by groups in the Niger Delta and by international advocacy coalitions against the devastation caused by Shell, most famously led by the Movement for the

Survival of the Ogoni People (MOSOP) and their charismatic leader, Ken Saro-Wiwa, who managed to force Shell to stop drilling and withdraw from Ogoniland (only one small part of the Delta) in 1993. The backlash from the Nigerian state was ferocious and resulted in the execution of Saro-Wiwa and the Ogoni Nine on 10 November 1995. Since then the struggle for environmental justice in the Delta has been fought in Nigerian national and federal elections, in international boardrooms, and in the waterways of the region by new militants like the Movement for the Emancipation of the Niger Delta (MEND) and environmental NGOs like Environmental Rights Action (Friends of the Earth Nigeria). Complex networks of power, activism, and accountability have been created, subverted, and invoked by the myriad of actors involved, sometimes bypassing the Nigerian federal state and sometimes working through it or confronting it. International courtrooms have been the venue for some of the major contests: in 2009 Shell reached an out-of-court settlement for $15.5 million in compensation for the relatives of the Ogoni Nine, and in January 2013 a district court in The Hague ruled that Shell was liable to pay compensation for not preventing the pollution of farmlands at Ikot Ada Udo, Akwa Ibom State.[2]

The Niger Delta case raises important questions about the production of green states in Africa, and particularly about the role of cooperation and conflict between states. This chapter focuses on the international dimensions of the production of green state effects in Africa, which is not to suggest that the three preceding chapters—on the production of territories, populations, and economies—have not also treated international and transnational themes. However, there are specific practices and discourses associated with IR which play a central role in producing green states in Africa. I show here how these practices and discourses of cooperation and conflict work to produce exemplary leaders, on the one hand, alongside pollution enclaves on the other. The arguments of increasing international homogeneity articulated in various forms by theorists of structural neorealism, neoliberalism, and ecological modernisation are all shown to neglect the ways in which heterogeneity and difference are produced. I then turn to attempts to mitigate this heterogeneity through transnational environmental solidarity. The core argument of this chapter, coming at the culmination of the four chapters on the production of green state effects in Africa, is that international and transnational politics is crucial to explaining both African environmental politics and the production of Africa's green states in all their similarity and variety.

The case of the Niger Delta is apposite in introducing this chapter for three reasons. The first has to do with the scale of the ecological devastation in the region. The Niger Delta is the world's most severely petroleum-impacted ecosystem, and since 1956, when Shell first struck oil in commercial quantities in the Eastern Delta, more than 1.5 million tons of oil, or 11 million gallons a year, has been spilt, equivalent to one Exxon-Valdez disaster every year or three times the Gulf of Mexico BP Deepwater Horizon spill in 2010. These spills adversely affect human health, destroy fish stocks, pollute waterways, and contaminate farmland. Aside from the volume of oil spills, countless other environmental problems are related to the oil industry in the area. Nearly constant gas flaring emits dangerous chemicals, leads to acid rain, and gives the night an eerie glow. Other severe environmental issues in the region, such as deforestation, are less directly related to the oil industry, but they combine to produce a "hellish landscape." These ecological impacts in one of the world's poorest regions, a region where community capacity and livelihoods are systematically undermined and frustrated, are an important reminder of the environmental issues with which this book is centrally concerned. The violence of climate change and environmental degradation is not a risk to be borne in the future in most of the global South; rather in places like the Niger Delta "the day of reckoning already exists."[3]

The second reason the Niger Delta is an apt illustration is that it reinforces a key point of this book: environmental struggles in Africa are preeminently political. They involve conflicts and negotiations over interests, identities, and values, and sometimes they break out into open violence, of the state and of capital as well as that of paramilitary groups like MEND. These actors are themselves not homogenous or unified, as both the Nigerian state and groups like MOSOP, Environmental Rights Action, and MEND are riven by internal divides and conflicts. Shell's close relationship with the Nigerian military has led to charges of complicity in the systematic killing and torture of local residents, and the company has been accused of assisting armed militants through lucrative payments. One NGO report alleges that in 2009–10, "security personnel guarding Shell facilities were responsible for extra-judicial killing and torture in Ogoniland."[4] The interaction between local and transnational forces has made the Niger Delta one of the world's most dangerous places to be an environmental activist.

The third reason for the appropriateness of the Delta case here is the central importance of international institutions, actors, and regimes—including formal organisations like the UN, other states, multinational corporations, NGOs, and transnational movements—in the construction of green states in Africa. The Niger Delta example cannot be understood without accounting for the role of Shell and other oil companies, the United States, China, and other purchasers of Nigerian oil, courts based in the United States and the Netherlands which can hear lawsuits brought against Shell, the interventions of international organisations such as UNEP, and the transnational struggles of numerous other groups, including MOSOP, MEND, FoEI, Environmental Rights Action, Global Witness, the World Rain Forest Action Group, Amnesty International, the Body Shop, Greenpeace, and others. The Niger Delta is both a very local conflict over the nature of the Nigerian federal state and a quintessentially international, transnational conflict. Environmental Rights Action, for example, are one of the most active members of the FoEI network and have hosted biennial general meetings and conducted solidarity campaigns with other communities affected by the oil industry worldwide, including the Shell-to-Sea case in Ireland. The coalition of civil society organisations, politicians, professional and special interest associations, and student and human rights groups which protested the sudden rise in the pump price of petroleum in Nigeria in January 2012 also invoked transnational links by labelling itself Occupy Nigeria.[5]

Naomi Klein argues that the Niger Delta is where global environmental antiextraction activism really started in the 1990s, and she suggests that transnational networks of antiextraction solidarity will be the new front lines in forthcoming struggles against environmental degradation and social injustice. To Klein, the success of MOSOP in forcing Shell out of Ogoniland is "one of the most significant achievements of grassroots environmental activism anywhere in the world," and, further, she maintains that since the drilling stopped in this small area of the Delta the land has begun to heal and farming has improved.[6] Whatever the actual environmental situation in Ogoniland, it seems clear that even limited campaign victories can, in Klein's word, cause "battles to multiply, with each act of courage, and each victory, inspiring others to strengthen their resolve."[7] As she points out, these new sites of extraction are no longer confined to the global South, and networks of solidarity can extend from South to North as well as vice versa.

THE PRODUCTION OF SOVEREIGNTY

Just as the previous chapters have shown how discourses and practices of governing territories, populations, and economies combine to constitute state effects, this chapter shows how international and transnational practices between states and across state borders—trade, exploration, diplomatic relations, solidarity campaigns, warfare, negotiations, etc.—are crucial producers of state effects. Nation-states are themselves "the effects of 'international' practices."[8] States are not produced in isolation but are fundamentally relational and social entities: a state is a state because of other states. It is not accurate, therefore, to claim that "global environmental change increases the mutual dependence of nation states, thereby further undermining the idea of sovereignty as enshrined in the traditional Westphalian system."[9] Rather, forms of environmental cooperation and conflict involve the reproduction and reperformance of state sovereignty.

States interact with other states through diplomacy, negotiations, and in the formulation of international law. The first International Congress for the Protection of Nature took place in Paris in 1909. More recent conferences, especially since the 1950s, have taken place over issues like transboundary pollution, species loss, sustainable development, nuclear proliferation, climate change, and many others. Since 1972 the headquarters of UNEP have been in Nairobi, Kenya, which also hosted the first session of the United Nations Environment Assembly in June 2014. As Robert Falkner argues, over the past century "international society has slowly but steadily been 'greened,'" and "environmental ideas and norms have gradually been woven into the normative fabric of the states system."[10] This process has included "the creation of an increasingly complex set of international environmental institutions, the expansion of international environmental law, and the emergence of a distinctive practice of multilateral environmental diplomacy."[11] Thus, "to be fully recognised 'environmental citizens' of international society, states are now expected to participate in the ever-expanding scope of environmental standard-setting and treaty-making."[12]

In contrast, green states are also produced through conflict and warfare. "War makes states," Charles Tilly famously asserted, and "coercive exploitation played a large part in the creation of the European states."[13] Timothy Mitchell observes that the "First World War was the first great carbon-fuelled conflict," and conflicts since then have been crucial to the expansion and extension of industrial oil- and coal-powered capitalism.[14] As long as states have existed they have developed extensive security apparatuses and assemblages in order to secure their environments and natural resources. As we have seen in previous chapters, many environmental conservation initiatives involve paramilitary or security forces securing land against rural populations for commercial agriculture or forestry, preventing poaching, and providing disaster relief. Wars over natural resources continue to take place, as in Sierra Leone and the DRC, or remain an ever-present threat on the horizon, as in the Nile Basin. Darfur has been pronounced "the first modern climate change conflict," and while this claim must be regarded with some suspicion where it is used to depoliticise accounts of the conflict in favour of environmental determinism, it is nevertheless commonplace to hear politicians warn that climate change, or environmental stresses, present new security threats.[15] State theorists like Richard Lachmann worry that global warming will lead to the world becoming "divided into regions of very strong, increasingly autarkic states and other regions of localised power, amid a Hobbesian war of all against all and massive population decline."[16] War making, state making, and environment making are closely bound together, and environmental security discourses predict they will become ever more entwined in the future.

IR as a discipline has been classically divided between theorists who have stressed the primacy of conflict and national security in producing and shaping states (realists) and those who have focused on the role of law, institutions, and norms in producing a society of states (idealists). To IR theorists of war like Kenneth Waltz, the constant threat and frequent presence of interstate conflict throughout human history has produced an evolutionary dynamic where the fittest states survive. As Waltz explains, "Competition produces a tendency toward the sameness of the competitors. . . . Contending states imitate the military innovations contrived by the country of greatest capability and ingenuity. And so the weapons of major contenders, and even their strategies, begin to look much the same all over the world."[17] Waltz views the form of the state as being determined by its function: survival in an anarchical, competitive system. Idealists have reached similar conclusions about the production of functionally similar states but have emphasised the importance of shared norms, legal regimes, and economic interdependence, exacerbated by globalisation and the spread of interconnected financial markets. Theorists of ecological modernisation, who share many of these liberal assumptions, maintain that "the ethics and principles of environmental behavior as regards the investments, production and trade of transnational companies and investment banks are increasingly applied in a similar way to practices anywhere around the globe."[18] In diverse ways and through various mechanisms, therefore, many theorists see the production of homogeneity as a key effect of international cooperation and conflict.

Three mechanisms by which homogeneity is apparently produced in the sphere of environmental governance are multilateral legal regimes, aid conditionality, and epistemic communities. First, as Marian Miller observes, "international regimes, by their very nature, modify the norms and practices of state sovereignty," especially in developing countries.[19] Evolutions in environmental norms—for example, whaling, once seen as a legitimate industry, is now the target of moral and legal sanctions; or the growing expectations that states will control transboundary pollution and make provision for citizen participation in governance—alter what it means to be a modern, responsible state. The climate change regime, or regime complex, is perhaps one of the best examples of a collection of norms, discourses, worldviews, institutions, regulations, and practices which govern the local specificities of climate and carbon policy in quite similar ways across the world. By 2015 the UNFCCC had received thirty-four National Adaptation Programmes of Action from African states, the most recent being from Equatorial Guinea in November 2013, and fifty-three African states submitted Intended Nationally Determined Contributions on their climate action targets for COP21 in December 2015. Although there were only 237 projects in the CDM pipeline in Africa in 2012, or 2.8 percent of the total, the principles and norms established through the CDM, such as additionality, commensurability, carbon trading, have structured the landscape for climate change adaptation projects in Africa. The climate regime also represents one of the potentially most lucrative new sources of aid for developing countries, with projections that adaptation financing will require at least $100 billion per year in transfers from richer to poorer countries. Despite heated negotiations over finance during the COP21 meeting in Paris in December 2015, flows of aid are falling well short of the $100 billion target. But the processes by which projects are assessed and aid disbursed will further entrench common codes of conduct in environmental governance.[20]

Aid conditionality is the second driver of increasingly similar or homogenous African green state effects. Development aid is an important source of funding for environmental projects, agencies, and ministries in Africa. For example, the Tanzanian Ministry of Environment is highly dependent on external aid: major donors include Denmark and UN Habitat, although funds have also been received from the World Bank, FAO, USAID, and the Global Environment Facility. In another case, Peter Newell notes that Germany wrote off £500 million of Kenya's debt in exchange for nature conservation projects. These funds come with conditions, norms, and expectations of how they will be used. As Vigdis Broch-Due concludes, "[The] development industry has been a major generator of preconstructed frameworks like templates and blueprints that can be deployed as tools to simplify and control across continents a range of diverse and complex environments."[21]

In their detailed review of the sector, Hicks et al. analysed 428,000 individual aid projects across 170 countries in 1980–99. They suggest that the grand bargain reached at the Rio Conference on Environment and Development in 1992 was that "wealthy countries agreed to underwrite the participation of less developed countries in any global environmental accord to come out of the meetings."[22] While this bargain was often not met, they find a strong overall trend toward the greening of development aid: "At the beginning of the 1980s, bilateral donors on average gave eleven times as much money for dirty projects as for environmentally beneficial ones. By the early 1990s, this ratio was below 4:1, and by the end of the decade it was 2:1. By the late 1990s, no major bilateral donors were out of line with this standard, and some were even funding more environmental projects than dirty projects."[23] Aid for environmental projects remained low throughout this period—although certain large donors like Germany, Norway, and Japan are leaders in this sector—but the proportion of what they term dirty aid fell in comparison to neutral aid. The Development Assistance Committee (DAC) *Aid to Environment Development Co-operation Report 2012* found that "aid targeting environmental sustainability as the 'principal objective' grew more than three-fold over the period, amounting to USD 11.3 billion in 2009–10."[24] An even greater increase was seen in aid that targeted environmental sustainability as a significant objective, and "Germany, Japan, Norway and Spain have shown a strong increase in activities in support of the environment."[25] According to DAC, over a quarter of all bilateral aid targeted environmental sustainability as a principal or significant objective, and a third of this environmental aid went to Africa. In view of the limited group of donors funding environmental projects and programmes in a wide range of developing countries and the similar discourses and ideologies informing many of these relationships, implicit or explicit aid conditionality can work to produce forms of international homogeneity in green state effects.

The third mechanism for producing more homogenous green states in Africa is the network of epistemic communities which inhabit global environmental governance, described by Keeley and Scoones as "internationalised discourse coalitions."[26] Members of these communities and NGOs frequently have the same training, read the same books, meet at the same conferences, and get their funding from the same places. Ashford perhaps overstates the case when he avers that, when it comes to environmental innovation, developing countries "to an increasing extent follow, copy, and adapt technologies from the developed world rather than develop new ones."[27] But it is certainly true that governmental techniques and technologies developed in the West and promoted by international agencies often shape the forms of environmental governance in Africa and in other developing regions. For example, programmes to mainstream environmental issues into Poverty Reduction Strategy Papers (PRSP) and the formulation of national climate adaptation strategies often seem to reproduce particular examples and phrases, and similar initiatives and programmes are advocated irrespective of the national context. In 2003 a World Bank study of environmental mainstreaming of PRSPs across fifty developing countries found similar assumptions about environment-society-economy relations and similar technical tools for monitoring and intervention across the sample. As James Scott puts it, "The forces of standardisation are today represented by international organisations," continuing the "great project of homogenisation" begun by nation-states in the promulgation of uniform languages, knowledge, cadastral systems, modes of proper behaviour, and so on.[28] The World Bank has proclaimed itself "*the* global knowledge bank" and is influential within networks of consultants and researchers working on issues like land reform and governance, REDD+, and PES. According to Michael Goldman, "The Bank's form of environmental knowledge production has rapidly become hegemonic."[29]

Taken together, these mechanisms of multilateral legal regimes, aid conditionality, and epistemic communities can produce increasingly similar governance states. Such green conditionality means that, according to Keeley and Scoones, "very often—adopting wholesale the core narratives of the international debates—is a basic requirement for gaining access to such funds."[30] Graham Harrison observes that in some cases "the donor—state relation is too intimate and interrelated to be understood as a dichotomy. Donors do not just impose conditionalities; they also work in routinised fashion at the centre of policy-making."[31] According to Harrison, Africa is where the production of governance states is most advanced, World Bank staffers are deeply embedded at the heart of the state, and sovereignty has only ever been conditional and contingent. Not only the imposition of conditionalities, or even just the shaping of recipient states' preferences and interests, but also the very production of state identities and capacities by practices of environmental aid and development assistance is a critical element of state greening.

The production of homogeneity in state forms has been typically claimed by neorealists, neoliberals, and ecological modernisation theorists, although more critical authors like Harrison note the way in which neoliberal governance and capitalist expansion have led to certain forms of homogeneity. By contrast, many critical theorists have sought to show how cooperation between certain actors, such as between Great Powers, or sovereign states, or capitalist elites, or male patriarchs, or European missionaries, has facilitated and perpetuated conflict and violence at the expense of subaltern groups. Thus, rather than the smooth, essentially homogenous world of neorealism and neoliberal theory, critical theorists see a world which is fundamentally uneven or heterogeneous: in Justin Rosenberg's formulation, the world consists of "a multiplicity of temporally coexisting instances, levels and forms of society."[32] To Marxist theorists, an uneven international has been produced through core–periphery relations, combined and uneven development, imperialism, and internal colonisation. Feminists have drawn attention to the role of gendered power relations and patriarchy in producing unequal bodies, practices, and spaces. Postcolonial theorists have emphasised the role of language, race, and religion in structuring disparities between civilisations, and the perpetuation of these differences through the spread of specific value systems, modes of education and culture, and technology. From these perspectives, ungovernable spaces combine with unprofitable relations and undesirable peoples to produce a fundamentally patchy and lumpy world order, one defined more by heterogeneity than by homogeneity.[33]

This binary choice between either homogeneity or heterogeneity is a tenuous one, and real-world politics involves a complex interrelationship or dialectic between the two. Phil Cerny draws attention to dynamics of both homogenisation (competition and emulation) and differentiation (competitive advantage) amongst developing states in the international economy.[34] However, here I emphasise the differentiating dynamics within international environmental politics which is tending to divide African states into leaders and laggards. In contrast to the linear, unidirectional narratives of neorealists, neoliberals, and ecological modernisers, I show how African green state effects are highly differentiated and produce a heterogeneous landscape of inspirational examples and pollution enclaves.

The best way to initially illustrate this dynamic of heterogeneity and differentiation is through the proliferation of environmental indexing, ranking and benchmarking schemes and ratings which have sprung up as mechanisms of global environmental governance since at least the 1990s. The sheer number of these indicators and rankings creates a complex web of norms and standards by which states agree to be measured and assessed, and they cooperate in submitting the necessary information and restructuring their governance structures in order to perform competitively across a range of environmental indicators. The power of these indexes is best described as "disciplinary neoliberalism," which, for Stephen Gill, combines capillary power reshaping the micropractices of free individual conduct within a broader structural context of panoptic surveillance.[35] States are notionally free to be part of these rankings or not, but the power of the indexes lies in shaping "the conduct of conduct" of responsible members of international society. The indexes are competitive and hence constitute a lens through which the conduct of states is examined and compared, judging them as failing, competitive, corrupt, unequal, tolerant, and so forth. They foster diversity and differentiation within a broader, universalising schema. The same basic units and categories are compared, but the result is a highly differentiated political order.

In the environmental field, some of the most well-known measures, as mentioned earlier, are Yale's EPI, which ranks how well countries perform in two environmental policy areas, protection of human health from environmental harm and protection of ecosystems, and Columbia University's Environmental Sustainability Index, which "benchmarks the ability of nations to protect the environment over the next several decades" and focuses on environmental policymaking. The SSI follows the Brundtland Report's definition of sustainable development quite closely and measures human well-being, environmental well-being, and economic well-being, and the HPI, produced by the New Economics Foundation, calculates "the extent to which countries deliver long, happy, sustainable lives for the people that live in them" by ranking countries on how many such lives they produce per unit of environmental input: well-being and life expectancy divided by ecological footprint.[36] The Africa Living Planet Index charts the levels of biodiversity and species loss between the 1970s and the 2000s, and the African Ecological Footprint Index ranks states according to their per capita footprint (Mauritius has the highest, Eritrea the lowest).[37] There are many other indicators, indexes, and ranking systems used for other specific issues, including water quality, carbon dioxide emissions, regulatory environment, etc., among them those produced by the World Resources Institute, the Climate Risk Index, and the Green Economy Index.

These indexes represent a massive investment of time and energy in monitoring and measuring and ranking vast quantities of data about countries, their ecosystems, economies, and policies. To provide a snapshot of how some of the African countries discussed in this book are placed in these indexes, I compare a small group of states across several of them (table 1). The columns list their overall ranking on the EPI 2014, their ranking according to percentage ten-year change on the EPI Change 2014, the SSI 2014, ranked by environmental well-being, and the HPI 2012.

A number of observations can be made from these data. First, African countries tend to rank quite low on most of these indexes, apart from the environmental well-being component of the SSI, which measures biodiversity, consumption, water resources, energy use, GHGs, and so forth. South Africa is the only country to do better on the EPI, which focuses on environmental regulation and government capacity, than on the SSI, which focuses on sustainable resource use. Whereas European and North American countries

TABLE 1. AFRICAN COUNTRY RANKINGS ON ENVIRONMENTAL INDEXES

	EPI (2014)	EPI Change (2014)	SSI (2014)	HPI (2012)
Angola	160	28	32	127
Botswana	100	49	51	151
Congo	130	7	53	121
Ethiopia	131	51	16	94
Kenya	140	15	14	98
Madagascar	166	12	19	49
Malawi	128	40	2	72
Mozambique	158	157	4	114
Namibia	117	6	49	96
Niger	142	1	33	144
Nigeria	134	103	28	125
Rwanda	146	26	7	108
Sierra Leone	173	5	12	139
South Africa	72	71	91	142
Tanzania	143	159	11	133
Uganda	134	32	13	131
Zimbabwe	94	99	17	115

tend to do best in terms of economic well-being, development, and environmental regulation, the HPI puts Costa Rica, Vietnam, Colombia, and Belize top owing to their ability to produce high levels of experienced well-being and life expectancy despite having very low ecological footprints. Their very low ecological footprints notwithstanding, African countries tend to score badly on this index because of their lower life expectancies; Algeria is the highest-placed African country on the HPI at 26th place, followed by Tunisia and Morocco; the highest-placed sub-Saharan countries are Madagascar and Malawi, at 49 and 72.

A second observation is the considerable variation of individual countries across indexes. Botswana, for example, is a mid-ranking country on the EPI but in last place (151st) on the HPI owing to a relatively high ecological footprint compared to lower life expectancy and well-being. Similar variations can be observed for Ethiopia, Tanzania and Zimbabwe. The absence of uniformity is not surprising, as the indexes are often measuring very diverse things, but it does reveal the potential for countries to strategically select indexes and measurements, game the system, and brand themselves accordingly. It also discloses the lack of agreement about what should be measured in assessing environmental health and sustainability: there is an almost infinite variety of potential indicators, and an overall evaluation of what constitutes good environmental governance and performance is highly contested and subjective.

Finally, the indexes do demonstrate some consistency in their very inconsistency. There is clearly much heterogeneity both within countries and across the region. The African continent includes high-performing countries like Malawi, Mozambique, and Rwanda, all in the top ten of the SSI, and Niger, Sierra Leone, Namibia, and the Congo, all in the top ten most improved countries in the EPI. Yet Angola, Madagascar, and Sierra Leone are towards the very bottom of the 2014 EPI, and countries as diverse as Niger, South Africa, and Botswana are grouped together toward the very bottom of the HPI. There is no common trajectory across the continent: in contrast to the dramatic improvements of Niger, Sierra Leone, Namibia, and the Congo, according to the EPI, Tanzania and Mozambique are among the least improved globally in the first decade and a half of the twenty-first century.

However, the most meaningful feature of these indexes is not what they tell us about the reality of African environments or environmental policy or even the relative position of various countries.[38] Rather, the types of criteria measured and the techniques of measurement are important practices of government and the conduct of conduct in international society. Their visibility and comparability and intrusive methods of data collection mean that states are judged and start to judge each other by applying these criteria, and new norms of what it means to be a responsible or green state are produced, invoked, and resisted. Through such indices it is possible to disaggregate and compare Africa's green states, and these rating systems encourage the division of Africa's states into leaders and laggards.

EXEMPLARY ENVIRONMENTAL LEADERS

International environmental leadership is evident within Africa, and here I want to examine the ways in which various states, individuals, regions, and projects have sought to position themselves as international exemplars. In many cases they have received international recognition for their leadership. While the rankings discussed above offer little evidence for making a broader claim about African states' leading on environmental performance or sustainability (some unevenly good scores on the EPI change rankings and the SSI environmental component notwithstanding), other forms of leadership exist. Tanzania, for example, is seen as having "consistently been a world leader in conservation."[39] In terms of tree planting and restoring deforested landscapes (see chapter 4), the IUCN note that "there are a lot of inspirational examples in Africa."[40] According to Doyle and Doherty, whereas "the poorest countries in Africa still inhabit a political sphere where climate change politics is secondary, some African countries like South Africa and Nigeria are actually taking the lead in climate campaigns."[41] South Africa has sought to use climate change negotiations and other international events such as the Johannesburg World Summit in 2002 and the FIFA World Cup of 2010 to promote an image of the country as modern, progressive, responsible, and green; and Nigeria launched two Earth observation satellites in June 2011 with the purpose of helping to monitor climate change and human vulnerability in the Sahel. According to then-President Goodluck Jonathan, this was "another milestone in our nation's effort to solve national problems through space technology."[42]

These two examples illustrate the phenomenon of competition states discussed by Cerny in the 1990s, as states look for ways to brand themselves attractively in order to secure resources, both material and immaterial, within a competitive global economy.[43] Green discourses and global environmental governance therefore pave the way for African states to attract potential resources, which can be mobilised through long-standing practices of extraversion and gatekeeping. There is a clear set of incentives for African states to emphasise both their environmental vulnerability and their capacity for exemplary leadership, and the diverse results profiled in the rankings above can be selectively and strategically invoked by states in the pursuit of either of these goals. Two examples of African environmental leadership, from South Africa and Tanzania, can be provided, notwithstanding the very different positions they hold on the EPI rankings.

South Africa has always attempted to portray itself as an exceptional state: more developed, more democratic, more modern than its neighbours. Since the early 2000s green discourses of environmental governance and diplomacy have contributed to this exceptionalism, as illustrated by a key passage from the National Climate Change Response Paper of 2004: "As South Africa is now an active player in the international arena in many areas, it is important that national climate change response plans are acceptable to the broader global community. At the very least, this means demonstrated adherence to all international treaties, conventions and protocols to which South Africa is a party. However, being seen to be taking a leading role amongst the ranks of the developing countries could considerably enhance South Africa's standing in the international community."[44] Accordingly, hosting major international negotiations—such as the Johannesburg Summit of 2002 (Rio+10), the IUCN World Parks Congress in 2003, and the Durban climate conference in 2011 (COP17)—has become a major plank of South Africa's leadership role in global environmental politics. The presence of South Africa in the coalition which produced the Copenhagen Accord in 2009, after the failure of the EU to exercise international leadership in taking the climate regime forward, was widely seen as evidence of a shift in global climate geopolitics. The Durban climate conference in 2011 was portrayed as "an opportunity to showcase the country," in particular green economy strategies such as the successful tendering process for renewable energy providers (see chapter 5). In 2012 the Global Green Economy Index ranked South Africa first out of the twenty-seven countries listed (between them comprising over 90 percent of the global green economy) in terms of leadership performance on the green economy. This ranking has fallen in subsequent years but the perception of South Africa's leadership continues to outrank its performance on environmental indicators.

When it comes to conservation, South Africa is widely regarded as being at the cutting edge of the latest techniques of biodiversity protection, preservation, and the integrating of historically marginalised communities. One example is that of the Makuleke community and the comanagement scheme agreed with KNP, which is widely regarded as a landmark case both in South Africa and globally (see chapter 3). De Villiers writes, "The Makuleke agreement is the first agreement under which the right of a community to land situated within a national park—the KNP—is restored and where the community has declared itself willing to let the land remain part of the park on condition that joint management takes place."[45] Another widely cited South African story of supposed best practice is the policy of free basic water in Durban, whereby poor communities in informal communities have been granted their constitutional right to a basic level of free water supply. Beyond this basic level, low-tech solutions such as flow limiters ensure conservation or at least sustainable use of what is a scarce national resource.[46] While both of these examples are more politically complex, contested, and controversial than they are frequently presented as being, what is significant here is that they *are* so frequently presented to international audiences as pioneering examples of world-leading projects for just sustainability emerging from Africa.

The FIFA World Cup in 2010 was also intended to showcase a modern, successful, competent South Africa, encapsulating the African Renaissance. "We want to show that Africa's time has come," President Mbeki proclaimed in 2003.[47] One plank of this project was the Green Goal 2010 programme, which sought to create a positive legacy from the tournament across the three pillars of sustainable development: social, economic, and environmental. The envisaged outcomes of the Green Goal strategy were to reduce the environmental footprint of the event, to leave a green legacy, to communicate the importance of environmental management to citizens, and to reduce carbon emissions.

As previous research on these programmes has shown, the strategy and implementation of the greening initiatives were patchy and could best be described as a missed opportunity. Nevertheless, individual host cities, including Cape Town and Durban, managed to generate some momentum behind the project, and the City of Cape Town Green Goal programme attracted some praise. This comprised approximately forty-three projects, from waste minimisation and recycling initiatives, to biodiversity protection and education campaigns, to city beautification and public transport improvements. The tree planting and recycling bins associated with the Green Goal project did little to mitigate the adverse effects of a megaevent characterised by the diversion of scarce public funds into white elephant stadium construction,

15. Green Goal 2010 programme, Cape Town, July 2010. Photo by author.

the forced removal of communities, quasi-imperial control by FIFA and their multinational partners over every aspect of the tournament marketing, legacies of bribery and corruption, and the overhyped anticipation of economic benefits and national unity. Yet such critiques at least partly miss the underlying rationale for using such an event to promote green discourses and practices, which depended upon the theatrics, extravagance, and scale of the World Cup circus. As Archbishop Desmond Tutu put it, "People live on more than just bread. . . . It is the first time this prestigious tournament has been held on the African continent, and therefore important for who we are, for our self-esteem as a continent and as South Africans."[48] From this perspective the prominence and visibility of gigantic projects like the stadiums, Gautrain, and airport upgrades were essential aspects of setting an inspirational example, white elephants or not. South Africa has been explicitly searching for a postapartheid international role and an opportunity to take the moral high ground internationally, and, as a result, climate change leadership, along with regional peacekeeping, has become an important plank of South African state branding.

Tanzania is also an interesting example of environmental leadership, although a very different one from South Africa as regards levels of wealth, development, and state capacity. Conservation is central to Tanzania's international identity, and well over 30 percent of Tanzania's land is under some form of national protection (see chapter 3). Yet Tanzania has received international praise for its progressive mainstreaming of environmental issues into the development policy-making process. The National Strategy for Growth and the Reduction of Poverty, developed in 2005, has been described as "an ambitious and unprecedented Tanzanian initiative to integrate environmental issues into development policy and practice"; further, it "offers an iconic and enduring (and perhaps rather rare) example of a nationally-developed policy process which delivers—in practice—what the World Bank's Poverty Reduction Strategy principles describe in theory."[49] It included 15 directly environmental targets (out of 108 in total) which are quantitative and measurable and were developed through one of the most extensive participatory processes in Tanzanian history. The strategy was motivated by the broader vision of sustainable development set out in Tanzania's national development strategy, *Vision 2025*. While, as in the case of South Africa's Green Goal programme, the actual impact of such initiatives on broader environmental sustainability and justice is unclear and probably doubtful, what is significant is that such exemplary interventions are being increasingly promoted as the route to sustainable development in the global South. Tanzania's environmental mainstreaming process has accordingly been held up as an "inspiration to other developing countries, especially in Africa."[50]

These two cases illustrate a striking feature of African environmental leadership. Leadership in international politics can take many forms and modes: transforming the material or institutional structures within international society; setting agendas and consciousness raising; building bridges and coalitions between other actors; and leading by example. South Africa has actively pursued a coalition-building mode of leadership in the climate and sustainable development negotiations, and this has contributed to the common African position discussed below. In most of the other cases, however, the form of leadership is exemplary: making the first move in order to demonstrate the feasibility, value, and superiority of particular policy solutions. IR theorists like Waltz have noted how the "exemplary effect" can work to conduct behaviour in global politics, as "states to imitate the behaviour of their most successful competitors."[51]

The logic of exemplary leadership is a characteristic feature of green African states. It relies upon an approach to environment and development politics predicated on demonstration farms, best-practice cases, pilot projects, model villages, and so-called lighthouse exemplars. This dynamic is explicitly advocated by Eckersley as part of her argument for a transnational, cosmopolitan, postliberal green state. She contends that the spread of green values within international society by "western green democratic states" towards other states "should be by the 'demonstration effect' (by the force of the better example or the better argument) not by diplomatic manipulation, blackmail, or conventional force."[52] In order to avoid charges of green imperialism, she suggests, green states should spread by emulation, not imposition. The logic of this, Eckersley concedes, means that "the resulting international order would be variegated, made up of what might be clusters of transnational green states operating within a larger, less green and more traditional set of interstate relationships." These clusters—such as in the EU, in Eckersley's view—would grow or be copied by means of "respectful persuasion or example (possibly hastened by the unwelcome assistance of ecological collapse)."[53]

Whereas Eckersley assumes these examples will primarily come from advanced, industrialised countries, it is possible to see this logic at work in a number of African cases. The South African use of environmental summits or conferences is an illustration of this form of leadership, which has also been adopted by the UNFCCC itself. The Momentum for Change programme uses each climate conference to profile a number of public–private lighthouse activities in the hope of "inspiring mitigation and adaptation activities, and to spur innovation and increase capacity for future initiatives."[54] Recent lighthouse projects include climate adaptation in Namibia and Senegal and "Solar Sister," a door-to-door green (solar) energy social enterprise in Uganda. These are instances of "new forms of climate governance" that go well beyond formal multilateral diplomacy.[55] Yet while advocates of these innovative, more flexible modes of governance emphasise their independence from states and state-centric politics, they remain easily appropriated by state assemblages in the service of a broader attempt to brand countries as international environmental leaders. This rationality of inspirational leadership takes a number of forms, including at the levels of individuals, locations, and projects.

First, inspirational examples often rely upon heroic personalities or celebrities. Philanthropic initiatives by the superrich are increasingly lauded as powerful mechanisms for funding development and environmental programmes that combine feel-good narratives of charity and apolitical do-gooding with the human face of the successful entrepreneur cast as eco-hero. UNEP Goodwill Ambassadors are a case in point. Their role is "to help generate public awareness and understanding of environmental causes," and they include the international football star Yaya Touré, the Brazilian supermodel Gisele Bündchen, the American actor Don Cheadle, the Chinese actress Li Bingbing, the French photographer Yann Arthus Bertrand, and the Indian economist Pavan Sukhdev.[56] Politicians can also function as inspirational figures. Meles Zenawi of Ethiopia and Paul Kagame of Rwanda have both been praised by the media and donors in recent years.

But there are risks in holding individuals up as eco-heroes. The widespread commendation afforded the supposed entrepreneurial leadership of President Bingu wa Mutharika of Malawi under the benign patrimony of the Bill and Melinda Gates Foundation illustrates this point. In a paean to Mutharika, Calestous Juma opens by quoting Mark Twain:

> In a prophetic depiction of the power of inspirational models, Mark Twain famously said: "Few things are harder to put up with than the annoyance of a good example." Malawi's remarkable efforts to address the challenges of food security were implemented against the rulebook of economic dogma that preaches against agricultural subsidies to farmers. Malawi's President Bingu wa Mutharika defied these teachings and put in place a series of policy measures that addressed agricultural development and overall economic development. He serves as an example for other African leaders of how aggressive agricultural investment (16 percent of government spending) can yield increased production and results.[57]

According to Juma, Mutharika bravely defied prevailing economic orthodoxy by granting massive subsidies, particularly in fertiliser, to farmers through the Farm Input Subsidy Program in 2005. This step followed years of food insecurity, which at their high point during the famine of 2001–2 caused between forty-seven thousand and eighty-five thousand deaths. Maize production "grew from 1.2 million metric tons in 2005 to 3.4 million metric tons by 2007," and Malawi exported its surplus to other food-insecure countries in the region such as Zimbabwe, Lesotho, and Swaziland.[58]

Yet in the face of Mutharika's rapid fall from donors' favour, rising domestic protests against his authoritarianism, and the chaos surrounding the political transition after his death, the "power of a good example" seems less self-evident. Moreover, the spending on artificial fertilisers would not be regarded by many as environmentally sustainable, and it also had a number of perverse economic and social consequences. One NGO reports that the effects included "farmers trapped in a cycle of debt and dependency on costly external inputs, and an eroding natural resource base."[59] Resnick et al. note that "because fertiliser use has been promoted through a subsidy scheme that is highly popular among poor farmers and therefore an electoral boon to many politicians from the ruling party, shifting towards a more environmentally friendly mode of enhancing soil fertility will be extremely challenging."[60] Malawi experienced macroeconomic instability in 2011–12 and a contraction in the agricultural sector by 3 percent in 2012. Heroic individuals can be quickly invoked by international agencies and states as part of their green branding, but this is a risky strategy. It feeds into a personalised politics of individual agency which is easily assimilated by the myth of the neopatrimonial "Big Man." When a good example goes awry, the unreliability of such theories of social change becomes painfully evident, yet the logic of the inspirational example seems hardwired into the governing rationalities of green states and global environmental regimes.

The type of inspiration associated with particular locations is best illustrated by the Millennium Villages campaign, part of the heroic vision of Jeffrey Sachs, "neurotic neoliberal" economist and director of Columbia University's Earth Institute. This intervention initially targeted fourteen clusters of villages in ten countries in sub-Saharan Africa, introducing a package of reforms and investments in order to achieve the Millennium Development Goals and kick-start rural entrepreneurship and sustainable development. The vision consists of investing $120 annually in each village inhabitant for a period of five to ten years, after which period funding is withdrawn in the hope that development will be self-sustaining. It is a form of "utopian social engineering" designed to produce an idealised society. Yet, as Japhy Wilson notes, "The miniature scale at which the projects operate implies that the development gains will be insignificant in comparison to the fate of the vast populations that surround them," and furthermore there is little explicit attention given to how these projects are to be disseminated or scaled-up beyond the force of the good example.[61] Moreover, many of the projects, such as Ruhiira village in Uganda, seem to function primarily to impress and inspire foreign visitors and development practitioners rather than to markedly improve the lives of the majority of villagers in the project area. This is another case wherein the good example turns out, on closer inspection, to rarely live up to expectations.

A parallel case, also instructive in regard to how local examples are mobilised as part of wider exemplary logics, comes from the GMO cotton trials on the Makhathini Flats in northern KwaZulu-Natal (South Africa) from 1998 onwards. The first GMO crop to be legally grown by smallholder farmers in Africa was the insect-resistant GM cotton using the *Bacillus thuringensis* (Bt) gene developed by Monsanto. Early research "revealed that after only two growing seasons, adoption rates among these smallholder farmers had swelled from 7 percent to over 90 percent. They reported two significant explanations for these sky-high adoption rates: increased yields (equivalent to a 40 percent increase for smallholder farmers), and reduced pesticide applications (which lowered costs, reduced exposure, and lessened labor requirements)."[62] Also entailing financial savings for the farmers concerned, the idea seemed to be an all-round triumph for GM crops in Africa.

The trial farm was promoted enthusiastically across the continent. The chairperson of the Ubongwa Farmers' Association "was flown to thirteen different countries to give his first-hand account of how the lives of his family and community had improved since adopting GM."[63] The Makhathini trial was explicitly and energetically promoted as a model to be emulated elsewhere by African cotton farmers. Yet despite the portrayal of the model or pilot as "a space without place," one of the reasons for the success of this trial was exactly the local context, and in particular the availability of cheap, reliable credit and access to markets and infrastructure in the region. When lines of easy credit later dried up, the successes of the GM cotton trials began to fall apart. Attempts to develop high-volume cotton production elsewhere—and even to sustain it in Makhathini over the long term—have not proved as successful.[64] Despite the local specificities of the villages in which the Millennium Villages Programme is rolled out or in which GM cotton is experimented with, these cases—and national support for or obstruction of them—become a means of identifying cooperative, responsible, leading green states in sub-Saharan Africa. Through their attitudes to these sorts of model projects, states can be quickly categorised as part of the solution or part of the problem by international donors and agencies.

The third and final level of the inspirational example is that of the project. Cases here could include Ethiopia's promotion of low-carbon zones intended to act "as beacons for low carbon development not only in Ethiopia, but across Africa: demonstrating success and providing a target for green investment."[65] Other instances emerge from CSR projects. The UN Global Compact encourages companies to adopt higher standards on employment practices, environmental impacts, and so on and "relies on persuasion and the example of good practices rather than on hierarchy and coercion."[66] The DBSA recommended the promotion of "flagship programmes to demonstrate green economic activity" as a first step toward the development of a more integrated, comprehensive approach to the green economy.[67] Mol writes, "The popular Chinese strategies of benchmarking, promoting 'model' enterprises, and giving awards is [*sic*] used in evaluating the sustainability performance of Chinese TNCs [transnational corporations] operating in Africa, such as the 2010 Green Banking Innovation Awards and the 2010 Top Chinese Enterprises in Africa Award."[68]

The widespread critiques of the political implications of such CSR schemes highlight some of the broader weaknesses of the exemplary mode of inspirational leadership. As Peter Utting has remarked, much of the evidence presented for the benefits of CSR schemes is uneven, anecdotal, and contested.[69] Blowfield and Frynas note that World Bank staff "have argued that CSR can be a useful step on the way to better national legislation in countries that have failed to enforce their laws."[70] Yet they conclude, "We know very little about the impact of CSR initiatives in developing countries, and what we do know raises questions about both the efficiency of CSR approaches and the tangible benefits for the poor and marginalised."[71] Exemplary initiatives produce highly uneven and variegated development, in which lucky cases selected for projects may benefit in some ways (although there are also costs associated with the increased visibility and attention), whereas the vast majority of spaces and populations remain outside the ambit of these projects. Inconvenient outcomes, including dissenting populations and fractious social movements, become problems that require concealment, criminalisation, and marginalisation.

Any one of the three levels of inspirational example—the individual, location, and project—is therefore easily appropriated by green competition states eager to brand themselves as exemplary leaders and thereby attract both material and symbolic resources from international society. The same examples are repeated ad nauseam across international reports, reviews, and assessments. Yet the model of development at work here is that of the green enclave. James Ferguson characterised the engagement of oil companies in Africa as enclaves, suggesting, in reference to Angola, that "capital does not 'flow' from London to Cabinda; it hops, neatly skipping over most of what lies in between."[72] A similar conclusion could be drawn about the manner in which exemplary environmental interventions produce enclaves of highly visible, purportedly successful projects, leaving vast areas "ungreened" in between them. In the case of biodiversity conservation, Brockington and Scholfield echo Ferguson in arguing that "globalised interest in conservation in Africa may be characterised best by the way it hops over space to particular areas of interest, leaving out vast areas in between."[73] Attention tends to focus on the spectacular and the charismatic, places of outstanding natural beauty, biodiversity hot spots, and UNESCO-accredited world heritage sites. The Tanzanian State of the Environment Report states ambitiously, "The ruins at Kilwa Kisiwani and Songo Mnara, designated as UNESCO World Heritage Sites, have unlimited potential to attract tourists."[74] South Africa was not admitted to the UNESCO system until after 1994, and since then the proclamation of each of a number of World Heritage Sites in the country "has been greeted locally with enthusiasm and pride."[75] Yet few would seriously consider a national development strategy based around world heritage sites as a viable approach to broad-based sustainability or poverty eradication. Instead, they produce an international landscape which is fundamentally uneven, differentiated, and lumpy. Heterogeneity rather than homogeneity is the defining characteristic of green state effects in Africa, driven in no small part by the logic of the inspirational example.

ENVIRONMENTAL LAGGARDS AND POLLUTION ENCLAVES

If the exemplary leader is one form of green state effect produced through international environmental politics, then its converse is the environmental laggard. A lumpy and heterogeneous international landscape comprises both inspirational examples and enclaves of pollution. These twin dynamics occur simultaneously and in parallel to each other, often overlapping. Klein uses the term "sacrifice zones" to refer to areas given over to highly polluting extractive industry, and she suggests that while these used to be primarily located in the poorer regions of the global South they are increasingly encroaching into the hitherto relatively insulated regions of the global North, including the United States, Canada, the United Kingdom, and even the Arctic. The AfDB and WWF use the term "hot spots" or "ecological frontiers [which] . . . will emerge across the continent where expanding industrial, extractive and economic activity intersect with sensitive ecosystems."[76] As environmental justice theorists have long pointed out, environmental risks and vulnerabilities are not equally shared but disproportionately impact communities of colour, women, the poor, the young and the elderly, indigenous peoples, and other structurally marginalised groups. The uneven distribution of ecological harm is a core feature of the production of green state effects.

Cases of egregious environmental harm, pollution enclaves, and structural injustice in Africa are not hard to find. High-profile instances of waste dumping by European companies contribute to a sense in which there is a race to the bottom in African environmental politics. Fifteen to seventeen people died and up to one hundred thousand had to be treated for nausea, headaches, breathing difficulties, stinging eyes, and burning skin when a tanker chartered by the Dutch shipping company Trafigura off-loaded toxic waste that was subsequently dumped in the streets of Abidjan, Côte d'Ivoire, in 2006.[77] In most African cities there is a stark, immediately obvious contrast between the relatively clean streets surrounding the diplomatic and financial quarters and the chronic pollution, traffic, noise, rubbish, and waste water in informal settlements and poor districts. Zones of intensive mineral extraction like Zambia's copper belt, South Africa's Highveld, Ghana's Ashanti region, Sierra Leone's diamond fields in Kono, Eastern Katanga in the DRC, and many others are often plagued by localised environmental degradation and pollution.

As the world's most severely petroleum-impacted ecosystem within a petrostate in which environmental governance is a low priority, the Niger Delta is a typical pollution enclave. Nigeria was one of twenty-five African states in 2010 which had provided no information to the UN on the status of their national strategy for sustainable development. The Nigerian Federal Ministry of the Environment concluded in 2010 that the national policy framework on climate change was largely undeveloped and was "not in position to provide the country the required focused response to climate change concerns."[78] Nigeria has little of the eye-catching flora and fauna of southern and East Africa, and only 14 percent of its land is under environmental protection. In a rather backhanded compliment the nineteenth-century traveller Mary Kingsley wrote, "I believe that the great swamp region of the Bight of Biafra [Niger Delta] is the greatest in the World, and that in its immensity and gloom, it has the grandeur equal to that of the Himalayas."[79] Few travellers in the twenty-first century would concur with this comparison.

Nigeria's status as an environmental laggard is both reflected in and perpetuated by the challenges environmental activists in the country face. Despite the international prominence of campaigners like Saro-Wiwa and Bassey, environmental protest in Nigeria is the exception rather than the rule. The environmental movement is patchy, and some of the most well-known groups, such as MOSOP, were associated not with broader environmental justice campaigns but with a single ethnic group in a highly factionalised country. More recent movements in the Delta, such as MEND, use little or no environmental rhetoric or framing. Their avowed goals are "to localise control of Nigeria's oil and to secure reparations from the federal government for decades of pollution caused by the oil industry."[80] In response to MEND's attacks on oil infrastructure in the Niger Delta, the Nigerian "state–transnational oil alliance" has militarised and securitised the region. As a result, the Delta is described as being "over-policed and under-secured," creating a highly problematic context for environmental campaigners.[81] As Frynas observes, conditions of political instability, opaque governance, and limited accountability can present certain advantages to major multinational corporations like Shell, not least because of the relative ease with which protestors can be bought off, marginalised, or repressed.

This is not to minimise or sideline the achievements of impressive environmental groups such as Environmental Rights Action, who have played a crucial role in the FoEI network through Bassey, a well-known international activist, the director of Environmental Rights Action, and chair of FoEI in 2008–12. They have built upon the legacy of MOSOP and Saro-Wiwa, bringing the Delta repeatedly to international attention and pressing the government and the oil companies to take action (albeit limited) on environmental degradation. One consequence of their tenacity was the commissioning of the UNEP report, published in 2011, which assessed the ecological damage to Ogoniland by the Nigerian government and presented recommendations.[82] Environmental activists in Nigeria have benefitted from the notoriety afforded by the legacy of the MOSOP struggles in the 1990s, and they have travelled to other areas of struggle to develop transnational bonds. As one activist reports, "Movement and interaction with others have helped our struggle. Now the whole world knows about our plight. We are not alone. The work that Ken started is still on. Whether it is in the UN or the OAU, we are known, and the world is now watching Nigeria."[83] Yet the lack of progress on environmental justice and the absence of serious challenges to extractive industries, by either the Nigerian state or the oil companies, confirm the relative weakness of environmental campaigners in the Delta.

South Africa, by contrast, demonstrated exemplary environmental leadership on some issues, but, like Nigeria, it has sizable pollution enclaves. The country has a range of serious environmental problems, including urban air pollution, rural land degradation, water scarcity, rhino poaching, inadequate sanitation in many poorer areas, an inefficient and sometimes dangerous public transport system, and large, dirty mining and manufacturing industries that threaten the health of local communities. In 2010 South Africa emitted 9.2 tCO_2 per capita compared to 1.7 in India, 2.2 in Brazil, 6.2 in China, and 7.9 in the United Kingdom.[84] Around 77 percent of all energy needs in the country are met by coal, and Sasol's Secunda plant is one of the largest point sources of CO_2 emissions in the world. The inequality and injustice of the distribution of these pollution enclaves are starkly illustrated by Nomavenda Mathiane's account of an apartheid-era informal township: "As you enter a black area one of the first things you see are notices about how to kill mosquitoes and rats. You would never see notices like that in a white area. There is no way one blocked toilet in a white area could affect an entire street. There is no way refuse could lie around uncollected for weeks. There is no way a white suburb could be built next to a fertiliser plant."[85]

A prime example of a pollution enclave within South Africa is the South Durban basin, which contains several large refineries and plants alongside residential communities in which the locals have "abnormally high rates of respiratory problems, asthma, leukaemia and cancer."[86] The basin is not only a pollution hot spot, however, but is also an international focal point for protest by environmental activists. One victory came in 2011 with the closure of the hazardous Bulbul landfill site in Chatsworth after a campaign by community groups assisted by GroundWork. Mottiar and Bond report that "by mid-2012, Durban became South Africa's most active protest site, ranging from high-profile middle-class demonstrations close to the town centre—a peaceful march against rhino poachers and a picket against animal abuse at the Brian Boswell Circus—to working class revolts."[87] The Centre for Civil Society, based in the University of KwaZulu-Natal, attracts activists and scholars from all around the world and seeks to link social movements and justice campaigners through regular conferences and seminars, local tours, and transnational solidarity.

Leading NGOs and CBOs in South Durban include GroundWork and the South Durban Community Environmental Alliance (SDCEA). The heads of these organisations, Bobby Peek and Des D'Sa, respectively, have been internationally recognised for their activism and both have been awarded the Goldman Environmental Prize for grassroots activism. These international links and recognition have proved useful: a key long-running strategy of the SDCEA has been the use of bucket brigades, involving samples of air and water being collected in a specialised bucket, which is then sent by courier to a laboratory in the United States to be tested for pollutants. The results are returned to the community and used to contest corporate and government pollution figures. Samples collected in late 2000 and sent to the US Environmental Protection Agency revealed a "cocktail of carcinogenic pollutants." Highly visible moments have also been used to garner international attention: the Fossil Fools Day protests on 1 April featured events staged around the world to "combine a pallet of traditional direct action tactics, with a dose of humour to both 'name and shame' key players in the oil and gas industry, and the financial institutions and politicians who support them."[88] On St Patrick's Day in 2008 groups in South Durban demonstrated against Shell in solidarity with communities who were also involved in protests against Shell in Ireland. The COP17 climate meeting in Durban in 2011 was attended by some six thousand international and local civil society participants (almost a third of the official delegates), and the organisers staged a Global Day of Action, a Peoples' Space, and a Climate Refugee Camp. In 2012 protests in Umlazi township, outside Durban, drew upon transnational waves of activism and explicitly invoked the Occupy! slogans of the 99 percent and showed the film *Occupy Wall Street*.[89] At the COP19 climate conference in Warsaw in November 2013, activists from South Durban held a solidarity People's Climate Camp, both to highlight the global struggle for climate justice and in protest against a proposed multibillion-dollar port expansion of the South Durban harbour.

These cases from Nigeria and South Africa illustrate a number of ways in which the crucial dynamics of cooperation and conflict and similarity and difference work to produce environmental leaders and laggards. First, states can be both leaders and laggards on environmental issues, and exemplary leadership in one policy area can be accompanied by pollution enclaves just down the road. Second, activism can highlight some of the most egregious cases of environmental degradation and injustice, but such groups can also function as part of a structure which produces a more uneven international and exacerbates existing differences.[90] Perversely, one of the products of local and transnational environmental activism can be a centrifugal dynamic whereby certain sites and struggles become highly visible and intensely politicised whereas other sites and struggles tend to be neglected and forgotten. Across the continent, within and between states, it tends to be localities with strong environmental movements and communities, conspicuous grievances, and favourable political contexts which attract further transnational support and attention. Such backing attracts more media coverage, puts more pressure on governments, and sometimes even produces high-profile victories. The winning of victories reinforces this dynamic and stimulates further mobilisation. The dynamic works equally effectively in the opposite direction: the harassment and persecution of movements, together with the absence of sufficiently shocking or symbolic grievances, means that international pressure and attention go elsewhere. FoEI groups in Uganda, Swaziland, and Mozambique, for example, have reported government harassment and marginalisation.[91] Reactionary behavior like this permits elites to marginalise and divert opposition, further weakening the options for successful mobilisation on environmental issues. The politics of transnational environmental activism in Africa often works to reinforce the production of a variegated and heterogeneous set of green state effects and contributes to the structuring of an uneven international topography.

TRANSNATIONAL ENVIRONMENTAL SOLIDARITY

In contrast to prevailing narratives of homogeneity articulated in various forms by neorealists, neoliberals, and ecological modernisers, green state effects in Africa, as we have seen, can be characterised as variegated and heterogeneous, within an uneven international landscape. This argument echoes those of many critical theorists who have shown how international anarchy or international society is actually distinguished by hierarchies of power, wealth, race, gender, religion, and so forth. The systematic production of environmental leaders and laggards through global environmental governance and global political economies contributes to this fundamental unevenness "of socio-cultural forms, of developmental levels, of geographical scales and of historical temporalities."[92] Klein's response to this situation is to advocate greater transnational solidarity between groups struggling against extractivism: what she terms an expanding "Blockadia." Such actions would embody an attitude of "not just 'not in my backyard' but, as the French anti-fracking activists say: *Ni ici, ni ailleurs*—neither here, nor elsewhere. In other words: no new carbon frontiers."[93]

Picking up this challenge, I want to consider the ways in which new forms of transnational environmental solidarity could be conceptualised as another set of discourses and practices which produce green state effects in Africa, and how far practices of critical solidarity might go to mitigate some of the injustices and heterogeneities profiled above. Klein has little time for international negotiations and state politics (although she does acknowledge the

New Deal in the 1930s and the call for a "Marshall Plan for the Earth"), but it is important to show how, in some cases, state assemblages can also help to forge transnational linkages between causes and struggles. For this reason, the first example is the Common African Position on climate change, which has been used by the African Group of Negotiators (AGN) as a way to mitigate their structural marginality within the UNFCCC process.

The idea of a common African negotiating position is linked to the quest for continental unity expressed in the twentieth century by movements for Pan-Africanism and the African Renaissance and by institutions like the Organisation for African Unity (OAU), AU, and the New Partnership for African Development (NEPAD). It has also manifested in attempts to forge a united African stance on issues like UN reform, the post-2015 Millennium Development Goals agenda, indigenous rights, and climate change. In terms of explicitly environmental issues, the OAU adopted the African Convention on the Conservation of Nature and Natural Resources in Algiers in September 1968, and in 1985 African governments established the African Ministerial Conference on the Environment (AMCEN) as "a policy forum to enable ministers in charge of environment issues to better formulate, harmonise and coordinate their activities and programmes."[94] AMCEN remains an active, influential body in coordinating African environmental policy, alongside the AU's Action Plan for the Environment Initiative of NEPAD, agreed in 2003. In January 2014 the AU adopted the Common African Position on the Post-2015 Development Agenda, focusing on the importance of achieving sustainable development, green growth, and water and food security.[95]

The climate change negotiations, however, are a particular and special case of striving for continental solidarity. The AGN is a prominent regional coalition in the UNFCCC negotiations, and when the Committee of the African Heads of State on Climate Change developed a "Common Position" on climate change in 2008–9 it was one of the first times a continental position had become a major platform for the climate negotiations. The African position was developed at the Algiers meeting of AMCEN in November 2008 and was cemented in 2009 in Nairobi in the run-up to the Copenhagen COP15 in November. The African stance drew on the broader positions set out by the G77+China and the Least Developed Countries (LDCs) but differed from them in its emphasis. The first demand of the African position was for financial compensation for damage caused to natural, economic, and social resources due to climate change caused by the developed countries: "According to the African Group the financial commitment of developed countries should be at least 1.5 percent of their global GDP."[96] Other demands included affirming the centrality of the principle of common but differentiated responsibilities, and the importance of the two-track negotiation process whereby historic emitters would make binding commitments (Annex I countries) and others (Annex II countries) would not make emissions commitments but would receive assistance with climate adaptation. In this the AGN shared the LDC view that a transparent, rules-based, and legally binding multilateral regime was by far the most effective way to address climate change. African countries also demanded that developed countries "needed to reduce their greenhouse gas emissions by at least 40 percent below 1990 levels by 2020. By 2050 the GHG-emissions of developed countries should be at least 80 percent to 95 percent below 1990 levels, in order to achieve the lowest level of stabilisation assessed by the IPCC's Fourth Assessment Report."[97] For many African countries, as for the LDCs generally, the importance of aiming to keep global temperature rises under 1.5°C was vital.

This common position and the image of a continent united attracted considerable attention but also led to serious tensions both within Africa and with other partners, for instance, with the G77+China. In a moment of summit theatre, the AGN walked out of the Barcelona negotiations in November 2009 to signal their disgust that the 40 percent target for reduced emissions was not being met. During the Copenhagen process in 2011 the common African position seemed to fracture under the pressure of the negotiations. South Africa was accused of having sold out by signing up to the Copenhagen Accord, which sought to limit temperature rises only to under 2°C and failed to commit the developed world to the required levels of emission cuts. The Sudanese chair of the G77 bloc, Lumumba Di-Aping, pronounced that the agreement asked "Africa to sign a suicide pact, an incineration pact in order to maintain the economic dominance of a few countries. It is a solution based on values, the very same values in our opinion that funnelled six million people in Europe into furnaces."[98] South Africa came in for special criticism by Di-Aping for having "actively sought to disrupt the bloc's unity" during the negotiations and for the lack of leadership displayed by President Jacob Zuma. When Prime Minister Zenawi, together with President José Manuel Barroso of the European Commission and Prime Minister Frederik Reinfeldt of Sweden, announced at a press conference that a mixture of both public and private sources could provide the $100 billion required annually to pay for adaptation to the effects of climate change and help countries move toward a green development path, he too attracted the condemnation of Di-Aping, who accused him of capitulating to EU pressure. Although it proved impossible to maintain a unified continental position through these negotiations, it was clear that the ideal of continental solidarity was a meaningful aspiration, both within Africa and in terms of how African negotiators were seen by other actors.[99]

This African diplomatic prominence was reflected in the decision to hold COP17 in 2011 in Durban. Local media reported that this was "both a mark of South Africa's growing diplomatic status and another opportunity to shine on the world stage."[100] South Africa sought to continue their role as a bridge builder between developed and developing countries, and they achieved their primary goal of not letting the Kyoto Protocol die on African soil. Support from many smaller African states was crucial in buttressing the EU's demand for clearer and more committed action from all signatories, including those classed as Annex II countries such as India and China. This concession, however, and the rising visibility of African negotiators, were ironically paralleled by backsliding from developed country commitments on binding climate action. At the COP19 meeting, Japan announced a new and far less ambitious post-Fukushima mitigation target, Australia and Canada confirmed their effective rejection of the UNFCCC process, and other rich countries displayed an unwillingness to make progress on agreements to compensate for loss and damage. African prominence and visibility—and a "One Continent, One Voice" negotiating strategy—have not been matched by the capacity to produce meaningful international agreements or to make headway in climate negotiations, especially in the halting steps forward on adaptation funding. The negotiation of the Paris Agreement in 2015 did reintroduce the 1.5°C target as an aspiration, to the delight of many African negotiators, but on the other hand there are no binding mechanisms to commit states to GHG reductions and no mention of decarbonisation. Loss and damage are recognized, but the agreement explicitly prohibits attempts to gain compensation or prove liability for already existing harms caused by climate change.

Despite its difficulties, the attempt to maintain a continental position on climate change is highly significant for the production of green state effects. Green states in Africa, whether inspirational leaders or laggards, are products of international processes through which they are constructed as distinctively African, implying in this context a commitment to Pan-African solidarity and the overturning of historic marginalisation. Yet such attempts to achieve continental unity demonstrate that the production of green state effects is difficult and encounters resistance. Moreover, even moments of relative success do not necessarily translate into actual improvements in the effective governance of climate change or the realization of environmental justice.

Transnational environmental solidarity is not limited to alliances between heads of state at international conferences, however. In the environmental field perhaps more than any other, transnational networks stretch across state institutions and actors and incorporate civil society groups, social movement activists, scientists and researchers, church and faith leaders, private philanthropists, and international bureaucrats. These transnational networks play a crucial role in the production of contemporary green state effects in Africa. This is true of green state effects anywhere, not just in Africa, but the rhetorical and historical force of the Pan-Africanist discourse gives practices of African solidarity more weight than in some other regions.

African solidarity can be illustrated by mobilisation around one outstanding issue: the impact of Chinese investment and construction on local environments. In 2013 the Human Development Report of the United Nations Development Programme notes that "between 1992 and 2011, China's trade with Sub-Saharan Africa rose from $1 billion to more than $140 billion."[101] China designated 2006 the Year of Africa, and in 2011 it was estimated that China had over nine hundred investment projects in Africa. China's partnerships with various African governments have spread across the continent, from oil-backed credit lines in Angola to hydropower construction in Ethiopia. In May 2014 Kenya announced fifteen agreements and memoranda of understanding with China on environment, agriculture, health, transport, culture, and investment. In response to these closer ties between African governments and China, many activist groups have sought to monitor and hold them accountable to environmental and social standards. The media outlet Fahamu has developed a "China–Africa Watch" as part of its Pambazuka News publications (it had published 416 articles as of June 2015); the Tanzania Consumer Advocacy Society used the passing of the Olympic torch through Dar es Salam in 2008 to highlight not only China's role in making counterfeit products but also the health and environmental implications of such items; campaigners in Niger demanded more transparency in environmental and labour standards where Chinese projects were concerned; and in Zambia NGOs "investigated environmental performance of Chinese and other firms in the Copperbelt."[102]

Some of these campaigns have had concrete effects on state practices. As Mol writes,

> In September 2006 conservation groups forced Sinopec, one of the three major Chinese oil companies, to suspend oil prospecting in Loango National Park in Gabon. Also in 2006, Zambian authorities shut down Chinese-owned Collum Coal Mine Industries in Sinazongwe for establishing sub-standard working conditions and failing to implement environmental and safety regulations. In May 2007 the Zambian government closed a manganese mine in Kabwe, run by Chiman Manufacturing, a Chinese TNC, following local concerns over high levels of air pollution and failures to implement pollution control measures. And in 2010 the Gabonese environmental NGO Brainforest successfully campaigned against a massive China ExIm Bank supported iron ore development project cum hydropower dam, with poor environmental guidelines and threatening a national park.[103]

Local groups have often been championed by transnational ones such as Greenpeace, WWF, FoEI, and International Rivers as they hold national governments and Chinese firms to account for the environmental degradation they cause. On 29 April 2006 MEND resorted to violence and "detonated a car bomb close to the Warri oil refinery in the western part of the volatile oil-rich Niger Delta," timed to coincide with the "visit of the Chinese President Hu Jintao to Nigeria, and the granting of four oil drilling licences valued at $4 billion to Chinese oil companies."[104] These cases show how a shared discourse of preoccupation with the effects of Chinese investment—not limited to environmental issues but certainly including them—can be identified across many countries in the region.

The transnational activist solidarity networks produce other green state effects through their dissemination of shared environmental discourses and practices. International networks work to conduct the conduct of African environmental practices and discourses, yet African groups and movements are increasingly prominent within global NGO networks once entirely dominated by northern groups. Two of them are climate justice networks and FoEI. African movements and voices, almost unheard of prior to the 2000s in climate change circles, have become more evident since the Durban Declaration on Climate Justice in 2004 and the formation of the Durban Group for Climate Justice. The Pan-African Climate Justice Alliance (PACJA) is an African civil society network composed of groups from forty-three countries and numbering some five hundred members. It seeks to "advocate, lobby and create awareness on the need to integrate climate change into laws, policies and practices in broader sustainable development and poverty reduction strategies in African countries."[105] At the COP19 climate meeting the PACJA launched a "week of action," with activities in Kenya, Ethiopia, Cameroon, Somalia, Ghana, Nigeria, Uganda, Togo, Mauritius, Benin, and South Africa. Kumi Naidoo, the executive director of Greenpeace International, is a South African with roots in the civic antiapartheid movement. During this struggle he developed a notion of "critical solidarity," which informs his position on climate change.[106] The campaign for fossil fuel divestment being championed by Greenpeace among others is modelled in part on the global boycotts and divestment campaigns against apartheid South Africa in the 1980s.

In contrast to Greenpeace, which is more vertically structured, FoEI have an organisational system which is oriented towards horizontal transnational networks of solidarity. African voices, once marginal, are increasingly audible. Doherty's and Doyle's detailed study of FoEI argues that the network has "increasingly been driven by the major concerns of its southern members."[107] Highly active African branches include Environmental Rights Action in Nigeria, with three staff and three hundred members; GroundWork in South Africa, with six staff; the Centre for Environment and Development in Cameroon, with thirteen staff and twelve hundred members; and FoE Ghana, with nineteen staff. There are also branches, some with even larger staffs, in Mali, Mozambique, Sierra Leone, Swaziland, Tanzania, Togo, Tunisia, and Uganda. FoEI biennial general meetings have been held in Ghana (1990), Togo (1995), Benin (2001), and Nigeria (2006). Doherty and Doyle point out that southern groups are able to drive and shape the agenda of the international network, and they emphasise the diversity of campaigns, ideologies, and repertoires. Equally evident is that being part of the FoEI network shapes the conduct of its members in certain ways. Branches in South Africa and Burkina Faso have been expelled from the network—the former for failing to move beyond an all-white membership, the latter for inactivity—whereas others, like Sierra Leone, have remained members but have been monitored. Groups are encouraged to participate in international campaigns, and acting in solidarity with other members of the network is highly prized and valued. More important, FoEI not only offers a network through which to share information, contacts, and perspectives as well as near constant email updates and news but also functions as a route into many of the intergovernmental negotiations and regimes discussed above. Doherty's and Doyle's analysis shows how differences within the network over attitudes towards capitalism, corporate power, democracy, and justice were debated and accommodated and how a collective identity was forged despite political differences over visions, strategies, and tactics. A crucial element of critical solidarity is the capacity for agonistic differences, debates, and even disputes within a broader context of mutual respect and affinity. At a heated FoEI biennial general meeting in Abuja in October 2006, as disagreements over the types of democracy the organisation wanted to promote in the world threatened to lead to lasting fractures, a Nigerian delegate brought the discussion to some kind of consensus with an appeal for negotiation and deliberation rather than heated personal attacks. "We are heavily in solidarity in this room," he said. "Our solidarity in not in doubt."[108]

Appeals to solidarity can function as reassuring or comforting tactics, and sometimes they work to depoliticise unequal power relations. The solidarity of African heads of state—most obviously with respect to the quiet diplomacy over Mugabe's regime in Zimbabwe and the ignoring of outstanding International Criminal Court arrest warrants—is deeply problematic. The politics of groups like FoEI and Greenpeace are better captured, at their best, by the notion of critical solidarity, described by Chris Rossdale as a "process intimately concerned with challenging the identities and positions of those engaged, of calling ourselves into question."[109] Critical solidarity cannot be a way of asserting an unchallenged position or of establishing one's innocence or occupation of the moral high ground, but is instead a commitment to a perpetual process of self-examination and critique. Solidarity can emerge from an acknowledgment that, given our involvement and implication in processes of transnational environmental harm through our travel, consumption, social reproduction, etc., we have an obligation to lend support and offer affinity to others impacted by environmental injustice. Critical solidarity is therefore about forging connections which are able to withstand agonistic political contestation and reciprocal examination.[110]

Practices of critical solidarity have been crucial to producing green state effects in Africa, as transnational activists have built connections over such issues as slavery, colonialism, human rights, race relations, apartheid, trade, debt, patriarchy, arms, poverty, and environmental degradation.[111] This is not simply a situation in which activists from the global North are standing in solidarity with African struggles. Rather, the prominence of leaders like Bassey and Naidoo within FoEI and Greenpeace, respectively, and the growing visibility of African activists and movements within global antiextractivist battles are testimony to a multidirectional network. In one notable example, Saro-Wiwa's brother, Owens Wiwa, attended the trial of the Rossport Five in June

2005 in Ireland when they were jailed for contempt of court after interfering with the construction of the Shell-to-Sea gas pipeline in County Mayo. In return, members of the Shell-to-Sea campaign attended trials in New York against Shell for their complicity in crimes in the Niger Delta. Terence Conway of the Shell-to-Sea campaign said, "The lesson we've learned from the Ogoni is not to give in no matter how impossible it seems, no matter what the odds."[112]

GREEN STATES WITHIN AN UNEVEN INTERNATIONAL TOPOGRAPHY

International politics is a crucial site for the production of green state effects, alongside the governance of territories, populations, and economies. Membership in an international society of states who cooperate and compete according to a range of rules and norms is part of what it means to be a state. The governance of environmental issues is a key element of this. This chapter has shown how various international practices, including diplomatic

16. Artwork in RioCentro, Rio+20 Earth Summit. Photograph courtesy of IISD/Earth Negotiations Bulletin.

negotiations, conflicts, and indexes and ratings schemes, are part of the production of green state effects.

More than this, however, the chapter has shown how international dynamics of conflict and cooperation are crucial in explaining how certain types of green African state are produced, in all their similarities and differences. Some states, such as South Africa and Tanzania, have enthusiastically pursued a variety of environmental interventions in diverse fields and invoked green discourses as a means of international branding. They have pursued a form of environmental leadership best described as exemplary, although the ability of this mode of leadership to produce broad-ranging improvements in environmental indicators is doubtful. Other states, such as Nigeria, seem, in contrast, to be described more accurately as environmental laggards. Yet this state-centric view does not properly capture the uneven character of African environmental governance: states like South Africa and Nigeria contain sites of exemplary leadership alongside pollution enclaves.

African environmental governance is therefore characterised by considerable diversity, difference, and unevenness. Even theorists of ecological modernisation recognise that it is a process which develops unevenly. Thus, Mol concedes that "this 'meta-theoretical homogenisation' of ecological modernisation, unequally determined by western industrialised societies and their institutions and actors, but by no means fully controlled by them, converts into heterogeneous practices, trajectories and processes of environmental reform in the different countries and regions."[113] This view of the world is akin to what Stephen Collier describes as topological, meaning "a heterogeneous space, constituted through multiple determinations, and not reducible to a given form of knowledge-power."[114] These contradictory trends and dynamics are a central effect of the global discourse of liberal environmentalism, in which state sovereignty over natural resources, free trade and economic competitiveness, institution building and regime construction, and governance by inspirational example all produce an uneven international. Sneddon et al. note that one feature of such a system is that decisions with regard to environmental governance are "a function of both fragmenting and integrating forces occurring at multiple scales."[115] Whereas liberal norms, institutions, discourses, and epistemic communities tend to produce convergence and homogeneity, the separation between responsible and irresponsible states, subjects, and populations produces an uneven international topography, one of "jagged peaks and profound valleys," as Tilly described the general upward trend of European state formation toward greater accumulation and concentration.

As Sending and Neumann suggest, this produces "a more differentiated set of states and other polities, thereby conditioning sovereignty and taking us beyond Waltz's image of international politics, where all relevant units were said to be the same."[116]

What political implications can we draw from this dynamic tension between homogeneity and diversity? Many aspects of it should be of deep concern. Problems include both the reproduction of global discourses and trampling over local knowledge, contexts, and conditions as well as a focus on exemplary or favourable cases to the neglect of the most vulnerable and fragile. Neither democratic values nor a commitment to protecting the weakest in society plays much of a role in any of the dynamics discussed here. Local communities and the least visible and least influential states are caught between homogenising dynamics which threaten to erode their particular concerns and exemplary logics which threaten to ignore them unless they can compete for visibility.

Moreover, these dynamics also point to widespread challenges to and transformations of the very notion of state sovereignty. Many environmental and ecological theorists have a deep-seated antipathy to the state and assertions of sovereignty in environmental politics (see chapter 1). War and state assertions of sovereignty over natural resources seem part of the root causes of the environmental crisis, certainly in the light of the marginal, glacier-slow, incremental gains achieved through processes of international negotiation. Smith writes, "Sustaining a place for ecological politics and saving the natural world both depend on rejecting the anti-political and anti-ecological principle of sovereignty."[117] Green state theorists like Eckersley have responded to this line of argument by saying that states can be greened through international norms, legislation, and forms of cooperation to produce a more enlightened multilateral order.[118] I have outlined a different response here, one which sees sovereign politics as contingent, fractured, malleable, and contextual. Sovereignty is a practice as well as a principle, a set of discourses as well as a divine belief. Sovereignty is a tool and form of government, of governmentality, by which subjects can be divided, classified, and made responsible. The ecological implications of practices of sovereignty are neither straightforwardly good nor bad.

As we have seen, conflict and cooperation in international politics can produce various forms of green state effects—leaders and laggards, inspirational examples, and pollution enclaves—each of which has particular implications for ecological and progressive politics. Together they constitute a complex world of peaks and valleys, inspirational examples and pollution enclaves, and more or less governed places. Such disorder and heterogeneity should not completely disappoint us. As Scott argues, "The great emancipatory gains for human freedom have not been the result of orderly, institutional procedures but of disorderly, unpredictable, spontaneous action cracking open the social order from below."[119] One response to heterogeneity is an attempt to build new forms of transnational solidarity in protest against ecological degradation, unsustainable development, and social injustice. Green state effects in Africa have been produced through practices of green solidarity in the past, such as attempts to maintain a common African position on climate change, and the green states of the future could be shaped even more profoundly by forms of progressive and critical solidarity.

CHAPTER 7

Afro-Ecologism

Africa is essentially a rural, magical, phantom Africa, partly bucolic, partly nightmarish, inhabited by peasant folk, composed of a community of sufferers who have nothing in common other than their common position on the margins of history, prostrate as they are in an outer-world—that of sorcerers and griots, of magical beings who keep fountains, sing in rivers and hide in the trees, of the village dead and ancestors whose voices can be heard, of masks and forests full of symbols, of the clichés that are so-called "African solidarity," "community spirit," "warmth" and respect for elders and chiefs.

—Achille Mbembe, *Nicholas Sarkozy's Africa*

Maybe the state is only a composite reality and a mythicized abstraction whose importance is much less than we think.

—Michel Foucault, *Security, Territory, Population*

In a book of this breadth and scope there is a constant risk of generalisation and overabstraction. In struggling against this, I have emphasised the importance of seeing the green state in Africa as an effect of micropractices and discourses of environmental governance and contestation. In turn, this approach sometimes risks missing the big picture: the state is not just an assemblage of practices and discourses like any other. It has a mythical and symbolic enframing character which constitutes a landscape and context for much of political life. Similarly, the focus on specific national and local African examples can sometimes obscure the power of broader assumptions about the place of Africa within global environmental politics. Many environmentalists, ecologists, and conservationists have a reverence for Africa's wild spaces and peasant communities which is similar to the mythical Africa presented by Nicholas Sarkozy and satirised by Achille Mbembe (see chapter 1).[1] These narratives have power and consequences with respect to Africa's place in global regimes and structures as well as to the types of green state effects produced across the continent. I want to address these more general questions here. What *is* the green state in Africa? How does it differ from green states elsewhere? What are the political implications of how environmental issues are governed and contested across the continent?

The central argument of this book is that African states are all green states in some form. The governance and resistance of environments in Africa are central to the production of state effects, and state assemblages are central to environmental politics in Africa. If we want to talk about African environments, then we have to talk about African states—and vice versa. I have shown how discourses and practices such as peace parks in southern Africa, environmental education programmes, green economy strategies, and international climate negotiations all involve, implicate, and transform the African state, and it is through them that what can be described as the green state in Africa is produced. The green state in Africa is the effect of an assemblage of environmental rationalities, discourses, and technologies of government through which territories, populations, economies, and international relations have been brought within the scope of sedimented power relations.

WHAT IS THE GREEN STATE IN AFRICA?

On the above terms, all African states are green states. Moreover, all states, everywhere in the world, govern territories, populations, economies, and international relations through environmental discourses and practices. The degree to which these governmentalities are explicitly identified as green, environmental, or ecological varies across societies and regimes and is highly culturally specific and subjective. But one of the central arguments in this book has been that since the 1990s these explicitly green discourses have become more prominent and visible in Africa. The really crucial questions, however, concern how environmental discourses and practices are mobilised and with what sorts of political consequences. Green state effects take very different forms—in Africa and beyond—and this book has provided a framework for assessing them and exploring their political implications.

This argument sets several challenges to existing literatures on green states and global politics. First, it is necessary to be much more honest about the complexities involved in the word "green."[2] Eckersley's postliberal green state is normatively ecocentric and therefore differs markedly from the emphasis in Dryzek or Meadowcroft on states in which environmental issues like conservation or water security have become linked to core state imperatives. In this book I have advanced a conception of green states that is more about the way in which green discourses and practices are invoked by states and state assemblages and thus leads to a far wider range of potential green state effects. Crucially, this means that states in the developing world become part of and even central to discussions about global transformations in environmental statehood. The second, more substantial set of challenges to green state theory is, therefore, What role do developing states play in changing forms of environmental statehood? Is the green state of ecological modernisation theory a Western concept? How does international society shape practices of green statehood in the global South? What innovations in green governmentalities in the global South will shape environmental politics in the global North? A whole new field of green state theory is opened up by these questions, which go well beyond Eckersley's throwaway remark that "it is for developing countries to find their own green path in accordance with their own traditions."[3]

This book has provided one way of answering some of these questions and mapped some of the green paths taken in Africa. Another way of putting the question, however, is as follows: If all states are produced in some form through green discourses and practices, what is specifically *African* about the discussions in this book? The Africa Progress Report in 2014 makes a great deal of the need for a *uniquely* African green revolution, emphasising both the centrality of agriculture to African development and the need to avoid the mistakes of the green revolution in Asia as well as the specific challenges and opportunities posed by the combinations of demography, geography, and technology in Africa.[4] While there are some similar drivers of green state effects globally and some similar manifestations and implications, my argument is that global environmental governance is characterised by an uneven international topography, by heterogeneity rather than homogeneity (see chapter 6). At a certain level of generality, therefore, green state effects in Africa are distinctively different from green state effects elsewhere, as a result of Africa's unique position in the global economy and international society and the specific historical constitution of African states and societies. There are four dimensions to this Afro-ecologism. First, in generalised and schematic terms, green state effects in Africa have been more centrally dependent on the governance and contestation of land and conservation than in many other states worldwide. Second, the biopolitics of rural under- and overpopulation, often framed in terms of the peasant question, is more prominent in Africa than elsewhere. Third, as the least economically developed region, according to modernisation theorists, natural resource extraction and the hopes attached to rapid, muscular green growth and modernisation are fundamental to understanding attempts to govern economies in Africa. Fourth and finally, discourses and practices of African solidarity and Pan-African unity have shaped the international relations of Africa's environmental politics to a degree rarely seen on other continents.

Certain key examples from individual countries have emerged at several points in the preceding chapters, and although my aim is not to impute a totality or homogeneity to these countries and essentialise their core character, they do illuminate various aspects of green state politics in Africa. Tanzania, for example, illustrates the centrality of the governance and contestation of land and conservation to state formation as well as (above all during the *ujamaa* period) efforts to produce an educated, enlightened population of rural farmers. The defining image of the green state in Tanzania is the failed road project through the Serengeti, where sovereign power faltered in the face of regional and global environmental pressure. Twenty-first century green state effects in Tanzania have been primarily shaped by the politics of land investments and commercial agriculture, which have also produced a backlash against immigrant populations, or those "not from the soil", as well as by the centrality of international environmental aid donors, whose discourses and practices have profoundly remoulded the green state in Tanzania. International authority is most evident in the greening of the poverty reduction strategy paper in the 2000s, which was crafted by international consultants and then presented as an inspirational example to other developing countries.

Contrasting sets of green state effects can be seen in more authoritarian countries like Rwanda and Ethiopia. Both have prominent green economy strategies, and in the climate negotiations Meles Zenawi and Paul Kagame were leading voices on the importance of funding climate mitigation and adaptation in Africa. Both have implemented large-scale mass public works programmes covering projects like tree planting, land terracing, litter eradication, and other environmental issues. They are strong, relatively autonomous states with long histories of modernist development projects, often aimed at managing more sustainable resource use, securing accumulation, and mitigating environmental threats. As such, they have received international praise as powerful examples, and they fulfil many of the criteria for developmental states.[5] On the other hand, they pose considerable challenges to mainstream green state theory. Rwanda and Ethiopia are certainly not postliberal states championing Eckersley's enlightened ecological citizenship. Their authoritarian political cultures, poor human rights records, and lack of tolerance of dissent vividly confirm that the green state in some parts of Africa has more than family resemblances to the colonial or authoritarian state. Yet in other respects they meet the criteria of a notable governmental focus on managing environmental burdens, and in both countries the governance of environmental issues is central and closely linked to core imperatives of survival (Ethiopian hydropower), maintenance of domestic order (environmental volunteering in Rwanda), generation of finance (aid projects, ecotourism, and conservation), capital accumulation (green agricultural modernisation), and political legitimation (invocation of the green economy discourse as part of the drive for modernisation). These strong green states are best seen not as pawns of international aid donors but have demonstrated an ability to strategically mobilise green discourses in support of a national modernisation project in the aftermath of traumatic experiences of famine and genocide.

Another set of green state effects is identifiable in South Africa, which is closest to the ecological modernisation ideal of a state which has the capacity to implement some of the latest technological solutions to environmental problems. In pursuit of ambitious GHG reduction goals South Africa has developed an impressive renewable energy sector, funded through independent power producers. South Africa has the best-funded conservation sector on the continent, with the capacity to deploy extensive security measures to combat poaching, including drones, ranger units, satellite tracking, and dyes and poisons for rhino horn, and it has a substantial ecotourism sector reliant on green branding, socially responsible community partnerships, and extensive private ranches and reserves. Major public works programmes such as Working for Water employ millions in environmental services, and the Green Economy Accord hopes that one million climate jobs will emerge from targeted investment in environmental sectors. Most visibly, South Africa has used prominent moments like the Johannesburg World Summit on Sustainable Development of 2002, the Durban IUCN World Parks Congress in 2003, the Durban climate conference of 2011, and the FIFA World Cup in 2010 to promote an image of exemplary environmental leadership.

A final example, one exhibiting a very different set of green state effects, is Nigeria, which also has considerable capacity, financial muscle, and technological expertise. Certain projects there, such as the launching of two Earth observation satellites in 2011 and the bus-centered mass transit system implemented in Lagos in 2008, show the country's potential for environmental leadership. On the other hand, the scale of ecological devastation in the Niger Delta, one of the world's most severely petroleum-impacted ecosystems, and the inability of the federal state to deal satisfactorily with a long-running low-intensity civil war in the region, mark out Nigeria as an environmental laggard characterised by extreme pollution enclaves. This status is reflected in the Yale EPI, which ranks Nigeria at 134, and the HPI, which ranks Nigeria at 125.[6] More generally, explicitly green discourses and practices are far less prominent in Nigeria than in many of the other countries discussed in this book, meaning that while it is still possible to claim that the Nigerian state has been profoundly shaped by the governance and contestation of environmental issues—including oil extraction in the Delta, agriculture and land erosion in the North, the biopolitics of citizenship and belonging, and the international relations of environmental cooperation and transnational solidarity—Nigeria illustrates a form of the green state very different to Tanzania, Rwanda, Ethiopia, and South Africa.

These examples are not intended to be ideal types or to encompass the entire spectrum of green state effects in Africa. Botswana, Mozambique, Madagascar, Egypt, Sierra Leone, and each subsequent African state presents an alternative assemblage for the governance and contestation of land, populations, economies, and international relations. However, these examples do illustrate the ways in which the framework or analytical grid deployed in this book can illuminate African green state effects. Moreover, insofar as continental-scale generalisation is possible or desirable, I reiterate that Afro-ecologism can be summarized in terms of the prominence of land and conservation, the biopolitics of rural under- and overpopulation, muscular green growth and economic modernisation, and practices of African environmental solidarity.

States, in short, matter. The sorts of green state effects produced by forms of environmental governance and contestation also matter. In response to arguments that states are antiecological, authoritarian, capitalist, gendered, and racialised or simply that the political and economic significance of states in a globalising world is dwindling, I maintain that despite these truths, states retain considerable political and social legitimacy and capacity; they can be transformed and reformed by social forces to become less violent and unjust; and they represent one of the few plausible political responses to environmental degradation and unsustainable development pathways.[7] Such an argument, however, does not invalidate the need for the continual critique of statist politics and the biopolitical implications of green state effects.

BIOPOLITICS AND POSTCOLONIAL GOVERNMENTALITY

Some might conclude that building stronger green states in Africa is a necessary step on the road to a more ecologically sustainable and socially just world. This is certainly Eckersley's view, who writes, "A proliferation of transnationally oriented green states [is] likely to provide a surer path to a greener world."[8] I am more cautious and critical, however. Green states, understood from a postcolonial rather than a modernisation perspective, also entail a number of political risks and dangers. For example, one rather neglected element of this book has been the ways in which indigenous African knowledge, discourses, and practices have contributed to the governance and contestation of African environments. Many African cultures and languages are replete with cosmologies, ontologies, and epistemologies which could provide critical traction in contesting ecological degradation and injustice, as demonstrated in the work and philosophy of Maathai's Green Belt Movement. Jacklyn Cock observes a traditional "conservation ethic" among the Xhosa in South Africa that determines "which land could be cultivated; when to plant, plough and harvest; what water could be drunk; which trees could be cut; and which animals could be hunted."[9] Christian Lund notes the ecological and symbolic functions of the Earth priests in Ghana: they link the community to the original occupiers and perform rites to appease the gods and establish and sanctify the connection between the user and the land. In Zimbabwe, Terence Ranger suggests, ancestor spirits "cleansed the land from the stain of incest, made rain, and gave out ritually treated seed. The graves of dead senior ancestors were surrounded by sacred groves, which were never to be cut."[10] Encapsulating many of the relational ontologies associated with African indigenous cultures, the Malagasy word for environment, *tontolo iainana,* can be translated as "the world in which we live."[11] There are two reasons I have not engaged more extensively here with how such discourses and practices shape environmental governance. First, it would require more closely researched, fine-grained, local, linguistic, and cultural analysis than is possible in a book of this type. Second, alternative and subjugated knowledges are, almost by definition, less easily articulated through state assemblages and institutions. There is a codifying, universalising, rationalising character to the way states see and govern, and the marginalisation of alternative belief systems is one of the risks and dangers posed by a state-centric politics and mode of analysis.[12]

Identifying such risks and dangers is a crucial part of critique. Foucault's defence of a critical ethos is influential here. He was clear that nothing is evil in itself but everything is dangerous, and the "ethical political choice we have to make each day is to determine which is the main danger."[13] This is not a simplistic denunciation of the green state in Africa as being therefore bad and dangerous. My argument is *not* that "if the green state is not as good as the ecological modernisers suggest, then it must be bad." We must constantly attempt to subvert the binary of good versus evil. James Ferguson's intervention into the governmentality debates is useful in this regard, as he notes that "critical development studies" have often used "Foucauldian analysis to reveal the way that interventions, projects, etc., which claim to be merely technical or benevolent, really involve relations of power. . . . Power has been 'critiqued,' an oppressive system has been exposed as such, and that seems to be taken as a satisfactory end to the matter."[14] In contrast to such a limited form of critique, he urges us to follow Foucault in his (admittedly hesitant) calls for new arts of government and an "autonomous governmentality." To Ferguson, "If we are indeed to arrive at viable left 'arts of government,' we will need to be open to the unexpected, ready to 'increase the experiments wherever possible,' and attentive to the ways that governmental techniques originally deployed for nefarious purposes can be appropriated toward other ends."[15] Nothing is more in need of being rescued from its "nefarious purposes" than the state, and in this spirit the framework deployed in this book can be used to highlight some of the principal dangers and most encouraging possibilities in the construction of Africa's green states.

The state as a totality is not something we can either accept or reject, as Hansen and Stepputat point out, "for the simple reason that we cannot escape it."[16] A similar point is made by Andrew Vincent, for whom we are "State-creatures whose development, welfare and future cannot be divorced from the State. It is not something that we can shrug off."[17] Rather, following Foucault and an approach to states as assemblages and effects, we should focus on the dangers and possibilities of particular discourses, technologies, and governmental rationalities in specific fields. As an indication of the sorts of partial, contingent, and subjective normative assertions which this approach could enable, I end by making some suggestions about the sorts of forms of environmental governance which might turn out to be better than those we have at present. They are intended as stimulants to future thought and research, not as cardinal principles of a normative theory of the African green state.

The manner in which green states produce and are produced by different modes of environmental land-use and bordering highlights certain exclusive and exclusionary modes of territorialisation as well as some more hybrid, flexible, and ambiguous forms. Modes of governance which tend toward the former seem more dangerous and less likely to win popular consent. Coercive conservation has a long and troubled history in Africa, and despite its resurgence, along with the violence of so-called land grabs, it is more politically desirable to advocate hybrid, flexible, and ambiguous practices. These can easily be appropriated by neoliberal capitalism in the form of community-based conservation and the zoning of investment projects, but they can also be accomplished in ways more sensitive to local land use patterns and ecological contingencies. They also allow reversibility, adaptability, and flexibility, which lessen the risk that highly inequitable, unjust forms of land use will become entrenched.[18] The defining images of African environmental governance in this book are the road, which cuts swathes through protected areas

17. "Winter in Soweto, Central Western Jabavu," Santu Mofokeng (b. 1956). © Santu Mofokeng, c. 1985 silverprint edition 5. Images courtesy Lunetta Bartz, MAKER, Johannesburg.

of Africa's wilderness, and the periurban slum, which is wild but not wilderness. Both exemplify the hermaphrodite landscapes of contemporary Africa. These spaces are neither ungoverned nor conventional state territories. Instead, they are products of rhizome modes of state governance through which green land is shaped and represented in Africa. The green states of the future need to bring roads and slums as well as protected areas and agricultural land to the heart of debates over Africa's environmental governance.

Green states produce a variety of populations, and solution-subjects which include the educated, entrepreneurial farmer, the green consumer, and the environmental citizen. People and their bodies are often absent from programmatic and scientific accounts of African conservation and environmental politics, but as the example of Wangari Maathai and her tree-planting movement illustrates, real people play crucial roles as educators, tree planters, dissidents, politicians, villains, and heroes. Each of these subjectivities brings dangers and possibilities, and none of them can be described as either completely good or bad. Yet attempts to transform Africa's peasantry have a long, coercive, largely unsuccessful history, and staking the future of the green state on the production of green consumers is unrealistic and dangerous and unlikely to achieve genuine environmental and social transformation. Environmental citizenship schemes have many advantages, but they also run the risk of being articulated in ways that stress the dangers of foreign bodies and exacerbate the hostility and violence of xenophobic assertions of autochthony. Thus the production of environmental citizenship might rather be undertaken in ways which permit flexible forms of belonging, and amenability to practices of subversion and resistance. Here the environmental dissident—the activist, green politician, troublemaker—is a powerful figure. Green states which facilitate practices of environmental dissidence, or being otherwise, constitute some of the most attractive, powerful governing assemblages.[19]

Discourses of green transformation and revolution pose the biggest challenges to existing models of development and growth. The green growth narrative is currently dominant, but it threatens to worsen existing highly inequitable and ecologically damaging growth patterns and further discredit environmentalism in the process by legitimating big infrastructural projects like dams, mining, and commercial agriculture. Green resilience is certainly necessary in the face of impending climate chaos, and the concept has radical potential and a progressive genealogy, but as currently articulated it represents a conservative defence of the status quo. Revolutionary economic interventions seem highly unlikely in the terms environmental activists desire and propose, and examples of programmes such as Fast Track Land Reform in Zimbabwe highlight the perils and risks of such projects. In the absence of revolutionary economic change, quasi-Keynesian strategies of social, economic, and environmental transformation and significant public, state-led investment in and regulation of environmental goods, services, and markets seem to be among the most encouraging prospects for the construction of green developmental states. Again, simplistic distinctions between good and bad make little sense in distinguishing between these four green economy discourses, and all such evaluations must be context specific and contingent. The framework does provide, however, a set of questions and considerations that help in making these contextual evaluations in particular cases.

Intuitively it seems obvious that the more exemplary international environmental leaders there are, the better. Yet inspirational projects and demonstration initiatives are the inevitable corollary of the production and often of the obscuring of pollution enclaves and zones of environmental degradation. In this respect, efforts to build international and transnational solidarity between states and social movements and in the process disseminate successful interventions and support weaker states and partners have much to recommend them. While there are concomitant hazards in attempts to impose a consensus position, particularly when directed from Pretoria or Abuja, the African Renaissance vision of a positive African contribution to world politics based around dialogue and cooperation can work to counter many of the negative stereotypes of African politics. Transnational activist solidarity networks such as FoEI and antiextractivist mobilisations, or what Klein calls Blockadia, which can connect South Durban to the Niger Delta as well as to New York and to the west coast of Ireland, can both incorporate and reproduce green state effects in transgressive ways. A struggle to achieve green state effects and environmental justice could provide a powerful vision of a postcolonial, Pan-African political project in the twenty-first century and has the potential to go well beyond Africa to encompass greater South–South and North–South solidarity.

GREEN STATES IN THE GLOBAL SOUTH

In summation, therefore, my analysis of the production of green state effects in Africa has tended to suggest that while we should be sceptical about the claims of ecological modernisation theorists that the green state is the next stage of history, we should also marshal political resources and activism in

18. Tea pickers, Murang'a District, Kenya. Photo by David Blumenkrantz.

support of attempts to build green states through practices of hybrid territorialisations, the production of dissenting environmental citizens, discourses of radical green transformation, and relations of transnational critical environmental solidarity. A truly environmental politics implies not the end of the state but a state that is reshaped, refashioned, and transformed to enable better prospects for human and nonhuman flourishing, while acknowledging that our human capacity to ever know the consequences of our actions is limited.[20]

Foucault famously observed that "modern man is an animal whose politics places his existence as a living being in question."[21] This was true when Foucault was writing in the 1970s, and it is even truer in the twenty-first century as climate change becomes more evident and earth scientists proclaim we have entered the era of the Anthropocene. In light of that fact, the project of creating green states must necessarily go well beyond the contours of Africa. Indeed, much of the existing literature on green states focuses on how to green the industrialised states of the global North, societies which are responsible for many of the environmental challenges faced by Foucault's "modern man." Such research agendas as well as political campaigns are crucial and essential. But just as African states, hitherto neglected in debates over the green state, have a vital role to play, so developing states within the broader global South must be at the heart of green politics.[22] Developing states in Africa and Asia and Latin America as well as enclaves of poverty and injustice and unsustainability in the global North will be the crucial sites for the greening of politics in coming years. The framework proposed in this book, based on a postcolonial rather than a modernisation perspective of the state, is an appropriate one for the study of developing states well beyond Africa. Theorists like Eckersley have presented the green state in Europe and North America as "a democratic state whose regulatory ideals and democratic procedures are informed by *ecological* democracy rather than *liberal* democracy."[23] By contrast, the green state in the South should be seen as the effect of an assemblage of environmental rationalities, discourses, and technologies of government through which the governance and contestation of territories, populations, economies, and international relations have been brought within the scope of sedimented power relations. Such an approach enables the empirical study of environmental politics in a more genuinely global manner than has been possible to date. It also raises the distinct possibility that the states of the South may have more to teach the North than green state theorists have tended to assume.

Notes

INTRODUCTION

1. Iliffe, *Africans,* 1. The term "longue durée" is associated with the French Annales school of historians, including Fernand Braudel, Marc Bloch, and Lucien Febvre, and emphasises the continuity of structures of thought and society, where "the movement of history is slow and covers vast reaches of time." Braudel, *A History of Civilisations,* 34. See also Watts, *Silent Violence,* xx, 82–3.
2. Klein, *This Changes Everything.*
3. Dalby, "Biopolitics and Climate Security in the Anthropocene"; Houston, "Crisis Is Where We Live"; Leach, "What Is Green?" 32; Mitchell, *Carbon Democracy,* 260.
4. Kuehls, *Beyond Sovereign Territory;* Litfin, ed., *The Greening of Sovereignty in World Politics;* Scott, *Seeing Like a State;* Whitehead et al., *The Nature of the State.*
5. Bayart, *The State in Africa;* Cooper, *Africa since 1940;* Scott, *Seeing Like a State.*
6. Eckersley, *The Green State;* Meadowcroft, "From Welfare State to Ecostate." In contrast, see Death, "Green States in Africa."
7. Scoones et al., "The Politics of Green Transformations," 1. See also Swilling and Annecke, *Just Transitions.*
8. Death and Gabay, "Introduction," 1. See also Africa Progress Panel, *Grain, Fish, Money;* African Development Bank and WWF, *African Ecological Futures 2015,* 18; Dowden, *Africa;* Economist, "The Hopeful Continent"; Rotberg, *Africa Emerges.*
9. Bayart, "Africa in the World."
10. See table 1 in chapter 6; Benjamin, "South Africa Comes Last in Sustainable Development Index"; Maathai, *The Challenge for Africa,* chapter 12; UNEP, *Africa Environment Outlook 3,* 11. On COP21 see http://www.uneca.org/cop21/pages/why-cop21-important-africa (accessed 21 December 2015).

11. Cited in Africa Progress Panel, *Grain, Fish, Money,* 11. See also Iliffe, *Africans,* 1; Patel, "Africa."
12. See table 1 in chapter 6; Bassey, *To Cook a Continent;* UNISDR, "Climate threat to Africa's resilience"; Deressa, *Climate Change and Growth in Africa,* 29; Africa Progress Panel, *Grain, Fish, Money,* 16; African Development Bank and WWF, *African Ecological Futures 2015,* 18; Devereux, "Why Does Famine Persist in Africa?"; UNECA, *MDG Report 2013;* Death, "The Green Economy in South Africa"; Benjamin, "South Africa Comes Last in Sustainable Development Index"; UNEP, *Africa Environment Outlook 3,* 22; UNEP, *Environmental Assessment of Ogoniland;* BBC, "Rwandan Opposition Politician Found Dead"; Lakhani, "Surge in Deaths of Environmental Activists Over Past Decade, Report Finds."
13. The research is empirically informed, and the acknowledgments mention those whose conversations have shaped my understanding of African environmental politics. Although this book does use descriptive statistics in places, and the evidence presented goes well beyond the anecdotal, there is no quantitative analysis. This is partly because of the weaknesses of many African datasets but, more important, because the discourses and practices which drive states and other actors to collect data of certain kinds are often more interesting than the actual statistics themselves. See Jerven, "Measuring African Development"; Scott, *Seeing Like a State.*
14. Barry and Eckersley, eds., *The State and the Global Ecological Crisis;* Dryzek et al., *Green States and Social Movements;* Eckersley, *The Green State.* See also the special issue of *Environmental Politics* 25, no. 1 (2016), entitled "Greening Leviathan? The Emergence of the Environmental State," edited by Peter Feindt, James Meadowcroft, and Andreas Duit.
15. Death, "Green States in Africa"; Duit et al., "Greening Leviathan," 6; Vogler, "Green Statehood and Environmental Crisis," 106–7.
16. Foucault, *The Birth of Biopolitics,* 77.
17. Death, "Governmentality at the Limits of the International."
18. Brockington et al., *Nature Unbound,* 30.
19. Mamdani, *Citizen and Subject,* 31.
20. Barry and Eckersley, eds., *The State and the Global Ecological Crisis;* Dryzek et al., *Green States and Social Movements;* Eckersley, *The Green State.*
21. Space limits do not allow a systematic discussion of how the governance and contestation of water have also produced environmental (blue?) state effects in Africa. My argument is that land, populations, economies, and international relations are more fundamental to producing green state effects in Africa than the governance and contestation of water per se. However, examples of interesting riverine and marine cases and literature are cited throughout. On disputed claims about "hydraulic civilisations," see Whitehead et al., *The Nature of the State,* 57. For fascinating accounts of water politics in South Africa, see, among others, Hellberg, "Water, Life and Politics"; Loftus, "Rethinking Political Ecologies of Water"; Roberts, "Privatizing Social Reproduction."
22. Death and Gabay, "Introduction."

23. See my discussion of eco-hero-worship in Death, "Can We Save the Planet?" On the links between "celebritisation" and the masculinization of environmentalism, see MacGregor, "Only Resist," 622–23.
24. Tutu, "We Need an Apartheid-Style Boycott to Save the Planet."
25. Dryzek, "Resistance Is Fertile"; MacGregor, "Only Resist."

CHAPTER 1. GLOBAL ENVIRONMENTAL GOVERNANCE AND THE GREEN STATE

1. Cox, "Social Forces, States, and World Orders," 128.
2. Inayatullah, ed., *Autobiographical International Relations.* Some of the arguments here were rehearsed in an earlier form in Death, "Green States in Africa."
3. Keohane, "Analyzing the Effectiveness of International Environmental Institutions," 3.
4. Ibid., 5.
5. Sarkozy, Address at the University of Cheikh Anta Diop. See also Mbembe, "Nicholas Sarkozy's Africa."
6. Abrahamsen, "A Breeding Ground for Terrorists?"; Bachmann, "Governmentality and Counterterrorism"; Booth, *Governance for Development in Africa;* Edigheji, ed., *Constructing a Democratic Developmental State in South Africa;* UNDP, *Human Development Report 2013.*
7. Barry, *The Politics of Actually Existing Unsustainability;* Eckersley, *The Green State;* Newell and Paterson, *Climate Capitalism.*
8. Young, *The African Colonial State in Comparative Perspective,* 1–2.
9. Sarkozy, Address at the University of Cheikh Anta Diop.
10. Barry, *Rethinking Green Politics,* 77–78; Barry and Eckersley, "An Introduction to Reinstating the State," xi; Biermann and Dingwerth, "Global Environmental Change and the Nation State"; Hurrell, "The State," 170; Bryant and Bailey, *Third World Political Ecology,* 51–52; Mol and Buttel, "The Environmental State Under Pressure," 5.
11. Castree and Braun, "The Construction of Nature and the Nature of Construction"; Cronon, "The Trouble with Wilderness"; Whitehead et al., *The Nature of the State,* 28–33.
12. Brenton, *The Greening of Machiavelli,* 2–3; Rosenau, "Environmental Challenges in a Turbulent World," 76; Rudy and White, "Hybridity"; Whitehead et al., *The Nature of the State,* 1.
13. The World Commission on Environment and Development, *Our Common Future,* 27.
14. Smith, *Against Ecological Sovereignty,* 193.
15. Haas, "Addressing the Global Governance Deficit," 7; Young, *International Governance,* 2.
16. Barry, *Rethinking Green Politics,* 78; Dobson, *Green Political Thought,* 105–6; Kuehls, "States," 243; Whitehead et al., *The Nature of the State,* 28–33.
17. Beck, *Risk Society;* Linklater, *Critical Theory and World Politics,* 45–46.

18. Quoted in Eckersley, *The Green State,* 107.
19. Tilly, "War Making and State Making as Organized Crime," 169. See also Poggi, *The State,* 65–66; Shaw, *Theory of the Global State,* 190–91.
20. Cerny, *The Changing Architecture of Politics,* 35.
21. Bookchin, *Remaking Society.*
22. Escobar, *Encountering Development,* 193.
23. Conca, "Old States in New Bottles?," 181.
24. O'Riordan, "Reflections on the Pathways to Sustainability," 326. See also Luke, *Ecocritique,* 78; Scott, *Two Cheers for Anarchism;* Whitehead, "Cold Monsters and Ecological Leviathans," 423.
25. Cited in Barrow, "The Miliband–Poulantzas Debate," 10.
26. Cited in Vincent, *Theories of the State,* 169.
27. Barrow, "The Miliband–Poulantzas Debate"; Bryant and Bailey, *Third World Political Ecology;* Dalby, "Ecological Politics, Violence, and the Theme of Empire"; Falkner, "American Hegemony and the Global Environment"; Peet et al., eds., *Global Political Ecology;* Selwyn, *The Global Development Crisis,* 22–23; Skocpol, "Bringing the State Back In," 5; Wainwright and Mann, "Climate Leviathan."
28. O'Connor, "Capitalism, Nature, Socialism." See also Foster, "Capitalism and Ecology"; Luke, "The System of Sustainable Degradation," 99; Paterson, "Commodification," 56.
29. Paterson, "Globalisation, Ecology, and Resistance," 139.
30. Davidson, "The Insuperable Imperative," 48.
31. Eckersley, *The Green State,* 86–87; MacGregor, "Only Resist"; McClintock, *Imperial Leather;* Mies and Shiva, *Ecofeminism.*
32. Doyle and Doherty, "Green Public Spheres and the Green Governance State," 884.
33. Paterson, *Understanding Global Environmental Politics,* 62.
34. Clapp and Dauvergne, *Paths to a Green World;* Eckersley, *The Green State,* 65–69; Harvey, *A Brief History of Neoliberalism;* Wilson, *Jeffrey Sachs;* Wolf, "Will the Nation-State Survive Globalisation?"
35. Beck, *What Is Globalization?,* 1–2.
36. Strange, "The Defective State," 56–57.
37. Biermann and Dingwerth, "Global Environmental Change and the Nation State"; Evans, "The Eclipse of the State?"; Mann, "Has Globalization Ended the Rise and Rise of the Nation-State?"; Strange, *The Retreat of the State,* 1–2.
38. Falkner, "Private Environmental Governance and International Relations," 74; Litfin, *Ecovillages;* Mol, "The Environmental Nation State in Decline"; Mol and Buttel, "The Environmental State Under Pressure," 4; Rosenau, "Environmental Challenges in a Turbulent World."
39. Clark, *Globalization and International Relations Theory,* 54.
40. Adger and Jordan, "Sustainability," 10–11.
41. Baker, *Sustainable Development,* 53. See also Eckersley, *The Green State,* 66.
42. Berger, "States of Nature and the Nature of States," 1204.
43. Brenner et al., "Introduction," 3.

44. Barry, *Rethinking Green Politics,* 111; Sonnenfeld and Mol, "Ecological Modernisation, Governance and Globalization," 1457–58.
45. Newell and Paterson, *Climate Capitalism;* Wainwright and Mann, "Climate Leviathan."
46. Eckersley, *The Green State,* 7. See also Duit et al., "Greening Leviathan," 3.
47. Eckersley, "Moving Forward in the Climate Negotiations."
48. Eckersley, *The Green State,* 96.
49. Ibid., 112.
50. Eckersley, "The State as Gatekeeper," 134.
51. Barry, *The Politics of Actually Existing Unsustainability,* 259–60; Dobson, *Citizenship and the Environment;* Meadowcroft, "Greening the State?"
52. Newell and Paterson, *Climate Capitalism,* 144–51.
53. Ibid., 172–78. See also Klein, *This Changes Everything,* 458.
54. Cited in Poggi, *The State,* 78. See also Vincent, *Theories of the State,* 119.
55. Christoff, "Out of Chaos, a Shining Star?"; Meadowcroft, "From Welfare State to Ecostate"; Meadowcroft, "The Politics of Sustainable Development"; Paehlke and Torgerson, eds., *Managing Leviathan.* See also the special issue of *Environmental Politics* 25, no. 1 (2016) entitled "Greening Leviathan? The Emergence of the Environmental State", edited by Peter Feindt, James Meadowcroft, and Andreas Duit.
56. Weidner, "Capacity Building for Ecological Modernisation," 1344.
57. Dryzek et al., "The Environmental Transformation of the State," 679.
58. Ibid., 660. See also Dryzek et al., *Green States and Social Movements;* Hunold and Dryzek, "Green Political Theory and the State"; Hunold and Dryzek, "Green Political Strategy and the State."
59. Brenton, *The Greening of Machiavelli,* 8. See also Barnett, *The Meaning of Environmental Security;* Chasek, *Earth Negotiations,* 11; Dalby, *Security and Environmental Change.*
60. Young, "The Politics of International Regime Formation"; Young, *International Governance.* See also Haas et al., eds., *Institutions for the Earth;* Keohane, "Analyzing the Effectiveness of International Environmental Institutions."
61. Cited in Eckersley, *The Green State,* 213.
62. Weidner, "Capacity Building for Ecological Modernisation," 1341.
63. Keohane, "Analyzing the Effectiveness of International Environmental Institutions," 27. See also Mol, "The Environmental Nation State in Decline."
64. Mann, "The Autonomous Power of the State," 53.
65. Cerny, *The Changing Architecture of Politics;* Beck, *What Is Globalization?;* Robinson, "Social Theory and Globalisation"; Clark, *Globalization and International Relations Theory,* 7; Hobson and Ramesh, "Globalisation Makes of States What States Make of It," 10; Shaw, *Theory of the Global State;* Harrison, *The World Bank and Africa;* Hobson, *The State and International Relations.*
66. Buttel, "Ecological Modernization as Social Theory," 61; Eckersley, *The Green State,* 69–79.
67. Buttel, "Ecological Modernization as Social Theory," 58–59.

68. Ashford, "Government and Environmental Innovation in Europe and North America," 1419.
69. Warner, "Ecological Modernisation Theory," 547.
70. Mol and Sonnenfeld, "Ecological Modernisation around the World," 6.
71. Sonnenfeld and Mol, "Ecological Modernization, Governance and Globalization," 1457.
72. Eckersley, *The Green State,* 252–53. Eckersley clarifies in a subsequent article that her focus on the developed world is informed by principles of justice: "Developed states are primarily responsible for past carbon emissions, they have a larger per capita 'ecological footprint,' and they have greater wealth and institutional capacity." Thus developed states must "take the lead." See Eckersley, "The State as Gatekeeper," 136; Vogler, "Green Statehood and Environmental Crisis."
73. Barry and Eckersley, "W(h)ither the Green State?," 272.
74. Sonnenfeld and Mol, "Globalization and the Transformation of Environmental Governance," 1324.
75. Mol, "Ecological Modernization and the Global Economy," 110. Partial but dated exceptions include Conca, "Rethinking the Ecology–Sovereignty Debate"; Kuehls, *Beyond Sovereign Territory;* Langhelle, "Why Sustainable Development and Ecological Modernization Should Not Be Conflated," 309; Lipschutz and Conca, eds., *The State and Social Power in Global Environmental Politics;* Miller, "Sovereignty Reconfigured"; Weidner, "Capacity Building for Ecological Modernization."
76. Sarkozy, Address at the University of Cheikh Anta Diop.
77. Joseph, "The Limits of Governmentality," 237. See also Bayart, *The State in Africa;* Clapham, "Degrees of Statehood"; Grovogui, "Sovereignty in Africa"; Warner, "The Rise of the State System in Africa."
78. Ashford, "Government and Environmental Innovation in Europe and North America," 1420; Mol, "Ecological Modernization and the Global Economy," 110; Weidner, "Capacity Building for Ecological Modernization," 1352.
79. Evans, "The Eclipse of the State?," 63.
80. Mann, "Has Globalization Ended the Rise and Rise of the Nation-State?," 487.
81. Buttel, "Ecological Modernization as Social Theory"; Habermas, "New Social Movements"; Inglehart, "Post-Materialism in an Environment of Insecurity"; Meadowcroft, "Greening the State?"; Mol, "Ecological Modernization and the Global Economy."
82. Mol, "Ecological Modernization and the Global Economy," 107.
83. See table 1 in chapter 6.
84. Godfrey et al., *Africa Talks Climate,* 2.
85. Patey, "Crude Days Ahead?," 633.
86. African Development Bank and WWF, *African Ecological Futures 2015,* 21; Cornelissen et al., "Introduction," 5.
87. Mitchell, *Rule of Experts;* Scott, *Seeing Like a State*; Watts, *Silent Violence,* chapter 2.
88. Grove, *Green Imperialism.* See also Bassey, *To Cook a Continent,* chapter 8; Brockington et al., *Nature Unbound,* 21; Doyle, *Environmental Movement in Minority and Majority*

Worlds; MacKenzie, *The Empire of Nature;* Martinez-Alier, *Environmentalism of the Poor;* Peluso and Watts, eds., *Violent Environments.*

89. Doherty and Doyle, *Environmentalism, Resistance and Solidarity,* 25.
90. Sowers, *Environmental Politics in Egypt.*
91. See table 1 in chapter 6.
92. Zarsky, "Stuck in the Mud?," 83.

CHAPTER 2. POSTCOLONIAL THEORY AND THE GREEN STATE IN AFRICA

1. Evans et al., eds., *Bringing the State Back In;* Hobson, *The State and International Relations,* 4; Jessop, "Bringing the State Back In (Yet Again)"; Jessop, *State Theory,* 339; Mitchell, "The Limits of the State"; Vincent, *Theories of the State,* 3.
2. Weber, "Politics as a Vocation," 78.
3. Bull, *The Anarchical Society,* 8.
4. Dryzek et al., *Green States and Social Movements,* 1.
5. Jessop, "Bringing the State Back In (Yet Again)," 152; Vincent, *Theories of the State,* chapter 5; Whitehead et al., *The Nature of the State,* 40–3.
6. Cited in Jessop, *The Capitalist State,* 9. See the role of the state in the history of primitive accumulation as described in Marx, *Capital,* part 8.
7. Cited in Vincent, *Theories of the State,* 167–69.
8. Jessop, *The Capitalist State,* 16–17. See also Jessop, *State Theory,* chapter 8; Bruff, "The Relevance of Nicos Poulantzas for Contemporary Debates on 'The International'"; Bieler and Morton, "The Will-o'-the-Wisp of the Transnational State."
9. Jessop, *The Capitalist State,* 222.
10. Jessop, *State Theory,* 341.
11. Weber, "Politics as a Vocation," 82–84.
12. Mitchell, "The Limits of the State," 78.
13. Eschle, *Global Democracy, Social Movements, and Feminism;* Jessop, "Bringing the State Back In (Yet Again)," 160; Jessop, "Putting Neoliberalism in Its Time and Place," 70; Legg, "Assemblage/Apparatus"; McClintock, *Imperial Leather;* Mitchell, *Rule of Experts,* 300; Mitchell, "Rethinking Economy."
14. Waltz, *Theory of International Politics,* 113. See also Hobson, *The State and International Relations,* 9.
15. Jessop, *State Theory,* 15. On states and war, see Jessop, "Bringing the State Back In (Yet Again)," 154. On the relationship between IR and political sociology, see Bayart, *Global Subjects,* 9–10; Cox, "Social Forces, States, and World Orders," 126–27; Dean, *Governing Societies,* 27–35.
16. Armstrong, "The Evolution of International Society," 46. See also Buzan and Little, *International Systems in World History;* Tilly, *Coercion, Capital and European States, AD 990–1992,* 166–67. For alternative accounts of Westphalia and the emergence of international society, see Grovogui, "Sovereignty in Africa"; Hobson, "The Other Side of the Westphalian Frontier"; Keene, *Beyond the Anarchical Society;* Shilliam, "Non-Western Thought and International Relations."

17. Hirst and Thompson, "Globalization and the Future of the Nation State," 410.
18. Bull, *The Anarchical Society,* 9.
19. Kuehls, *Beyond Sovereign Territory,* 72. See also Whitehead, "Cold Monsters and Ecological Leviathans," 425.
20. Jessop, *The Future of the Capitalist State,* 247.
21. Abrahamsen and Williams, *Security Beyond the State,* 89.
22. Beck, *What Is Globalization?,* 14, 110.
23. Shilliam, "Non-Western Thought and International Relations," 4. See also Bayart, *Global Subjects,* 14–23; Hobson, "The Other Side of the Westphalian Frontier."
24. Comaroff and Comaroff, *Theory from the South;* Grovogui, "Sovereignty in Africa"; Keene, *Beyond the Anarchical Society.*
25. Bayart, *The State in Africa,* 263.
26. Herbst, *States and Power in Africa.*
27. Cooper, *Africa since 1940,* 5, 156.
28. Clapham, "Discerning the New Africa," 269.
29. Clapham, "Degrees of Statehood," 156. See also Migdal, *Strong Societies and Weak States,* xvi.
30. Hyden, *Beyond Ujamaa in Tanzania;* Jensen, "Shosholoza"; Mamdani, *Citizen and Subject;* Mbembe, "At the Edge of the World"; Migdal, *Strong Societies and Weak States,* 33–39; Munro, "Power, Peasants and Political Development."
31. Bayart, *The State in Africa,* 74–79; Chabal and Daloz, *Africa Works;* Clapham, *Africa and the International System,* 15; Ezrow and Frantz, "Revisiting the Concept of the Failed State," 1324; Jackson, *Quasi-States;* Lemay-Hébert and Mathieu, "The OECD's Discourse on Fragile States," 235–36.
32. Dunn, "Madlib #32"; Grovogui, "Sovereignty in Africa"; Hyden, *African Politics in Comparative Perspective,* chapter 3; Whitehead, "Cold Monsters and Ecological Leviathans," 423.
33. Fisher, "When It Pays to Be a 'Fragile State,'" 317.
34. Bayart, "Africa in the World," 218. See also Bilgin and Morton, "Historicizing Representations of 'Failed States'"; Grimm et al., "'Fragile States,'" 202.
35. Hagmann and Péclard, "Negotiating Statehood," 542.
36. Abrahamsen and Williams, *Security Beyond the State,* 87.
37. Bayart, *The State in Africa,* 210. For a few entry points into the huge literature on class in Africa, see Bernstein, "Commercial Agriculture in South Africa since 1994"; Harrison, *Neoliberal Africa;* McMichael, "Peasants Make Their Own History, But Not Just as They Please . . ."; Seddon and Zeilig, "Class and Protest in Africa"; Sklar, "The Nature of Class Domination in Africa."
38. Neumann, *Imposing Wilderness,* 97. See also Cooper, *Africa since 1940,* 5; Mamdani, *Citizen and Subject;* Watts, *Silent Violence,* chapter 4.
39. Bayart, "Africa in the World," 264.
40. Mbembe, *On the Postcolony,* 102. See also Comaroff and Comaroff, *Theory from the South.*
41. Ahluwalia, *Politics and Post-Colonial Theory;* Davis, *Late Victorian Holocausts;* Jensen, "Shosholoza"; Krishna, *Globalization and Postcolonialism;* Harrison, "Economic

Faith, Social Project and a Misreading of African Society"; Young, "'A Project to Be Realised.'"

42. Clapham, *Africa and the International System,* 20. See also Brown, "Sovereignty Matters"; Jackson and Rosberg, "Why Africa's Weak States Persist."
43. Ayoob, "The Third World in the System of States," 70.
44. Bayart, *The State in Africa,* xliv.
45. Dunn, "Madlib #32," 49. See also Brown, "Africa and International Relations"; Death, "Governmentality at the Limits of the International."
46. Bayart, *The State in Africa,* xxviii.
47. Ibid., xxix.
48. Ibid., 220. For an explicitly "arboreal" approach to the state, see Krasner, "Approaches to the State," 240. For a critique of such approaches, see Deleuze and Guattari, *A Thousand Plateaus.*
49. Mbembe, "Provisional Notes on the Postcolony," 3–4.
50. Foucault, *Security, Territory, Population,* 277. See also Dean, *Governmentality,* 23–24; Jones, "State Encounters."
51. Mitchell, "The Limits of the State," 95. See also Barry, *Political Machines,* 5; Comaroff, "Reflections on the Colonial State, in South Africa and Elsewhere"; Ferguson and Gupta, "Spatializing States"; Legg, "Assemblage/Apparatus"; Watts, "Development and Governmentality."
52. Jessop, *State Theory,* 233.
53. Ibid., 360.
54. Hansen and Stepputat, "Introduction," 14, 37.
55. Foucault, *Power/Knowledge,* 121.
56. Foucault, *The Birth of Biopolitics,* 76–77.
57. Jessop, "From Micro-Powers to Governmentality," 36; Jessop, *State Theory,* 342.
58. Death, "Governmentality at the Limits of the International," 764. See also Barnett, "The Consolations of 'Neoliberalism'"; Dean, *Governmentality,* 131; Jessop, "Putting Neoliberalism in Its Time and Place"; Okereke et al., "Conceptualising Climate Governance beyond the International Regime"; Neumann and Sending, *Governing the Global Polity;* Zanotti, "Governmentality, Ontology, Methodology," 289.
59. Dean, *Governing Societies,* 201. See also Dean, *Governmentality,* 9; Dunn, "Contested State Spaces"; Ferguson, "Toward a Left Art of Government"; Foucault, *The Will to Knowledge,* 95.
60. Foucault, *The Birth of Biopolitics,* 77. See also Foucault, *Security, Territory, Population,* 109.
61. Foucault, *The Birth of Biopolitics,* 6.
62. Ibid., 116, 270.
63. Foucault, *Security, Territory, Population,* 1.
64. Dean, *Governmentality,* 98–99. See also Nadesan, *Governmentality, Biopower and Everyday Life.*
65. Foucault, *Society Must Be Defended,* 242–47; Meadowcroft, "Greening the State?," 64; Scott, *Seeing Like a State.*

66. Mol and Buttel, "The Environmental State Under Pressure," 6. See also Iliffe, *Africans;* McCann, *Green Land, Brown Land, Black Land;* Watts, *Silent Violence.*
67. Dean, *Governmentality,* 98–99. See also Cavanagh, "Biopolitics, Environmental Change, and Development Studies."
68. Bryant and Bailey, *Third World Political Ecology,* 52. See also Peluso and Vandergeest, "Political Ecologies of War and Forests."
69. Nadesan, *Governmentality, Biopower and Everyday Life,* 1.
70. Mitchell, *Colonising Egypt,* 35. See also Foucault, *Security, Territory, Population,* 11–15; Gruffydd Jones, "Civilising African Cities"; Scott, *Seeing Like a State.*
71. Mitchell, *Colonising Egypt,* 67.
72. Barry, *The Politics of Actually Existing Unsustainability,* 79.
73. Mitchell, *Rule of Experts,* 9.
74. Ibid., 86; Mitchell, *Colonising Egypt,* 175.
75. Dryzek et al., *Green States and Social Movements.* See also Eckersley, *The Green State,* xi; Meadowcroft, "From Welfare State to Ecostate," 4.
76. Sowers, *Environmental Politics in Egypt;* Whitehead et al., *The Nature of the State,* 57.
77. Beinart, *The Rise of Conservation in South Africa,* xv.
78. Ibid., 20. See also Anderson, "Depression, Dust Bowl, Demography, and Drought"; Bonneuil, "Development as Experience"; Grove, *Green Imperialism.*
79. Ntsebeza, *Democracy Compromised.*
80. Beinart, *The Rise of Conservation in South Africa,* 380.
81. Beinart and Coates, *Environment and History,* 77.
82. Ibid., 90. See also Carruthers, *The Kruger National Park;* Carruthers, "Tracking in Game Trails"; Cock, *The War Against Ourselves;* Dunn, "Contested State Spaces"; MacKenzie, *The Empire of Nature.*
83. Bull, *The Anarchical Society,* 8.
84. Kuehls, "States," 240.
85. Agnew and Corbridge, *Mastering Space,* 79–84. See also Brenner and Elden, "Henri Lefebvre on State, Space, Territory"; Engel and Olsen, "Authority, Sovereignty and Africa's Changing Regimes of Territorialization"; Moisio and Paasi, "Beyond State-Centricity"; Peluso and Vandergeest, "Political Ecologies of War and Forests"; Sassen, "When Territory Deborders Territoriality."
86. See Bruff, "The Relevance of Nicos Poulantzas for Contemporary Debates on 'The International,'" 180.
87. Elden, "How Should We Do the History of Territory?," 14; Peluso and Lund, "New Frontiers of Land Control," 673.
88. Bull, *The Anarchical Society,* 8.
89. Kuehls, "States," 240.
90. Jessop, *State Theory,* 361.
91. Dean, *Governmentality,* 12. See also Comaroff and Comaroff, *Theory from the South,* 20–21; Legg, "Foucault's Population Geographies."
92. Mitchell, *Rule of Experts,* 3–4.
93. Mitchell, "Rethinking Economy," 1116–17.
94. Ibid., 1119.

95. Scott, *Seeing Like a State,* 2.
96. Sharma and Gupta, "Introduction," 7.
97. Mitchell, "The Limits of the State," 94.
98. Larner and Walters, "The Political Rationality of 'New Regionalism,'" 392.
99. Epstein, *The Power of Words in International Relations,* 254.
100. Schroeder, "Geographies of Environmental Intervention in Africa."
101. Tilly, "War Making and State Making as Organized Crime," 170. See also Chaturvedi and Doyle, *Climate Terror*; Comaroff and Comaroff, *Theory from the South*; Marx, *Capital,* 940.
102. Cited in Poggi, *The State,* 78.
103. Bruff, "The Rise of Authoritarian Neoliberalism," 125–27.
104. Chandler, *Empire in Denial;* Chaturvedi and Doyle, *Climate Terror;* Gabay and Death, ed., *Critical Perspectives on African Politics.*

CHAPTER 3. GREEN LAND AND STATE TERRITORY

1. Royal Society for the Protection of Birds, "Serengeti Highway."
2. Revkin, "East African Court Blocks Paved Serengeti Highway."
3. Serengeti Watch, "Court Decision Bars Paved Road Across Serengeti." See also Dobson et al., "Road Will Ruin Serengeti"; Homewood et al., "Alternative View of Serengeti Road"; Neumann, *Imposing Wilderness.*
4. Shivji, "Serengeti Shall Not Kill!," 244.
5. UNEP, *Africa Environment Outlook 3,* 11; World Bank, "Terrestrial Protected Areas (Percent of Total Land Area)."
6. Anderson and Grove, "Introduction"; Barrett, "Markets of Exceptionalism"; Berry, *No Condition Is Permanent;* Brockington, *Fortress Conservation,* 5–6; Brockington et al., *Nature Unbound;* Cronon, "The Trouble with Wilderness"; Evers, "Lex Loci Meets Lex Fori"; McCann, *Green Land, Brown Land, Black Land;* Neumann, *Imposing Wilderness;* Watts, *Silent Violence.*
7. Serengeti Watch, "Court Decision Bars Paved Road Across Serengeti."
8. Barry, *Political Machines;* Klaeger, "The Perils and Possibilities of African Roads"; Lee, "Death in Slow Motion"; Manji, "Bulldozers, Homes and Highways"; Paterson, "Car Culture and Global Environmental Politics."
9. Weber, "Politics as a Vocation," 78.
10. Agnew and Corbridge, *Mastering Space,* 80.
11. Kuehls, "States," 240; Smith, *Uneven Development,* chapter 3; Whitehead et al., *The Nature of the State,* chapter 4.
12. Elden, "How Should We Do the History of Territory?," 6.
13. Brenner and Elden, "Henri Lefebvre on State, Space, Territory," 358.
14. Black, *Maps and Politics,* 130–31. See also Iliffe, *Africans*; Warner, "The Rise of the State System in Africa."
15. Cited in Vivan, "Geography, Literature, and the African Territory," 51.
16. Kaplan and Schroeder, "Africa's New Map." See also Bayart, *The State in Africa,* 3; Mbembe, *On the Postcolony.*

17. Hughes, "Cadastral Politics," 744.
18. Warner, "The Rise of the State System in Africa"; Young, "The African Colonial State and Its Political Legacy."
19. Vaughan-Williams, "Borders, Territory, Law," 325.
20. Nelson, "Introduction," 3.
21. Anderson, "'Yours in Struggle for Majimbo'"; Chinigò, "The Politics of Land Registration in Ethiopia"; Fanon, *The Wretched of the Earth;* Mamdani, *Citizen and Subject.*
22. For example, the absence of reflection on conservation or on land and territory in the work of Dryzek and his colleagues is notable. E.g., Dryzek et al., *Green States and Social Movements.* In contrast, consider Kuehls, *Beyond Sovereign Territory*; Maathai, *The Challenge for Africa.*
23. Dryzek et al., *Green States and Social Movements,* 164.
24. See Karkkainen, "Post-Sovereign Environmental Governance"; Sassen, "Territory and Territoriality in the Global Economy"; Strange, *The Retreat of the State.*
25. Strange, "The Defective State," 55, 63.
26. Beck, *What Is Globalization?,* 209.
27. Beinart and Coates, *Environment and History,* 72.
28. Mitchell, "The Limits of the State," 94.
29. Dunn, "Contested State Spaces." See also Barrett, "Markets of Exceptionalism"; Mbembe, "At the Edge of the World," 58; Moisio and Paasi, "Beyond State-Centricity."
30. Dorling and Fairbairn, *Mapping,* 89; Engel and Olsen, "Authority, Sovereignty and Africa's Changing Regimes of Territorialization," 64; Ferguson, "Seeing Like an Oil Company"; Meagher, "A Back Door to Globalisation?"; Ramutsindela, "The Changing Meanings of South Africa's Internal Boundaries"; Ramutsindela, *Transfrontier Conservation in Africa,* 48; Tosa, "Anarchical Governance."
31. Kuehls, "The Environment of Sovereignty"; Kuehls, "States," 244.
32. Boone, *Property and Political Order in Africa;* Shipton, *Mortgaging the Ancestors.*
33. IUCN, "Protected Areas Categories System." See also Brockington et al., *Nature Unbound,* 21–23.
34. Schroeder, "Geographies of Environmental Intervention in Africa," 364.
35. Corson, "Territorialization, Enclosure and Neoliberalism"; Evers, "Lex Loci Meets Lex Fori," 136; Sheridan, "The Environmental and Social History of African Sacred Groves"; Shipton, *Mortgaging the Ancestors.*
36. Lund, "The Past and Space," 14.
37. Mitchell, *Rule of Experts,* 74.
38. Lund and Boone, "Introduction," 3. See also Boone, *Property and Political Order in Africa.*
39. Black, *Maps and Politics,* 138; Scott, *Seeing Like a State;* Mitchell, *Rule of Experts,* 9; Whitehead et al., *The Nature of the State,* chapter 4.
40. Africa Progress Panel, *Grain, Fish, Money,* 74. See also Boone, *Property and Political Order in Africa;* Chinigò, "The Politics of Land Registration in Ethiopia"; Evers, "Lex Loci Meets Lex Fori"; Manji, *The Politics of Land Reform in Africa.*

41. Harley, "Cartography, Ethics and Social Theory," 5.
42. Brockington et al., *Nature Unbound,* 28.
43. Schroeder, "Geographies of Environmental Intervention in Africa."
44. Adams and Hutton, "People, Parks and Poverty"; Brockington, *Fortress Conservation;* Brockington et al., *Nature Unbound;* Jones, "A Political Ecology of Wildlife Conservation in Africa"; Neumann, *Imposing Wilderness;* Spierenburg and Wels, " 'Securing Space,' " 297.
45. Cloete, "Going to the Bush," 46; Cronon, "The Trouble with Wilderness"; Draper, "Zen and the Art of Garden Province Maintenance"; Grove, *Green Imperialism;* MacKenzie, *The Empire of Nature.*
46. Neumann, *Imposing Wilderness,* 128–29.
47. United Republic of Tanzania, *State of the Environment Report 2006,* 53–55; Benjaminsen et al., "Wildlife Management in Tanzania," 1088; Brockington, "The Politics and Ethnography of Environmentalism in Tanzania," 102; Neumann, *Imposing Wilderness,* 138.
48. Brooks, "Re-Reading the Hluhluwe–Umfolozi Game Reserve," 76. See also Brooks, "Images of 'Wild Africa' "; Draper, "Zen and the Art of Garden Province Maintenance."
49. Brooks, "Re-Reading the Hluhluwe–Umfolozi Game Reserve," 75.
50. Ibid.
51. Brooks, "Images of 'Wild Africa,' " 232.
52. Beinart and Coates, *Environment and History,* 77; Bunn, "An Unnatural State"; Carruthers, *The Kruger National Park;* Cock, *The War Against Ourselves,* 151; MacKenzie, *The Empire of Nature,* 266–77.
53. Kings, "Rhino Deaths Reach Tipping Point"; Welz, "The War on African Poaching." See also Duffy, "Waging a War to Save Biodiversity."
54. Peace Parks Foundation, "Combatting Wildlife Crime," 6. See also Beinart, *The Rise of Conservation in South Africa,* chapter 6; Spierenburg and Wels, " 'Securing Space.' "
55. Peluso, "Coercing Conservation," 46. See also Nelson and Agrawal, "Patronage or Participation?," 573.
56. Henk, *The Botswana Defense Force in the Struggle for an African Environment.*
57. Peace Parks Foundation, "Combatting Wildlife Crime," 6. See also Büscher and Ramutsindela, "Green Violence."
58. Dunn, "Contested State Spaces," 40; Neumann, *Imposing Wilderness,* 97; Peluso and Vandergeest, "Political Ecologies of War and Forests."
59. Ellis, "Of Elephants and Men." See also Draper, "Zen and the Art of Garden Province Maintenance," 821; Spierenburg and Wels, " 'Securing Space,' " 296.
60. Brockington et al., *Nature Unbound,* 3. See also Brenner, "Beyond State-Centrism?"; Harvey, *A Brief History of Neoliberalism.*
61. Adams and Hutton, "People, Parks and Poverty"; Büscher and Dietz, "Conjunctions of Governance"; Büscher and Ramutsindela, "Green Violence"; Duffy, "Waging a War to Save Biodiversity."
62. Amanor and Moyo, eds., *Land and Sustainable Development in Africa;* Carmody, *The New Scramble for Africa;* Manji, *The Politics of Land Reform in Africa;* Margulis et al.,

"Land Grabbing and Global Governance"; McMichael, "Land Grabbing as Security Mercantilism in International Relations."

63. Bonneuil, "Development as Experience," 271; Mitchell, *Colonising Egypt;* Scott, *Seeing Like a State.*
64. De Wet, *Moving Together, Drifting Apart,* 27–28.
65. Ibid., 29.
66. Scoones, "Range Management Science and Policy," 45.
67. Anderson, "Depression, Dust Bowl, Demography, and Drought"; Beinart, *The Rise of Conservation in South Africa;* Hebinck et al., "Land and Agrarian Reform in South Africa's Eastern Cape Province"; McCann, *Green Land, Brown Land, Black Land;* Ntsebeza, *Democracy Compromised.*
68. Dunn, "Contested State Spaces," 439. See also Blaikie, "Is Small Really Beautiful?," 1948; Cheru, "The Silent Revolution and the Weapons of the Weak."
69. Haynes, "Power, Politics and Environmental Movements in the Third World," 237–38. See also Le Billion, *Wars of Plunder,* 77–80.
70. Patey, "Crude Days Ahead?"; Verhoeven, "Climate Change, Conflict and Development in Sudan."
71. Benjaminsen et al., "Wildlife Management in Tanzania," 1102; Manji and Ekine, eds., *African Awakening;* Mngxitama, "The Taming of Land Resistance"; Ntsebeza and Hall, eds., *The Land Question in South Africa;* Scoones et al., "The New Politics of Zimbabwe's Lowveld."
72. Alexander and McGregor, "Wildlife and Politics," 609.
73. Conca, "Old States in New Bottles?" 202. See also Death, "Environmental Mainstreaming and Post-Sovereign Governance in Tanzania."
74. Death, *Governing Sustainable Development;* Nelson, "Introduction"; Ribot and Larson, eds., *Democratic Decentralisation through a Natural Resource Lens.*
75. Blaikie, "Is Small Really Beautiful?"; Nelson and Agrawal, "Patronage or Participation?"; Schafer and Bell, "The State and Community-Based Natural Resource Management"; Swatuk, "From Project to Context."
76. Alexander and McGregor, "Wildlife and Politics," 605–606.
77. Moyo and Matondi, "Interrogating Sustainable Development and Resource Control in Zimbabwe," 66. See also Brockington et al., *Nature Unbound,* 95–98; Duffy, *Killing for Conservation;* Dzingirai, "The New Scramble for the African Countryside"; Hill, "Zimbabwe's Wildlife Utilization Programs," 108; Keeley and Scoones, *Understanding Environmental Policy Processes,* chapter 6.
78. Alexander and McGregor, "Wildlife and Politics," 607.
79. Cited in Nelson and Agrawal, "Patronage or Participation?," 561.
80. Benjaminsen et al., "Wildlife Management in Tanzania," 1089. See also Nelson et al., "The Evolution and Reform of Tanzanian Wildlife Management."
81. De Villiers, *Land Claims and National Parks,* 60. See also Brockington et al., *Nature Unbound,* 105–6; Cock, *The War Against Ourselves,* 153; Robins and van der Waal, "'Model Tribes' and Iconic Conservationists?"
82. Robins and van der Waal, "'Model Tribes' and Iconic Conservationists?" 170–71.

83. Chapin, "A Challenge to Conservationists," 25. See also Levine, "Convergence or Convenience?," 1047; Nelson, *Emergent or Illusory?,* 18; Nelson and Agrawal, "Patronage or Participation?," 577.
84. Seagle, "Discourse, Development and Legitimacy," 211.
85. Corson, "Territorialization, Enclosure and Neoliberalism," 703–4; Duffy, "Non-Governmental Organisations and Governance States," 737; Vinciguerra, "How the Daewoo Attempted Land Acquisition Contributed to Madagascar's Political Crisis in 2009."
86. Blaikie, "Is Small Really Beautiful?," 1943; Mamdani, *Citizen and Subject;* Ntsebeza, *Democracy Compromised.*
87. Ali, ed., *Peace Parks;* Barrett, "Markets of Exceptionalism"; Büscher, *Transforming the Frontier,* 42–48; Duffy, "The Potential and Pitfalls of Global Environmental Governance"; Ramutsindela, *Transfrontier Conservation in Africa;* Spierenburg and Wels, " 'Securing Space,' " 297; van Amerom and Büscher, "Peace Parks in Southern Africa."
88. Büscher, "Seeking 'Telos' in the 'Transfrontier'?"
89. Peace Parks Foundation, "Great Limpopo Transfrontier Park." See also Wolmer, "Transboundary Conservation."
90. Ramutsindela, *Transfrontier Conservation in Africa,* 76.
91. Duffy, "The Potential and Pitfalls of Global Environmental Governance," 106–7; van Amerom and Büscher, "Peace Parks in Southern Africa," 173–74.
92. Peace Parks Foundation, "Kavango Zambezi." See also African Development Bank and WWF, *Africa Ecological Footprint Report,* 44; Barrett, "Markets of Exceptionalism," 461–63.
93. Adams and Hutton, "People, Parks and Poverty." See also Ramutsindela, *Transfrontier Conservation in Africa,* chapter 7.
94. Duffy, "The Environmental Challenge to the Nation-State," 441.
95. Pinnock, "Southern African Elephant Corridors Blocked by Poachers."
96. Cloete, "Africa's 'Charismatic Megafauna' and Berlin's 'Two Concepts of Liberty,' " 271.
97. Büscher, "Derivative Nature."
98. Peace Parks Foundation, "Information Systems and GIS," 7. See also Barrett, "Markets of Exceptionalism," 468–69; Spierenburg and Wels, " 'Securing Space,' " 301.
99. Spierenburg and Wels, " 'Securing Space,' " 305. See also Moyo and Matondi, "Interrogating Sustainable Development and Resource Control in Zimbabwe," 71.
100. Duffy, "The Environmental Challenge to the Nation-State," 451.
101. Mbembe, "At the Edge of the World," 76.
102. Ramutsindela, "Glocalisation and Nature Conservation Strategies in 21st-Century Southern Africa," 64.
103. Ramutsindela, "The Changing Meanings of South Africa's Internal Boundaries"; Ramutsindela, *Transfrontier Conservation in Africa,* 48.
104. Swatuk, "From Project to Context," 116.

105. van Amerom and Büscher, "Peace Parks in Southern Africa," 167.
106. Karkkainen, "Post-Sovereign Environmental Governance."
107. Duffy, "The Potential and Pitfalls of Global Environmental Governance," 101.
108. Büscher and Dietz, "Conjunctions of Governance," 11.
109. Clapp, *Food,* 148. See also Borras Jr. et al., "Towards a Better Understanding of Global Land Grabbing"; Carmody, *The New Scramble for Africa;* Wolford et al., "Governing Global Land Deals."
110. Amanor, "Introduction," 13. See also McMichael, "Land Grabbing as Security Mercantilism in International Relations," 60; Mittal, *Lives on Hold.*
111. Southern Agricultural Growth Corridor of Tanzania. See also Africa Progress Panel, *Grain, Fish, Money,* 64; African Development Bank and WWF, *African Ecological Futures 2015,* 24, 66; Jenkins, *Mobilizing the Southern Agricultural Growth Corridor of Tanzania;* Paul and Steinbrecher, "African Agricultural Growth Corridors and the New Alliance for Food Security and Nutrition."
112. Bonneuil, "Development as Experience"; Leach et al., "Green Grabs and Biochar."
113. Bachram, "Climate Fraud and Carbon Colonialism"; Büscher and Fletcher, "Accumulation by Conservation"; Gomera et al., "A Changing Climate for Community Resource Governance"; Leach et al., "Green Grabs and Biochar"; Nel and Hill, "Constructing Walls of Carbon"; Newell and Paterson, *Climate Capitalism,* 132–33.
114. McMichael, "Land Grabbing as Security Mercantilism in International Relations," 58; Sassen, "Land Grabs Today."
115. Aliber and Cousins, "Livelihoods after Land Reform in South Africa," 140. See also Chinigò, "The Politics of Land Registration in Ethiopia."
116. Fraser, "Hybridity Emergent," 300; Kepe, "Globalization, Science, and the Making of an Environmental Discourse on the Wild Coast, South Africa."
117. Department of Rural Development and Land Reform, *Policy for the Integration of Environmental Planning into Land Reform and Rural Development Projects,* 4.
118. Phuhlisani Solutions, *Final Report,* 37.
119. Ibid., 28.
120. Ibid., 58.
121. Mbembe, "At the Edge of the World," 77.
122. James, "Citizenship and Land in South Africa," 27–28. See also Fletcher, "Neoliberal Environmentality."
123. Nelson, "Democratizing Natural Resource Governance," 310.
124. Davis, *Planet of Slums,* 9.
125. Toulmin, *Climate Change in Africa,* 88.
126. Pieterse, "Grasping the Unknowable," 20.
127. Chatterjee, *The Politics of the Governed;* Di Muzio, "Governing Global Slums"; Gruffydd Jones, "Civilising African Cities"; Hetherington, *The Badlands of Modernity;* Johnson, "Unravelling Foucault's 'Different Spaces'"; Lindell and Ihalainen, "The Politics of Confinement and Mobility"; Manji, "Bulldozers, Homes and Highways"; Mathiane, "Blighted Environment"; Sassen, "When Territory Deborders Territoriality"; Scott, *Seeing Like a State,* 261.

128. Lund and Boone, "Introduction," 10.
129. Strange, *The Retreat of the State,* 2.

CHAPTER 4. GREEN CITIZENS AND PROBLEMATIC POPULATIONS

1. Nobel Prize, "Wangari Maathai—The Facts." See also Maathai, *The Challenge for Africa,* 257–58; Patel, "Africa," 8.
2. Maathai, *Unbowed,* 45–46, 121.
3. Ibid., 125.
4. Ibid.
5. Ibid., 135.
6. Ibid., 137. See also Maathai, *The Challenge for Africa.*
7. The Green Belt Movement, "See Where We Work."
8. Nixon, "Slow Violence, Gender, and the Environmentalism of the Poor," 260. See also Maathai, *Unbowed,* 159.
9. Comaroff, "Reflections on the Colonial State, in South Africa and Elsewhere," 328–29. See also Agrawal, *Environmentality;* Arora-Jonsson, "Virtue and Vulnerability"; Cronon, "The Trouble with Wilderness"; Dean, *Governmentality,* 12; Iliffe, *Africans,* 9; Legg, "Foucault's Population Geographies"; Scott, *Seeing Like a State.* Chapter 1 in Maathai, *The Challenge for Africa,* is entitled "The Farmer of Yaoundé."
10. Schmitt, *The Concept of the Political;* Césaire, cited in Fanon, *The Wretched of the Earth,* 138.
11. Foucault, *Security, Territory, Population,* 1.
12. Nixon, "Slow Violence, Gender, and the Environmentalism of the Poor," 264.
13. Critchley, *More People, More Trees,* 10.
14. TIST, "Planting Trees and Improving Agriculture for Better Lives." See also Kröger, "The Political Economy of Global Tree Plantation Expansion"; Maniates, "Individualization"; Peluso and Vandergeest, "Political Ecologies of War and Forests."
15. Cited in Highfield, "No Longer Praying on Borrowed Wine," 149.
16. Bunn, "An Unnatural State," 204.
17. Foucault, *The Will to Knowledge,* 143. See also Biermann and Mansfield, "Biodiversity, Purity, and Death"; Cavanagh, "Biopolitics, Environmental Change, and Development Studies."
18. Cited in Keen, *Complex Emergencies,* 100. See also Africa Progress Panel, *Grain, Fish, Money,* 31; AllAfrica, "Africa"; Population Reference Bureau, "2013 World Population Data Sheet"; Coole, "Too Many Bodies?"; Hartmann, "Converging on Disaster"; Rotberg, *Africa Emerges,* chapter 2.
19. Neville, *South Africa Talks Climate,* 21.
20. African Development Bank and WWF, *Africa Ecological Footprint Report,* 6, 34–35.
21. Mitchell, *Rule of Experts,* 209.
22. Diamond, *Collapse,* 22. Chapter 10 is entitled "Malthus in Africa: Rwanda's Genocide," but it (eventually) provides a much more nuanced and balanced account of the genocide and its various causal factors than these headings suggest. See also Paarlberg, "Politics and Food Insecurity in Africa," 505.

23. Boserup, "Environment, Population, and Technology in Primitive Societies."
24. Iliffe, *A Modern History of Tanganyika,* 4.
25. World Bank, "Population Density (People per sq. km of Land Area)."
26. Diamond, *Collapse,* 328. Better accounts and explanations of the genocide are available: see Hintjens, "Explaining the 1994 Genocide in Rwanda"; Mamdani, *When Victims Become Killers;* Prunier, *The Rwanda Crisis.*
27. Critchley, *More People, More Trees;* Tiffen et al., *More People, Less Erosion.* See also Ford, "The Population–Environment Nexus and Vulnerability Assessment in Africa," 210.
28. Cited in Africa Progress Panel, *Grain, Fish, Money,* 11.
29. Stebbing, "The Man-Made Desert in Africa," 24. See also Brockington, *Fortress Conservation;* Hartmann, "Converging on Disaster"; Leach and Mearns, "Environmental Change and Policy," 2; Maathai, *The Challenge for Africa,* 13–14; Ranger, *Voices from the Rocks,* 56–57; Watts, *Silent Violence,* 352.
30. Stebbing, "The Man-Made Desert in Africa," 40.
31. Cited in Moore and Vaughan, *Cutting Down Trees,* 7.
32. Adem, "The Local Politics of Ethiopia's Green Revolution in South Wollo," 87. See also Lautze and Maxwell, "Why Do Famines Persist in the Horn of Africa?" 234; Vidal, "Regreening Program to Restore One-Sixth of Ethiopia's Land."
33. Crummey and Winter-Nelson, "Farmer Tree-Planting in Wällo, Ethiopia," 94.
34. Cited in McCann, *Green Land, Brown Land, Black Land,* 79. See also Maathai, *The Challenge for Africa,* 243; Rotberg, *Africa Emerges,* 40.
35. Keller, "Drought, War, and the Politics of Famine in Ethiopia and Eritrea," 609.
36. McCann, *Green Land, Brown Land, Black Land,* 60.
37. Moore and Vaughan, *Cutting Down Trees,* 115.
38. Nally, "The Biopolitics of Food Provisioning," 43. See also Arora-Jonsson, "Virtue and Vulnerability"; Watts, *Silent Violence,* lxxxii.
39. Juma, *The New Harvest,* xiv.
40. Peluso and Vandergeest, "Political Ecologies of War and Forests." See also Foucault, *Security, Territory, Population,* 46–47, 128; Schama, *Landscape and Memory;* Scott, *Seeing Like a State.*
41. Rahmato, "Littering the Landscape," 206.
42. Ibid., 214–15. See also Keeley and Scoones, *Understanding Environmental Policy Processes,* chapter 4.
43. Lefort, "Free Market Economy, 'Developmental State' and Party–State Hegemony in Ethiopia," 682.
44. Ibid., 688–89. See also Chinigò, "The Politics of Land Registration in Ethiopia"; Lavers, "Food Security and Social Protection in Highland Ethiopia"; Vidal, "Regreening Program to Restore One-Sixth of Ethiopia's Land."
45. Rahmato, "Littering the Landscape," 210. See also Cheru, "The Silent Revolution and the Weapons of the Weak"; Crummey and Winter-Nelson, "Farmer Tree-Planting in Wällo, Ethiopia," 96.
46. Rahmato, "Littering the Landscape," 219.
47. Luttrell and Pantaleo, *Budget Support, Aid Instruments and the Environment,* 30.

48. Godfrey et al., *Africa Talks Climate,* 9, 15.
49. Ibid., 10–11.
50. Vidal, "Regreening Program to Restore One-Sixth of Ethiopia's Land."
51. FAO, "The Great Green Wall for the Sahara and the Sahel Initiative." See also AU, EU, and FAO, *The Great Green Wall for the Sahara and the Sahel Initiative,* 4.
52. IISD, "GEF Commits $4.6 Million to Regional Component of Great Green Wall Initiative."
53. Critchley, *More People, More Trees,* 24, 65–67. See also Kröger, "The Political Economy of Global Tree Plantation Expansion"; Maathai, *The Challenge for Africa,* 243–48; Tiffen et al., *More People, Less Erosion;* Pye-Smith, *The Quiet Revolution,* vi.
54. Cited in Bank and Minkley, "Going Nowhere Slowly?," 6.
55. Bernstein and Woodhouse, "Telling Environmental Change Like It Is?," 288.
56. Business and Biodiversity Campaign, "Bartering With Trees in the World Cup Host Country South Africa"; Death, "'Greening' the 2010 FIFA World Cup."
57. Musyoki, *The Emerging Policy for Green Economy and Social Development in Limpopo, South Africa,* 8.
58. Ibid., 9.
59. Hyden, *Beyond Ujamaa in Tanzania,* 9.
60. Conca et al., "Confronting Consumption," 2. See also Maniates, "Individualization."
61. Foresight, *The Future of Food and Farming,* 9–10.
62. UNECA, *MDG Report 2013,* 7.
63. Devereux, "Why Does Famine Persist in Africa?"; UNECA, *MDG Report 2013,* 7–8; Edkins, *Whose Hunger?* 4; Watts, *Silent Violence.*
64. Bayart, *The State in Africa,* xxii.
65. Ibid., 235. See also Mbembe, *On the Postcolony.*
66. McDonald, *Food Security,* 85; Posel, "Races to Consume."
67. United Republic of Tanzania, *State of the Environment Report 2006,* 110. See also Africa Progress Panel, *Grain, Fish, Money,* 31; African Development Bank and WWF, *Africa Ecological Footprint Report,* 36.
68. Hitimana et al., *West African Urbanisation Trends,* 3.
69. Mathiane, "Blighted Environment," 116.
70. United Republic of Tanzania, *State of the Environment Report 2006,* 114. See also Gruffydd Jones, "Civilising African Cities"; McDonald, "Three Steps Forward, Two Steps Back"; Simon and Leck, "Urbanising the Global Environmental Change and Human Security Agendas"; Swartz, *The Moral Ecology of South Africa's Township Youth,* 4.
71. Chari, "State Racism and Biopolitical Struggle," 78–79. See also Gruffydd Jones, "Civilising African Cities"; Mamdani, *Citizen and Subject,* 18.
72. Cited in Posel, "Races to Consume," 158. See also James, "Money-Go-Round"; Robins, "The 2011 Toilet Wars in South Africa"; Simon, "Climate and Environmental Change and the Potential for Greening African Cities"; Zikode, "Despite the State's Violence, Our Fight to Escape the Mud, Shit and Fire of South Africa's Slums Will Continue."
73. Foucault, *The Birth of Biopolitics,* 270.

74. Comaroff and Comaroff, *Theory from the South,* 154.
75. Dobson, "Environmental Citizenship," 282.
76. MacGregor, "Only Resist," 625.
77. Goldman, "Water for All!," 150. See also Bakker, "Commons versus Commodities"; Loftus, "Rethinking Political Ecologies of Water"; Roberts, "Privatizing Social Reproduction."
78. Ghana Web, "Energy Not Wasted Will Not Be Paid For—Energy Commission."
79. Goldman, "Water for All!," 161. See also Muller, "Parish Pump Politics."
80. Juwaheer et al., "Analysing the Impact of Green Marketing Strategies on Consumer Purchasing Patterns in Mauritius," 37.
81. Consumers International, "Green Action Fund Winners Revealed"; Green Africa Directory, "African Entrepreneurs Recognised for Social and Environmental Innovation."
82. Global Footprint Network, "World Footprint."
83. Middlemiss, "Reframing Individual Responsibility for Sustainable Consumption," 154.
84. Paterson and Stripple, "My Space," 347.
85. African Development Bank and WWF, *Africa Ecological Footprint Report,* 6.
86. Ibid., 12.
87. Ibid., 14, 37.
88. Ibid., 37.
89. Ibid., 14, 32.
90. African Development Bank and WWF, *African Ecological Futures 2015,* 18. See also UNDP, *Human Development Report 2013,* 35.
91. Republic of South Africa, *National Climate Change Response White Paper,* 38–39.
92. Ibid., 44.
93. Ibid., 48. On neoliberal techniques of "responsibilisation," see Rose, *Powers of Freedom,* 74.
94. South African Government News Agency, "Dept to Negotiate on Indalo Yethu Trust Dissolution." See also Death, *Governing Sustainable Development,* 114.
95. Struwig, "South Africans' Attitudes Towards the Environment," 208.
96. Neville, *South Africa Talks Climate,* 15.
97. Ibid., 16. See also Maniates, "Individualization."
98. Steyn, "Popular Environmental Struggles in South Africa, 1972–1992," 133; Simon, "Climate and Environmental Change and the Potential for Greening African Cities."
99. Dauvergne and LeBaron, "The Social Cost of Environmental Solutions."
100. Grove, *Green Imperialism,* 14.
101. Leopold, *A Sand County Almanac,* 189.
102. Hultgren, "Natural Exceptions to Green Sovereignty?"; Nixon, "Environmentalism and Postcolonialism," 236–37.
103. McInnes, "HIV/Aids and Security," 324.
104. Crook, "Gays, Gods and Governments." See also Cock, *The War Against Ourselves,* 69; Comaroff and Comaroff, *Theory from the South,* chapter 8; Harman, "The Dual

Feminisation of HIV/AIDS"; Hodes, "'It's a Beautiful Struggle'"; Iliffe, *Africans;* Mbali, "The 'New Struggle.'"

105. Struwig, "South Africans' Attitudes Towards the Environment," 208.
106. Clapp, "The Political Economy of Food Aid in an Era of Agricultural Biotechnology," 467.
107. Mwale, "The Babelisation of Debate on GM Maize via the Media in Southern Africa in 2002," 116.
108. Clapp, "The Political Economy of Food Aid in an Era of Agricultural Biotechnology," 472.
109. Chenje and Mohamed-Katerere, "Invasive Alien Species," 332.
110. Ibid., 336–37. See also Crummey and Winter-Nelson, "Farmer Tree-Planting in Wällo, Ethiopia," 120; Maathai, *The Challenge for Africa,* 243–48; Middleton, "Land Rights and Alien Plants in Dryland Madagascar."
111. Bennett, "Naturalising Australian Trees in South Africa," 279. See also Neely, "'Blame It on the Weeds.'"
112. Comaroff and Comaroff, "Naturing the Nation," 629.
113. Ibid., 630.
114. Ibid., 644.
115. Neely, "'Blame It on the Weeds'" 871.
116. Comaroff and Comaroff, "Naturing the Nation," 646. See also Mottiar and Bond, "The Politics of Discontent and Social Protest in Durban," 312–13.
117. Jackson, "Sons of Which Soil?," 97–98.
118. Mamdani, *When Victims Become Killers,* 14. See also Bøås, "Autochthony and Citizenship"; Evers, "Lex Loci Meets Lex Fori," 135–36; Jenkins, "Ethnicity, Violence, and the Immigrant-Guest Metaphor in Kenya."
119. United Republic of Tanzania, *State of the Environment Report 2006,* 16.
120. Brockington, *Fortress Conservation,* 2.
121. Mittal, *Lives on Hold,* 3.
122. Ibid., 4.
123. Ibid., 8.
124. Ibid.
125. Ibid.
126. Quoted in Ernest, "Removal of 'Foreigners' from Tanzania Met with Outrage."
127. Godfrey et al., *Africa Talks Climate,* 3.
128. Cited in Baldwin, "Racialisation and the Figure of the Climate-Change Migrant," 1484.
129. Ibid., 1474. See also Chaturvedi and Doyle, *Climate Terror,* chapter 5; Jackson, "Sons of Which Soil?," 115.
130. Baldwin, "Orientalising Environmental Citizenship," 631–32. See also Arora-Jonsson, "Virtue and Vulnerability"; MacGregor, "Only Resist."
131. Kepe, "Shaped by Race," 872. See also de-Shalit, "Sustainability and Population Policies," 195; McDonald, "Three Steps Forward, Two Steps Back"; McDuff, "Thirty Years of Environmental Education in Africa," 390; Patel, "Environmental Justice in South Africa"; Posel, "Races to Consume"; Ramphele, "New Day Rising."

132. Baldwin, "Orientalising Environmental Citizenship," 626.
133. Barry, *The Politics of Actually Existing Unsustainability,* 257–67; BBC, "Rwanda Gets Tough on Plastic Bags"; Huggins, "'Control Grabbing' and Small-Scale Agricultural Intensification." See also Maathai, *The Challenge for Africa,* 67.
134. Cited in Kuehls, *Beyond Sovereign Territory,* 66. See also Rose, *Powers of Freedom.*
135. USAID, *Africa Environmental Education Assessment I.* See also Gough and Gough, "Environmental Education Research in Southern Africa"; Hattingh et al., eds., *Environmental Education, Ethics and Action in Southern Africa;* Lotz-Sisitka, "Environmental Education Research and Social Change."
136. Maathai, *The Challenge for Africa,* 167; SADC-REEP, "SADC Regional Environmental Education Programme"; Taylor, "Environmental Education in Primary Education."
137. USAID, *Africa Environmental Education Assessment I.* See also Cloete, "Going to the Bush"; Maila and Loubser, "Emancipatory Indigenous Knowledge Systems."
138. Ringia and Porter, *Access to Environmental Information in Tanzania,* 3.
139. ANC, *Reconstruction and Development Plan.* See also Ramphele and McDowell, eds., *Restoring the Land.*
140. Lotz-Sisitka, "Curriculum Patterning in Environmental Education," 104; Steyn, "Popular Environmental Struggles in South Africa, 1972–1992," 133, 141.
141. Brockington and Scholfield, "The Work of Conservation Organisations in Sub-Saharan Africa," 8, 21.
142. McDuff, "Thirty Years of Environmental Education in Africa," 383.
143. Ibid., 384.
144. Steyn, "Popular Environmental Struggles in South Africa, 1972–1992"; Cock, *The War Against Ourselves,* 55, 176; Death, "Environmental Movements, Climate Change, and Consumption in South Africa"; Patel, "Environmental Justice in South Africa"; Ramphele and McDowell, eds., *Restoring the Land.*
145. Dryzek et al., *Green States and Social Movements,* 192.
146. Cock, "The Challenge of Ecological Transformation in Post-Apartheid South Africa," 189–90.
147. Duffield, *Development, Security and Unending War,* 8–9.
148. Cloete, "Going to the Bush," 35.
149. Ibid., 47. See also Maathai, *The Challenge for Africa,* 161.
150. Müller, "Education and the Formation of Geopolitical Subjects," 1.
151. Beinart, *The Rise of Conservation in South Africa,* 380.
152. Houston, "Crisis Is Where We Live."
153. Dean, *Governmentality,* 98–99; Hannah, "Biopower, Life and Left Politics."
154. Bonneuil, "Development as Experience"; Biermann and Mansfield, "Biodiversity, Purity, and Death"; Cavanagh, "Biopolitics, Environmental Change, and Development Studies"; Chari, "State Racism and Biopolitical Struggle"; Mbembe, "Aesthetics of Superfluity."
155. Butler, *Gender Trouble,* 146. See also Comaroff, "Reflections on the Colonial State, in South Africa and Elsewhere," 339; Scott, *Weapons of the Weak.*
156. Maathai, *Unbowed,* 159.

157. Maathai, *The Challenge for Africa,* 162, 203–5. See also Scott, *Two Cheers for Anarchism.*
158. Barry, *The Politics of Actually Existing Unsustainability,* 284.
159. Dryzek et al., *Green States and Social Movements,* 192.
160. Ranger, *Voices from the Rocks,* 284; Harness, "What a South African Activist Sees as 'The Greatest Threat since Apartheid'"; Human Rights Watch, "Dispatches."
161. Global Greens, "Dakar 2012 Global Greens Congress Wrap Up."
162. Howden, "Rwanda's Democratic Credentials under Fire." See also BBC, "Rwandan Opposition Politician Found Dead"; Maathai, *The Challenge for Africa,* 196; Schreurs and Papadakis, *Historical Dictionary of the Green Movement,* lx.
163. Van de Walle, "Presidentialism and Clientalism in Africa's Emerging Party Systems"; Tripp, "Women's Movements and Challenges to Neopatrimonial Rule."
164. Igoe and Kelsall, "Introduction," 25.
165. Agrawal, *Environmentality,* 217.
166. Darier, "Environmental Governmentality," 603. See also Dean, *Governmentality,* 34–35; Edkins, *Poststructuralism and International Relations,* 6.
167. Maniates, "Individualization."
168. Schama, *Landscape and Memory,* 114. See also Deleuze and Guattari, *A Thousand Plateaus,* 15–18.
169. Huggan and Tiffin, "Green Postcolonialism," 9.
170. Van Veuren, "Tooth and Nail," 576.
171. Veracini, "District 9 and Avatar," 364.
172. Ibid., 365.
173. Jackson, "Sons of Which Soil?," 114.
174. Musila, "Laughing at the Rainbow's Cracks?," 152.
175. Mofokeng, "Climate Change."

CHAPTER 5. GREEN ECONOMIES AND ENVIRONMENTAL MARKETS

1. Cited in van Onselen, *The Seed Is Mine,* 528.
2. Ibid.
3. In November 2015 the South African National Treasury issued a draft of the carbon tax bill for public comment, with an expectation that it may be introduced in the finance minister's budget in February 2016. But it has been delayed and revised several times previously. See http://www.treasury.gov.za/comm_media/press/2015/2015110201%20-%20Media%20Statement%20Carbon%20Tax%20Bill.pdf (accessed 21 December 2015).
4. National Treasury (Republic of South Africa), "Press Release." See also Fakir and Gulati, "Carbon Tax"; Satgar, "South Africa's Emergent 'Green Developmental State'?," 141–42.
5. Cited in Resnick et al., "The Political Economy of Green Growth," 220. See also Blaine, "Carbon Tax 'An Overkill,' Say Major Electricity Users"; Bond, "South Africa's Carbon Tax Debate Disappoints"; Lloyd, "Carbon Tax Shoots Itself in the Foot."

6. Ki-moon, "UN Secretary General, Remarks to the Fifth Tokyo International Conference on African Development (Ticad V)." See also Death, "Leading by Example."
7. Fine, "Assessing South Africa's New Growth Path," 558. See also Fine, *South Africa's Political Economy.*
8. Resnick et al., "The Political Economy of Green Growth," 219.
9. Nally, "The Biopolitics of Food Provisioning," 40.
10. Ibid.
11. Lemke, "'The Birth of Bio-Politics,'" 193. See also Mazzucato, *The Entrepreneurial State,* 8; Mitchell, "Rethinking Economy."
12. Konings, "Renewing State Theory," 174.
13. UNEP, *Towards a Green Economy,* 16.
14. Scott, *Seeing Like a State,* chapter 1; Whitehead, "Sustainability."
15. Marx, *Capital,* chapter 1; Mitchell, *Rule of Experts,* 9; Paterson, "Commodification"; Whitehead et al., *The Nature of the State,* 38.
16. Mitchell, *Rule of Experts,* 5.
17. Ibid., 21. See also Foucault, *The Birth of Biopolitics,* 51–73; Nally, "Biopolitics of Food Provisioning"; Sowers, *Environmental Politics in Egypt.*
18. Hirst and Thompson, "Globalization and the Future of the Nation State"; Newell, "The Political Economy of Global Environmental Governance"; Leach et al., "Green Grabs and Biochar"; Mitchell, *Carbon Democracy.*
19. Goodland, "The Concept of Environmental Sustainability," 2.
20. Stern, *The Economics of Climate Change.* See also Barry, *The Politics of Actually Existing Unsustainability;* Clapp and Dauvergne, *Paths to a Green World,* 5–6; Robinson, "Squaring the Circle?"; Sachs, *Planet Dialectics.*
21. Buttel, "Ecological Modernization as Social Theory," 61.
22. Mol, "Ecological Modernization and the Global Economy," 93. See also Ferguson, "The Green Economy Agenda."
23. Bachram, "Climate Fraud and Carbon Colonialism"; Lohmann, *Carbon Trading;* Newell and Paterson, *Climate Capitalism,* 25–29; Spaargaren and Mol, "Carbon Flows, Carbon Markets, and Low-Carbon Lifestyles"; Stephan and Paterson, "The Politics of Carbon Markets."
24. Newell and Paterson, *Climate Capitalism,* 104. See also Methmann, "The Sky is the Limit."
25. Lohmann, *Carbon Trading,* 297–99; Reyes, "Unclean Development Mechanism," 15.
26. The Gold Standard, "The First Ever Cookstove CDM—POA Registered in Africa."
27. Newell and Paterson, *Climate Capitalism,* 129–30.
28. Gomera et al., "A Changing Climate for Community Resource Governance," 304. See also Toulmin, *Climate Change in Africa,* 81–84.
29. UNEP, *Towards a Green Economy,* 17.
30. DED et al., *Green Economy Summit Discussion Document,* 35.
31. Büscher and Fletcher, "Accumulation by Conservation." See also Leach et al., "Green Grabs and Biochar"; Nel and Hill, "Constructing Walls of Carbon."
32. Newell and Paterson, *Climate Capitalism,* 1.

33. Hallegatte et al., *From Growth to Green Growth;* Luke, "The System of Sustainable Degradation"; Middleton and O'Keefe, *Redefining Sustainable Development;* Paterson, "Commodification"; Büscher, "Derivative Nature"; Bachram, "Climate Fraud and Carbon Colonialism."
34. Meadowcroft, "Planning, Democracy and the Challenge of Sustainable Development," 167–68.
35. Mol and Buttel, "The Environmental State Under Pressure," 2.
36. Ibid.
37. Meadowcroft, "Planning, Democracy and the Challenge of Sustainable Development," 181.
38. Blowfield and Frynas, "Setting New Agendas," 503.
39. Falkner, "Private Environmental Governance and International Relations," 77.
40. Meadowcroft, "Greening the State?," 69. See also Bond, "Social Movements and Corporate Social Responsibility in South Africa"; Eckersley, *The Green State,* 65–69; Meadowcroft, "Who Is in Charge Here?"; Okereke et al., "Conceptualising Climate Governance beyond the International Regime."
41. Deegan, *Africa Today,* 58. See also UNCTAD, *Economic Development in Africa Report 2012,* 2; Parker, "Poverty Report Indicates Africa Is Stagnating"; Murphy, "Lessons to Be Learned from the Challenges to Achieving the MDGs in Africa."
42. Aké, *Democracy and Development in Africa,* 2–4; Bayart, "Africa in the World"; Berry, *No Condition Is Permanent;* Maathai, *The Challenge for Africa,* chapter 5; Neumann, *Imposing Wilderness,* 97; Reed, *Economic Change, Governance and Natural Resource Wealth,* 16; Selwyn, *The Global Development Crisis.*
43. Mol and Buttel, "The Environmental State Under Pressure," 6. See also Collier, *Bottom Billion;* Sachs, *The End of Poverty;* Okereke and Agupusi, *Homegrown Development in Africa;* Rostow, *The Stages of Economic Growth;* van de Walle, *African Economies and the Politics of Permanent Crisis, 1979—1999,* 16.
44. Clapham, "Governmentality and Economic Policy in Sub-Saharan Africa," 813. See also Abrahamsen, *Disciplining Democracy,* chapters 5, 6; Chabal and Daloz, *Africa Works,* 121; Harrison, *Neoliberal Africa.*
45. Clapham, "Degrees of Statehood," 149. See also Harrison, *The World Bank and Africa.*
46. McMichael, "Land Grabbing as Security Mercantilism in International Relations," 55.
47. McCarthy and Prudham, "Neoliberal Nature and the Nature of Neoliberalism," 278. See also Devereux, "Why Does Famine Persist in Africa?," 29; Hall, "A Political Economy of Land Reform in South Africa," 220.
48. Resnick et al., "The Political Economy of Green Growth," 216.
49. UNEP, *Global Green New Deal,* 1, 4.
50. UN, *The Future We Want,* 56; Barbier, "Global Governance," 12. See also Death, "Four Discourses of the Green Economy in the Global South"; Tienhaara, "Varieties of Green Capitalism."
51. World Bank, *Inclusive Green Growth,* 2.
52. Pearce, *Blueprint 3,* 4–5. See also Pearce et al., *Blueprint for a Green Economy.*

53. Barbier, "The Policy Challenges for Green Economy and Sustainable Economic Development," 234.
54. Godfrey et al., *Africa Talks Climate;* Toulmin, *Climate Change in Africa;* Jessop, "Economic and Ecological Crises"; Stern, *The Economics of Climate Change.*
55. UNEP, *Global Green New Deal,* 1.
56. UNEP, *Towards a Green Economy,* 14.
57. Ibid., 15.
58. Jessop, "Economic and Ecological Crises," 21.
59. Tienhaara, "Varieties of Green Capitalism."
60. Bär et al., *Green Economy Discourses in the Run-Up to Rio 2012,* 24–25. See also Bina, "The Green Economy and Sustainable Development"; Ferguson, "The Green Economy Agenda"; Goodman and Salleh, "The 'Green Economy' "; Tienhaara, "Varieties of Green Capitalism"; Wanner, "The New 'Passive Revolution' of the Green Economy and Growth Discourse."
61. See also Death, "Four Discourses of the Green Economy in the Global South"; Death, "The Green Economy in South Africa."
62. De la Court, *Beyond Brundtland,* 25. See also Clapp and Dauvergne, *Paths to a Green World,* 9–11; Jessop, "Economic and Ecological Crises," 23; Bookchin, *Toward an Ecological Society;* Schumacher, *Small Is Beautiful.*
63. Barry, *The Politics of Actually Existing Unsustainability,* 278.
64. Ferguson, "The Green Economy Agenda," 13. See also Goodman and Salleh, "The 'Green Economy' "; Jackson, *Prosperity Without Growth;* Litfin, *Ecovillages;* Litfin, "Localism"; Stevenson, "Representing Green Radicalism"; Swilling and Annecke, *Just Transitions.*
65. Barbier, "Global Governance," 3.
66. ILO, *Sustainable Development, Decent Work and Green Jobs,* xiv. See also Newell and Paterson, *Climate Capitalism,* 179; Tienhaara, "Varieties of Green Capitalism," 190; UNCTAD, *Economic Development in Africa Report 2012.*
67. UNEP, *Towards a Green Economy,* 20.
68. The World Commission on Environment and Development, *Our Common Future,* 48.
69. UNCTAD, *Economic Development in Africa Report 2012,* 27. On the politics of green transformations more broadly, see Scoones et al., *The Politics of Green Transformations.*
70. World Bank, *Inclusive Green Growth,* 3.
71. Methmann, " 'Climate Protection' as Empty Signifier," 365; Newell and Paterson, *Climate Capitalism,* chapter 4.
72. Paterson, "Global Governance for Sustainable Capitalism?," 115. See also Hallegatte et al., *From Growth to Green Growth,* 2.
73. Brassett et al., "Introduction"; Foresight, *The Future of Food and Farming;* Grove, "Insuring 'Our Common Future'?"; Jones and Carabine, *Exploring Political and Socio-Economic Drivers of Transformational Climate Policy,* 2; Methmann and Oels, "Vulnerability."

74. Cited in Development Bank of Southern Africa (DBSA), *Programmes in Support of Transitioning South Africa to a Green Economy,* 7. See also Petersen, "Developing Climate Adaptation."
75. Khor, "Challenges of the Green Economy Concept and Policies in the Context of Sustainable Development, Poverty and Equity." See also Bär et al., *Green Economy Discourses in the Run-Up to Rio 2012.*
76. AMCEN, "Bamako Declaration on the Environment for Sustainable Development," 1.
77. Death, "The Green Economy in South Africa"; Federal Democratic Republic of Ethiopia, *Ethiopia's Climate-Resilient Green Economy;* Republic of Rwanda, *Green Growth and Climate Resilience;* Maurice Ile Durable, "Policy, Strategy and Action Plan."
78. Ghana News Agency, "Ghana Committed to Green Economy—Oteng-Agyei"; UNDP, *Human Development Report 2013,* 108; Shipanga, "Namibia Towards a Green Economy"; Muyanwa, "Govt to Pursue Green Economy"; Banda and Bass, *Inclusive Green Growth in Zambia;* Muwamba, "Malawi Tips Countries to Promote Green Economy"; UNEP, "Senegal Joins the Partnership for Action on Green Economy"; Nhema, "Green Economy Now a Must"; Editor, "Kenya's Green Economy on a 'Positive' Growth."
79. Anderson and Browne, "The Politics of Oil in Eastern Africa"; Brockington et al., *Nature Unbound,* 4; Carmody, *The New Scramble for Africa;* Global Witness, *Rigged?;* Klein, *This Changes Everything;* Kopinski et al., "Resource Curse or Resource Disease?"; Maathai, *The Challenge for Africa,* 99; Patey, "Crude Days Ahead?"; Seagle, "Discourse, Development and Legitimacy."
80. African Development Bank, "AfDB, Largest Financier of Clean Energy on the African Continent with $4.3 Billion in Energy Projects"; African Development Bank and WWF, *Africa Ecological Footprint Report,* 54; World Bank, *Inclusive Green Growth,* 165; Hamouchene, "Desertec"; Western Sahara Resource Watch, "Green Energy to Uphold Occupation in Western Sahara"; Gets, *Powering the Future,* 29; Njeru, "Kenya to Generate Over Half of Its Electricity through Solar Power by 2016"; Baker, "Renewable Energy in South Africa's Minerals-Energy Complex"; Baker, "Opportunity and Crisis in South Africa's Electricity."
81. Cited in Pearce, "Will Huge New Hydro Projects Bring Power to Africa's People?"
82. UNCTAD, *Economic Development in Africa Report 2012,* 108; Pearce, "Will Huge New Hydro Projects Bring Power to Africa's People?"; IRIN, "Lesotho."
83. Africa Progress Panel, *Grain, Fish, Money;* Foresight, *The Future of Food and Farming,* 28; McMichael and Schneider, "Food Security Politics and the Millennium Development Goals"; Thompson, "Alliance for a Green Revolution in Africa (AGRA)"; NEPAD, "Comprehensive Africa Agriculture Development Programme (CAADP)"; Watts, *Silent Violence,* 498–505; Resnick et al., "The Political Economy of Green Growth," 221–22; Pearce, "Can 'Climate-Smart' Agriculture Help Both Africa and the Planet?"; Atela, *The Politics of Agricultural Carbon Finance.*

84. Africa Progress Panel, *Grain, Fish, Money,* 125–26; African Development Bank and WWF, *African Ecological Futures 2015,* 24; Fourie, "Three Trends in African Development—Drawn from the East Asian Experience"; Harman and Williams, "International Development in Transition"; Manji, "Bulldozers, Homes and Highways," 209–10; Okereke and Agupusi, *Homegrown Development in Africa;* Rotberg, *Africa Emerges,* chapter 7.
85. United Republic of Tanzania, *Poverty and Human Development Report 2009,* 22.
86. Horne, *Understanding Land Investment Deals in Africa,* 1. See also Baxter, *Understanding Land Investment Deals in Africa,* 2; Patey, "Crude Days Ahead?," 633.
87. Ziervogel and Parnell, "South African Coastal Cities," 235.
88. Cited in Africa Progress Panel, *Grain, Fish, Money,* 11. See also Iliffe, *Africans,* 1.
89. Ziervogel and Parnell, "South African Coastal Cities," 233.
90. Ibid.
91. World Bank, "World Bank Climate Change Strategy for Africa Calls for Adaptation, Mitigation and Additional Financing." See also Africa Progress Panel, *Grain, Fish, Money,* 55.
92. Federal Democratic Republic of Ethiopia, *Ethiopia's Climate-Resilient Green Economy,* 1, 81; Lautze and Maxwell, "Why Do Famines Persist in the Horn of Africa?"; World Bank, "Ethiopia Economic Update—Laying the Foundation for Achieving Middle Income Status"; Jones and Carabine, *Exploring Political and Socio-Economic Drivers of Transformational Climate Policy.*
93. UNEP, *Towards a Green Economy,* 20.
94. Petersen, "Developing Climate Adaptation." See also Africa Progress Panel, *Grain, Fish, Money,* 50; ILO, *Sustainable Development, Decent Work and Green Jobs,* 66; Lavers, "Food Security and Social Protection in Highland Ethiopia"; UNDP, *Human Development Report 2011,* 78.
95. Petersen, "Developing Climate Adaptation," 575. See also Watts, *Silent Violence,* 218.
96. Roberts, "Financing Social Reproduction." On Ethiopian politics, see Adem, "The Local Politics of Ethiopia's Green Revolution in South Wollo"; Cheru, "The Silent Revolution and the Weapons of the Weak"; Keeley and Scoones, *Understanding Environmental Policy Processes,* chapter 4; Jones and Carabine, *Exploring Political and Socio-Economic Drivers of Transformational Climate Policy;* Lefort, "Free Market Economy, 'Developmental State' and Party-State Hegemony in Ethiopia."
97. Adaption Fund, "About." See also Traynor, "EU Puts €100bn-A-Year Price on Tackling Climate Change."
98. UNEP, *Green Economy Assessment Report—Kenya,* 2.
99. Hall, "Land-Grabbing in Southern Africa," 197. See also Feed the Future, "Malawi."
100. Resnick et al., "The Political Economy of Green Growth," 223–24.
101. Bofin et al., *REDD Integrity,* 22, 65. See also African Development Bank, "Democratic Republic of Congo Gets $21.5 Million Green Light to Transform its Vast Forests."
102. Ruitenbeek and Cartier, *Putting Tanzania's Hidden Economy to Work,* 18. See also Chachage, *Land Acquisition and Accumulation in Tanzania.*
103. IISD, "Africa to Become World's Largest Market for Solar Lanterns by 2015."

104. Development Bank of Southern Africa (DBSA) *Programmes in Support of Transitioning South Africa to a Green Economy,* 6.
105. Cited in Parker, "SA's New Green Economy Accord Met with Scepticism." See also Fine, "Assessing South Africa's New Growth Path"; Republic of South Africa, *Green Economy Accord;* Satgar, "South Africa's Emergent 'Green Developmental State'?"; UNEP, *Green Economy Modelling Report of South Africa,* 1.
106. African Development Bank and WWF, *Africa Ecological Footprint Report,* 54; Baker, "Renewable Energy in South Africa's Minerals-Energy Complex"; Baker, "Opportunity and Crisis in South Africa's Electricity"; Baker et al., "The Political Economy of Energy Transitions"; Gets, *Powering the Future;* Kings, "SA's Renewable Energy Sector a Beacon in Africa"; Reuters, "S. Africa Okays $5.4 Bln in Clean Energy Projects"; Scholvin, "South Africa's Energy Policy."
107. Reuters, "S. Africa Okays $5.4 Bln in Clean Energy Projects"; Satgar, "South Africa's Emergent 'Green Developmental State'?"; Sole and Evans, "Medupi, the Murder and the Mega Fraud."
108. Cited in England, "Bid to Wean Country Off Coal," 2. See also Büscher, "Derivative Nature"; Death, "Leading by Example"; Death, "'Greening' the 2010 FIFA World Cup"; Dowden, *Africa;* Economist, "The Hopeful Continent"; Rotberg, *Africa Emerges.*
109. UNECA et al., "African Consensus Statement to Rio+20," #21.
110. Jones and Carabine, *Exploring Political and Socio-Economic Drivers of Transformational Climate Policy,* 17.
111. Development Bank of Southern Africa (DBSA), *Programmes in Support of Transitioning South Africa to a Green Economy,* 5.
112. Republic of South Africa, "State of the Nation Address of the President of South Africa, Thabo Mbeki." See also Cousins, "Agrarian Reform and the 'Two Economies.'"
113. Cited in Neely, "'Blame It on the Weeds,'" 875. See also Hawn, "South Africa Puts the Unemployed to Work, Restoring Land and Water"; Resnick et al., "The Political Economy of Green Growth," 216; ILO, *Sustainable Development, Decent Work and Green Jobs,* 44; Musyoki, *The Emerging Policy for Green Economy and Social Development in Limpopo,* 3; Satgar, "South Africa's Emergent 'Green Developmental State'?" 137–38.
114. Republic of Rwanda, *Green Growth and Climate Resilience,* ii.
115. Ibid., iv. See also African Development Bank and OECD, *Enabling Green Growth in Africa,* 7; Huggins, "'Control Grabbing' and Small-Scale Agricultural Intensification."
116. ILO, *Sustainable Development, Decent Work and Green Jobs,* 36; UNCTAD, *Economic Development in Africa Report 2012,* 125; UNEP, *Global Green New Deal,* 26; UNEP, *Green Economy Success Stories.* In contrast, see Africa Progress Panel, *Grain, Fish, Money;* Juma, *The New Harvest.*
117. World Bank, "Lighting Africa."
118. Resnick et al., "The Political Economy of Green Growth," 216.

119. Steward et al., *Towards a Green Food System,* 1. See also Bond, "Justice"; Death, "Environmental Movements, Climate Change, and Consumption in South Africa"; Deen, "Rio+20"; Manji and Ekine, eds., *African Awakening.*
120. The Economist, "Zimbabwe after Hyperinflation." See also Moyo, "The Land Question in Southern Africa"; Moyo and Matondi, "Interrogating Sustainable Development and Resource Control in Zimbabwe"; Scoones et al., *Zimbabwe's Land Reform;* Scoones et al., "The New Politics of Zimbabwe's Lowveld."
121. Gallagher, "The Battle for Zimbabwe in 2013"; Raftopoulos, "The 2013 Elections in Zimbabwe"; Scoones et al., *Zimbabwe's Land Reform,* 3–4, 52–54.
122. Aliber and Cousins, "Livelihoods after Land Reform in South Africa," 164.
123. Cited in Greenberg, "The Landless People's Movement and the Failure of Post-Apartheid Land Reform," 149.
124. See Cieplak, "Shunting Hectares"; SAPA, "Nkwinti Praises Mugabe Land Reform."
125. Bank and Minkley, "Going Nowhere Slowly?," 2; Cousins, "Agrarian Reform and the 'Two Economies,'" 220–21.
126. Van Onselen, *The Seed Is Mine,* vii. See also Africa Progress Panel, *Grain, Fish, Money,* 55.
127. UNEP, *Global Green New Deal,* 4. See also Evans, "Constructing the 21st Century Developmental State"; Mazzucato, *The Entrepreneurial State;* UNDP, *Human Development Report 2013;* Williams, ed., *The End of the Developmental State?*
128. UNCTAD, *Economic Development in Africa Report 2012,* 5.
129. Ibid., 86.

CHAPTER 6. GREEN AFRICAN STATES AND INTERNATIONAL RELATIONS

1. UNEP, *Environmental Assessment of Ogoniland,* 6.
2. Friends of the Earth International, "Friends of the Earth Groups Call on Shell to Clean Up Nigeria Oil Spills." See also Anugwom, "Beyond Oil"; Bassey, *To Cook a Continent,* 79–85; EJOLT, *Crude Justice and Ecocide in the Niger Delta;* Obi, "Oil and the Post-Amnesty Programme (PAP)"; Pilkington, "Shell Pays Out $15.5m Over Saro-Wiwa Killing."
3. Chaturvedi and Doyle, *Climate Terror,* 47. See also Amunwa, *Counting the Cost,* 6; Nossiter, "Far from Gulf, a Spill Scourge 5 Decades Old"; UNEP, *Environmental Assessment of Ogoniland.*
4. Amunwa, *Counting the Cost,* 13. See also Agbiboa, "Have We Heard the Last?"; Frynas, "Political Instability and Business"; Frynas, "Shell in Nigeria"; Obi, "Oil and the Post-Amnesty Programme (PAP)"; Watts, "Development and Governmentality."
5. Bowman, "Shell to Sea"; Doherty and Doyle, *Environmentalism, Resistance and Solidarity,* 174–78; Mitchell, *Carbon Democracy;* Obi, "Transnationalism, Africa's 'Resource Curse' and 'Contested Sovereignties'"; Watts, *Silent Violence,* xiv; Willems and Obadare, "Introduction," 1.
6. Klein, *This Changes Everything,* 306.
7. Ibid., 324.

8. Larner and Walters, "The Political Rationality of 'New Regionalism,'" 392. See also Mitchell, "The Limits of the State," 94.
9. Biermann and Dingwerth, "Global Environmental Change and the Nation State," 2. See also Conca, "Rethinking the Ecology—Sovereignty Debate," 702; Litfin, "The Greening of Sovereignty"; Okereke et al., "Conceptualising Climate Governance beyond the International Regime."
10. Falkner, "Global Environmentalism and the Greening of International Society," 503, 516. See also Brenton, *The Greening of Machiavelli;* Chasek, *Earth Negotiations.*
11. Falkner, "Global Environmentalism and the Greening of International Society," 505.
12. Ibid., 517.
13. Tilly, "War Making and State Making as Organized Crime," 169–70.
14. Mitchell, *Carbon Democracy,* 66.
15. Mazo, *Climate Conflict,* 74. See also Barnett, *The Meaning of Environmental Security;* Black, "Climate 'Drives African Conflict'"; Dalby, *Security and Environmental Change;* Peluso, "Coercing Conservation."
16. Lachmann, *States and Power,* 206.
17. Waltz, *Theory of International Politics,* 127.
18. Mol, "Ecological Modernization and the Global Economy," 100, 108. See also Bernstein, "Liberal Environmentalism and Global Environmental Governance."
19. Miller, "Sovereignty Reconfigured," 173. See also Duit et al., "Greening Leviathan," 10; Epstein, *The Power of Words in International Relations;* Keohane and Victor, "The Regime Complex for Climate Change"; Mason, *The New Accountability.*
20. UNFCCC, "NAPAs received by the Secretariat"; UNEP DTU Partnership, "Total in the CDM Pipeline." See also http://www.au.int/en/pressreleases/19465/implementation-indcs-another-red-line-africa-will-not-cross-cop-21-negotiations (accessed 21 December 2015).
21. Broch-Due, "Producing Nature and Poverty in Africa," 38. See also Luttrell and Pantaleo, *Budget Support, Aid Instruments and the Environment,* 25; Newell, *Globalization and the Environment,* 121–23.
22. Hicks et al., *Greening Aid?,* 1.
23. Ibid., 16.
24. DAC, *Aid to Environment Development Co-operation Report 2012,* 1.
25. Ibid., 1–2.
26. Keeley and Scoones, *Understanding Environmental Policy Processes,* 169.
27. Ashford, "Government and Environmental Innovation in Europe and North America," 1420.
28. Scott, *Two Cheers for Anarchism,* 54–55. See also Bojö and Reddy, *Status and Evolution of Environmental Priorities in the Poverty Reduction Strategies,* 2; Corson, "Shifting Environmental Governance in a Neoliberal World"; Death, "Environmental Mainstreaming and Post-Sovereign Governance in Tanzania."
29. Goldman, "The Birth of a Discipline," 209.
30. Keeley and Scoones, *Understanding Environmental Policy Processes,* 170.

31. Harrison, "Post-Conditionality Politics and Administrative Reform," 671. See also Abrahamsen, "The Power of Partnerships in Global Governance"; Harrison, *The World Bank and Africa.*
32. Rosenberg, "Why Is There No International Historical Sociology?," 314.
33. Chaturvedi and Doyle, *Climate Terror;* Cox, "Social Forces, States, and World Orders"; Doty, *Imperial Encounters;* Mbembe, *On the Postcolony;* Ferguson, *Global Shadows;* McClintock, *Imperial Leather;* Smith, *Uneven Development.*
34. Cerny, *The Changing Architecture of Politics,* 102, 237.
35. Gill, "Globalisation, Market Civilisation, and Disciplinary Neoliberalism," 411–15. See also Abrahamsen, "The Power of Partnerships in Global Governance," 1463; Fougner, "Neoliberal Governance of States"; Löwenheim, "Examining the State."
36. Yale, "Environmental Performance Index"; SEDAC, "Environmental Sustainability Index"; Sustainable Society Foundation, "Sustainable Society Index"; NEF, "Happy Planet Index."
37. African Development Bank and WWF, *Africa Ecological Footprint Report,* 6, 12.
38. Indeed, it is best to be circumspect about many datasets on African development and environmental indicators. What is far more significant is the desire to generate statistics, and how this produces a certain set of "state effects," as James Scott has shown. For a review of some of the issues with African datasets, see Jerven, "Measuring African Development."
39. Dobson et al., "Road Will Ruin Serengeti."
40. Vidal, "Regreening Program to Restore One-Sixth of Ethiopia's Land."
41. Doherty and Doyle, *Environmentalism, Resistance and Solidarity,* 173.
42. Cited in African Development Bank and WWF, *Africa Ecological Footprint Report,* 7.
43. Cerny, *The Changing Architecture of Politics,* 53, 241. See also van Ham, "Branding Territory."
44. Republic of South Africa, *A National Climate Change Response Strategy for South Africa,* 28. See also Death, *Governing Sustainable Development;* Death, "A Predictable Disaster for the Climate—But Who Else Won and Lost in Durban at COP17?"; Death, "Leading by Example"; Development Bank of Southern Africa (DBSA), *Programmes in Support of Transitioning South Africa to a Green Economy,* 36; Dual Citizen, *The Global Green Economy Index;* Hurrell and Sengupta, "Emerging Powers, North–South Relations, and Global Climate Politics"; Patel, "Environmental Justice in South Africa."
45. De Villiers, *Land Claims and National Parks,* 5. See also Brockington et al., *Nature Unbound,* 105–6; Cock, *The War Against Ourselves,* 153; Robins and van der Waal, " 'Model Tribes' and Iconic Conservationists?"
46. Hellberg, "Water, Life and Politics"; Loftus, "Rethinking Political Ecologies of Water"; Muller, "Parish Pump Politics."
47. Cited in Desai and Vahed, "World Cup 2010," 154.
48. Cited in Smith, "Desmond Tutu." See also Death, " 'Greening' the 2010 FIFA World Cup"; Pillay and Bass, "Mega-Events as a Response to Poverty Reduction"; van der Westhuizen, "Glitz, Glamour and the Gautrain."
49. Assey et al., *Environment at the Heart of Tanzania's Development,* iv.

50. Ibid. See also Death, "Environmental Mainstreaming and Post-Sovereign Governance in Tanzania."
51. Cited in Wilson, "Darwinian Reasoning and Waltz's Theory of International Politics," 418. See also Nye, *The Powers to Lead;* Parker et al., "Climate Change Leaders and Followers"; Young, "Political Leadership and Regime Formation."
52. Eckersley, *The Green State,* 201.
53. Ibid. See also Eckersley, "The State as Gatekeeper," 136.
54. UNFCCC, "Momentum for Change."
55. Hoffmann, *Climate Governance at the Crossroads;* Newell and Paterson, *Climate Capitalism,* chapter 7.
56. UNEP, "Our Goodwill Ambassadors." See also Brockington, *Celebrity and the Environment,* 99–101; Maathai, *The Challenge for Africa,* 63–64.
57. Juma, *The New Harvest,* 1–2.
58. Devereux, "Why Does Famine Persist in Africa?"; Resnick et al., "The Political Economy of Green Growth," 221.
59. African Centre for Biodiversity, *Running to Stand Still,* vi.
60. Resnick et al., "The Political Economy of Green Growth," 215. See also African Centre for Biodiversity, *Running to Stand Still;* Gabay, "Two 'Transitions' "; Wroe, "Donors, Dependency, and Political Crisis in Malawi"; African Development Bank, "Malawi Economic Outlook."
61. Wilson, "Model Villages in the Neoliberal Era," 110, 120. See also Maathai, *The Challenge for Africa,* 71–73; Wilson, "A Strange Kind of Science"; Wilson, *Jeffrey Sachs.* On a very different type of "inspirational village," see Swilling and Annecke, *Just Transitions.*
62. Schnurr, "Inventing Makhathini," 784. See also Scoones, "Can GM Crops Prevent Famine in Africa?," 313.
63. Schnurr, "Inventing Makhathini," 785.
64. Schnurr, "Biotechnology and Bio-Hegemony in Uganda"; Scoones, "Can GM Crops Prevent Famine in Africa?," 323.
65. Bailey, "Establishing Low Carbon Growth in Ethiopia."
66. Thérien and Pouliot, "The Global Compact," 65.
67. Development Bank of Southern Africa (DBSA), *Programmes in Support of Transitioning South Africa to a Green Economy,* 5.
68. Mol, "China's Ascent and Africa's Environment," 791.
69. Utting, "Corporate Environmentalism in the South," 268, 274.
70. Blowfield and Frynas, "Setting New Agendas," 503.
71. Ibid., 506–7. See also Bond, "Social Movements and Corporate Social Responsibility in South Africa"; Brown, " 'Fair Trade' with Africa"; Fig, "Manufacturing Amnesia."
72. Ferguson, "Seeing Like an Oil Company," 379.
73. Brockington and Scholfield, "The Work of Conservation Organisations in Sub-Saharan Africa," 19.
74. United Republic of Tanzania, *State of the Environment Report 2006,* 63. See also Chapin, "A Challenge to Conservationists," 22–23; Cock, *The War Against Ourselves,* 14–15.

75. Carruthers, "Tracking in Game Trails," 810.
76. Klein, *This Changes Everything,* 310; African Development Bank and WWF, *African Ecological Futures 2015,* 18. See also Bullard, *Dumping in Dixie;* Harvey, "The Environment of Justice"; Schlosberg, *Environmental Justice and the New Pluralism.*
77. Greenpeace International, "The Toxic Truth." See also Clapp and Dauvergne, *Paths to a Green World,* 130; Davis, *Planet of Slums.*
78. Federal Ministry of Environment, *National Environmental, Economic and Development Study (Needs) for Climate Change in Nigeria,* 4; UN, *National Sustainable Development Strategies.*
79. Cited in Agbiboa, "Have We Heard the Last?," 448. See also World Bank, "Terrestrial Protected Areas (Percent of Total Land Area)."
80. Agbiboa, "Have We Heard the Last?," 457. See also Doherty and Doyle, *Environmentalism, Resistance and Solidarity,* 174–78; Bob, "Marketing Rebellion," 319–21; Haynes, "Power, Politics and Environmental Movements in the Third World"; Watts, *Silent Violence.*
81. Amunwa, *Counting the Cost,* 12. See also Abrahamsen and Williams, *Security Beyond the State,* 126–48; Frynas, "Political Instability and Business"; Obi, "Structuring Transnational Spaces of Identity, Rights and Power in the Niger Delta of Nigeria," 478.
82. Bassey, *To Cook a Continent;* Doherty and Doyle, *Environmentalism, Resistance and Solidarity,* 174–78; UNEP, *Environmental Assessment of Ogoniland.*
83. Anugwom, "Beyond Oil," 27.
84. World Bank, "Data." See also Bond, *Unsustainable South Africa;* Cock, *The War Against Ourselves;* McDonald, *Environmental Justice in South Africa;* Patel, "Environmental Justice in South Africa"; Ramphele and McDowell, ed., *Restoring the Land;* Resnick et al., "The Political Economy of Green Growth," 219; Satgar, "South Africa's Emergent 'Green Developmental State'?"; Swilling and Annecke, *Just Transitions;* Yeld, "Fall in Line on Climate Change, Sasol Told."
85. Mathiane, "Blighted Environment," 116.
86. Aylett, "Conflict, Collaboration and Climate Change," 484.
87. Mottiar and Bond, "The Politics of Discontent and Social Protest in Durban," 322. See also Barnett and Scott, "Spaces of Opposition"; Bassey, *To Cook a Continent,* 97–99; Bond, *Durban's Climate Gamble;* Patel, "Environmental Justice in South Africa."
88. Aylett, "Conflict, Collaboration and Climate Change," 485–86. See also Scott and Barnett, "Something in the Air," 379; Doherty and Doyle, *Environmentalism, Resistance and Solidarity,* 181–82.
89. Mottiar, "From 'Popcorn' to 'Occupy,'" 611–13. See also Death, "Counter-Conducts as a Mode of Resistance"; Hallowes et al., *COP In, COP Out, COP 17,* 17; Nkabane, "Isipingo Marchers Protest against Dig-Out Port."
90. Bloomfield, "Shame Campaigns and Environmental Justice"; Bob, "Marketing Rebellion"; Haynes, "Power, Politics and Environmental Movements in the Third World"; Sowers, *Environmental Politics in Egypt.*
91. Doherty and Doyle, *Environmentalism, Resistance and Solidarity,* 141–42.

92. Rosenberg, "Why Is There No International Historical Sociology?," 316.
93. Klein, *This Changes Everything,* 335.
94. Sherman, *Environment and Development Decision Making in Africa 2006–2008,* 1. See also Ahluwalia, *Politics and Post-Colonial Theory;* Ajulu, "Thabo Mbeki's African Renaissance in a Globalising World Economy"; Nhamo, "Climate Change."
95. UNECA et al., "African Consensus Statement to Rio+20."
96. Hoste, *Where Was United Africa in the Climate Change Negotiations?,* 1.
97. Ibid., 2. See also Qobo, "Is Environmentally Sustainable and Inclusive Growth Possible?," 349; Vickers, "Africa and the Rising Powers," 687–88; Mathema et al., *Understanding Key Positions of the Least Developed Countries in Climate Change Negotiations.*
98. BBC, "Copenhagen Deal Reaction in Quotes." See also Death, "Leading by Example," 465; Vickers, "Africa and the Rising Powers," 687–88.
99. Hurrell and Sengupta, "Emerging Powers, North–South Relations, and Global Climate Politics," 463. See also Hoste, *Where Was United Africa in the Climate Change Negotiations?,* 4; Salgado, "SA Accused of Undermining G77."
100. Groenewalde, "COP17." See also Hurrell and Sengupta, "Emerging Powers, North–South Relations, and Global Climate Politics," 472; Vickers, "Africa and the Rising Powers," 688–89.
101. UNDP, *Human Development Report 2013,* 45. See also Carmody, *The New Scramble for Africa,* chapter 3; Dent, "Africa and China," 6–8; Maathai, *The Challenge for Africa,* 106–10; Mohan, "Beyond the Enclave."
102. Mol, "China's Ascent and Africa's Environment," 790.
103. Ibid.
104. Obi, "Enter the Dragon?," 418.
105. Norrington-Davies and Thornton, *Climate Change Financing and Aid Effectiveness,* 19. See also Bond, "Justice."
106. Vidal, "Kumi Naidoo."
107. Doherty and Doyle, *Environmentalism, Resistance and Solidarity,* 25.
108. Ibid., 5–7, 61, 68, 94. See also Bassey, *To Cook a Continent.*
109. Rossdale, "Between Innocence and Deconstruction."
110. The concept and politics of solidarity are far more complex than can be adequately discussed here. For more nuanced discussions of solidarity, public spheres, and subaltern counterpublics, see Calhoun, "Imagining Solidarity"; Doyle and Doherty, "Green Public Spheres and the Green Governance State"; Flesher Fominaya, "International Solidarity in Social Movements"; Schlosberg, *Environmental Justice and the New Pluralism.* On agonistic politics, ethics, and response, see Edkins, *Poststructuralism and International Relations;* Edkins, *Whose Hunger?;* MacGregor, "Only Resist," 630. For thoughts on how Foucault's concept of "care of the self" might connect to critical resistance, see Death, "Counter-Conducts as a Mode of Resistance."
111. Clark, *International Legitimacy and World Society;* Cooper, *Africa since 1940,* 203; Keck and Sikkink, *Activists Beyond Borders.*

112. Bowman, "Shell to Sea." See also Anugwom, "Beyond Oil"; Bassey, *To Cook a Continent,* 157–62.
113. Mol, "Ecological Modernization and the Global Economy," 110.
114. Collier, "Topologies of Power," 99. See also Deleuze and Guattari, *A Thousand Plateaus.*
115. Sneddon et al., "Sustainable Development in a Post-Brundtland World," 263. See also Bernstein, "Liberal Environmentalism and Global Environmental Governance."
116. Neumann and Sending, *Governing the Global Polity,* 165. See also Tilly, *Coercion, Capital and European States, AD 990–1992,* 28.
117. Smith, *Against Ecological Sovereignty,* xx.
118. Eckersley, *The Green State,* 2.
119. Scott, *Two Cheers for Anarchism,* 141.

CHAPTER 7. AFRO-ECOLOGISM

1. Brockington et al., *Nature Unbound;* Cronon, "The Trouble with Wilderness"; Neumann, *Imposing Wilderness;* Mbembe, "Nicholas Sarkozy's Africa."
2. See, among others, Leach, "What Is Green?"
3. Eckersley, "The State as Gatekeeper," 136–37.
4. Africa Progress Panel, *Grain, Fish, Money,* 15.
5. Ibid., 46–47. See also Rotberg, *Africa Emerges,* chapter 11; Scoones et al., eds., *The Politics of Green Transformations;* Williams, ed., *The End of the Developmental State?*
6. See table 1, chapter 6.
7. Barry and Eckersley, eds., *The State and the Global Ecological Crisis;* Eckersley, *The Green State;* Dryzek et al., *Green States and Social Movements.*
8. Eckersley, *The Green State,* 202.
9. Cock, *The War Against Ourselves,* 31. See also Maathai, *The Challenge for Africa,* 173–80.
10. Lund, "The Past and Space," 17–18; Ranger, "Women and Environment in African Religion," 73; Ranger, *Voices from the Rocks.*
11. Seagle, "Discourse, Development and Legitimacy," 196. See also Hodgson, "Becoming Indigenous in Africa"; Keeley and Scoones, *Understanding Environmental Policy Processes,* 29–30; Maila and Loubser, "Emancipatory Indigenous Knowledge Systems."
12. Scott, *Seeing Like a State.*
13. Foucault, "On the Genealogy of Ethics," 256. See also Gordon, "Introduction," xix.
14. Ferguson, "Toward a Left Art of Government," 62.
15. Ibid., 67. See also Kuehls, *Beyond Sovereign Territory,* 5–23; Neumann and Sending, *Governing the Global Polity,* 43–44.
16. Hansen and Stepputat, "Introduction," 9.
17. Vincent, *Theories of the State,* 224.
18. Scott, *Seeing Like a State,* 345.
19. Barry, *The Politics of Actually Existing Unsustainability,* 283–85. On counter-conducts as a form of "being otherwise," see Death, "Counter-Conducts as a Mode of Resistance."

20. Kuehls, "States," 246.
21. Foucault, *The Will to Knowledge,* 143. See also Dalby, "Biopolitics and Climate Security in the Anthropocene."
22. Death, "Four Discourses of the Green Economy in the Global South."
23. Eckersley, *The Green State,* 2.

Bibliography

Abrahamsen, Rita. "A Breeding Ground for Terrorists? Africa and Britain's 'War on Terrorism.'" *Review of African Political Economy* 31, no. 102 (2004), 677–84.

———. *Disciplining Democracy: Development Discourse and Good Governance in Africa.* London: Zed Books, 2000.

———. "The Power of Partnerships in Global Governance." *Third World Quarterly* 25, no. 8 (2004), 1453–67.

———, and Michael C. Williams. *Security Beyond the State: Private Security in International Politics.* Cambridge: Cambridge University Press, 2011.

Adams, William M., and Jon Hutton. "People, Parks and Poverty: Political Ecology and Biodiversity Conservation." *Conservation and Society* 5, no. 2 (2007), 147–83.

Adaption Fund. "About." Available at https://www.adaptation-fund.org/about (accessed 26 June 2015).

Adem, Teferi Abate. "The Local Politics of Ethiopia's Green Revolution in South Wollo." *African Studies Review* 55, no. 3 (2012), 81–102.

Adger, W. Neil, and Andrew Jordan. "Sustainability: Exploring the Processes and Outcomes of Governance." In *Governing Sustainability,* ed. W. Neil Adger and Andrew Jordan, 3–31. Cambridge: Cambridge University Press, 2009.

Adichie, Chimamanda Ngozi. *Purple Hibiscus.* Chapel Hill: Algonquin Books, 2003.

Africa Progress Panel. *Grain, Fish, Money: Financing Africa's Green and Blue Revolutions.* Africa Progress Report 2014. Geneva: Africa Progress Panel, 2014.

African Centre for Biodiversity. *Running to Stand Still: Small-Scale Farmers and the Green Revolution in Malawi.* Johannesburg: African Centre for Biodiversity, 2014.

African Development Bank. "AfDB, Largest Financier of Clean Energy on the African Continent with $4.3 Billion in Energy Projects." 3 October 2013. Available at http://www.afdb.org/en/news-and-events/article/afdb-largest-financier-of-clean-energy-on-the-african-continent-with-4-3-billion-in-energy-projects-12327/ (accessed 4 July 2014).

———. "Democratic Republic of Congo gets $21.5 million green light to transform its vast forests." 30 August 2013. Available at http://www.afdb.org/en/news-and-events/article/democratic-republic-of-congo-gets-21-5-million-green-light-to-transform-its-vast-forests-12219/ (accessed 4 July 2014).

———. "Malawi Economic Outlook: 2013." Available at http://www.afdb.org/en/countries/southern-africa/malawi/malawi-economic-outlook/ (accessed 9 October 2013).

———, and OECD. *Enabling Green Growth in Africa: Joint AfDB–OECD Report from the Workshop held in Lusaka, Zambia,* 15–16 January 2013. Available at http://www.oecd.org/dac/environment-development/AfDB-OECD%20Enabling%20green%20growth%20in%20Africa%20workshop%20report.pdf (accessed 5 July 2015).

———, and WWF. *Africa Ecological Footprint Report: Green Infrastructure for Africa's Ecological Security.* Tunis: AfDB and WWF, 2012.

———. *African Ecological Futures 2015.* Abidjan: AfDB and WWF, 2015.

Agbiboa, Daniel Egiegba. "Have we heard the last? Oil, environmental insecurity, and the impact of the amnesty programme on the Niger Delta resistance movement." *Review of African Political Economy* 40, no. 137 (2013), 447–65.

Agnew, John, and Stuart Corbridge. *Mastering Space: Hegemony, Territory, and International Political Economy.* London: Routledge, 1995.

Agrawal, Arun. *Environmentality: Technologies of Government and the Making of Subjects.* Durham: Duke University Press, 2005.

Ahluwalia, Pal. *Politics and Post-Colonial Theory: African Inflections.* London: Routledge, 2001.

Ajulu, Rok. "Thabo Mbeki's African Renaissance in a Globalising World Economy: The Struggle for the Soul of the Continent." *Review of African Political Economy* 28, no. 87 (2001), 27–42.

Aké, Claude. *Democracy and Development in Africa.* Washington, D.C.: Brookings Institution Press, 1996.

Alexander, Jocelyn, and JoAnn McGregor. "Wildlife and Politics: CAMPFIRE in Zimbabwe." *Development and Change* 31 (2000), 605–27.

Ali, Saleem Hassan, ed. *Peace Parks: Conservation and Conflict Resolution.* Cambridge: MIT Press, 2007.

Aliber, Michael, and Ben Cousins. "Livelihoods after land reform in South Africa." *Journal of Agrarian Change* 13, no. 1 (2013), 140–65.

AllAfrica. "Africa: Continent's population reaches one billion." Available at http://allafrica.com/stories/200908200660.html (accessed 16 July 2014).

Amanor, Kojo Sebastian. "Introduction: Land and Sustainable Development Issues in Africa." In *Land and Sustainable Development in Africa,* ed. Kojo Sebastian Amanor and Sam Moyo, 1–32. London: Zed Books, 2008.

———, and Sam Moyo, eds. *Land and Sustainable Development in Africa.* London: Zed Books, 2008.

AMCEN. "Bamako Declaration on the Environment for Sustainable Development." 23–25 June 2010. Available at http://www.unep.org/roa/amcen/Amcen_Events /13th_Session/Docs/AMCEN-13-CRP-2_ENG.pdf (accessed 5 July 2015).

Amunwa, Ben. *Counting the Cost: Corporations and Human Rights Abuses in the Niger Delta.* London: Platform, 2011.

ANC. *Reconstruction and Development Plan.* Johannesburg: ANC, 1994. Available at http://www.polity.org.za/polity/govdocs/rdp/rdp2.html#2.10 (accessed 16 July 2014).

Anderson, David. "Depression, Dust Bowl, Demography, and Drought: The Colonial State and Soil Conservation in East Africa during the 1930s." *African Affairs* 83, no. 332 (1984), 321–43.

———. "'Yours in Struggle for Majimbo': Nationalism and the Party Politics of Decolonization in Kenya, 1955–1964." *Journal of Contemporary History* 40 (2005), 547–64.

———, and Adrian J. Browne. "The Politics of Oil in Eastern Africa." *Journal of Eastern African Studies* 5, no. 2 (2011), 369–410.

———, and Richard Grove. "Introduction: The Scramble for Eden: Past, Present and Future in African Conservation." In *Conservation in Africa: People, Policies and Practice,* ed. David Anderson and Richard Grove, 1–12. Cambridge: Cambridge University Press, 1987.

Anugwom, Edlyne E. "Beyond Oil: Environmental Rights, Travel, Local Knowledge, and Youth Conflict in the Oil-Rich Niger Delta of Nigeria." *Africa Today* 61, no. 2 (2015), 20–39.

Armstrong, David. "The Evolution of International Society." In *The Globalization of World Politics: An Introduction to International Relations,* ed. John Baylis, Steve Smith, and Patricia Owens, 36–52. 4th ed. Oxford: Oxford University Press, 2008.

Arora-Jonsson, Seema. "Virtue and Vulnerability: Discourses on Women, Gender and Climate Change." *Global Environmental Change* 21 (2011), 744–51.

Ashford, Nicholas A. "Government and environmental innovation in Europe and North America." *American Behavioural Scientist* 45, no. 9 (2002), 1417–34.

Assey, Paschal, Stephen Bass, Blandina Cheche, David Howlett, George Jambiya, Idris Kikula, Servacius Likwelile, Amon Manyama, Eric Mugurusi, Ruzika Muheto, and Longinus Rutasitara. *Environment at the Heart of Tanzania's Development: Lessons from Tanzania National Strategy for Growth and Reduction of Poverty (MKUKUTA),* Natural Resource Issues Series No. 6. London: International Institute for Environment and Development, 2007.

Atela, Joanes O. *The Politics of Agricultural Carbon Finance: The Case of the Kenya Agricultural Carbon Project.* Brighton: STEPS Centre, 2012.

AU, EU, and FAO. *The Great Green Wall for the Sahara and the Sahel Initiative.* Undated. Available at http://www.fao.org/docrep/016/ap603e/ap603e.pdf (accessed 16 July 2014).

Aylett, Alex. "Conflict, Collaboration and Climate Change: Participatory Democracy and Urban Environmental Struggles in Durban, South Africa." *International Journal of Urban and Regional Research* 34, no. 3 (2010), 478–95.

Ayoob, Mohammed. "The Third World in the System of States: Acute Schizophrenia or Growing Pains?" *International Studies Quarterly* 33, no. 1 (1989), 67–79.

Bachmann, Jan. "Governmentality and Counterterrorism: Appropriating International Security Projects in Kenya." *Journal of Intervention and Statebuilding* 6, no. 1 (2012), 41–56.

Bachram, Heidi. "Climate Fraud and Carbon Colonialism: The New Trade in Greenhouse Gases." *Capitalism, Nature, Socialism* 15, no. 4 (2004), 5–20.

Bailey, Rob. "Establishing Low Carbon Growth in Ethiopia." *NAI Forum,* 3 September 2013.

Baker, Lucy. "Opportunity and Crisis in South Africa's Electricity." June 2015. Available at http://blogs.sussex.ac.uk/sussexenergygroup/2015/06/02/opportunity-and-crisis-in-south-africas-electricity/ (accessed 26 June 2015).

———. "Renewable Energy in South Africa's Minerals-Energy Complex: A 'Low Carbon' Transition?" *Review of African Political Economy* 42, no. 144 (2015), 245–61.

———, Peter Newell, and Jon Phillips. "The Political Economy of Energy Transitions: The Case of South Africa." *New Political Economy* 19, no. 6 (2014), 791–818.

Baker, Susan. *Sustainable Development.* Abingdon: Routledge, 2006.

Bakker, Karen. "Commons versus Commodities: Political Ecologies of Water Privatization." In *Global Political Ecology,* ed. Richard Peet, Paul Robbins, and Michael J. Watts, 347–70. Abingdon: Routledge, 2011.

Baldwin, Andrew. "Orientalising Environmental Citizenship: Climate Change, Migration and the Potentiality of Race." *Citizenship Studies* 16, no. 5–6 (2012), 625–40.

———. "Racialisation and the Figure of the Climate-Change Migrant." *Environment and Planning A* 45 (2013), 1474–90.

Banda, Tasila, and Steve Bass. *Inclusive Green Growth in Zambia: Scoping the Needs and Potentials.* London: IIED, 2014.

Bank, Leslie, and Gary Minkley. "Going Nowhere Slowly? Land, Livelihoods and Rural Development in the Eastern Cape." *Social Dynamics: A Journal of African Studies* 31, no. 1 (2005), 1–38.

Bär, Holger, Klaus Jacob, and Stefan Werland. *Green Economy Discourses in the Run-Up to Rio 2012.* Berlin: Environmental Policy Research Centre, Freie Universität Berlin, 2011.

Barbier, Edward B. "Global Governance: The G20 and a Global Green New Deal." *Economics: The e-journal,* 4 (2010), 1–32.

———. "The Policy Challenges for Green Economy and Sustainable Economic Development." *Natural Resources Forum* 35 (2011), 233–45.

Barnett, Clive. "The consolations of 'neoliberalism.'" *Geoforum* 36 (2005), 7–12.

———, and Dianne Scott. "Spaces of Opposition: Activism and Deliberation in Post-Apartheid Environmental Politics." *Environment and Planning A* 39 (2007), 2612–31.

Barnett, Jon. *The Meaning of Environmental Security: Ecological Politics and Policy in the New Security Era.* London: Zed Books, 2001.

Barrett, George. "Markets of Exceptionalism: Peace Parks in Southern Africa." *Journal of Contemporary African Studies* 31, no. 3 (2013), 457–80.

Barrow, Clyde W. "The Miliband–Poulantzas Debate: An Intellectual History." In *Paradigm Lost: State Theory Reconsidered,* ed. Stanley Aronowitz and Peter Bratsis, 3–52. Minneapolis: University of Minnesota Press, 2002.

Barry, Andrew. *Political Machines.* London: Athlone, 2001.

Barry, John. *Rethinking Green Politics: Nature, Virtue, Progress.* London: Sage, 1999.

———. *The Politics of Actually Existing Unsustainability: Human Flourishing in a Climate-Changed, Carbon-Constrained World.* Oxford: Oxford University Press, 2012.

———, and Robyn Eckersley. "An Introduction to Reinstating the State." In *The State and the Global Ecological Crisis,* ed. John Barry and Robyn Eckersley, ix–xxv. Cambridge: MIT Press, 2005.

———, eds. *The State and the Global Ecological Crisis.* Cambridge: MIT Press, 2005.

———. "W(h)ither the Green State?" In *The State and the Global Ecological Crisis,* ed. John Barry and Robyn Eckersley, 255–72. Cambridge: MIT Press, 2005.

Bassey, Nnimmo. *To Cook a Continent: Destructive Extraction and the Climate Crisis in Africa.* Cape Town: Pambazuka Press, 2012.

Baxter, Joan. *Understanding Land Investment Deals in Africa: Country Report Mali.* Oakland, Calif.: Oakland Institute, 2011.

Bayart, Jean-François. "Africa in the World: A History of Extraversion." *African Affairs* 99, no. 395 (2000), 217–67.

———. *Global Subjects: A Political Critique of Globalization.* Cambridge: Polity, 2007.

———. *The State in Africa: The Politics of the Belly.* 2d ed. Cambridge: Polity, 2009.

BBC. "Copenhagen deal reaction in quotes." *BBC News* (UK), 19 December 2009.

———. "Rwanda gets tough on plastic bags." *BBC News* (UK), 17 January 2006.

———. "Rwandan opposition politician found dead." *BBC News* (UK), 14 July 2010.

Beck, Ulrich. *Risk Society: Toward a New Modernity.* London: Sage, 1992.

———. *What Is Globalization?* Cambridge: Polity, 2000.

Beinart, William. *The Rise of Conservation in South Africa: Settlers, Livestock, and the Environment 1770–1950.* Oxford: Oxford University Press, 2003.

———, and Peter Coates. *Environment and History: The Taming of Nature in the USA and South Africa.* London: Routledge, 1995.

Benjamin, Chantelle. "South Africa comes last in sustainable development index." *Mail and Guardian* (SA), 20 September 2013.

Benjaminsen, Tor A., Mara J. Goldman, Maya Y. Minwary, and Faustin P. Maganga. "Wildlife Management in Tanzania: State Control, Rent Seeking and Community Resistance." *Development and Change* 44, no. 5 (2013), 1087–1109.

Bennett, Brett M. "Naturalising Australian Trees in South Africa: Climate, Exotics and Experimentation." *Journal of Southern African Studies* 37, no. 2 (2011), 265–80.

Berger, Mark T. "States of Nature and the Nature of States: The Fate of Nations, the Collapse of States, and the Future of the World." *Third World Quarterly* 28, no. 6, (2007), 1203–14.

Bernstein, Henry. "Commercial Agriculture in South Africa since 1994: 'Natural, Simply Capitalism.'" *Journal of Agrarian Change* 13, no. 1 (2013), 23–46.

———, and Philip Woodhouse. "Telling Environmental Change Like It Is? Reflections on a Study in Sub-Saharan Africa." *Journal of Agrarian Change* 1, no. 2 (2001), 283–324.

Bernstein, Steven. "Liberal environmentalism and global environmental governance." *Global Environmental Politics* 2, no. 3 (2002), 1–16.

Berry, Sara. *No Condition Is Permanent: The Social Dynamics of Agrarian Change in Sub-Saharan Africa.* Madison: University of Wisconsin Press, 1993.

Bieler, Andreas, and Adam David Morton. "The Will-o'-the-Wisp of the Transnational State." *Journal of Australian Political Economy* 72 (2013), 23–51.

Biermann, Christine, and Becky Mansfield. "Biodiversity, Purity, and Death: Conservation Biology as Biopolitics." *Environment and Planning D: Society and Space* 32 (2014), 257–73.

Biermann, Frank, and Klaus Dingwerth. "Global Environmental Change and the Nation State." *Global Environmental Politics* 4, no. 1 (2004), 1–22.

Bilgin, Pinar, and Adam David Morton. "Historicizing Representations of 'Failed States': Beyond the Cold War Annexation of the Social Sciences?" *Third World Quarterly* 23, no. 1 (2002), 55–80.

Bina, Olivia. "The Green Economy and Sustainable Development: An Uneasy Balance?" *Environment and Planning C: Government and Policy* 31 (2013), 1023–47.

Black, Jeremy. *Maps and Politics.* London: Reaktion, 1997.

Black, Richard. "Climate 'Drives African Conflict,'" *BBC News* (UK), 24 November 2009.

Blaikie, Piers. "Is Small Really Beautiful? Community-Based Natural Resource Management in Malawi and Botswana." *World Development* 34, no. 11 (2006), 1942–57.

Blaine, Sue. "Carbon Tax 'An Overkill,' Say Major Electricity Users." *Business Day* (SA), 27 September 2013.

Bloomfield, Michael John. "Shame Campaigns and Environmental Justice: Corporate Shaming as Activist Strategy." *Environmental Politics* 23, no. 2 (2014), 263–81.

Blowfield, Michael, and Jedrzej George Frynas. "Setting New Agendas: Critical Perspectives on Corporate Social Responsibility in the Developing World." *International Affairs* 81, no. 3 (2005), 499–513.

Bøås, Morten. "Autochthony and Citizenship: 'Civil Society' as Vernacular Architecture?" *Journal of Intervention and Statebuilding* 6, no. 1 (2012), 91–105.

Bob, Clifford. "Marketing Rebellion: Insurgent Groups, International Media and NGO Support." *International Politics* 38 (2001), 311–34.

Bofin, Peter, Marie-Lise du Preez, André Standing, and Aled Williams. *REDD Integrity: Addressing Governance and Corruption Challenges in Schemes for Reducing Emissions from Deforestation and Forest Degradation (REDD).* Bergen: Chr. Michelsen Institute, 2011.

Bojö, Jan, and Rama Chandra Reddy. *Status and Evolution of Environmental Priorities in the Poverty Reduction Strategies: An Assessment of Fifty Poverty Reduction Strategy Papers.* Washington, D.C.: World Bank, 2003.

Bond, Patrick. *Durban's Climate Gamble: Trading Carbon, Betting the Earth.* Pretoria: UNISA, 2011.

———. "Justice." In *Critical Environmental Politics,* ed. Carl Death, 133–45. Abingdon: Routledge, 2014.

———. "Social Movements and Corporate Social Responsibility in South Africa." *Development and Change* 39, no. 6 (2008), 1037–52.

———. "South Africa's Carbon Tax Debate Disappoints." *TripleCrisis,* 12 March 2012. Available at http://triplecrisis.com/south-africas-carbon-tax-debate-disappoints/ (accessed 7 October 2013).

———. *Unsustainable South Africa: Environment, Development and Social Protest.* Pietermaritzburg: University of Natal Press, 2002.

Bonneuil, Christophe. "Development as Experience: Science and State-Building in Late Colonial and Postcolonial Africa, 1930–70." *Osiris* 15 (2000), 258–81.

Bookchin, Murray. *Remaking Society: Pathways to a Green Future.* Boston: South End Press, 1990.

———. *Toward an Ecological Society.* Montreal: Black Rose Books, 1980.

Boone, Catherine. *Property and Political Order in Africa: Land Rights and the Structure of Politics.* Cambridge: Cambridge University Press, 2014.

Booth, David. *Governance for Development in Africa: Building on What Works.* London: Overseas Development Institute, 2011.

Borras, Saturnino M., Jr., Ruth Hall, Ian Scoones, Ben White, and Wendy Wolford. "Towards a Better Understanding of Global Land Grabbing: An Editorial Introduction." *Journal of Peasant Studies* 38, no. 2 (2011), 209–16.

Boserup, Esther. "Environment, Population, and Technology in Primitive Societies." *Population and Development Review* 2 (1976), 21–36.

Bowman, Andy. "Shell to Sea." *Red Pepper,* December 2008.

Brassett, James, Stuart Croft, and Nick Vaughan-Williams. "Introduction: An Agenda for Resilience Research in Politics and International Relations." *Politics* 33, no. 4 (2013), 221–28.

Braudel, Fernand. *A History of Civilisations.* London: Penguin, 1993.

Brenner, Neil. "Beyond State-Centrism? Space, Territoriality and Geographical Scale in Globalization Studies." *Theory and Society* 29 (1999), 39–78.

———, and Stuart Elden. "Henri Lefebvre on State, Space, Territory." *International Political Sociology* 3 (2009), 353–77.

———, Bob Jessop, Martin Jones, and Gordon Macleod. "Introduction: State Space in Question." In *State/Space: A Reader,* ed. Neil Brenner, Bob Jessop, Martin Jones, and Gordon Macleod, 1–26. Oxford: Blackwell, 2003.

Brenton, Tony. *The Greening of Machiavelli: The Evolution of International Environmental Politics.* London: RIIA and Earthscan, 1994.

Broch-Due, Vigdis. "Producing Nature and Poverty in Africa: An Introduction." In *Producing Nature and Poverty in Africa,* ed. Vigdis Broch-Due and Richard A. Schroeder, 9–52. Uppsala: Nordiska Afrikainstitutet, 2000.

Brockington, Dan. *Celebrity and the Environment: Fame, Wealth and Power in Conservation.* London: Zed Books, 2009.

———. *Fortress Conservation: The Preservation of the Mkomazi Game Reserve, Tanzania.* Oxford: James Currey, 2002.

———. "The politics and ethnography of environmentalism in Tanzania." *African Affairs* 105, no. 418 (2006), 97–116.

———, Rosaleen Duffy, and Jim Igoe. *Nature Unbound: Conservation, Capitalism and the Future of Protected Areas.* London: Earthscan, 2008.

———, and Katherine Scholfield. "The Work of Conservation Organisations in Sub-Saharan Africa." *Journal of Modern African Studies* 48, no. 1 (2010), 1–33.

Brooks, Shirley. "Images of 'Wild Africa': Nature Tourism and the (Re)Creation of Hluhluwe Game Reserve, 1930–1945." *Journal of Historical Geography* 31 (2005), 220–40.

———. "Re-Reading the Hluhluwe–Umfolozi Game Reserve: Constructions of a 'Natural' Space." *Transformation* 44 (2000), 63–79.

Brown, Michael Barratt. "'Fair Trade' with Africa." *Review of African Political Economy* 34, no. 112 (2007), 267–77.

Brown, William. "Africa and International Relations: A Comment on IR Theory, Anarchy and Statehood." *Review of International Studies* 32, no. 1 (2006), 119–43.

———. "Sovereignty Matters: Africa, Donors, and the Aid Relationship." *African Affairs* 112, no. 447 (2013), 262–82.

Bruff, Ian. "The relevance of Nicos Poulantzas for contemporary debates on 'the international.'" *International Politics* 49, no. 2 (2012), 177–94.

Bryant, Raymond L., and Sinéad Bailey. *Third World Political Ecology.* London: Routledge, 1997.

Bull, Hedley. *The Anarchical Society: A Study of Order in Modern Politics.* New York: Columbia University Press, 1977.

Bullard, Robert D. *Dumping in Dixie: Race, Class and Environmental Quality.* Boulder: Westview Press, 1990.

Bunn, David. "An Unnatural State: Tourism, Water and Wildlife Photography in the Early Kruger National Park." In *Social History and African Environments,* ed. William Beinart and Joann McGregor, 199–220. Oxford: James Currey, 2003.

Büscher, Bram. "Derivative Nature: Interrogating the Value of Conservation in 'Boundless Southern Africa,'" *Third World Quarterly* 31, no. 2 (2010), 259–76.

———. "Seeking 'Telos' in the 'Transfrontier'? Neoliberalism and the Transcending of Community Conservation in Southern Africa." *Environment and Planning A* 42 (2010), 644–60.

———. *Transforming the Frontier: Peace Parks and the Politics of Neoliberal Conservation in Southern Africa.* Durham: Duke University Press, 2013.

———, and Ton Dietz. "Conjunctions of Governance: The State and the Conservation–Development Nexus in Southern Africa." *Journal of Transdisciplinary Environmental Studies* 4, no. 2 (2005), 1–15.

———, and Robert Fletcher. "Accumulation by Conservation." *New Political Economy* 20, no. 2 (2015), 273–98.

———, and Maano Ramutsindela. "Green Violence: Rhino Poaching and the War to Save Southern Africa's Peace Parks." *African Affairs* online first (2015), 1–22.

Business and Biodiversity Campaign. "Bartering With Trees in the World Cup Host Country South Africa." 5 July 2010. Available at http://www.business-biodiversity.eu/default.asp?Menue=155andNews=99 (accessed 6 July 2015).

Butler, Judith. *Gender Trouble: Feminism and the Subversion of Identity.* London: Routledge, 1990.

Buttel, F. H. "Ecological modernization as social theory." *Geoforum* 31, no. 1 (2000), 57–65.

Buzan, Barry, and Richard Little. *International Systems in World History: Remaking the Study of International Relations.* Oxford: Oxford University Press, 2000.

Calhoun, Craig J. "Imagining Solidarity: Cosmopolitanism, Constitutional Patriotism, and the Public Sphere." *Public Culture* 14, no. 1 (2002), 147–71.

Carmody, Pádraig. *The New Scramble for Africa.* Cambridge: Polity, 2011.

Carruthers, Jane. *The Kruger National Park: A Social and Political History.* Scottsville: University of Natal Press, 1995.

———. "Tracking in Game Trails: Looking Afresh at the Politics of Environmental History in South Africa." *Environmental History* 11 (2006), 804–29.

Castree, Noel, and Bruce Braun. "The Construction of Nature and the Nature of Construction: Analytical and Political Tools for Building Survivable Futures." In *Remaking Reality: Nature at the Millennium,* ed. Bruce Braun and Noel Castree, 3–42. London: Routledge, 1998.

Cavanagh, Connor J. "Biopolitics, Environmental Change, and Development Studies." *Forum for Development Studies* 41, no. 2 (2014), 273–94.

Cerny, Philip G. *The Changing Architecture of Politics: Structure, Agency and the Future of the State.* London: Sage, 1990.

Chabal, Patrick, and Jean-Pascal Daloz. *Africa Works: Disorder as Political Instrument.* Oxford: James Currey, 1999.

Chachage, Chambi. *Land Acquisition and Accumulation in Tanzania: The Case of Morogoro, Iringa and Pwani Regions.* Research paper commissioned for Pelum Tanzania, October 2010.

Chandler, David. *Empire in Denial: The Politics of State-Building.* London: Pluto Press, 2006.

Chapin, Mac. "A challenge to conservationists." *Worldwatch Magazine,* November/December 2004, 17–31.

Chari, Sharad. "State Racism and Biopolitical Struggle: The Evasive Commons in Twentieth-Century Durban, South Africa." *Radical History Review* 108 (2010), 73–90.

Chasek, Pamela S. *Earth Negotiations: Analyzing Thirty Years of Environmental Diplomacy.* Tokyo: UNUP, 2001.

Chatterjee, Partha. *The Politics of the Governed: Reflections on Popular Politics in Most of the World.* New York: Columbia University Press, 2004.

Chaturvedi, Sanjay, and Timothy Doyle. *Climate Terror: A Critical Geopolitics of Climate Change.* London: Palgrave Macmillan, 2015.

Chenje, Munyaradzi, and Jennifer Mohamed-Katerere. "Invasive Alien Species." In *African Environmental Outlook 2: Our Environment, Our Wealth.* Nairobi: UNEP, 2006.

Cheru, Fantu. “The Silent Revolution and the Weapons of the Weak: Transformation and Innovation from Below.” In *The Global Resistance Reader*, ed. Louise Amoore, 74–85. London: Routledge, 2005.

Chinigò, Davide. “The Politics of Land Registration in Ethiopia: Territorialising State Power in the Rural Milieu.” *Review of African Political Economy* 42, no. 144 (2015), 174–89.

Christoff, Peter. “Out of Chaos, a Shining Star? Toward a Typology of Green States.” In *The State and the Global Ecological Crisis,* ed. John Barry and Robyn Eckersley, 25–52. Cambridge: MIT Press, 2005.

Cieplak, Piotr. “Shunting Hectares: Land Reform in South Africa.” *Africa Research Institute,* 18 June 2013.

Clapham, Christopher. *Africa and the International System: The Politics of State Survival.* Cambridge: Cambridge University Press, 1996.

———. “Degrees of Statehood.” *Review of International Studies* 24 (1998), 143–57.

———. “Discerning the New Africa.” *International Affairs* 74, no. 2 (1998), 263–69.

———. “Governmentality and Economic Policy in Sub-Saharan Africa.” *Third World Quarterly* 17, no. 4 (1996), 809–24.

Clapp, Jennifer. *Food.* Cambridge: Polity, 2012.

———. “The Political Economy of Food Aid in an Era of Agricultural Biotechnology.” *Global Governance* 11 (2005), 467–85.

———, and Peter Dauvergne. *Paths to a Green World: The Political Economy of the Global Environment.* Cambridge: MIT Press, 2005.

Clark, Ian. *Globalization and International Relations Theory.* Oxford: Oxford University Press, 1999.

———. *International Legitimacy and World Society.* Oxford; Oxford University Press, 2007.

Cloete, Elsie L. “Africa’s ‘Charismatic Megafauna’ and Berlin’s ‘Two Concepts of Liberty’: Postcolony Routes to Utopia?” *Politikon: South African Journal of Political Studies* 35, no. 3 (2008), 257–76.

———. “Going to the Bush: Language, Power and the Conserved Environment in Southern Africa.” *Environmental Education Research* 17, no. 1 (2011), 35–51.

Cock, Jacklyn. “The Challenge of Ecological Transformation in Post-Apartheid South Africa: The Re-Emergence of an Environmental Justice Movement.” In *Contesting Transformation: Popular Resistance in Twenty-First-Century South Africa,* ed. Marcelle C. Dawson and Luke Sinwell, 183–200. London: Pluto, 2012.

———. *The War Against Ourselves: Nature, Power and Justice.* Johannesburg: Wits University Press, 2007.

Collier, Paul. *Bottom Billion: Why the Poorest Countries Are Failing and What Can Be Done About It.* Oxford: Oxford University Press, 2007.

Collier, Stephen J. "Topologies of Power: Foucault's Analysis of Political Government Beyond Governmentality." *Theory, Culture, Society* 26, no. 6 (2009), 78–108.

Comaroff, Jean, and John L. Comaroff. "Naturing the Nation: Aliens, Apocalypse and the Postcolonial State." *Journal of Southern African Studies* 27, no. 3 (2001), 627–51.

———. *Theory from the South: or, How Euro-America Is Evolving Toward Africa.* Boulder: Paradigm, 2012.

Comaroff, John L. "Reflections on the Colonial State, in South Africa and Elsewhere: Factions, Fragments, Facts and Fictions." *Social Identities* 4, no. 3 (1998), 321–61.

Conca, Ken. "Old States in New Bottles? The Hybridization of Authority in Global Environmental Governance." In *The State and the Global Ecological Crisis,* ed. John Barry and Robyn Eckersley, 181–205. Cambridge: MIT Press, 2005.

———. "Rethinking the Ecology–Sovereignty Debate." *Millennium* 23, no. 3 (1994), 701–11.

———, Thomas Princen, and Michael F. Maniates. "Confronting Consumption." *Global Environmental Politics* 1, no. 3 (2001), 1–10.

Consumers International. "Green Action Fund winners revealed." available at http://www.consumersinternational.org/news-and-media/news/2012/07/green-fund/#.UnuEeHfuqZM (accessed 16 July 2014).

Coole, Diana. "Too Many Bodies? The Return and Disavowal of the Population Question." *Environmental Politics* 22, no. 2 (2013), 195–215.

Cooper, Frederick. *Africa since 1940: The Past of the Present.* Cambridge: Cambridge University Press, 2002.

Cornelissen, Scarlett, Fantu Cheru, and Timothy M. Shaw. "Introduction: Africa and International Relations in the 21st Century: Still Challenging Theory?" In *Africa and International Relations in the 21st Century,* ed. Scarlett Cornelissen, Fantu Cheru, and Timothy M. Shaw, 1–17. Basingstoke: Palgrave Macmillan, 2012.

Corson, Catherine. "Shifting Environmental Governance in a Neoliberal World: US AID for Conservation." *Antipode* 42, no. 3 (2010), 576–602.

———. "Territorialization, Enclosure and Neoliberalism: Non-State Influence in Struggles over Madagascar's Forests." *Journal of Peasant Studies* 38, no. 4 (2011), 703–26.

Cousins, Ben. "Agrarian Reform and the 'Two Economies': Transforming South Africa's Countryside." In *The Land Question in South Africa: The Challenge of Transformation and Redistribution,* ed. Lungisile Ntsebeza and Ruth Hall, 220–41. Cape Town: HSRC Press, 2007.

Cox, Robert W. "Social Forces, States, and World Orders: Beyond International Relations Theory." *Millennium* 10, no. 2 (1981), 126–55.

Critchley, William. *More People, More Trees: Environmental Recovery in Africa.* Rugby: Practical Action, 2010.

Cronon, William. "The Trouble with Wilderness: or, Getting Back to the Wrong Nature." *Environmental History* 1, no. 1 (1996), 7–28.

Crook, Rachel. "Gays, Gods and Governments: Homophobia in Uganda." *OpenDemocracy* (UK), 20 February 2012.

Crummey, Donald, and Alex Winter-Nelson. "Farmer Tree-Planting in Wällo, Ethiopia." In *African Savannas: Global Narratives and Local Knowledge of Environmental Change,* ed. Thomas J. Bassett and Donald Crummey, 91–120. Oxford: James Currey, 2003.

DAC. *Aid to Environment Development Co-operation Report 2012.* Paris: OECD, 2012.

Dalby, Simon. "Biopolitics and Climate Security in the Anthropocene." *Geoforum* 49 (2013), 184–92.

———. "Ecological Politics, Violence, and the Theme of Empire." *Global Environmental Politics* 4, no. 2 (2004), 1–11.

———. *Security and Environmental Change.* Cambridge: Polity, 2009.

Darier, Eric. "Environmental Governmentality: The Case of Canada's Green Plan." *Environmental Politics* 5, no. 4 (1996), 585–606.

Dauvergne, Peter, and Genevieve LeBaron. "The Social Cost of Environmental Solutions." *New Political Economy* 18, no. 3 (2013), 410–30.

Davidson, Stewart. "The Insuperable Imperative: A Critique of the Ecologically Modernizing State." *Capitalism Nature Socialism* 23, no. 2 (2012), 31–50.

Davis, Mike. *Late Victorian Holocausts: El Niño Famines and the Making of the Third World.* London: Verso, 2001.

———. *Planet of Slums.* London: Verso, 2006.

Dean, Mitchell. *Governing Societies: Political Perspectives on Domestic and International Rule.* Maidenhead: Open University Press, 2007.

———. *Governmentality: Power and Rule in Modern Society.* London: Sage, 1999.

Death, Carl. "A Predictable Disaster for the Climate–But Who Else Won and Lost in Durban at COP17?" *Environmental Politics* 21, no. 6 (2012), 980–86.

———. "Can We Save the Planet?" In *Global Politics: A New Introduction,* ed. Jenny Edkins and Maja Zehfuss, 61–84. Abingdon: Routledge, 2013.

———. "Counter-Conducts as a Mode of Resistance: Ways of 'Not Being Like That' in South Africa." *Global Society* (forthcoming).

———. "Environmental Mainstreaming and Post-Sovereign Governance in Tanzania." *Journal of Eastern African Studies* 7, no. 1 (2013), 1–20.

———. "Environmental Movements, Climate Change, and Consumption in South Africa." *Journal of Southern African Studies* 40, no. 6 (2014), 1215–34.

———. "Four Discourses of the Green Economy in the Global South." *Third World Quarterly* 36, no. 12 (2015), 2207–24.

———. *Governing Sustainable Development: Partnerships, Protests and Power.* Abingdon: Routledge, 2010.

———. "Governmentality at the Limits of the International: African Politics and Foucauldian Theory." *Review of International Studies* 39, no. 3 (2013), 763–87.

———. "Green States in Africa: Beyond the Usual Suspects." *Environmental Politics* 25, no. 1 (2016), 116–35.

———. " 'Greening' the 2010 FIFA World Cup: Environmental Sustainability and the Mega-Event in South Africa." *Journal of Environmental Policy and Planning* 13, no. 2 (2011), 99–117.

———. "Leading by Example: South African Foreign Policy and Global Environmental Politics." *International Relations* 25, no. 4 (2011), 453–76.

———. "The Green Economy in South Africa: Global Discourses and Local Politics." *Politikon: South African Journal of Political Studies* 41, no. 1 (2014), 1–22.

———, and Clive Gabay. "Introduction: Critical Perspectives on Liberal Interventions and Governmentality in Africa." In *Critical Perspectives on African Politics: Liberal Interventions, State-Building and Civil Society,* ed. Clive Gabay and Carl Death, 1–17. Abingdon: Routledge, 2014.

DED, DEA, DSI, and DTI. *Green Economy Summit Discussion Document.* Republic of South Africa, 2010. Available at http://www.sustainabilityinstitute.net/component/docman/cat_view/44-related-research-initiatives/43-green-economy (accessed 30 April 2013).

Deegan, Heather. *Africa Today: Culture, Economics, Religion, Security.* Abingdon: Routledge, 2009.

Deen, Thalif. "Rio+20: Promised Green Economy Was a Fake, Say Activists." *IPS,* 22 June 2012.

de la Court, Thijs. *Beyond Brundtland: Green Development in the 1990s.* London: Zed Books, 1990.

de Villiers, Bertus. *Land Claims and National Parks: The Makuleke Experience.* Pretoria: HSRC, 1999.

Deleuze, Gilles, and Félix Guattari. *A Thousand Plateaus: Capitalism and Schizophrenia.* London: Athlone, 1988.

Dent, Christopher M. "Africa and China: A New Kind of Development Partnership." In *China and Africa Development Relations,* ed. Christopher M. Dent, 1–20. Abingdon: Routledge, 2011.

Department of Rural Development and Land Reform. *Policy for the Integration of Environmental Planning into Land Reform and Rural Development Projects.* RSA: Pretoria, 2012.

Deressa, Temesgen Tadesse. *Climate Change and Growth in Africa: Challenges and the Way Forward.* Africa Growth Initiative Report. Washington, D.C.: Brookings Institution, 2014.

Desai, Ashwin, and Goolam Vahed. "World Cup 2010: Africa's Turn or the Turn on Africa?" *Soccer and Society* 11, no. 1 (2010), 154–67.

de-Shalit, Avner. "Sustainability and Population Policies: Myths, Truths and Half-Baked Ideas." In *Global Sustainable Development in the 21st Century*, ed. Keekok Lee, Alan Holland, and Desmond MacNeill, 188–98. Edinburgh: Edinburgh University Press, 2000.

Development Bank of Southern Africa. *Programmes in Support of Transitioning South Africa to a Green Economy.* Johannesburg: DBSA, 2011.

Devereux, Stephen. "Why does famine persist in Africa?" *Food Security* 1, no. 1 (2009), 25–35.

de Wet, Chris. *Moving Together, Drifting Apart: Betterment Planning and Villagisation in a South African Homeland.* Johannesburg: Witwatersrand University Press, 1995.

Diamond, Jared. *Collapse: How Societies Choose to Fail or Survive.* London: Penguin, 2011.

Di Muzio, Tim. "Governing Global Slums: The Biopolitics of Target 11." *Global Governance* 14 (2008), 305–26.

Dobson, Andrew. *Citizenship and the Environment.* Oxford: Oxford University Press, 2003.

———. "Environmental Citizenship: Towards Sustainable Development." *Sustainable Development* 15 (2007), 276–85.

———. *Green Political Thought.* 4th ed. Abingdon: Routledge, 2007.

Dobson, Andrew P., Markus Borner, Anthony R. E. Sinclair, et al. "Road Will Ruin Serengeti." *Nature* 467 (2010), 272–73.

Doherty, Brian, and Timothy Doyle. *Environmentalism, Resistance and Solidarity: The Politics of Friends of the Earth International.* Basingstoke: Palgrave Macmillan, 2014.

Dorling, Daniel, and David Fairbairn. *Mapping: Ways of Representing the World.* Harlow: Longman, 1997.

Doty, Roxanne Lynne. *Imperial Encounters: The Politics of Representation in North–South Relations.* Minneapolis: University of Minnesota Press, 1996.

Dowden, Richard. *Africa: Altered States, Ordinary Miracles.* London: Portobello Books, 2009.

Doyle, Timothy. *Environmental Movements in Minority and Majority Worlds: A Global Perspective.* New Brunswick: Rutgers University Press, 2004.

———, and Brian Doherty. "Green Public Spheres and the Green Governance State: The Politics of Emancipation and Ecological Conditionality." *Environmental Politics* 15, no. 5 (2006), 881–92.

Draper, Malcolm. "Zen and the Art of Garden Province Maintenance: The Soft Intimacy of Hard Men in the Wilderness of KwaZulu-Natal, South Africa, 1952–1997." *Journal of Southern African Studies* 24, no. 4 (1998), 801–28.

Dryzek, John S. "Resistance Is Fertile." *Global Environmental Politics* 1, no. 1 (2001), 11–17.

———, David Downes, Christian Hunold, David Schlosberg, and Hans-Kristian Hernes. *Green States and Social Movements: Environmentalism in the United States, United Kingdom, Germany, and Norway.* Oxford: Oxford University Press, 2003.

———, Christian Hunold, David Schlosberg, David Downes, and Hans-Kristian Hernes. "The Environmental Transformation of the State: The USA, Norway, Germany and the UK." *Political Studies* 50, no. 4 (2002), 659–82.

Dual Citizen. *The Global Green Economy Index.* Washington, D.C.: Dual Citizen, 2012.

Duffield, Mark. *Development, Security and Unending War: Governing the World of Peoples.* Cambridge: Polity, 2007.

Duffy, Rosaleen. *Killing for Conservation: Wildlife Policy in Zimbabwe.* Oxford: James Currey, 2000.

———. "Non-Governmental Organisations and Governance States: The Impact of Transnational Environmental Management Networks in Madagascar." *Environmental Politics* 15, no. 5 (2006), 731–49.

———. "The Environmental Challenge to the Nation-State: Superparks and National Parks Policy in Zimbabwe." *Journal of Southern African Studies* 23, no. 3 (1997), 441–51.

———. "The Potential and Pitfalls of Global Environmental Governance: The Politics of Transfrontier Conservation Areas in Southern Africa." *Political Geography* 25 (2006), 89–112.

———. "Waging a War to Save Biodiversity: The Rise of Militarized Conservation." *International Affairs* 90, no. 4 (2014), 819–34.

Duit, Andreas, Peter H. Feindt, and James Meadowcroft. "Greening Leviathan: The Rise of the Environmental State?" *Environmental Politics* 25, no. 1 (2016), 1–23.

Dunn, Kevin C. "Contested State Spaces: African National Parks and the State." *European Journal of International Relations* 15, no. 3 (2009), 423–46.

———. "Madlib #32. The (Blank) African State: Rethinking the Sovereign State in International Relations Theory." In *Africa's Challenge to International Relations Theory,* ed. Kevin C. Dunn and Timothy M. Shaw, 46–63. Basingstoke: Palgrave Macmillan, 2001.

Dzingirai, Vupenyu. "The New Scramble for the African Countryside." *Development and Change* 34, no. 2 (2003), 243–63.

Eckersley, Robyn. "Moving Forward in the Climate Negotiations: Multilateralism or Minilateralism?" *Global Environmental Politics* 12, no. 2 (2012), 24–42.

———. *The Green State: Rethinking Democracy and Sovereignty.* Cambridge: MIT Press, 2004.

———. "The State as Gatekeeper: A Reply." *Politics and Ethics Review* 2, no. 2 (2006), 127–38.

Economist, The. "The Hopeful Continent: Africa Rising." *The Economist* (UK), 3 December 2011.

———. "Zimbabwe After Hyperinflation: In Dollars They Trust." *The Economist* (UK), 27 April 2013.

Edigheji Omano, ed. *Constructing a Democratic Developmental State in South Africa: Potentials and Challenges.* Cape Town: HSRC Press, 2010.

Editor. "Kenya's Green Economy on a 'Positive' Growth." *Business Daily* (Kenya), 7 May 2013.

Edkins, Jenny. *Poststructuralism and International Relations: Bringing the Political Back In.* London: Lynne Rienner, 1999.

———. *Whose Hunger? Concepts of Famine, Practices of Aid.* Minneapolis: University of Minnesota Press, 2000.

EJOLT. *Crude Justice and Ecocide in the Niger Delta.* Environmental Justice Organizations, Liabilities and Trade (EJOLT) report, 4 April 2013. Available at http://www.ejolt.org/2013/04/crude-justice-ecocide-in-the-niger-delta/ (accessed 19 December 2013).

Elden, Stuart. "How Should We Do the History of Territory?" *Territory, Politics, Governance* 1, no. 1 (2013), 5–20.

Ellis, Stephen. "Of Elephants and Men: Politics and Nature Conservation in South Africa." *Journal of Southern African Studies* 20, no. 1 (1994), 53–69.

Engel, Ulf, and Gorm Rye Olsen. "Authority, Sovereignty and Africa's Changing Regimes of Territorialization." In *Africa and International Relations in the 21st Century,* ed. Scarlett Cornelissen, Fantu Cheru, and Timothy M. Shaw, 51–65. Basingstoke: Palgrave Macmillan, 2012.

England, Andrew. "Bid to Wean Country Off Coal." *Financial Times* (UK), 2 December 2011.

Epstein, Charlotte. *The Power of Words in International Relations: Birth of an Anti-Whaling Discourse.* Cambridge: MIT Press, 2008.

Ernest, Sylvester. "Removal of 'Foreigners' from Tanzania Met With Outrage." *Mail and Guardian* (SA), 27 September 2013.

Eschle, Catherine. *Global Democracy, Social Movements, and Feminism.* Boulder: Westview, 2001.

Escobar, Arturo. *Encountering Development: The Making and Unmaking of the Third World.* Princeton: Princeton University Press, 1995.

Ezrow, Natasha, and Erica Frantz. "Revisiting the Concept of the Failed State: Bringing the State Back In." *Third World Quarterly* 34, no. 8 (2013), 1323–38.

Evans, Peter B. "Constructing the 21st Century Developmental State: Potentials and Pitfalls." In *Constructing a Democratic Developmental State in South Africa: Potentials and Challenges,* ed. Omano Edigheji, 37–58. Cape Town: HSRC Press, 2010.

———. "The Eclipse of the State? Reflections on Stateness in an Era of Globalization." *World Politics* 50, no. 1 (1997), 62–87.

———, Dietrich Rueschemeyer, and Theda Skocpol, eds. *Bringing the State Back In.* Cambridge: Cambridge University Press, 1985.

Evers, Sandra J. T. M. "Lex Loci Meets Lex Fori: Merging Customary Law and National Land Legislation in Madagascar." In *Contest for Land in Madagascar: Environment, Ancestors and Development,* ed. Sandra J. T. M. Evers, Gwyn Campbell, and Michael Lambek, 119–40. Leiden: Brill, 2013.

Fakir, Saliem, and Manisha Gulati. "Carbon Tax: Don't Throw the Baby Out With the Bath Water." *Mail and Guardian* (SA), 2 September 2013.

Falkner, Robert. "American Hegemony and the Global Environment." *International Studies Review* 7 (2005), 585–599.

———. "Global Environmentalism and the Greening of International Society." *International Affairs* 88, no. 3 (2012), 503–22.

———. "Private Environmental Governance and International Relations: Exploring the Links." *Global Environmental Politics* 3, no. 2 (2003), 72–87.

Fanon, Frantz. *The Wretched of the Earth.* New York: Grove, 2004.

FAO. "The Great Green Wall for the Sahara and the Sahel Initiative." Undated. Available at http://www.fao.org/partnerships/great-green-wall/in-action/vision/en/ (accessed 16 July 2014).

Federal Democratic Republic of Ethiopia. *Ethiopia's Climate-Resilient Green Economy.* Addis Ababa: Federal Democratic Republic of Ethiopia, 2011.

Federal Ministry of Environment. *National Environmental, Economic and Development Study (Needs) for Climate Change in Nigeria.* Abuja: Federal Ministry of Environment, 2010.

Feed the Future. "Malawi." Undated. Available at http://www.feedthefuture.gov/country/malawi (accessed 9 October 2013).

Ferguson, James. *Global Shadows: Africa in the Neoliberal World Order.* London: Duke University Press, 2007.

———. "Seeing Like an Oil Company: Space, Security and Global Capital in Neoliberal Africa." *American Anthropologist* 107, no. 3 (2005), 377–82.

———. "Toward a Left Art of Government: From 'Foucauldian Critique' to Foucauldian Politics." *History of the Human Sciences* 24, no. 4 (2011), 61–68.

———, and Akhil Gupta. "Spatializing States: Towards an Ethnography of Neoliberal Governmentality." *American Ethnologist* 29, no. 4 (2002), 981–1002.

Ferguson, Peter. "The Green Economy Agenda: Business as Usual or Transformational Discourse?" *Environmental Politics* 24, no. 1 (2015), 17–37.

Fig, David. "Manufacturing Amnesia: Corporate Social Responsibility in South Africa." *International Affairs* 81, no. 3 (2005), 599–617.

Fine, Ben. "Assessing South Africa's New Growth Path: Framework for Change?" *Review of African Political Economy* 39, no. 134 (2012), 551–68.

———. *South Africa's Political Economy: From Minerals–Energy Complex to Industrialisation.* London: Hurst, 1997.

Fisher, Jonathan. "When It Pays to Be a 'Fragile State': Uganda's Use and Abuse of a Dubious Concept." *Third World Quarterly* 35, no. 2 (2014), 316–32.

Flesher Fominaya, Cristina. "International Solidarity in Social Movements." *Interface* 6, no. 2 (2014), 16–25.

Fletcher, Robert. "Neoliberal Environmentality: Towards a Poststructuralist Political Ecology of the Conservation Debate." *Conservation and Society* 8, no. 3 (2010), 171–81.

Ford, Robert T. "The Population–Environment Nexus and Vulnerability Assessment in Africa." *Geojournal* 35, no. 2 (1995), 207–16.

Foresight. *The Future of Food and Farming: Challenges and Choices for Global Sustainability.* London: Government Office for Science, 2011.

Foster, John Bellamy. "Capitalism and Ecology: The Nature of the Contradiction." *Monthly Review* 54, no. 4 (2002), 6–16.

Foucault, Michel. "On the Genealogy of Ethics: An Overview of Work in Progress." In *Ethics, Subjectivity and Truth: Essential Works of Foucault 1954–1984.* Volume 1. Edited by Paul Rabinow. New York: New Press, 1997.

———. *Power/Knowledge: Selected Interviews and Other Writings, 1972–77.* New York: Pantheon, 1980.

———. *Security, Territory, Population: Lectures at the Collège de France 1977–1978.* Edited by Michel Senellart. Basingstoke: Palgrave Macmillan, 2007.

———. *Society Must Be Defended: Lectures at the Collège de France 1975–1976.* Edited by Mauro Bertani. London: Allen Lane, 2003.

———. *The Birth of Biopolitics: Lectures at the Collège de France 1978–1979.* Edited by Michel Senellart. Basingstoke: Palgrave Macmillan, 2008.

———. *The Will to Knowledge: The History of Sexuality 1.* London: Penguin, 1998.

Fougner, Tore. "Neoliberal Governance of States: The Role of Competitive Indexing and Country Benchmarking." *Millennium* 37, no. 2 (2008), 303–26.

Fourie, Elsje. "Three Trends in African Development–Drawn from the East Asian Experience." *NAI Forum* (Sweden), 11 May 2013.

Fraser, Alistair. "Hybridity Emergent: Geo-History, Learning, and Land Restitution in South Africa." *Geoforum* 38 (2007), 299–311.

Friends of the Earth International. "Friends of the Earth Groups Call on Shell to Clean Up Nigeria Oil Spills." *Pambazuka Press,* 7 August 2013.

Frynas, Jedrzej George. "Political Instability and Business: Focus on Shell in Nigeria." *Third World Quarterly* 19, no. 3 (1998), 457–78.

———. "Shell in Nigeria: A Further Contribution." *Third World Quarterly* 21, no. 1 (2000), 157–64.

Gabay, Clive. "Two 'Transitions': The Political Economy of Joyce Banda's Rise to Power and the Related Role of Civil Society Organisations in Malawi." *Review of African Political Economy* 41, no. 141 (2014), 374–88.

———, and Carl Death, eds. *Critical Perspectives on African Politics: Liberal Interventions, State-Building and Civil Society.* Abingdon: Routledge, 2014.

Gallagher, Julia. "The Battle for Zimbabwe in 2013: From Polarisation to Ambivalence." *Journal of Modern African Studies* 53, no. 1 (2015), 27–49.

Gets, Alastair. *Powering the Future: Renewable Energy Roll-out in South Africa.* Johannesburg: Greenpeace Africa: 2013.

Ghana News Agency. "Ghana Committed to Green Economy–Oteng-Agyei." *Ghana News Agency,* 21 August 2013.

Ghana Web. "Energy Not Wasted Will Not Be Paid For–Energy Commission." *Ghana Web,* 20 October 2013.

Gill, Stephen. "Globalisation, Market Civilisation, and Disciplinary Neoliberalism." *Millennium* 24, no. 3 (1995), 399–423.

Global Footprint Network. "World Footprint: Do We All Fit on the Planet?" Undated. Available at http://www.footprintnetwork.org/en/index.php/gfn/page/world_footprint/ (accessed 16 July 2014).

Global Greens. "Dakar 2012 Global Greens Congress Wrap Up." 1 April 2012. Available at http://www.globalgreens.org/news/dakar-congress-wrap (accessed 16 July 2014).

Global Witness. *Rigged? The Scramble for Africa's Oil, Gas and Minerals.* London: Global Witness, 2012.

Godfrey, Anna, Emily Le Roux-Rutledge, Susan Cooke, and Miriam Burton. *Africa Talks Climate: The Public Understanding of Climate Change in Ten Countries.* Executive Summary. London: BBC World Service Trust, 2010.

Goldman, Michael. "The Birth of a Discipline: Producing Authoritative Green Knowledge, World Bank–Style." *Ethnography* 2, no. 2 (2001), 191–217.

———. "Water for All! The Phenomenal Rise of Transnational Knowledge and Policy Networks." In *Environmental Governance: Power and Knowledge in a Local–Global World,* ed. Gabriela Kütting and Ronnie Lipschutz, 145–69. Abingdon: Routledge, 2009.

Gold Standard, The. "The First Ever Cookstove CDM–POA Registered in Africa." Undated. Available at http://www.cdmgoldstandard.org/the-first-ever-cookstove-cdm-poa-registered-in-africa (accessed 9 October 2012).

Gomera, Maxwell, Liz Rihoy, and Fred Nelson. "A Changing Climate for Community Resource Governance: Threats and Opportunities from Climate Change and the Emerging Carbon Market." In *Community Rights, Conservation and Contested Land: The Politics of Natural Resource Governance in Africa,* ed. Fred Nelson, 293–309. Abingdon: Earthscan, 2010.

Goodland, Robert. "The Concept of Environmental Sustainability." *Annual Review of Ecological Systems* 26, (1995), 1–24.

Goodman, James, and Ariel Salleh. "The 'Green Economy': Class Hegemony and Counter-Hegemony." *Globalizations* 10, no. 3 (2013), 411–24.

Gordimer, Nadine. *The Conservationist.* London: Bloomsbury, 2005.

Gordon, Colin. "Introduction." In *Power: Essential Works of Foucault 1954–1984.* Volume 3. Edited by James D. Faubion. New York: New Press, 2000.

Gough, Annette, and Noel Gough. "Environmental Education Research in Southern Africa: Dilemmas of Interpretation." *Environmental Education Research* 10, no. 3 (2004), 409–24.

Green Africa Directory. "African Entrepreneurs Recognised for Social and Environmental Innovation." 4 November 2013. Available at http://www.greenafricadirectory.org/african-entrepreneurs-recognised-for-social-and-environmental-innovation/ (accessed 16 July 2014).

Green Belt Movement, The. "See where we work." Undated. Available at http://www.greenbeltmovement.org/what-we-do/see-where-we-work (accessed 1 November 2013).

Greenberg, Stephen. "The Landless People's Movement and the Failure of Post-Apartheid Land Reform." In *Voices of Protest: Social Movements in Post-Apartheid South Africa,* ed. Richard Ballard, Adam Habib, and Imraan Valodia, 133–53. Scottsville: UKZN Press, 2006.

Greenpeace International. "The Toxic Truth." 12 September 2012. Available at http://www.greenpeace.org/international/en/publications/Campaign-reports/Toxics-reports/The-Toxic-Truth/ (accessed 21 July 2014).

Grimm, Sonja, Nicolas Lemay-Hébert, and Olivier Nay. " 'Fragile States': Introducing a Political Concept." *Third World Quarterly* 35, no. 2 (2014), 197–209.

Groenewalde, Yolandi. "COP17: SA's Chance to Shine." *Mail and Guardian* (SA), 10 January 2011.

Grove, Kevin J. "Insuring 'Our Common Future?' Dangerous Climate Change and the Biopolitics of Environmental Security." *Geopolitics* 15, no. 3 (2010), 536–63.

Grove, Richard H. *Green Imperialism: Colonial Expansion, Tropical Island Edens and the Origins of Environmentalism, 1600–1800.* Cambridge: Cambridge University Press, 1995.

Grovogui, Siba N. "Sovereignty in Africa: Quasi-Statehood and Other Myths in International Theory." In *Africa's Challenge to International Relations Theory,* ed. Kevin C. Dunn and Timothy M. Shaw, 29–45. Basingstoke: Palgrave, 2001.

Gruffydd Jones, Branwen. "Civilising African Cities: International Housing and Urban Policy from Colonial to Neoliberal Times." *Journal of Intervention and Statebuilding* 6, no. 1 (2012), 23–40.

Haas, Peter M. "Addressing the Global Governance Deficit." *Global Environmental Politics* 4, no. 4 (2004), 1–15.

———, Robert O. Keohane, and Marc A. Levy, eds. *Institutions for the Earth: Sources of Effective International Environmental Protection.* Cambridge: MIT Press, 1993.

Habermas, Jürgen. "New social movements." *Telos* 49 (1981), 33–37.

Hagmann, Tobias, and Didier Péclard. "Negotiating Statehood: Dynamics of Power and Domination in Africa." *Development and Change* 41, no. 4 (2010), 539–62.

Hall, Ruth. "A political economy of land reform in South Africa." *Review of African Political Economy* 31, no. 100 (2004), 213–27.

———. "Land-Grabbing in Southern Africa: The Many Faces of the Investor Rush." *Review of African Political Economy* 38, no. 128 (2011), 193–214.

Hallegatte, Stéphane, Geoffrey Heal, Marianne Fay, and David Treguer. *From Growth to Green Growth: A Framework.* Washington, D.C.: World Bank, 2011.

Hallowes, David, Trusha Reddy, and Oscar Reyes. *COP In, COP Out, COP 17: A Review of Civil Society Participation in the UN Conference on Climate Change, Durban 2011.* Johannesburg: Earthlife Africa, 2012.

Hamouchene, Hamza. "Desertec: The Renewable Energy Grab?" *Pambazuka Press,* 26 February 2015.

Hannah, Matthew G. "Biopower, Life and Left Politics." *Antipode* 43, no. 4 (2011), 1034–55.

Hansen, Thomas Blom, and Finn Stepputat. "Introduction: States of Imagination." In *States of Imagination: Ethnographic Explorations of the Postcolonial State,* ed. Thomas Blom Hansen and Finn Stepputat, 1–38. Durham: Duke University Press, 2001.

Harley, Jon. "Cartography, Ethics and Social Theory." *Cartographica* 27, no. 2 (1990), 1–23.

Harman, Sophie. "The Dual Feminisation of HIV/AIDS." *Globalizations* 8, no. 2 (2011), 213–28.

———, and David Williams. "International Development in Transition." *International Affairs* 90, no. 4 (2014), 925–41.

Harness, Tiffany. "What a South African Activist Sees as 'The Greatest Threat Since Apartheid.'" *Washington Post* (USA), 30 April 2014.

Harrison, Graham. "Economic Faith, Social Project and a Misreading of African Society: The Travails of Neoliberalism in Africa." *Third World Quarterly* 26, no. 8 (2005), 1303–20.

———. *Neoliberal Africa: The Impact of Global Social Engineering.* London: Zed Books, 2010.

———. "Post-Conditionality Politics and Administrative Reform: Reflections on the Cases of Uganda and Tanzania." *Development and Change* 32, no. 4 (2001), 657–79.

———. *The World Bank and Africa: The Construction of Governance States.* Abingdon: Routledge, 2004.

Hartmann, Betsy. "Converging on Disaster: Climate Security and the Malthusian Anticipatory Regime for Africa." *Geopolitics* 19, no. 4 (2014), 757–83.

Harvey, David. *A Brief History of Neoliberalism.* Oxford: Oxford University Press, 2005.

———. "The Environment of Justice." In *Living with Nature: Environmental Politics as Cultural Discourse,* ed. Frank Fischer and Maarten A. Hajer, 153–85. Oxford: Oxford University Press, 1999.

Hattingh, Johan, Heila Lotz-Sisitka, and Rob O'Donoghue, eds. *Environmental Education, Ethics and Action in Southern Africa.* Pretoria: HSRC, 2002.

Hawn, Amanda. "South Africa Puts the Unemployed to Work, Restoring Land and Water." *New York Times* (US), 26 July 2005.

Haynes, Jeff. "Power, Politics and Environmental Movements in the Third World." *Environmental Politics* 8, no. 1 (1999), 222–42.

Hebinck, Paul, Derick Fay, and Kwandiwe Kondlo. "Land and Agrarian Reform in South Africa's Eastern Cape Province: Caught by Continuities." *Journal of Agrarian Change* 11, no. 2 (2011), 220–40.

Hellberg, Sofie. "Water, Life and Politics: Exploring the Contested Case of Ethekwini Municipality through a Governmentality Lens." *Geoforum* 56 (2014), 226–326.

Henk, Dan. *The Botswana Defense Force in the Struggle for an African Environment.* Basingstoke: Palgrave Macmillan, 2007.

Herbst, Jeffrey. *States and Power in Africa: Comparative Lessons in Authority and Control.* Princeton: Princeton University Press, 2000.

Hetherington, Kevin. *The Badlands of Modernity: Heterotopia and Social Ordering.* London: Routledge, 1997.

Hicks, Robert L., Bradley C. Parks, J. Timmons Roberts, and Michael J. Tierney. *Greening Aid? Understanding the Environmental Impact of Development Assistance.* Oxford: Oxford University Press, 2008.

Highfield, Jonathan. "No Longer Praying on Borrowed Wine: Agroforestry and Food Sovereignty in Ben Okri's Famished Road Trilogy." In *Environment at the Margins: Literary and Environmental Studies in Africa,* ed. Byron Caminero-Santangelo and Garth Myers, 140–58. Athens: Ohio University Press, 2011.

Hill, Kevin A. "Zimbabwe's Wildlife Utilization Programs: Grassroots Democracy or an Extension of State Power?" *African Studies Review* 39, no. 1 (1996), 103–21.

Hintjens, Helen M. "Explaining the 1994 Genocide in Rwanda." *Journal of Modern African Studies* 37, no. 2 (1999), 241–86.

Hirst, Paul, and Grahame Thompson. "Globalization and the Future of the Nation State." *Economy and Society* 24, no. 3 (1995), 408–42.

Hitimana, Léonidas, Philipp Heinrigs, and Marie Trémolières. *West African Urbanisation Trends.* Paris: OECD, 2011.

Hobson, John M. "The Other Side of the Westphalian Frontier." In *Postcolonial Theory and International Relations: A Critical Introduction,* ed. Sanjay Seth, 32–48. Abingdon: Routledge, 2013.

———. *The State and International Relations.* Cambridge: Cambridge University Press, 2000.

———, and M. Ramesh. "Globalisation Makes of States What States Make of It: Between Agency and Structure in the State/Globalisation Debate." *New Political Economy* 7, no. 1 (2002), 5–22.

Hodes, Rebecca. "'It's a Beautiful Struggle': Siyayinqoba/Beat It! and the HIV/Aids Treatment Struggle on South African Television." In *Popular Politics and Resistance Movements in South Africa,* ed. William Beinart and Marcelle C. Dawson, 161–88. Johannesburg: Wits University Press, 2010.

Hodgson, Dorothy L. "Becoming Indigenous in Africa." *African Studies Review* 52, no. 3 (2009), 1–32.

Hoffmann, Matthew J. *Climate Governance at the Crossroads: Experimenting with a Global Response after Kyoto.* Oxford: Oxford University Press, 2011.

Homewood, Katherine, Dan Brockington, and Sian Sullivan. "Alternative View of Serengeti Road." *Nature* 467 (2010), 788–89.

Horne, Felix. *Understanding Land Investment Deals in Africa: Country Report Ethiopia.* Oakland, Calif.: Oakland Institute, 2011.

Hoste, Jean-Christophe. *Where Was United Africa in the Climate Change Negotiations? Africa Policy Brief.* Brussels: Egmont Institute, 2010.

Houston, Donna. "Crisis Is Where We Live: Environmental Justice for the Anthropocene." *Globalizations* 10, no. 3 (2013), 439–50.

Howden, Daniel. "Rwanda's Democratic Credentials under Fire." *Independent* (UK), 15 March 2010.

Huggan, Graham, and Helen Tiffin. "Green Postcolonialism." *Interventions: International Journal of Postcolonial Studies* 9, no. 1 (2007), 1–11.

Huggins, Christopher David. "'Control Grabbing' and Small-Scale Agricultural Intensification: Emerging Patterns of State-Facilitated 'Agricultural Investment' in Rwanda." *Journal of Peasant Studies* 41, no. 3 (2014), 365–84.

Hughes, David McDermott. "Cadastral Politics: The Making of Community-Based Resource Management in Zimbabwe and Mozambique." *Development and Change* 32 (2001), 741–68.

Hultgren, John. "Natural Exceptions to Green Sovereignty? American Environmentalism and the 'Immigration Problem.'" *Alternatives: Global, Local, Political* 37, no. 4 (2012), 300–316.

Human Rights Watch. "Dispatches: Standing up for Environmental Activists." 22 April 2015. Available at http://www.hrw.org/news/2015/04/22/dispatches-standing-environmental-activists (accessed 6 July 2015).

Hunold, Christian, and John Dryzek. "Green Political Strategy and the State: Combining Political Theory and Comparative History." In *The State and the Global Ecological Crisis,* ed. John Barry and Robyn Eckersley, 75–95. Cambridge: MIT Press, 2005.

———. "Green Political Theory and the State: Context Is Everything." *Global Environmental Politics* 2, no. 3 (2002), 17–39.

Hurrell, Andrew. "The State." In *Political Theory and the Ecological Challenge,* ed. Andrew Dobson and Robyn Eckersley, 165–82. Cambridge: Cambridge University Press, 2006.

———, and Sandeep Sengupta. "Emerging Powers, North–South Relations, and Global Climate Politics." *International Affairs* 88, no. 3 (2012), 463–84.

Hyden, Goran. *Beyond Ujamaa in Tanzania: Underdevelopment and an Uncaptured Peasantry.* London: Heinemann, 1980.

Igoe, Jim, and Tim Kelsall. "Introduction: Between a Rock and a Hard Place." In *Between a Rock and a Hard Place: African NGOs, Donors and the State,* ed. Jim Igoe and Tim Kelsall, 1–33. Durham: Carolina Academic Press, 2005.

IISD. "Africa to Become World's Largest Market for Solar Lanterns by 2015." 26 August 2013. Available at http://africasd.iisd.org/news/africa-to-become-worlds-largest-market-for-solar-lanterns-by-2015/ (accessed 4 October 2013).

———. "GEF Commits $4.6 Million to Regional Component of Great Green Wall Initiative." 15 October 2013. Available at http://africasd.iisd.org/news/gef-commits-4-6-million-to-regional-component-of-great-green-wall-initiative/ (accessed 16 July 2014).

Iliffe, John. *Africans: The History of a Continent.* Cambridge: Cambridge University Press, 2007.

———. *A Modern History of Tanganyika.* Cambridge: Cambridge University Press, 1979.

ILO. *Sustainable Development, Decent Work and Green Jobs.* Geneva: ILO, 2013.

Inayatullah, Naeem, ed. *Autobiographical International Relations: I, IR.* Abingdon: Routledge, 2011.

Inglehart, Ronald. "Post-Materialism in an Environment of Insecurity." *American Political Science Review* 75, no. 4 (1981), 880–900.

IRIN. "Lesotho: Dam-Building Continues Despite Controversy." *IRIN,* 11 November 2011.

IUCN. "Protected Areas Categories System." Undated. Available online at http://www.iucn.org/about/work/programmes/gpap_home/gpap_quality/gpap_pacategories/ (accessed 3 July 2014).

IUCN and UNEP-WCMC. *The World Database on Protected Areas* (WDPA), April 2015. Available at www.protectedplanet.net (accessed 3 July 2015).

Jackson, Robert H. *Quasi-States: Sovereignty, International Relations and the Third World.* Cambridge: Cambridge University Press, 1993.

———, and Carl J. Rosberg. "Why Africa's Weak States Persist: The Empirical and the Juridical in Statehood." *World Politics* 35, no. 1 (1982), 1–24.

Jackson, Stephen. "Sons of Which Soil? The Language and Politics of Autochthony in Eastern D.R. Congo." *African Studies Review* 49, no. 2 (2006), 95–123.

Jackson, Tim. *Prosperity Without Growth: Economics for a Finite Planet.* London: Earthscan, 2009.

James, Deborah. "Citizenship and Land in South Africa: From Rights to Responsibilities." *Critique of Anthropology* 33, no. 1 (2013), 26–46.

———. "Money-Go-Round: Personal Economies of Wealth, Aspiration and Indebtedness." *Africa* 82, no. 1 (2012), 20–40.

Jenkins, Beth. *Mobilizing the Southern Agricultural Growth Corridor of Tanzania: A Case Study.* Cambridge: Harvard Kennedy School, 2012.

Jenkins, Sarah. "Ethnicity, Violence, and the Immigrant-Guest Metaphor in Kenya." *African Affairs* 111, no. 445 (2012), 576–96.

Jensen, Steffen. "Shosholoza: Political Culture in South Africa between the Secular and the Occult." *Journal of Southern African Studies* 38, no. 1 (2012), 91–106.

Jerven, Morten. "Measuring African Development: Past and Present." *Canadian Journal of Development Studies* 35, no. 1 (2014), 1–8.

Jessop, Bob. "Bringing the State Back In (Yet Again): Reviews, Revisions, Rejections, and Redirections." *International Review of Sociology: Revue Internationale de Sociologie* 11, no. 2 (2001), 149–73.

———. "Economic and Ecological Crises: Green New Deals and No-Growth Economies." *Development* 55, no. 1 (2012), 17–24.

———. "From Micro-Powers to Governmentality: Foucault's Work on Statehood, State Formation, Statecraft and State Power." *Political Geography* 26, no. 1 (2007), 34–40.

———. "Putting Neoliberalism in Its Time and Place: A Response to the Debate." *Social Anthropology* 21, no. 1 (2013), 65–74.

———. *State Theory: Putting the Capitalist State in its Place.* Cambridge: Polity, 1990.

———. *The Capitalist State: Marxist Theories and Methods.* Oxford: Martin Robertson, 1982.

———. *The Future of the Capitalist State.* Cambridge: Polity, 2002.

Johnson, Peter. "Unravelling Foucault's 'Different Spaces,'" *History of the Human Sciences* 19, no. 4 (2006), 75–90.

Jones, Lindsey, and Elizabeth Carabine. *Exploring Political and Socio-Economic Drivers of Transformational Climate Policy: Early Insights from the Design of Ethiopia's Climate Resilient Green Economy Strategy.* London: ODI, 2013.

Jones, Rhys. "State Encounters." *Environment and Planning D: Society and Space* 30 (2012), 805–21.

Jones, Samantha. "A Political Ecology of Wildlife Conservation in Africa." *Review of African Political Economy* 33, no. 109 (2006), 483–95.

Joseph, Jonathan. "The Limits of Governmentality: Social Theory and the International." *European Journal of International Relations* 16, no. 2 (2010), 223–46.

Juffe-Bignoli, D., N. D. Burgess, H. Bingham, E. M. S. Belle, M. G. de Lima, M. Deguignet, B. Bertzky, A. N. Milam, J. Martinez-Lopez, E. Lewis, A. Eassom, S. Wicander, J. Geldmann, A. van Soesbergen, A. P. Arnell, B. O'Connor, S. Park, Y. N. Shi, F. S. Danks, B. MacSharry, and N. Kingston. *Protected Planet Report 2014.* Cambridge: UNEP-WCMC, 2014.

Juma, Calestous. *The New Harvest: Agricultural Innovation in Africa.* Oxford: Oxford University Press, 2011.

Juwaheer, Thanika Devi, Sharmila Pudaruth, and Marie Monique Emmanuelle Noyaux. "Analysing the Impact of Green Marketing Strategies on Consumer Purchasing Patterns in Mauritius." *World Journal of Entrepreneurship, Management and Sustainable Development* 8, no. 1 (2012), 36–59.

Kaplan, Robert D., and Mark Schroeder. "Africa's New Map." *Forbes.* Washington D.C., 23 October 2013.

Kapuściński, Ryszard. *The Shadow of the Sun: My African Life.* London: Penguin, 2001.

Karkkainen, Bradley C. "Post-Sovereign Environmental Governance." *Global Environmental Politics* 4, no. 1 (2004), 72–96.

Keck, Margaret E., and Kathryn Sikkink. *Activists Beyond Borders: Advocacy Networks in International Politics.* Ithaca: Cornell University Press, 1998.

Keeley, James, and Ian Scoones. *Understanding Environmental Policy Processes: Cases From Africa.* London: Earthscan, 2003.

Keen, David. *Complex Emergencies.* Cambridge: Polity, 2008.

Keene, Edward. *Beyond the Anarchical Society: Grotius, Colonialism and Order in World Politics.* Cambridge: Cambridge University Press, 2002.

Keller, Edmond J. "Drought, War, and the Politics of Famine in Ethiopia and Eritrea." *Journal of Modern African Studies* 30, no. 4 (1992), 609–24.

Keohane, Robert O. "Analyzing the Effectiveness of International Environmental Institutions." In *Institutions for Environmental Aid,* ed. Robert O. Keohane and Marc A. Levy, 3–27. Cambridge: MIT Press, 1996.

———, and David G. Victor. "The Regime Complex for Climate Change." *Perspectives on Politics* 9, no. 1 (2011), 7–23.

Kepe, Thembela. "Globalization, Science, and the Making of an Environmental Discourse on the Wild Coast, South Africa." *Environment and Planning A* 46 (2014), 2143–59.

———. "Shaped by Race: Why 'Race' Still Matters in the Challenges Facing Biodiversity Conservation in Africa." *Local Environment: The International Journal of Justice and Sustainability* 14, no. 9 (2009), 871–78.

Khor, Martin. "Challenges of the Green Economy Concept and Policies in the Context of Sustainable Development, Poverty and Equity." In *The Transition to a Green Economy: Benefits, Challenges and Risks from a Sustainable Development Perspective,* 69–72. New York: UN-DESA, UNEP, UNCTAD, 2011.

Ki-moon, Ban. "UN Secretary General, Remarks to the Fifth Tokyo International Conference on African Development (Ticad V): Private Sector, Trade and Investment as Engines of Development." Yokohama, Japan, 2 June 2013. Available at http://www.un.org/sg/statements/index.asp?nid=6864 (accessed 19 July 2014).

Kings, Sipho. "Rhino Deaths Reach Tipping Point." *Mail and Guardian* (SA), 27 September 2013.

———. "SA's Renewable Energy Sector a Beacon in Africa." *Mail and Guardian* (SA), 20 February 2013.

Klaeger, Gabriel. "The Perils and Possibilities of African Roads." *Africa: The Journal of the International African Institute* 83, no. 3 (2013), 359–66.

Klein, Naomi. *This Changes Everything: Capitalism vs. the Climate.* London: Allen Lane, 2014.

Konings, Martijn. "Renewing State Theory." *Politics* 30, no. 3 (2010), 174–82.

Kopinski, Dominik, Andrzej Polus, and Andwojciech Tycholiz. "Resource Curse or Resource Disease? Oil in Ghana." *African Affairs* 112, no. 449 (2013), 583–601.

Krasner, Stephen. "Approaches to the State: Alternative Conceptions and Historical Dynamics." *Comparative Politics* 16, no. 2 (1984), 223–46.

Krishna, Sankaran. *Globalization and Postcolonialism: Hegemony and Resistance in the Twenty-First Century.* Lanham: Rowman and Littlefield, 2009.

Kröger, Markus. "The Political Economy of Global Tree Plantation Expansion: A Review." *Journal of Peasant Studies* 41, no. 2 (2014), 235–61.

Kuehls, Thom. *Beyond Sovereign Territory: The Space of Ecopolitics.* Minneapolis: University of Minnesota Press, 1996.

Kuehls, Thom. "States." In *Critical Environmental Politics,* ed. Carl Death, 238–46. Abingdon: Routledge, 2014.

———. "The Environment of Sovereignty." In *A Political Space: Reading the Global through Clayoquot Sound,* ed. Warren Magnusson and Karena Shaw, 179–97. Minneapolis: University of Minnesota Press, 2003.

Lachmann, Richard. *States and Power.* Cambridge: Polity, 2010.

Lakhani, Nina. "Surge in Deaths of Environmental Activists Over Past Decade, Report Finds." *The Guardian* (UK), 15 April 2014.

Langhelle, Oluf. "Why Sustainable Development and Ecological Modernization Should Not Be Conflated." *Journal of Environmental Policy and Planning* 2, no. 4 (2000), 303–22.

Larner, Wendy, and William Walters. "The Political Rationality of 'New Regionalism': Toward a Genealogy of the Region." *Theory and Society* 31 (2002), 391–432.

Lautze, Sue, and Daniel Maxwell. "Why Do Famines Persist in the Horn of Africa? Ethiopia, 1999–2003." In *The New Famines: Why Famines Persist in an Era of Globalization,* ed. Stephen Devereux, 222–44. Abingdon: Routledge, 2007.

Lavers, Tom. "Food Security and Social Protection in Highland Ethiopia: Linking the Productive Safety Net to the Land Question." *Journal of Modern African Studies* 51, no. 3 (2013), 459–85.

Leach, Melissa. "What Is Green? Transformation Imperatives and Knowledge Politics." In *The Politics of Green Transformations,* ed. Ian Scoones, Melissa Leach, and Peter Newell, 25–38. Abingdon: Routledge, 2015.

———, James Fairhead, and James Fraser. "Green Grabs and Biochar: Revaluing African Soils and Farming in the New Carbon Economy." *Journal of Peasant Studies* 39, no. 2 (2012), 285–307.

———, and Robin Mearns. "Environmental Change and Policy: Challenging Received Wisdom in Africa." In *The Lie of the Land: Challenging Received Wisdom on the African Environment,* ed. Melissa Leach and Robin Mearns, 1–33. Oxford: James Currey, 1996.

Le Billion, Philippe. *Wars of Plunder: Conflicts, Profits and the Politics of Resources.* London: Hurst, 2012.

Lee, Rebekah. "Death in Slow Motion: Funerals, Ritual Practice and Road Danger in South Africa." *African Studies* 71, no. 2 (2012), 195–211.

Lefort, René. "Free Market Economy, 'Developmental State' and Party–State Hegemony in Ethiopia: The Case of the 'Model Farmers.'" *Journal of Modern African Studies* 50, no. 4 (2012), 681–706.

Legg, Stephen. "Assemblage/Apparatus: Using Deleuze and Foucault." *Area* 43, no. 2 (2011), 128–33.

———. "Foucault's Population Geographies: Classifications, Biopolitics and Governmental Spaces." *Population, Space and Place* 11 (2005), 137–56.

Lemay-Hébert, Nicolas, and Xavier Mathieu. "The OECD's Discourse on Fragile States: Expertise and the Normalisation of Knowledge Production." *Third World Quarterly* 35, no. 2 (2014), 232–51.

Lemke, Thomas. "'The Birth of Bio-Politics': Michel Foucault's Lecture at the Collège de France on Neo-Liberal Governmentality." *Economy and Society* 30, no. 2 (2001), 190–207.

Leopold, Aldo. *A Sand County Almanac: With Essays on Conservation.* Oxford: Oxford University Press, 1949.

Levine, Arielle. "Convergence or Convenience? International Conservation NGOs and Development Assistance in Tanzania." *World Development* 30, no. 6 (2002), 1043–55.

Lindell, Ilda, and Markus Ihalainen. "The Politics of Confinement and Mobility: Informality, Relocation and Urban Re-Making from Above and Below in Nairobi." In *Civic Agency in Africa: Arts of Resistance in the 21st Century*, ed. Ebenezer Obadare and Wendy Willems, 65–84. Woodbridge: James Currey, 2014.

Linklater, Andrew. *Critical Theory and World Politics: Citizenship, Sovereignty and Humanity* Abingdon: Routledge, 2007.

Lipschutz, Ronnie D., and Ken Conca, eds. *The State and Social Power in Global Environmental Politics.* New York: Columbia University Press, 1993.

Litfin, Karen T. *Ecovillages: Lessons for Sustainable Community.* Cambridge: Polity, 2014.

———. "Localism." In *Critical Environmental Politics,* ed. Carl Death, 156–64. Abingdon: Routledge, 2014.

———, ed. *The Greening of Sovereignty in World Politics.* Cambridge: MIT Press, 1998.

———. "The Greening of Sovereignty: An Introduction." In *The Greening of Sovereignty in World Politics,* ed. Karen T. Litfin, 1–27. Cambridge: MIT Press, 1998.

Lloyd, Philip. "Carbon Tax Shoots Itself in the Foot." *Mail and Guardian* (SA), 13 September 2013.

Loftus, Alex. "Rethinking Political Ecologies of Water." *Third World Quarterly* 30, no. 5 (2009), 953–68.

Lohmann, Larry. *Carbon Trading: A Critical Conversation on Climate Change, Privatisation and Power. Development Dialogue 48.* Uppsala: Dag Hammarskjold Centre and Corner House, 2006.

Lotz-Sisitka, Heila. "Curriculum Patterning in Environmental Education: A Review of Developments in Formal Education in South Africa." In *Environmental Education, Ethics and Action in Southern Africa,* ed. Johan Hattingh, Heila Lotz-Sisitka, and Rob O'Donoghue, 97–120. Pretoria: HSRC, 2002.

———. "Environmental Education Research and Social Change: Southern African Perspectives." *Environmental Education Research* 10, no. 3 (2004), 291–95.

Löwenheim, Oded. "Examining the State: A Foucauldian Perspective on International 'Governance Indicators.'" *Third World Quarterly* 29, 2 (2008), 255–74.

Luke, Timothy W. *Ecocritique: Contesting the Politics of Nature, Economy and Culture.* Minneapolis: University of Minnesota Press, 1997.

———. "The System of Sustainable Degradation." *Capitalism, Nature, Socialism* 17, no. 1 (2006), 99–112.

Lund, Christian. "The Past and Space: On Arguments in African Land Control." *Africa* 83, no. 1 (2013), 14–35.

———, and Catherine Boone. "Introduction: Land Politics in Africa–Constituting Authority over Territory, Property and Persons." *Africa* 83, no. 1 (2013), 1–13.

Luttrell, Cecilia, and Innocent Pantaleo. *Budget Support, Aid Instruments and the Environment: The Country Context, Tanzania Country Case Study.* London: ODI, 2008.

Maathai, Wangari Muta. *The Challenge for Africa.* New York: Random House, 2009.

———. *Unbowed: A Memoir.* London: William Heinemann, 2007.

Macfarlane, Robert. *The Old Ways: A Journey on Foot.* London: Penguin, 2012.

MacGregor, Sherilyn. "Only Resist: Feminist Ecological Citizenship and the Post-politics of Climate Change." *Hypatia* 29, no. 3 (2014), 617–33.

MacKenzie, John M. *The Empire of Nature: Hunting, Conservation and British Imperialism.* Manchester: Manchester University Press, 1988.

Maila, M. W., and C. P. Loubser. "Emancipatory Indigenous Knowledge Systems: Implications for Environmental Education in South Africa." *South African Journal of Education* 23, no. 4 (2003), 276–80.

Mamdani, Mahmood. *Citizen and Subject: Contemporary Africa and the Legacy of Late Colonialism.* London: James Currey, 1996.

———. *When Victims Become Killers: Colonialism, Nativism and the Genocide in Rwanda.* Oxford: James Currey, 2001.

Maniates, Michael. "Individualization: Plant a Tree, Buy a Bike, Save the World?" *Global Environmental Politics* 1, no. 3 (2001), 31–52.

Manji, Ambreena. "Bulldozers, Homes and Highways: Nairobi and the Right to the City." *Review of African Political Economy* 42, no. 144 (2015), 206–24.

———. *The Politics of Land Reform in Africa: From Communal Tenure to Free Markets.* London: Zed Books, 2006.

Manji, Firoze, and Sokari Ekine, eds. *African Awakening: The Emerging Revolutions.* Cape Town: Pambazuka Press, 2012.

Mann, Michael. "Has Globalization Ended the Rise and Rise of the Nation-State?" *Review of International Political Economy* 4, no. 3 (1997), 472–96.

———. "The Autonomous Power of the State: Its Origins, Mechanisms and Results." In *State / Space: A Reader,* ed. Neil Brenner, Bob Jessop, Martin Jones, and Gordon Macleod, 53–64. Oxford: Blackwell, 2003.

Margulis, Matias E., Nora McKeon, and Saturnino M. Borras Jr. "Land Grabbing and Global Governance: Critical Perspectives." *Globalizations* 10, no. 1 (2013), 1–23.

Martinez-Alier, Juan. *Environmentalism of the Poor: A Study of Ecological Conflicts and Valuation.* Cheltenham: Edward Elgar, 2003.

Marx, Karl. *Capital: A Critique of Political Economy.* Volume 1. London: Penguin, 1867/1990.

Mason, Michael. *The New Accountability: Environmental Responsibility Across Borders.* London: Earthscan, 2005.

Mathema, Prakash, Achala Abeysinghe, and Janna Tenzing. *Understanding Key Positions of the Least Developed Countries in Climate Change Negotiations.* London: IIED, 2014.

Mathiane, Nomavenda. "Blighted Environment." In *Restoring the Land: Environment and Change in Post-Apartheid South Africa,* ed. Mamphela Ramphele and Chris McDowell, 115–16. London; PANOS, 1991.

Maurice Ile Durable. "Policy, Strategy and Action Plan." Undated. Available at http://mid.govmu.org/portal/sites/mid/index.html (accessed 3 July 2015).

Mazo, Jeffrey. *Climate Conflict: How Global Warming Threatens Security and What to Do About It.* Abingdon: Routledge, 2010.

Mazzucato, Mariana. *The Entrepreneurial State: Debunking Public vs. Private Sector Myths.* London: Anthem Press, 2014.

Mbali, Mandisa. "The 'New Struggle': Resources, Networks, and the Formation of the Treatment Action Campaign (TAC), 1994–1998." In *Popular Politics and Resistance Movements in South Africa,* ed. William Beinart and Marcelle C. Dawson, 227–42. Johannesburg: Wits University Press, 2010.

Mbeki, Thabo. "I am an African." Speech by the Deputy President at the adoption of the Republic of South Africa Constitution Bill, Parliament, Cape Town, 8 May 1996.

Mbembe, Achille. "Aesthetics of Superfluity." *Public Culture* 16, no. 3 (2004), 373–405.

———. "At the Edge of the World: Boundaries, Territoriality and Sovereignty in Africa." In *Beyond State Crisis? Postcolonial Africa and Post-Soviet Eurasia in Comparative Perspective,* ed. M. R. Beissinger and C. Young, 53–80. Washington: Woodrow Wilson Centre Press, 2002.

———. "Nicholas Sarkozy's Africa." *Africultures,* 8 August 2007.

———. *On the Postcolony.* Berkeley: University of California Press, 2001.

———. "Provisional Notes on the Postcolony." *Africa: Journal of the International African Institute* 62, no. 1 (1992), 3–37.

McCann, James C. *Green Land, Brown Land, Black Land.* Oxford: James Currey, 1999.

McCarthy, James, and Scott Prudham. "Neoliberal Nature and the Nature of Neoliberalism." *Geoforum* 35 (2004), 272–83.

McClintock, Anne. *Imperial Leather: Race, Gender and Sexuality in the Colonial Contest.* London: Routledge, 1995.

McDonald, Bryan L. *Food Security.* Cambridge: Polity, 2010.

McDonald, David A., ed. *Environmental Justice in South Africa.* Athens: Ohio University Press, 2002.

———. "Three Steps Forward, Two Steps Back: Ideology and Urban Ecology in South Africa." *Review of African Political Economy* 25, no. 75 (1998), 73–88.

McDuff, Mallory. "Thirty Years of Environmental Education in Africa: The Role of the Wildlife Clubs of Kenya." *Environmental Education Research* 6, no. 4 (2000), 383–96.

McInnes, Colin. "HIV/Aids and Security." *International Affairs* 82, no. 2 (2006), 315–26.

McMichael, Philip. "Land Grabbing as Security Mercantilism in International Relations." *Globalizations* 10, no. 1 (2013), 47–64.

———. "Peasants Make Their Own History, But Not Just as They Please. . . ." *Journal of Agrarian Change* 8, no. 2–3 (2008), 205–28.

———, and Mindi Schneider. "Food Security Politics and the Millennium Development Goals." *Third World Quarterly* 32, no. 1 (2011), 119–39.

Mda, Zakes. *The Heart of Redness.* Oxford: Oxford University Press, 2000.

Meadowcroft, James. "From Welfare State to Ecostate." In *The State and the Global Ecological Crisis,* ed. John Barry and Robyn Eckersley, 3–23. Cambridge: MIT Press, 2005.

———. "Greening the State?" In *Comparative Environmental Politics: Theory, Practice, and Prospects,* ed. Paul F. Steinberg and Stacy D. VanDeVeer, 63–87. Cambridge: MIT Press, 2012.

———. "Planning, Democracy and the Challenge of Sustainable Development." *International Political Science Review* 18, no. 2 (1997), 167–89.

———. "The Politics of Sustainable Development: Emergent Arenas and Challenges for Political Science." *International Political Science Review* 20, no. 2 (1999), 219–37.

———. "Who Is in Charge Here? Governance for Sustainable Development in a Complex World." *Journal of Environmental Policy and Planning* 9, no. 3 (2007), 299–314.

Meagher, Kate. "A Back Door to Globalisation? Structural Adjustment, Globalisation and Transborder Trade in West Africa." *Review of African Political Economy* 30, no. 95 (2003), 57–75.

Methmann, Chris. "'Climate Protection' as Empty Signifier: A Discourse Theoretical Perspective on Climate Mainstreaming in World Politics." *Millennium* 39, no. 2 (2010), 345–72.

———. "The Sky Is the Limit: Global Warming as Global Governmentality." *European Journal of International Relations* 19, no. 1 (2013), 69–91.

———, and Angela Oels. "Vulnerability." In *Critical Environmental Politics,* ed. Carl Death, 277–86. Abingdon: Routledge, 2014.

Middlemiss, Lucie. "Reframing Individual Responsibility for Sustainable Consumption: Lessons from Environmental Justice and Ecological Citizenship." *Environmental Values* 19, no. 2 (2010), 147–67.

Middleton, Karen. "Land Rights and Alien Plants in Dryland Madagascar." In *Contest for Land in Madagascar: Environment, Ancestors and Development,* ed. Sandra J. T. M. Evers, Gwyn Campbell, and Michael Lambek, 141–70. Leiden: Brill, 2013.

Middleton, Neil, and Phil O'Keefe. *Redefining Sustainable Development.* London: Pluto Press, 2001.

Mies, Maria, and Vandana Shiva. *Ecofeminism.* London: Zed Books, 2014.

Migdal, Joel S. *Strong Societies and Weak States: State–Society Relations and State Capabilities in the Third World.* Princeton: Princeton University Press, 1988.

Miller, Marian A. L. "Sovereignty Reconfigured: Environmental Regimes and Third World States." In *The Greening of Sovereignty in World Politics,* ed. Karen T. Litfin, 173–92. Cambridge: MIT Press, 1998.

Mitchell, Timothy. *Carbon Democracy: Political Power in the Age of Oil.* London: Verso, 2011.

———. *Colonising Egypt.* Berkeley: University of California Press, 1988.

———. "Rethinking Economy." *Geoforum* 39 (2008), 1116–21.

———. *Rule of Experts: Egypt, Techno-Politics, Modernity.* Berkeley: University of California Press, 2002.

———. "The Limits of the State: Beyond Statist Approaches and Their Critics." *American Political Science Review* 85 no. 1, (1991), 77–96.

Mittal, Anuradha. *Lives on Hold: The Impact of Agrisol's Land Deal in Tanzania.* Oakland, Calif.: Oakland Institute, 2012.

Mngxitama, Andile. "The Taming of Land Resistance: Lessons from the National Land Committee." *Journal of Asian and African Studies* 41, no. 1/2 (2006), 39–69.

Mofokeng, Santu. "Climate change." Undated. Available at http://cargocollective.com/santumofokeng/filter/work/climate-change (accessed 26 June 2015).

Mohan, Giles. "Beyond the Enclave: Towards a Critical Political Economy of China and Africa." *Development and Change* 44, no. 6 (2013), 1255–72.

Moisio, Sami, and Anssi Paasi. "Beyond State-Centricity: Geopolitics of Changing State Spaces." *Geopolitics* 18, no. 2 (2013), 255–66.

Mol, Arthur P. J. "China's Ascent and Africa's Environment." *Global Environmental Change* 21 (2011), 795–94.

———. "Ecological Modernization and the Global Economy." *Global Environmental Politics* 2, no. 2 (2002), 92–115.

———. "The Environmental Nation State in Decline." *Environmental Politics* 25, no. 1 (2016), 48–68.

———, and Frederick H. Buttel. "The Environmental State Under Pressure: An Introduction." In *The Environmental State Under Pressure,* ed. Arthur P. J. Mol and Frederick H. Buttel, 1–12. Oxford: Elsevier, 2002.

———, and David A. Sonnenfeld. "Ecological Modernisation Around the World: An Introduction." *Environmental Politics* 9, no. 1 (2000), 1–14.

Moore, Henrietta L., and Megan Vaughan. *Cutting Down Trees: Gender, Nutrition, and Agricultural Change in the Northern Province of Zambia 1890–1990.* Portsmouth, N.H.: Heinemann, 1994.

Mottiar, Shauna. "From 'Popcorn' to 'Occupy': Protest in Durban, South Africa." *Development and Change* 44, no. 3 (2013), 603–19.

———, and Patrick Bond. "The Politics of Discontent and Social Protest in Durban." *Politikon: South African Journal of Political Studies* 39, no. 3 (2012), 309–30.

Moyo, Sam. "The Land Question in Southern Africa: A Comparative Review." In *The Land Question in South Africa: The Challenge of Transformation and Redistribution,* ed. Lungisile Ntsebeza and Ruth Hall, 60–84. Cape Town: HSRC Press, 2007.

———, and Prosper B. Matondi. "Interrogating Sustainable Development and Resource Control in Zimbabwe." In *Land and Sustainable Development in Africa,* ed. Kojo Sebastian Amanor and Sam Moyo, 55–82. London: Zed Books, 2008.

Müller, Martin. "Education and the Formation of Geopolitical Subjects." *International Political Sociology* 5 (2011), 1–17.

Muller, Mike. "Parish Pump Politics: The Politics of Water Supply in South Africa." *Progress in Development Studies* 7, no. 1 (2007), 33–45.

Munro, William A. "Power, Peasants and Political Development: Reconsidering State Construction in Africa." *Comparative Studies in Society and History* 38, no. 1 (1996), 112–48.

Murphy, Craig N. "Lessons to Be Learned from the Challenges to Achieving the MDGs in Africa." In *The Millennium Development Goals and Beyond: Global Development after 2015,* ed. Rorden Wilkinson and David Hulme, 131–45. Abingdon: Routledge, 2012.

Musila, Grace A. "Laughing at the Rainbow's Cracks? Blackness, Whiteness and the Ambivalences of South African Stand-Up Comedy." In *Civic Agency in Africa: Arts of Resistance in the 21st Century,* ed. Ebenezer Obadare and Wendy Willems, 147–66. Woodbridge: James Currey, 2014.

Musyoki, Agnes. *The Emerging Policy for Green Economy and Social Development in Limpopo, South Africa.* UNRISD and Friedrich Ebert Siftung occasional paper 8, June 2012.

Muwamba, Emmanuel. "Malawi Tips Countries to Promote Green Economy." *The Nation* (Malawi), 10 September 2013.

Muyanwa, James. "Govt to Pursue Green Economy." *Times of Zambia,* 3 June 2013.

Mwale, Pascal Newbourne. "The Babelisation of Debate on GM Maize via the Media in Southern Africa in 2002." *Social Dynamics: A Journal of African Studies* 36, no. 1 (2010), 112–21.

Nadesan, Majia Holmer. *Governmentality, Biopower and Everyday Life.* Abingdon: Routledge, 2008.

Nally, David. "The Biopolitics of Food Provisioning." *Transactions of the Institute of British Geographers* 36 (2011), 37–53.

National Treasury, Republic of South Africa. Press Release: "Carbon Tax Discussion Paper for Public Comment." Pretoria, 2 May 2013.

Ndebele, Njabulo. *The Cry of Winnie Mandela.* Banbury: Ayebia Clark, 2003.

Neely, Abigail H. "'Blame It on the Weeds': Politics, Poverty, and Ecology in the New South Africa." *Journal of Southern African Studies* 36, 4 (2010), 869–87.

NEF. "Happy Planet Index." Undated. Available at http://www.happyplanetindex.org/data/ (accessed 19 December 2013).

Nel, Adrian, and Douglas Hill. "Constructing Walls of Carbon–The Complexities of Community, Carbon Sequestration and Protected Areas in Uganda." *Journal of Contemporary African Studies* 31, no. 3 (2013), 421–40.

Nelson, Fred. "Democratizing Natural Resource Governance: Searching for Institutional Change." In *Community Rights, Conservation and Contested Land: The Politics of Natural Resource Governance in Africa,* ed. Fred Nelson, 310–33. Abingdon: Earthscan, 2010.

———. *Emergent or Illusory? Community Wildlife Management in Tanzania.* London: IIED, 2007.

———. "Introduction: The Politics of Natural Resource Governance in Africa." In *Community Rights, Conservation and Contested Land: The Politics of Natural Resource Governance in Africa,* ed. Fred Nelson, 3–31. Abingdon: Earthscan, 2010.

———, and Arun Agrawal. "Patronage or Participation? Community-Based Natural Resource Management Reform in Sub-Saharan Africa." *Development and Change* 39 no. 4 (2008), 557–85.

———, Rugemeleza Nshala, and W. A. Rodgers. "The Evolution and Reform of Tanzanian Wildlife Management." *Conservation and Society* 5, no. 2 (2007), 232–61.

NEPAD. "Comprehensive Africa Agriculture Development Programme (CAADP)." Undated. Available at http://www.nepad.org/foodsecurity/agriculture/about (accessed 9 October 2013).

Neumann, Iver B., and Ole Jacob Sending. *Governing the Global Polity: Practice, Mentality, Rationality.* Ann Arbor: University of Michigan Press, 2010.

Neumann, Roderick P. *Imposing Wilderness: Struggles over Livelihood and Nature Preservation in Africa.* Berkeley: University of California Press, 1998.

Neville, Lucy. *South Africa Talks Climate: The Public Understanding of Climate Change.* London: BBC World Service Trust 2010.

Newell, Peter. *Globalization and the Environment: Capitalism, Ecology and Power.* Cambridge: Polity, 2012.

———. "The Political Economy of Global Environmental Governance." *Review of International Studies* 34, no. 3 (2008), 507–29.

———, and Matthew Paterson. *Climate Capitalism: Global Warming and Transformation of the Global Economy.* Cambridge: Cambridge University Press, 2010.

Nhamo, Godwell. "Climate Change: Double-Edged Sword for African Trade and Development." *International Journal of African Renaissance Studies* 4, no. 2 (2009), 117–39.

Nhema, Francis. "Green Economy Now a Must." *The Herald* (Zimbabwe), 7 June 2012.

Nixon, Rob. "Environmentalism and Postcolonialism." In *Postcolonial Studies and Beyond,* ed. Ania Loomba, Suvir Kaul, Matti Bunzl, Antoinette Burton, and Jed Esty, 233–51. Durham: Duke University Press, 2005.

———. "Slow Violence, Gender, and the Environmentalism of the Poor." In *Environment at the Margins: Literary and Environmental Studies in Africa,* ed. Byron Caminero-Santangelo and Garth Myers, 257–85. Athens: Ohio University Press, 2011.

Njeru, Gitonga. "Kenya to Generate Over Half of Its Electricity Through Solar Power by 2016." *The Guardian* (UK), 17 January 2014.

Nkabane, Princess. "Isipingo Marchers Protest against Dig-Out Port." *The Mercury* (SA), 15 November 2013.

Nobel Prize. "Wangari Maathai–The Facts." Undated. Available at http://www.nobelprize.org/nobel_prizes/peace/laureates/2004/maathai-facts.html (accessed 16 July 2014).

Norrington-Davies, Gemma, and Nigel Thornton. *Climate Change Financing and Aid Effectiveness: Tanzania Case Study.* Paris: OECD, 2009.

Nossiter, Adam. "Far from Gulf, A Spill Scourge 5 Decades Old." *New York Times* (USA), 16 June 2010.

Ntsebeza, Lungisile. *Democracy Compromised: Chiefs and Politics of the Land in South Africa.* Leiden: Brill, 2005.

———, and Ruth Hall, eds. *The Land Question in South Africa: The Challenge of Transformation and Redistribution.* Cape Town: HSRC Press, 2007.

Nye, Joseph S. *The Powers to Lead.* Oxford: Oxford University Press, 2008.

Obi, Cyril I. "Enter the Dragon? Chinese Oil Companies and Resistance in the Niger Delta." *Review of African Political Economy* 35, no. 117 (2008), 417–34.

———. "Oil and the Post-Amnesty Programme (PAP): What Prospects for Sustainable Development and Peace in the Niger Delta?" *Review of African Political Economy* 41, no. 140 (2014), 249–63.

———. "Structuring Transnational Spaces of Identity, Rights and Power in the Niger Delta of Nigeria." *Globalizations* 6, no. 4 (2009), 467–81.

———. "Transnationalism, Africa's 'Resource Curse' and 'Contested Sovereignties': The Struggle for Nigeria's Niger Delta." In *Africa and International Relations in the 21st Century,* ed. Scarlett Cornelissen, Fantu Cheru, and Timothy M. Shaw, 147–61. Basingstoke: Palgrave Macmillan, 2012.

O'Connor, James. "Capitalism, Nature, Socialism: A Theoretical Introduction." *Capitalism, Nature, Socialism* 1 (1986), 11–38.

Okereke, Chukwumerije, and Patricia Agupusi. *Homegrown Development in Africa: Reality or Illusion?* Abingdon: Routledge, 2015.

———, Harriet Bulkeley, and Heike Schroeder. "Conceptualising Climate Governance beyond the International Regime." *Global Environmental Politics* 9, no. 1 (2009), 58–78.

O'Riordan, Tim. "Reflections on the Pathways to Sustainability." In *Governing Sustainability,* ed. W. Neil Adger and Andrew Jordan, 307–28. Cambridge: Cambridge University Press, 2009.

Paarlberg, Robert L. "Politics and Food Insecurity in Africa." *Review of Agricultural Economics* 21, no. 2 (1999) 499–511.

Paehlke, Robert, and Douglas Torgerson, eds. *Managing Leviathan: Environmental Politics and the Administrative State.* London: Belhaven Press, 1990.

Parker, Charles F., Christer Karlsson, and Mattias Hjerpe. "Climate Change Leaders and Followers: Leadership Recognition and Selection in the UNFCCC Negotiations." *International Relations,* 29, no. 4 (2015), 434–54.

Parker, Faranaaz. "Poverty Report Indicates Africa Is Stagnating." *Mail and Guardian* (SA), 1 October 2013.

Patel, Zarina. "Africa: A Continent of Hope?" *Local Environment* 11, no. 1 (2006), 7–15.

———. "Environmental Justice in South Africa: Tools and Trade-Offs." *Social Dynamics: A Journal of African Studies* 35, no. 1 (2009), 94–110.

Paterson, Mathew. "Car Culture and Global Environmental Politics." *Review of International Studies* 26, no. 2 (2000), 253–70.

———. "Commodification." In *Critical Environmental Politics,* ed. Carl Death, 53–62. Abingdon: Routledge, 2014.

———. "Globalisation, Ecology, and Resistance." *New Political Economy* 4, no. 1 (1999), 129–45.

———. "Global Governance for Sustainable Capitalism? The Political Economy of Global Environmental Governance." In *Governing Sustainability,* ed. W. N. Adger and A. Jordan, 99–122. Cambridge: Cambridge University Press, 2009.

———. *Understanding Global Environmental Politics: Domination, Accumulation, Resistance.* London: Macmillan, 2000.

———, and Johannes Stripple. "My Space: Governing Individuals' Carbon Emissions." *Environment and Planning D: Society and Space* 28, no. 2 (2010), 341–62.

Patey, Luke A. "Crude Days Ahead? Oil and the Resource Curse in Sudan." *African Affairs* 109, no. 437 (2010), 617–36.

Paul, Helena, and Ricarda Steinbrecher. "African Agricultural Growth Corridors and the New Alliance for Food Security and Nutrition: Who Benefits, Who Loses?" *EcoNexus Report,* June 2013. Available at http://www.econexus.info/

publication/african-agricultural-growth-corridors-and-new-alliance-food-security-and-nutrition-who-b (accessed 2 July 2014).

Peace Parks Foundation. "Combatting Wildlife Crime." In *Peace Parks Foundation Quarterly Review, January–March 2014*. Stellenbosch: PPF, 2014.

———. "Great Limpopo Transfrontier Park." Undated. Available at http://www.peaceparks.org/tfca.php?pid=19andmid=1005 (accessed 19 August 2013).

———. "Information Systems and GIS." In *Peace Parks Foundation Quarterly Review, October–December 2013*. Stellenbosch: PPF, 2013.

———. "Kavango Zambezi." Undated. Available at http://www.peaceparks.org/tfca.php?pid=19andmid=1008 (accessed 19 August 2013).

Pearce, David. *Blueprint 3: Measuring Sustainable Development*. London: Earthscan, 1993.

———, Anil Markandya, and Edward Barbier. *Blueprint for a Green Economy*. London: Earthscan, 1989.

Pearce, Fred. "Can 'Climate-Smart' Agriculture Help Both Africa and the Planet?" *Yale Environment 360*, 15 December 2011.

———. "Will Huge New Hydro Projects Bring Power to Africa's People?" *Yale Environment 360*, 30 May 2013.

Peet, Richard, Paul Robbins, and Michael J. Watts, eds. *Global Political Ecology*. Abingdon: Routledge, 2011.

Peluso, Nancy Lee. "Coercing Conservation: The Politics of State Resource Control."
In *The State and Social Power in Global Environmental Politics*, ed. Ronnie D. Lipschutz and Ken Conca, 46–70. New York: Columbia University Press, 1993.

———, and Christian Lund. "New Frontiers of Land Control: Introduction." *Journal of Peasant Studies* 38, no. 4 (2011), 667–81.

———, and Peter Vandergeest. "Political Ecologies of War and Forests: Counterinsurgencies and the Making of National Natures." *Annals of the Association of American Geographers* 101, no. 3 (2011), 587–608.

———, and Michael J. Watts, eds. *Violent Environments*. Ithaca: Cornell University Press, 2001.

Petersen, Nicole D. "Developing Climate Adaptation: The Intersection of Climate Research and Development Programmes in Index Insurance." *Development and Change* 43, no. 2 (2012), 557–84.

Phuhlisani Solutions. *Final Report: Tender DLA 05/02/C (2004/5) Appointment of a Service Provider to Provide Training (Capacity Building) and Facilitate the Implementation of the Departmental Policy and Guidelines on the Integration of Environmental Planning into Land Reform*. Cape Town: Phuhlisani Solutions, 2005.

Pieterse, Edgar. "Grasping the Unknowable: Coming to Grips with African Urbanisms." *Social Dynamics* 37, no. 1 (2011), 5–23.

Pilkington, Ed. "Shell Pays out $15.5m over Saro-Wiwa Killing." *The Guardian* (UK), 9 June 2009.

Pillay, Udesh, and Orli Bass. "Mega-Events as a Response to Poverty Reduction: The 2010 FIFA World Cup and Its Development Implications." *Urban Forum* 19, no. 3 (2008), 329–46.

Pinnock, Don. "Southern African Elephant Corridors Blocked by Poachers." *Daily Maverick* (SA), 9 January 2014.

Poggi, Gianfranco. *The State: Its Nature, Development and Prospects.* Cambridge: Polity, 1990.

Population Reference Bureau. "2013 World Population Data Sheet." Undated. Available at http://www.prb.org/Publications/Datasheets/2013/2013-world-population-data-sheet/data-sheet.aspx (accessed 2 November 2013).

Posel, Deborah. "Races to Consume: Revisiting South Africa's History of Race, Consumption and the Struggle for Freedom." *Ethnic and Racial Studies* 33, no. 2 (2010), 157–75.

Prunier, Gérard. *The Rwanda Crisis: History of a Genocide.* Cambridge: Cambridge University Press, 1995.

Pye-Smith, Charlie. *The Quiet Revolution: How Niger's Farmers Are Re-Greening the Parklands of the Sahel.* Nairobi: World Agroforestry Centre, 2013.

Qobo, Mzukisi. "Is Environmentally Sustainable and Inclusive Growth Possible? Sub-Saharan Africa and Emerging Global Norms on Development." *South African Journal of International Affairs* 20, no. 3 (2013), 339–56.

Raftopoulos, Brian. "The 2013 Elections in Zimbabwe: The End of an Era." *Journal of Southern African Studies* 39, no. 4 (2013), 971–88.

Rahmato, Dessalegn. "Littering the Landscape: Environmental Policy in Northeast Ethiopia." In *African Savannas: Global Narratives and Local Knowledge of Environmental Change,* eds. Thomas J. Bassett and Donald Crummey, 205–24. Oxford: James Currey, 2003.

Ramphele, Mamphela. "New Day Rising." In *Restoring the Land: Environment and Change in Post-Apartheid South Africa,* ed. Mamphela Ramphele and Chris McDowell, 1–12. London: PANOS, 1991.

———, and Chris McDowell, eds. *Restoring the Land: Environment and Change in Post-Apartheid South Africa.* London: PANOS, 1991.

Ramutsindela, Maano. "Glocalisation and Nature Conservation Strategies in 21st-Century Southern Africa." *Tijdschrift voor Economische en Sociale Geografie* 95, no. 1 (2004), 61–72.

———. "The Changing Meanings of South Africa's Internal Boundaries." *Area* 30, no. 4 (1998), 291–99.

———. *Transfrontier Conservation in Africa: At the Confluence of Capital, Politics and Nature.* Cambridge, Mass.: CABI, 2007.

Ranger, Terence. *Voices from the Rocks: Nature, Culture and History in the Matopos Hills of Zimbabwe.* Oxford: James Currey, 1999.

———. "Women and Environment in African Religion: The Case of Zimbabwe." In *Social History and African Environments,* ed. William Beinart and Joann McGregor, 72–86. Oxford: James Currey, 2003.

Reed, David. *Economic Change, Governance and Natural Resource Wealth: The Political Economy of Change in Southern Africa.* London: Earthscan, 2001.

Republic of Rwanda. *Green Growth and Climate Resilience: National Strategy for Climate Change and Low Carbon Development.* Kigali: Republic of Rwanda, 2011.

Republic of South Africa. *Green Economy Accord.* Pretoria: Republic of South Africa, 2011.

———. *A National Climate Change Response Strategy for South Africa.* Pretoria: DEAT, 2004.

———. *National Climate Change Response White Paper.* Pretoria: DEAT, 2011.

———. "State of the Nation Address of the President of South Africa, Thabo Mbeki." Houses of Parliament, Cape Town, 14 February 2003. Available at http://www.info.gov.za/speeches/2003/03021412521001.htm (accessed 9 October 2013).

Resnick, Danielle, Finn Tarp, and James Thurlow. "The Political Economy of Green Growth: Cases from Southern Africa." *Public Administration and Development* 32 (2012), 215–28.

Reuters. "S. Africa Okays $5.4 Bln in Clean Energy Projects." *Reuters,* 29 October 2012.

Revkin, Andrew C. "East African Court Blocks Paved Serengeti Highway." *New York Times* (USA), 25 June 2014.

Reyes, Oscar. "Unclean Development Mechanism: How African Carbon Markets Are Failing." In *Perspectives: Mobilising Climate Finance for Africa,* 4:11, Heinrich Böll Siftung (2011), 15–17.

Ribot, Jesse C., and Anne M. Larson, eds. *Democratic Decentralisation Through a Natural Resource Lens.* Abingdon: Routledge, 2005.

Ringia, Deogratias William, and Stephen J. Porter. *Access to Environmental Information in Tanzania.* Dar es Salaam: LEAT, 1999.

Roberts, Adrienne. "Financing Social Reproduction: The Gendered Relations of Debt and Mortgage Finance in Twenty-First-Century America." *New Political Economy* 18, no. 1 (2013), 21–42.

———. "Privatizing Social Reproduction: The Primitive Accumulation of Water in an Era of Neoliberalism." *Antipode* 40, no. 4 (2008), 535–60.

Robins, Steven. "The 2011 Toilet Wars in South Africa: Justice and Transition Between the Exceptional and the Everyday After Apartheid." *Development and Change* 45, no. 3 (2014), 479–501.

———, and Kees van der Waal. "'Model Tribes' and Iconic Conservationists? Tracking the Makuleke Restitution Case in Kruger National Park." In *Land, Memory, Reconstruction, and Justice: Perspectives on Land Claims in South Africa*, ed. Cherryl Walker, Anna Bohlin, Ruth Hall, and Thembela Kepe, 163–80. Athens: Ohio University Press, 2010.

Robinson, John. "Squaring the Circle? Some Thoughts on the Idea of Sustainable Development." *Ecological Economics* 48 (2004), 369–84.

Robinson, William I. "Social Theory and Globalisation: The Rise of a Transnational State." *Theory and Society* 30 (2001), 157–200.

Rose, Nikolas. *Powers of Freedom: Reframing Political Thought.* Cambridge: Cambridge University Press, 1999.

Rosenau, James N. "Environmental Challenges in a Turbulent World." In *The State and Social Power in Global Environmental Politics*, ed. Ronnie D. Lipschutz and Ken Conca, 71–93. New York: Columbia University Press, 1993.

Rosenberg, Justin. "Why Is There No International Historical Sociology?" *European Journal of International Relations* 12, no. 3 (2006), 307–40.

Rossdale, Chris. "Between Innocence and Deconstruction: Rethinking Political Solidarity." *The Disorder of Things*, 11 January 2015. Available at http://thedisorderofthings.com/2015/01/11/between-innocence-and-deconstruction-rethinking-political-solidarity/ (accessed 6 July 2015).

Rostow, Walt. *The Stages of Economic Growth: A Non-Communist Manifesto.* Cambridge: Cambridge University Press, 1960.

Rotberg, Robert I. *Africa Emerges: Consummate Challenges, Abundant Opportunities.* Cambridge: Polity, 2013.

RSPB. "Serengeti highway." Undated. Available online at http://www.rspb.org.uk/ourwork/casework/details.aspx?id=tcm:9-262997 (accessed 24 July 2013).

Rudy, Alan P., and Damian White. "Hybridity." In *Critical Environmental Politics*, ed. Carl Death, 121–32. Abingdon: Routledge, 2014.

Ruitenbeek, Jack, and Cynthia Cartier. *Putting Tanzania's Hidden Economy to Work: Reform, Management and Protection of its Natural Resource Sector.* Washington: World Bank, 2008.

Sachs, Jeffrey. *The End of Poverty: Economic Possibilities for Our Time.* London: Penguin, 2005.

Sachs, Wolfgang. *Planet Dialectics: Explorations in Environment and Development.* London: Zed Books, 1999.

SADC-REEP. "SADC Regional Environmental Education Programme." Undated. Available at http://www.sadc-reep.org.za/ (accessed 5 November 2013).

Salgado, Ingi. "SA Accused of Undermining G77." *Business Report* (SA), 11 December 2009.

SAPA. "Nkwinti Praises Mugabe Land Reform." *IOL News* (SA), 31 May 2013.

Sarkozy, Nicolas. Address at the University of Cheikh Anta Diop, Senegal, on 26 July 2007, by the President of the French Republic.

Sassen, Saskia. "Land Grabs Today: Feeding the Disassembling of National Territory." *Globalizations* 10, no. 1 (2013), 25–46.

———. "Territory and Territoriality in the Global Economy." *International Sociology* 15, no. 2 (2000), 372–93.

———. "When Territory Deborders Territoriality." *Territory, Politics, Governance* 1, no. 1 (2013), 21–45.

Satgar, Vishwas. "South Africa's Emergent 'Green Developmental State'?" In *The End of the Developmental State?*, ed. Michelle Williams, 126–53. Abingdon: Routledge, 2014.

Schafer, Jessica, and Richard Bell. "The State and Community-Based Natural Resource Management: The Case of the Moribane Forest Reserve, Mozambique." *Journal of Southern African Studies* 28, no. 2 (2002), 401–20.

Schama, Simon. *Landscape and Memory.* London: Fontana Press, 1996.

Schlosberg, David. *Environmental Justice and the New Pluralism.* Oxford: Oxford University Press, 1999.

Schmitt, Carl. *The Concept of the Political.* Chicago: University of Chicago Press, 2007.

Schnurr, Matthew A. "Inventing Makhathini: Creating a Prototype for the Dissemination of Genetically Modified Crops into Africa." *Geoforum* 43 (2012), 784–92.

———. "Biotechnology and Bio-Hegemony in Uganda: Unravelling the Social Relations Underpinning the Promotion of Genetically Modified Crops into New African Markets." *Journal of Peasant Studies* 40, no. 4 (2013), 639–58.

Scholvin, Sören. "South Africa's Energy Policy: Constrained by Nature and Path Dependency." *Journal of Southern African Studies* 40, no. 1 (2014), 185–202.

Schreurs, Miranda, and Elim Papadakis. *Historical Dictionary of the Green Movement.* Lanham Md.: Rowman and Littlefield, 2007.

Schroeder, Richard A. "Geographies of Environmental Intervention in Africa." *Progress in Human Geography* 23, no. 3 (1999), 359–78.

Schumacher, Ernst F. *Small Is Beautiful: A Study of Economics as If People Mattered.* New York: Harper and Row, 1973.

Scoones, Ian. "Can GM Crops Prevent Famine in Africa?" In *The New Famines: Why Famines Persist in an Era of Globalization,* ed. Stephen Devereux, 312–35. Routledge: Abingdon, 2007.

———. "Range Management Science and Policy: Politics, Polemics and Pasture in Southern Africa." In *The Lie of the Land: Challenging Received Wisdom on the African Environment,* ed. Melissa Leach and Robin Mearns, 34–53. Oxford: James Currey, 1996.

———, Joseph Chaumba, Blasio Mavedzenge, and William Wolmer. "The New Politics of Zimbabwe's Lowveld: Struggles Over Land at the Margins." *African Affairs* 111, no. 145 (2012), 527–50.

———, Nelson Marongwe, Blasio Mavedzenge, Jacob Mahenehene, Felix Murimbarimba, and Crispen Sukume. *Zimbabwe's Land Reform: Myths and Realities.* London: James Currey, 2010.

———, Melissa Leach, and Peter Newell, eds. *The Politics of Green Transformations.* Abingdon: Routledge, 2015.

———, Peter Newell, and Melissa Leach. "The Politics of Green Transformations." In *The Politics of Green Transformations,* ed. Ian Scoones, Melissa Leach, and Peter Newell, 1–24. Abingdon: Routledge, 2015.

Scott, Dianne, and Clive Barnett. "Something in the Air: Civic Science and Contentious Environmental Politics in Post-Apartheid South Africa." *Geoforum* 40 (2009), 373–82.

Scott, James C. *Seeing Like a State: How Certain Schemes to Improve the Human Condition Have Failed.* New Haven: Yale University Press, 1998.

———. *Two Cheers for Anarchism.* Princeton: Princeton University Press, 2012.

———. *Weapons of the Weak: Everyday Forms of Peasant Resistance.* New Haven: Yale University Press, 1985.

Seagle, Caroline. "Discourse, Development and Legitimacy: Nature / Culture Dualism of Mining Entanglements in Biodiversity Offsetting and Conservation in Madagascar." In *Contest for Land in Madagascar: Environment, Ancestors and Development,* ed. Sandra J. T. M. Evers, Gwyn Campbell, and Michael Lambek, 187–220. Leiden: Brill, 2013.

SEDAC. "Environmental Sustainability Index." Undated. Available at http://sedac.ciesin.columbia.edu/data/collection/esi/ (accessed 19 December 2013).

Selwyn, Ben. *The Global Development Crisis.* Cambridge: Polity, 2014.

Shipton, Parker. *Mortgaging the Ancestors: Ideologies of Attachment in Africa.* New Haven: Yale University Press, 2009.

Seddon, David, and Leo Zeilig. "Class and Protest in Africa: New Waves." *Review of African Political Economy* 32, no. 103 (2005), 9–27.

Serengeti Watch. "Court Decision Bars Paved Road across Serengeti." 20 June 2014. Available at http://www.savetheserengeti.org/general/court-decision-bars-paved-road-across-serengeti/ (accessed 2 July 2014).

Sharma, Aradhana, and Akhil Gupta. "Introduction: Rethinking Theories of the State in an Age of Globalization." In *The Anthropology of the State: A Reader,* ed. Aradhana Sharma and Akhil Gupta, 1–41. Oxford: Blackwell, 2006.

Shaw, Martin. *Theory of the Global State: Globality as an Unfinished Revolution.* Cambridge: Cambridge University Press, 2000.

Sheridan, Michael J. "The Environmental and Social History of African Sacred Groves: A Tanzanian Case Study." *African Studies Review* 52, no. 1 (2009), 73–98.

Sherman, Richard. *Environment and Development Decision Making in Africa 2006–2008.* Winnipeg: IISD, 2008.

Shilliam, Robbie. "Non-Western Thought and International Relations." In *International Relations and Non-Western Thought: Imperialism, Colonialism and Investigations of Global Modernity,* ed. Robbie Shilliam, 1–11. Abingdon: Routledge, 2011.

Shipanga, Selma. "Namibia Towards a Green Economy." *The Namibian,* 18 April 2013.

Shivji, Issa G. "Serengeti Shall Not Kill!" In *Let the People Speak: Tanzania Down the Road to Neo-Liberalism,* 243–45. Dakar: CODESRIA, 2006.

Simon, David. "Climate and Environmental Change and the Potential for Greening African Cities." *Local Economy* 28, no. 2 (2013), 203–17.

———, and Hayley Leck. "Urbanising the Global Environmental Change and Human Security Agendas." *Climate and Development* 2, no. 3 (2010), 263–75.

Sklar, Richard L. "The Nature of Class Domination in Africa." *Journal of Modern African Studies* 17, no. 4 (1979), 531–52.

Skocpol, Theda. "Bringing the State Back In: Strategies of Analysis in Current Research." In *Bringing the State Back In,* ed. Peter B. Evans, Dietrich Rueschemeyer, and Theda Skocpol, 3–37. Cambridge: Cambridge University Press, 1985.

Smith, David. "Desmond Tutu: Gutter Politics Would Hurt Nelson Mandela If He Knew." *The Guardian* (UK), 17 May 2010.

Smith, Mick. *Against Ecological Sovereignty: Ethics, Biopolitics, and Saving the Natural World.* Minneapolis: University of Minnesota Press, 2011.

Smith, Neil. *Uneven Development: Nature, Capital and the Production of Space.* Oxford: Basil Blackwell, 1984.

Sneddon, Chris, Richard B. Howarth, and Richard B. Norgaard. "Sustainable Development in a Post-Brundtland World." *Ecological Economics* 57 (2006), 253–68.

Sole, Sam, and Sally Evans. "Medupi, the Murder and the Mega Fraud." *Mail and Guardian* (SA), 2 August 2013.

Sonnenfeld, David A., and Arthur P. J. Mol. "Ecological Modernisation, Governance and Globalization: Epilogue." *American Behavioural Scientist* 45, no. 9 (2002), 1446–51.

———. "Globalization and the Transformation of Environmental Governance: An Introduction." *American Behavioural Scientist* 45, no. 9 (2002), 1318–39.

South African Government News Agency. "Dept to Negotiate on Indalo Yethu Trust Dissolution." 12 July 2012. Available at http://www.sanews.gov.za/south-africa/dept-negotiate-indalo-yethu-trust-dissolution (accessed 16 July 2014).

Southern Agricultural Growth Corridor of Tanzania. Undated. Available at http://www.sagcot.com/ (accessed 20 August 2013).

Sowers, Jeannie L. *Environmental Politics in Egypt: Activists, Experts and the State.* Abingdon: Routledge, 2013.

Spaargaren, Gert, and Arthur P. J. Mol. "Carbon Flows, Carbon Markets, and Low-Carbon Lifestyles: Reflecting on the Role of Markets in Climate Governance." *Environmental Politics* 22, no. 1 (2013), 174–93.

Spierenburg, Marja, and Harry Wels. " 'Securing Space': Mapping and Fencing in Transfrontier Conservation in Southern Africa." *Space and Culture* 9, no. 3 (2006), 294–312.

Stebbing, E. P. "The Man-Made Desert in Africa: Erosion and Drought." *African Affairs* 37, no. 146 (1938), 3–40.

Stephan, Benjamin, and Matthew Paterson. "The Politics of Carbon Markets: An Introduction." *Environmental Politics* 21, no. 4 (2012), 545–62.

Stern, Nicholas. *The Economics of Climate Change: The Stern Review.* Cambridge: Cambridge University Press, 2007.

Stevenson, Hayley. "Representing Green Radicalism: The Limits of Statebased Representation in Global Climate Governance." *Review of International Studies* 40, no. 1 (2014), 177–201.

Steward, Corrina, Maria Aguiar, Nikhil Aziz, Jonathan Leaning, and Daniel Moss. *Towards a Green Food System: How Food Sovereignty Can Save the Environment and Feed the World.* Boston: Grassroots International, 2008.

Steyn, Phia. "Popular Environmental Struggles in South Africa, 1972–1992." *Historia* 47, no. 1 (2002), 125–58.

Strange, Susan. "The Defective State." *Daedalus* 124, no. 2 (1995), 55–74.

———. *The Retreat of the State: The Diffusion of Power in the World Economy.* Cambridge: Cambridge University Press, 1996.

Struwig, Jaré. "South Africans' Attitudes Towards the Environment." In *South African Social Attitudes, Second Report: Reflections on the Age of Hope,* ed. Benjamin Roberts, Mbithi wa Kivilu, and Yul Derek Davids, 198–219. Cape Town: HSRC Press, 2010.

Sustainable Society Foundation. "Sustainable Society Index." Undated. Available at http://www.ssfindex.com/ssi/framework/ (accessed 19 December 2013).

Swartz, Sharlene. *The Moral Ecology of South Africa's Township Youth.* New York: Palgrave Macmillan, 2009.

Swatuk, Larry A. "From Project to Context: Community-Based Natural Resource Conservation in Botswana." *Global Environmental Politics* 5, no. 3 (2005), 95–124.

Swilling, Mark, and Eve Annecke. *Just Transitions: Explorations of Sustainability in an Unfair World.* Claremont: University of Cape Town Press, 2012.

Taylor, Christopher. "Environmental Education in Primary Education: Status and Trends in Southern and Eastern Africa." *Environmental Education Research* 4, no. 2 (1998), 201–15.

Thérien, Jean-Philippe, and Vincent Pouliot. "The Global Compact: Shifting the Politics of International Development." *Global Governance* 12, no. 1 (2006), 55–75.

Thompson, Carol B. "Alliance for a Green Revolution in Africa (AGRA): Advancing the Theft of African Genetic Wealth." *Review of African Political Economy* 39, no. 132 (2012), 345–50.

Tienhaara, Kyla. "Varieties of Green Capitalism: Economy and Environment in the Wake of the Global Financial Crisis." *Environmental Politics* 23, no. 2 (2014), 187–204.

Tiffen, Mary, Michael Mortimore, and Francis Gichuki. *More People, Less Erosion: Environmental Recovery in Kenya.* Chichester: Wiley, 1994.

Tilly, Charles. *Coercion, Capital and European States, AD 990–1992.* Oxford: Blackwell, 1992.

———. "War Making and State Making as Organized Crime." In *Bringing the State Back In,* ed. Peter B. Evans, Dietrich Rueschemeyer, and Theda Skocpol, 169–91. Cambridge: Cambridge University Press, 1985.

TIST. "Planting Trees and Improving Agriculture for Better Lives." Undated. Available at https://www.tist.org/i2/ (accessed 16 July 2014).

Toomey, Diane. "Greenpeace's Kumi Naidoo on Russia and the Climate Struggle." *Environment360,* 14 January 2014. Available at http://e360.yale.edu/feature/interview_greenpeace_kumi_naidoo_on_russia_and_the_climate_struggle/2728/ (accessed 16 June 2014).

Toulmin, Camilla. *Climate Change in Africa.* London: Zed Books, 2009.

Tosa, Hiroyuki. "Anarchical Governance: Neoliberal Governmentality in Resonance with the State of Exception." *International Political Sociology* 3, no. 4 (2009), 414–30.

Traynor, Ian. "EU Puts €100bn-a-Year Price on Tackling Climate Change." *The Guardian* (UK), 30 October 2009.

Tripp, Aili Mari. "Women's Movements and Challenges to Neopatrimonial Rule: Preliminary Observations from Africa." *Development and Change* 32, no. 4 (2001), 33–54.

Tutu, Desmond. "We Need an Apartheid-Style Boycott to Save the Planet." *The Guardian* (UK), 10 April 2014.

UN. *National Sustainable Development Strategies: The Global Picture 2010.* New York: Division for Sustainable Development, 2010.

———. *The Future We Want.* Outcome text of the UN Conference on Sustainable Development, Rio de Janeiro, 20–22 June 2012. Available at http://sustainabledevelopment.un.org/futurewewant.html (accessed 26 April 2013)

UNCTAD. *Economic Development in Africa Report 2012: Structural Transformation and Sustainable Development in Africa.* New York: UN, 2012.

UNDP. *Human Development Report 2011. Sustainability and Equity: A Better Future for All.* New York: UNDP, 2011.

———. *Human Development Report 2013. The Rise of the South: Human Progress in a Diverse World.* New York: UNDP, 2013.

UNECA. *MDG Report 2013: Assessing Progress in Africa Toward the Millennium Development Goals.* Addis Ababa: UNECA, 2013.

———, AfDB, and the AU. "African Consensus Statement to Rio+20." Addis Ababa, 20–25 October 2011.

UNEP. *Africa Environment Outlook 3: Our Environment, Our Health.* Nairobi: UNEP, 2013.

———. *Environmental Assessment of Ogoniland.* Nairobi: UNEP, 2011.

———. *Global Green New Deal.* Nairobi: UNEP, 2009.

———. *Green Economy Assessment Report–Kenya.* Nairobi: UNEP, 2014.

———. *Green Economy Modelling Report of South Africa: Focus on Natural Resource Management, Agriculture, Transport and Energy Sectors.* Nairobi: UNEP and DEA, 2013.

———. *Green Economy Success Stories: Organic Agriculture in Uganda.* Undated. Available at http://www.unep.org/greeneconomy/SuccessStories/OrganicagricultureinUganda/tabid/29866/Default.aspx (accessed 9 October 2013).

———. "Our Goodwill Ambassadors." Undated. Available at http://www.unep.org/gwa/ (accessed 19 December 2013).

———. "Senegal Joins the Partnership for Action on Green Economy." 18 November 2014. Available at http://www.unep.org/roa/InformationMaterial/NewsCentre/tabid/794456/EntryId/52504/Senegal-joins-the-Partnership-for-Action-on-Green-Economy.aspx (accessed 6 July 2015).

———. *Towards a Green Economy.* Nairobi: UNEP, 2011.

UNEP DTU Partnership. "Total in the CDM pipeline." undated. Available at http://www.cdmpipeline.org/regions_7.htm (accessed 23 June 2015).

UNFCCC. "Momentum for Change." undated. Available at http://unfccc.int/secretariat/momentum_for_change/items/6214.php (accessed 19 December 2013).

———. "NAPAs received by the Secretariat." Undated. Available at https://unfccc.int/adaptation/workstreams/national_adaptation_programmes_of_action/items/4585.php (accessed 23 June 2015).

UNISDR. "Climate threat to Africa's resilience." 16 May 2014. Available at http://www.unisdr.org/archive/37509 (accessed 19 May 2014).

United Republic of Tanzania. *Poverty and Human Development Report 2009.* Dar es Salaam: Ministry of Finance and Economic Affairs, 2009.

———. *State of the Environment Report 2006.* Dar es Salaam: Vice President's Office, Division of Environment, 2006.

USAID. *Africa Environmental Education Assessment I: The Gambia, Guinea, Madagascar, Namibia, and Uganda.* Undated. Available at http://pdf.usaid.gov/pdf_docs/PDACI961.pdf (accessed 16 July 2014).

Utting, Peter. "Corporate Environmentalism in the South: Assessing the Limits and Prospects." In *The Greening of Business in Developing Countries: Rhetoric, Reality and Prospects,* ed. Peter Utting, 268–88. London: Zed Books and UNRISD, 2002.

van Amerom, Marloes, and Bram Büscher. "Peace Parks in Southern Africa: Bringers of an African Renaissance?" *Journal of Modern African Studies* 43, no. 2 (2005), 159–82.

van de Walle, Nicholas. *African Economies and the Politics of Permanent Crisis, 1979–1999.* Cambridge: Cambridge University Press, 2001.

———. "Presidentialism and Clientalism in Africa's Emerging Party Systems." *Journal of Modern African Studies* 41, no. 2 (2003), 297–321.

van der Westhuizen, Janis. "Glitz, Glamour and the Gautrain: Mega-Projects as Political Symbols." *Politikon: South African Journal of Political Studies* 34, no. 3 (2007), 333–51.

van Ham, Peter. "Branding Territory: Inside the Wonderful Worlds of PR and IR Theory." *Millennium* 31, no. 2 (2002), 249–69.

van Onselen, Charles. *The Seed Is Mine: The Life of Kas Maine, A South African Sharecropper, 1894–1985.* Oxford: James Currey, 1996.

van Veuren, Mocke Jansen. "Tooth and Nail: Anxious Bodies in Neill Blomkamp's District 9." *Critical Arts: South–North Cultural and Media Studies* 26, no. 4 (2012), 570–86.

Vaughan-Williams, Nick. "Borders, Territory, Law." *International Political Sociology* 2 (2008), 322–38.

Veracini, Lorenzo. "District 9 and Avatar: Science Fiction and Settler Colonialism." *Journal of Intercultural Studies* 32, no. 4 (2011), 355–67.

Verhoeven, Harry. "Climate Change, Conflict and Development in Sudan: Global Neo-Malthusian Narratives and Local Power Struggles." *Development and Change* 42, no. 3 (2011), 679–707.

Vidal, John. "Kumi Naidoo: 'I Hope Sanity Will Prevail With Climate Change, Just As It Did With Apartheid.'" *The Guardian* (UK), 6 December 2011.

———. "Regreening Program to Restore One-Sixth of Ethiopia's Land." *The Guardian* (UK), 30 October 2014.

Vickers, Brendan. "Africa and the Rising Powers: Bargaining for the 'Marginalized Many,'" *International Affairs* 89, no. 3 (2013), 673–93.

Vincent, Andrew. *Theories of the State.* Oxford: Basil Blackwell, 1987.

Vinciguerra, Venusia. "How the Daewoo Attempted Land Acquisition Contributed to Madagascar's Political Crisis in 2009." In *Contest for Land in Madagascar: Environment, Ancestors and Development,* ed. Sandra J. T. M. Evers, Gwyn Campbell, and Michael Lambek, 221–46. Leiden: Brill, 2013.

Vivan, Itala. "Geography, Literature, and the African Territory: Some Observations on the Western Map and the Representation of Territory in the South African Literary Imagination." *Research in African Literatures* 31, no. 2 (2000), 49–70.

Vogler, John. "Green Statehood and Environmental Crisis." *Politics and Ethics Review* 2, no. 2 (2006), 101–8.

Wainwright, Joel, and Geoff Mann. "Climate Leviathan." *Antipode* 45, no. 1 (2013), 1–22.

Waltz, Kenneth. *Theory of International Politics.* London: McGraw Hill, 1979.

Wanner, Thomas. "The New 'Passive Revolution' of the Green Economy and Growth Discourse: Maintaining the 'Sustainable Development' of Neoliberal Capitalism." *New Political Economy* 20, no. 1 (2015), 21–41.

Warner, Carolyn M. "The Rise of the State System in Africa." *Review of International Studies* 27, no. 5 (2001), 65–89.

Warner, Rosalind. "Ecological Modernisation Theory: Towards a Critical Ecopolitics of Change?" *Environmental Politics* 19, no. 4 (2010), 538–56.

Watts, Michael J. "Development and Governmentality." *Singapore Journal of Tropical Geography* 24, no. 1 (2002), 6–34.

———. *Silent Violence: Food, Famine and Peasantry in Northern Nigeria.* Athens: University of Georgia Press, 2013.

Weber, Max. "Politics as a Vocation." In *From Max Weber: Essays in Sociology,* ed. H. H. Gerth and C. Wright Mills, 77–128. Abingdon: Routledge, 2009.

Weidner, Helmut. "Capacity Building for Ecological Modernisation: Lessons from Cross-National Research." *American Behavioural Scientist* 45, no. 9 (2002), 1340–68.

Welz, Adam. "The War on African Poaching: Is Militarization Fated to Fail?" *Yale Environment 360,* 12 August 2013.

Western Sahara Resource Watch. "Green Energy to Uphold Occupation in Western Sahara." *Pambazuka Press,* 5 September 2013.

Whitehead, Mark. "Cold Monsters and Ecological Leviathans: Reflections on the relationships Between States and the Environment." *Geography Compass* 2, no. 2 (2008), 414–32.

———. "Sustainability." In *Critical Environmental Politics,* ed. Carl Death, 257–66. Abingdon: Routledge, 2014.

———, Rhys Jones, and Martin Jones. *The Nature of the State: Excavating the Political Ecologies of the Modern State.* Oxford: Oxford University Press, 2007.

Willems, Wendy, and Ebenezer Obadare. "Introduction: African Resistance in an Age of Fractured Sovereignty." In *Civic Agency in Africa: Arts of Resistance in the 21st Century,* ed. Ebenezer Obadare and Wendy Willems, 1–23. Woodbridge: James Currey, 2014.

Williams Michelle, ed. *The End of the Developmental State?* Abingdon: Routledge, 2014.

Wilson, Iain. "Darwinian Reasoning and Waltz's Theory of International Politics: Elimination, Imitation and the Selection of Behaviours." *International Relations* 27, no. 4 (2013), 417–38.

Wilson, Japhy. "A Strange Kind of Science: Making Sense of the Millennium Villages Project." *Globalizations* 12, no. 4 (2015), 645–59.

———. *Jeffrey Sachs: The Strange Case of Dr Shock and Mr Aid.* London: Verso, 2014.

———. "Model Villages in the Neoliberal Era: The Millennium Development Goals and the Colonization of Everyday Life." *Journal of Peasant Studies* 41, no. 1 (2014), 107–25.

Wolf, Martin. "Will the Nation-State Survive Globalisation?" *Foreign Affairs* 80, no. 1 (2001), 178–90.

Wolford, Wendy, Saturnino M. Borras Jr., Ruth Hall, Ian Scoones, and Ben White. "Governing Global Land Deals: The Role of the State in the Rush for Land." *Development and Change* 44, no. 2 (2013), 189–210.

Wolmer, William. "Transboundary Conservation: The Politics of Ecological Integrity in the Great Limpopo Transfrontier Park." *Journal of Southern African Studies* 29, no. 1 (2003), 261–78.

World Bank. "Africa's Pulse." Volume 3, April 2011. Available at https://www.worldbank.org/en/region/afr (accessed 5 July 2015).

———. "Data: CO2 emissions (metric tons per capita)." Undated. Available at http://data.worldbank.org/indicator/EN.ATM.CO2E.PC (accessed 10 October 2013).

———. "Ethiopia Economic Update–Laying the Foundation for Achieving Middle Income Status." Press release, 18 June 2013.

———. *Inclusive Green Growth: The Pathway to Sustainable Development.* Washington: World Bank, 2012.

———. "Lighting Africa." Undated. Available at http://www.lightingafrica.org/ (accessed 9 October 2013).

———. "Population density (people per sq. km of land area)." Undated. Available at http://data.worldbank.org/indicator/EN.POP.DNST (accessed 2 November 2013).

———. "Terrestrial Protected Areas (Percent of Total Land Area)." Undated. Available online at http://data.worldbank.org/indicator/ER.LND.PTLD.ZS/countries?order=wbapi_data_value_2012%20wbapi_data_value%20wbapi_data_value-lastandsort=descanddisplay=default (accessed 3 July 2014).

———. "World Bank Climate Change Strategy for Africa Calls for Adaptation, Mitigation and Additional Financing." 30 November 2010. Available at http://go.worldbank.org/L47LGXV2A0 (accessed 8 October 2013).

World Commission on Environment and Development. *Our Common Future.* Oxford: Oxford University Press, 1987.

Wroe, Daniel. "Donors, Dependency, and Political Crisis in Malawi." *African Affairs* 111, no. 442 (2011), 135–44.

Yale. "Environmental Performance Index." Undated. Available at http://epi.yale.edu/ (accessed 3 July 2015).

Yeld, John. "Fall in Line on Climate Change, Sasol Told." *IOL* (SA), 11 November 2011.

Young, Crawford. "The African Colonial State and Its Political Legacy." In *The Precarious Balance: State and Society in Africa,* ed. Donald Rothchild and Naomi Chazan, 25–66. Boulder: Westview Press, 1988.

———. *The African Colonial State in Comparative Perspective.* New Haven: Yale University Press, 1994.

Young, Oran. *International Governance: Protecting the Environment in a Stateless Society.* Ithaca: Cornell University Press, 1994.

———. "Political Leadership and Regime Formation: On the Development of Institutions in International Society." *International Organization* 45, no. 3 (1991), 281–309.

———. "The Politics of International Regime Formation: Managing Natural Resources and the Environment." *International Organization* 43, no. 3 (1989), 349–75.

Young, Tom. "'A Project to Be Realised': Global Liberalism and Contemporary Africa." *Millennium* 24, no. 3 (1995), 527–46.

Zanotti, Laura. "Governmentality, Ontology, Methodology: Re-thinking Political Agency in the Global World." *Alternatives* 38, no. 4 (2013), 288–304.

Zarsky, Lyuba. "Stuck in the Mud? Nation-States, Globalization, and Environment." In *Green Planet Blues: Environmental Politics from Stockholm to Johannesburg,* ed. Ken Conca and Geoffrey D. Dalbelko, 82–93. Boulder: Westview Press, 2004.

Ziervogel, Gina, and Susan Parnell. "South African Coastal Cities: Governance Responses to Climate Change Adaptation." In *Climate Change at the City Scale: Impacts, Mitigation and Adaptation in Cape Town,* ed. Anton Cartwright, Susan Parnell, Gregg Oelofse, and Sarah Ward, 223–43. Abingdon: Routledge, 2012.

Zikode, S'bu. "Despite the State's Violence, Our Fight to Escape the Mud, Shit and Fire of South Africa's Slums Will Continue." *The Guardian* (UK), 12 November 2013.

Index

Figures and tables are indicated by f and t following page numbers. Illustrations and photographs are indicated by italicized page numbers.

Abidjan (Côte d'Ivoire), 125, 217
Abrahamsen, Rita, 53
Abuja (Nigeria), 127
Abuja Declaration on Fertiliser for an African Green Revolution (2006), 177–78
Abu Qir fertiliser factory (Egypt), 160
accountability issues, 178, 194, 218, 225. *See also* Niger Delta
Accra (Ghana), 125, 127
activism: anti–genetically modified organism (GMO) movements, 41, 134–35; and Chinese oil drilling licenses in Niger Delta, 226; dissidents' role, 8, 14, 18, 144–48, 242, 245; Ethiopian farmers resisting top-down governance, 120; global environmental movement, 142–43; green parties, 8, 146; indigenous peoples movements, 41; killings of environmental activists, 8; local movements, 28; and marginalized peoples, 151, 221, 224; and Shell pollution of Niger Delta, 193–96; support for, 17, 38–39; transnational waves of, 220; U.S. environmental movement, 156; Zimbabwe ecological movements, 145. *See also* green revolution; Maathai, Wangari
Adams, William M., 97
Addis Ababa (Ethiopia), 127
Adger, W. Neil, 29
Adichie, Chimamanda Ngozi, 19
Adorno, Theodor, 25
AfDB. *See* African Development Bank
Africa: Afro-ecologism, 16, 235–45; biopolitics in, 3; climate change's effect on and risk management in, 5, 7; engagement as necessary approach to states in, 5; environmental issues, formative role of, 2; and environmental performance indexes, 36–37, 39; fastest

Africa (*cont.*)
growing economies in, 40, 163, 171; green economy in, 7, 173–79; and green states literature, 4, 10, 36–37, 245; land and conservation politics in, 3; as least economically developed region, 3, 222–23; mischaracterisation of states in, 42–43, 52; natural resource extraction in, 3; pledges for climate action (Intended Nationally Determined Contributions), 6; perceived as premodern, backward region, 37; reforestation commitment in, 119–21; renewable energy initiatives in, 6; shared history across states of, 11–12; structural adjustment programmes, harm caused by, 164–65; weak states in, 37–38. *See also* colonialism, history of; developing states; green economy; green states; Pan-African unity; postcolonial theory; solidarity; *specific regions and countries*
Africa Environment Day (2013), 173
Africa Living Planet Index, 203
African Convention on the Conservation of Nature and Natural Resources (Algiers 1968), 222
African Development Bank (AfDB), 8, 40, 115, 130, 174, 175, 216; Climate Investment Fund, 182
African Ecological Footprint Index, 203
Africa Network for Animal Welfare (ANAW), 70
African Greens Federation, 146
African Group of Negotiators (AGN), 6; Common African Position on climate change, 222–23
African Ministerial Conference on the Environment (AMCEN 2010), 173, 222
African National Congress (ANC), 141
African Renaissance, 134, 136, 208, 222, 243
African Union (AU), 121; Common African Position on the Post-2015 Development Agenda, 222; Comprehensive Africa Agriculture Development Programme (CAADP), 177
Africa Progress Panel Report (2014), 81, 179, 187, 235
Africa Talks Climate survey, 120–21, 132, 138
Afro-ecologism, unique features of, 16, 235–39; biopolitics of under- and overpopulation, 236; examples from South Africa, Nigeria, Tanzania, Rwanda, and Ethiopia, 236–38; governance and contestation of land and conservation, 235–36; least economically developed region desiring rapid modernisation, 236; solidarity and Pan-African unity, 236; why states matter, 238–39. *See also* green states
AGN (African Group of Negotiators), 6, 222–23
Agnew, John, 64, 72
Agrawal, Arun, 93, 149
agriculture: budget cuts due to SAPs, 165; climate-smart agriculture, 171, 178; commercial farmers, 121, 181–82, 190; crop insurance, 180–81; crop science, 144; educated entrepreneurial farmers, 14, 118–23; exclusive territorialisation of farmland, 89–90; fertiliser and pesticide use, 177–78, 186–87, 213; foreign enterprises leasing or purchasing land for, 8; genetically modified foods, opposition to, 134–35, 187; green economy tied to, 177–78, 191; land grabbing of farmland, 100; monocrop industrial agriculture, 102; organic farming in Uganda, 187; pollination of crops, 160; resource limited farmers, 121; significance in African economy, 191; slash-and-burn cultivation, 117; smallholder farmers' access to fertilisers, high-yield seeds, and irrigation, 177; in South Africa, 62
AgriSol/AgriSol Energy, 100, 137
aid conditionality, 199–200

Alexander, Jocelyn, 91, 92
Algeria: environmental index on, 205; invasive alien species in, 135; renewable energy in, 6, 40, 176
Aliança Democrática, 147
Aliber, Michael, 190
Alliance for a Green Revolution in Africa, 177
Amanor, Kojo Sebastian, 100–101
AMCEN (African Ministerial Conference on the Environment 2010), 173, 222
Amnesty International, 196
anarchic international system, 54
ANAW (Africa Network for Animal Welfare), 70
ANC (African National Congress), 141
Anglo-Boer War (1898–1901), 88
Anglophone countries, 11
Angola: biofuel projects in, 182; borders of, 88; China's investments in, 225; environmental indexes on, 205; oil companies in, 215
Annan, Kofi, 7, 117, 179
anomie, 132–33
Anthropocene, 4, 114, 245
anti–genetically modified organism (GMO) movements, 41, 134–35
anti-instrumentalist perspectives, 23, 24–26, 27, 29, 31
antistatist perspectives, 21, 22–23, 27, 34, 56, 57
Arctic, 41, 216
armed conflict. *See* warfare
Ashford, Nicholas A., 35, 201
Asia, rapidly growing economy of, 171
Asian agribusiness in Africa, 100
Aswan Dam (Egypt), 61, 157, 176
AU. *See* African Union
Australia: and environmental performance indexes, 37; rejection of UNFCCC process, 224; trees from, introduced into South Africa, 135
authoritarian states, 25, 39; and green states' conservation, 88, 236–37; of neoliberal Europe, 68; state-building in Africa resulting in, 68
autochthony, 136, 143, 150
autonomous governmentality, 240
Ayoob, Mohammed, 54

Bailey, Sinéad, 60
Baker, Susan, 29
Balde, Abdoulaye, 174
Baldwin, Andrew, 138–39
Bali World Parks Congress (1982), 92
Bamako Declaration on the Environment for Sustainable Development (2010), 173
BanaPads Social Enterprise, 129
Bangladesh, leasing of South Sudanese agricultural land by, 100
Ban Ki-moon, 154
Bär, Holger, 168
Barbier, Edward, 170; *A New Blueprint for a Green Economy* (with Markandya), 166–67
Barroso, José Manuel, 223
Barry, John, 36, 68, 139, 145, 168
Bassey, Nnimmo, 7, 18, 41, 193, 217, 218, 228
Batoka Gorge dam (southern Africa), 177
Bayart, Jean-François, 13, 45, 50, 52–54, 55, 124
Beck, Ulrich, 24, 28, 49, 76
Beinart, William, 62
Belize, 205
Benin: FoEI activities in, 227; green party in, 147; land mapping in, 81; PACJA activities in, 227
Bennett, Brett M., 135
Berger, Mark, 29
Berlin Conference (1884–85), 74–75, 77
Bertrand, Yann Arthus, 212
Biafra, 90
Bill and Melinda Gates Foundation, 177, 212
Billion Trees Campaign, 108

biodiversity. *See* nature conservation and biodiversity
biofuels, 8, 101, 122–23, 182
biopolitics, 3, 58–59; of apartheid South Africa, 62–63, 67; colonial Egypt's biopolitics, 60–61, 63; contesting biopolitical subjectivities, 148–51; Dean on, 59; vs. environmentalism, 144; Foucault on, 58–59; and postcolonial governmentality, 239–43
Birdlife South Africa, 142
Black, Jeremy, 73
Blair, Tony, 28, 189
Bloch, Marc, 247n1
Blowfield, Michael, 162, 215
Body Shop, 196
Bokiaga, Didace Pembe, 147
Bond, Patrick, 219
Bookchin, Murray, 25
Boone, Catherine, 81, 106
borderline creation, 72, 74, 77–78, 87, 99; fears of giving up borders in transfrontier park creation, 96
Boserup, Esther, 115
Bosshard, W. C., 119
Botswana: borders of, 87, 99; carbon footprint in, 130; environmental education in, 140; environmental indexes on, 9, 204*t*, 205; fences in, 98; national parks and conservation in, 76; protected land in, 13, 71
Brainforest, 226
branding of states, 184, 206, 230
Braudel, Fernand, 247n1
Brazil: carbon credits in, 160; carbon emissions in, 219; and Copenhagen Accord, 6; in green states literature, 36; lending for dam construction from, 176; weak status for environmental reforms in, 38
Brenner, Neil, 88
Brenton, Tony: *Greening Machiavelli,* 33
Brian Boswell Circus, animal abuse at, 219
Britain. *See* United Kingdom
Broch-Due, Vigdis, 200
Brockington, Dan, 82, 137, 141–42, 216
Brooks, Shirley, 85
Brundtland Report, 23–24, 169, 170, 171, 203
Bryant, Raymond, 60
Buddhism, 41
Bujagali dam (Uganda), 176
Bulbul landfill (South Africa), 219
Bull, Hedley, 45, 48, 63, 64, 76
Bündchen, Gisele, 212
Bunn, David, 114
burial grounds, 80
Burkina Faso: agricultural economy in, 191; FoEI branch in, 227; Great Green Wall in, 121; green party in, 7, 146, 147; land mapping in, 81; population growth associated with regreening in, 116
Burundi: green party in, 147; refugees from, in Tanzania, 137–38
Büscher, Bram, 96, 99, 161
Butler, Judith, 144
Buttel, F. H., 35, 162, 164
Bwindi National Park (Uganda), 78

Cadbury, 164
Cairo, 125
Calvinist puritanism, 127
Cambodia, 134
Cameroon: borders of, 78; environmental activists in, 14; PACJA activities in, 227
CAMPFIRE (Communal Areas Management Programme for Indigenous Resources), 92–93
Canada: environmental performance indexes on, 37; pollution and hot spots in, 216; rejection of UNFCCC process, 224
capacity building, 20, 68, 192
Cape Town, 127, 208
capitalism, 23, 26–27, 30, 53, 88, 126, 127, 158
Carabine, Elizabeth, 185

carbon colonialism, 8, 102, 162
carbon emissions, 8, 102, 153, 157–60; carbon credits, 157, 160, 182; carbon-neutral economy as goal for South Africa, 185; comparison of South Africa with other countries, 219; developed states' responsibility as emitters, 223, 252n72; emissions trading, 159, 199; Kenya Agricultural Carbon Project, 178; low-carbon zones in Ethiopia, 214; Rwanda and fertiliser use, 186–87; transportation changes due to, 171. *See also* climate change
carbon footprint, 37, 130
carbon sinks, 101
carbon tax, 14, 153–55, 172, 269n3
CBNRM (Community Based Natural Resource Management), 92, 95
CDM (Clean Development Mechanism), 159–60, 162, 199
Central Africa: national parks and reserves in, 71; poverty in, 124
Central African Republic, 8
centralised authority: and colonialism, 75; natural resources, reconsolidating central authority over, 104, 75
Centre for Civil Society (University of KwaZulu-Natal), 219
Centre for Environment and Development (Cameroon), 227
Centre for the Study of Forced Migration and International Refugee Rights Initiative, 137–38
Cerny, Phil, 202, 206
Césaire, Aimé, 112
Chad, reforestation in, 121
Chapin, Mac, 94
Chase, Mike, 97
Cheadle, Don, 212
Chenda, Emmanuel, 174
Chicago School, 27
China: carbon credits in, 160; carbon emissions in, 219; at COP17 climate change conference (Durban 2011), 224; and Copenhagen Accord, 6; Export-Import Bank, 177, 226; flagship programmes in, 215; in green states literature, 36; investment's effect on African local environment, 225–26; lending for dam construction from, 176; population density in, 115; weak environmental reforms in, 38
Chipko Indians, 40
Civilian Conservation Corps, 170
civil society organisations, 39, 196, 226–27
Clapham, Christopher, 50–51, 54, 165
Clark, Ian, 29
class rule, 46
Clean Development Mechanism (CDM), 159–60, 162, 199
Climate Adaptation Fund (UNFCCC), 181
climate change: African attitudes on, 39, 151; African Group solidarity in negotiating over, 221–29; African leadership role on, 206; capacity building of green states to address, 21; climate-smart agriculture, 171, 178; environmental, political, and social transformations related to, 3–5; migration likely in the future due to, 138; mitigation and adaptation strategies, 167, 172, 179, 181, 199, 211, 223; and overpopulation, 115; principle of common but differentiated responsibilities of developing vs. developed countries, 223; South African Climate Change Strategy (2011), 130–32; vulnerability of Africa to, 5, 7, 8. *See also COP conferences*
Climate Investment Fund (AfDB), 40
climate justice networks, 41
Climate Risk Index, 203
climate summit (New York 2014), 121
Clinton, Bill, 28
Cloete, Elsie L., 143
coal-fired power plants (South Africa), 8, 155, 184

Coates, Peter, 62
Cock, Jacklyn, 142, 239
Collier, Stephen, 230
Collum Coal Mine Industries (Zambia), 226
Colombia, 205
colonialism, history of, 11, 21, 37, 51, 53; biopolitics of apartheid South Africa, 60, 62–63, 67, 88, 93, 126; biopolitics of colonial Egypt, 60–61, 63; and centralised political authority, 75; determinant factor in green state practices, 67, 188, 241; and exclusive territorialisation, 89–90, 95; national parks, creation of, 84; and resistance, 144; and slash-and-burn agriculture, 117; and state creation, 73, 81, 90; and underdevelopment, 163–64
Columbia University. *See* Environmental Sustainability Index
Comaroff, Jean and John, 13, 45, 111, 128, 135–36
Committee of the African Heads of State on Climate Change, 222
commodification, 65, 94, 101, 123, 157–62
Communal Areas Management Programme for Indigenous Resources (CAMPFIRE), 92–93
Communist Manifesto, 26
Community Based Natural Resource Management (CBNRM), 92, 95
community conservation and decentralised natural resource management, 93, 141, 241
competition, 198, 206
Conca, Ken, 26, 92
conceptual framework for green states, 63–66, 234, 238
Congo: environmental indexes on, 7, 42, 204*t*, 205; green party in, 7; palm oil business in, 164
Congo, Democratic Republic of. *See* Democratic Republic of Congo (DRC)
Congo River Basin, 6
Connolly, William, 75
Conrad, Joseph: *Heart of Darkness,* 73
conservation. *See* nature conservation and biodiversity
Conservation International, 94
consumerism: green consumer, 127–32. *See also* overconsumption issues
Consumers International, 129; Green Action Fund, 129
Convention on Biological Diversity, 71
Convention to Combat Desertification, 121
Conway, Terence, 229
cookstoves programme, 160
Cooper, Fredrick, 50
COP15 conference (Copenhagen 2009), 154, 169, 222. *See also* Copenhagen Accord (2009)
COP17 climate change conference (Durban 2011), 6, 154, 184, 207, 220, 224, 237
COP19 conference (Warsaw 2013), 175, 220, 224, 227
COP21 conference (Paris 2015), 6; and adaptation financing, 199; Intended Nationally Determined Contributions, 199. *See also* Paris Agreement (2015)
Copenhagen Accord (2009), 6, 207, 223
Corbridge, Stuart, 72
corporate social responsibility (CSR), 28, 162–63, 214–15
corruption, 52, 90, 127, 148, 209
Costa Rica, 205
Côte d'Ivoire: green party in, 147; invasive alien species in, 135; land mapping in, 81; toxic waste dumping in, 217
Cousins, Ben, 190
Cox, Robert, 19
Critchley, William, 122; *More People, More Trees,* 116, 121
critical solidarity, 227, 228, 245, 281n110
critical theorists, 16–17, 21, 32, 149–50, 202, 221, 240

crowd sourcing, 98
CSR (corporate social responsibility), 28, 162–63, 214–15
cuius regio, eius religio ("whose realm, his religion"), 48
cultural practices: associated with wilderness and frontier, 83, 127; and heterogeneity, 202. *See also* indigenous peoples

Daewoo, 95
dams, 15, 176–78, 180. *See also specific dams by name*
Darfur, 198
Darwin's Nightmare (film), 135
Daudi, Halima, 174
Dauvergne, Peter, 132
Davidson, Stewart, 27
Davies, Rob, 184
Davis, Mike, 105
DBSA (Development Bank of South Africa), 182, 185, 215
Dean, Mitchell, 13, 45, 58–60, 64
Deegan, Heather, 163
deep greens (ecological theorists), 22, 23, 27, 29, 31
deforestation, 118. *See also* Reducing Emissions from Deforestation and Forest Degradation (REDD+); reforestation
"degrowth," 168
Deleuze, Gilles, 55
Delisle, Guillaume: *Carte d'Afrique,* 73, 74*f*
Democratic Republic of Congo (DRC): autochthony in, 150; borders of, 78; dams in, 40; financing of forest governance in, 182; fragile state agenda in, 54; green party in, 147; mining in, 8, 217; reforestation in, 121; renewable energy in, 6, 176; territorial control in, 51; war in, 198
democratic states and green norms, 31–32, 245
Derg regime (Ethiopia), 119, 120
Desertec, 175
developed states: preaching to less developed states, 20; responsibility as emitters, 223, 252n72. *See also* development aid
developers vs. preservationists, 70
developing states: aid conditionality for, 199–200; capacity building in, 20, 68, 192; copying innovation of developed states, 201; environmental movements in, 39; framework of environmental politics for, 16; least developed countries (LDCs) in GHG-emissions negotiations, 222–23; negativity toward green economy in, 172; schizophrenia of, 54; as weak states, 38
development aid, conditionality of, 199–200
Development Assistance Committee's *Aid to Environment Development Co-operation Report* 2012, 200
Development Bank of South Africa (DBSA), 182, 185, 215
de Villiers, Bertus, 208
Devil weed, in Côte d'Ivoire, 135
de Wet, Chris, 89
Diamond, Jared, 115, 116, 263n22
Di-Aping, Lumumba, 223–24
Dietz, Ton, 99
diplomacy, 50, 197
disaster response, 179–81
disciplinary neoliberalism, 203
dissidents. *See* activism
District 9 (film), 150–51
Djibloho dam (Equatorial Guinea), 176–77
Djibouti, reforestation in, 121
Doherty, Brian, 27, 41, 206, 227
Doyle, Timothy, 27, 41, 206, 227
DRC. *See* Democratic Republic of Congo
Dryzek, John: on conception of state, 46; on environmental conservation imperative,

John Dryzek (*cont.*)
61, 75–76, 258n22; and green states literature, 12, 33; on interaction of states and social movements, 145; social movements' role in emerging green states, 142; on state imperatives linked to environmental issues, 235
D'Sa, Des, 18, 145, 219
Duffield, Mark, 143
Duffy, Rosaleen, 97–99
Dunn, Kevin, 55, 78, 90
Durban (South Africa), 96, 179, 208, 219
Durban conference (2011). *See* COP17 climate change conference
Durban Declaration on Climate Justice (2004), 226
Durban Group for Climate Justice, 226
DWAF, fire costs billed to, 103

East African Court of Justice (EACJ), 13, 70, 71
eastern Africa, 11, 69; borders and park boundaries in, 99; national parks and reserves in, 71; overpopulation in, 115; poverty in, 124
East Kivu forests and borders, 78
Eckersley, Robyn, 42; cautions voiced by, 68; on democratic nature of green states, 245; on developed states' role as environmental leaders, 252n72; on ecocentric nature of green states, 234–35; on enlightened ecological citizenship, 237; on EU as best option for green transnational state, 36, 211; on exemplary leadership's role in green states, 211; on greening of states in multilateral order, 231; and green states literature, 12; as normative theorist, 31–32; on transnationally oriented green states, benefits of, 239
ecological footprint, 252n72
ecological modernisation theory, 23–24, 158–59, 198, 202, 235, 237, 243
Ecological Party of Uganda, 147
eco-Marxists, 23, 26–27, 29, 31
economic protectionism, 172
economies of Africa, 163–65; conceptual framework of green states based on, 65; dependency in, 53–54; fastest growing in world among, 40, 163, 171; South African economy described by Mbeki, 185; transformation related to green states, 191–92. *See also* environmental markets; green economy; *specific sectors of the economy*
Ecopeace, 148
eco-protectionism, 172
ecosystem service valuing, 160
ecotourism, 88, 94, 97
education: budget cuts due to SAPs, 165; environmental education programmes, 140–41, 143; as Sustainable Development Goal, 141
Egypt: biopolitics of colonial period in, 60–61, 63, 67; boundary mapping of colonial period in, 81; combining natural and social environment in, 157; development projects in, 40; environmental politics in, 41; green party in, 147; invasive alien species in, 135; pollution controls on industry in, 160; reforestation in, 121; social conditions in, 132; sustainable development in, 7
EIA (environmental impact assessments), 39, 178
El Ali, Haidar, 146
Elden, Stuart, 73
electricity, 128, 176–77, 180
Elephants Without Borders, 97
Ellis, Stephen, 88
emissions trading, 159
employment: green jobs, creation of, 185, 237; nature conservation and biodiversity offering, 92, 94
empowerment, 92, 94
Endangered Wildlife Trust (South Africa), 142

Energizer, 182
energy dependence, 171
Engels, Friedrich, 46
English language dominance in environmental education programmes, 143
Enlightenment science and thought, 22, 23, 25, 29, 169
environmental education programmes, 140–42; English language dominance in, 143
environmental governance communities, 200–201
environmental impact assessments (EIA), 39, 178
environmental indicators. *See* environmental performance indexes
environmentalism vs. biopolitics, 144
environmental justice, 210, 216, 218, 219, 243, 252n72
environmental law enforcement, 178
environmental markets, 152–92; in African economies, 163–65; creation of, 156–58; decoupling of material flows from economic flows, 159; governance of, 161–63; overview, 152–56; planning needs of, 162; political nature of, 155–56; reconciliation of new markets with traditional environmental issues, 158–61. *See also* green economy
Environmental Performance Index (EPI; Yale University), 7, 8, 36–37, 39, 41–42, 203–6, 204*t*, 238
environmental performance indexes, 7–9, 36–37, 39, 41–42, 202–3, 278n38. *See also specific index by name*
environmental politics: critical to understanding Africa, 1–2, 11, 17; environmental movement and pacifism, 25; existing conservation policies of, 76; lack of fit between environmental issues and geographic boundaries of states, 22–23; and land politics, 106; positive aspects of, 5; and power relations, 149; race to the bottom, 217; reshaping of state for, 245; role of states in meeting environmental challenges, 10–11. *See also* biopolitics
Environmental Rights Action (Nigeria), 194, 196, 218, 227
environmental shocks, green resilience as factor in surviving, 179–81
Environmental Sustainability Index (Columbia University), 36–37, 203
EPI. *See* Environmental Performance Index (Yale University)
Epstein, Charlotte, 66
Equatorial Guinea: antipoaching operations in, 86; dam in, 176–77; National Adaptation Programmes of Action, 199
equity and equality, 148, 170, 171, 188; disparities produced by language, race, and religion, 202; environmental risks not equally shared, 216
Eritrea: carbon footprint in, 130; ecological footprint in, 203
erosion. *See* land degradation
Escobar, Arturo, 25
Eskom (South Africa electricity utility), 183
Ethiopia: agricultural modernisation in, 119–20; authoritarian regime in, 21; China's investments in, 225; Climate-Resilient Green Economic Strategy, 180–81; dam construction in, 176; deforestation in, 118; development projects in, 40; economic growth in, 163, 180; environmental education in, 140; environmental impact assessments (EIA) in, 178; environmental indexes on, 204*t*, 205; environmental marketing and branding of, 184; famine in, 124; green economy strategies in, 7, 14–15, 40, 173, 236–37; invasive alien species in, 135; land grabs and relocation in, 89; low-carbon zones in, 214; microinsurance in, 180–81;

Ethiopia (*cont.*)
overview, 236–37; PACJA activities in, 227; peasant farming in, 117; population density in, 115; reforestation in, 119–20, 121, 236; Rehabilitation of Forest, Grazing and Agricultural Lands Project (Project 2488), 119–20; renewable energy in, 6, 176; resistance to top-down governance of agriculture in, 120; rural intervention in, 119; sustainable development in, 185
EU. *See* Europe/European Union
Eurocentric thought, 5, 50, 73
European Commission, 69
Europe/European Union: and agribusiness and land grabs in Africa, 100; authoritarian neoliberalism in, 68; at Barcelona negotiations (2009), 167; as best option for green transnational state, 36, 211; conservation in, 76–77; environmental politics in, 106; EU Emissions Trading Scheme (EU ETS), 159; failure of leadership in global environmental politics, 207; and global financial crisis, 167; green economy in, 129, 173; green states in, 10; and green states literature, 33; North Africa supplying renewable energy to, 40; postmaterialist environmentalism in, 38; reforestation support from, 121; state transformation in, 34
Evans, Peter, 38
exploitation, 164
extractive industries. *See* mining; natural resource extraction
extreme poverty, 124, 163. *See also* poverty

Fahamu (media outlet), 225
failed states, 51–52
Falkner, Robert, 163, 197
famine: in Ethiopia, 180; frequency of, 8, 124; in Horn of Africa, 118
FAO. *See* Food and Agriculture Organisation
Febvre, Lucien, 247n1
Fédération Démocratique des Ecologistes du Sénégal, 7
feminist critique, 27, 128, 202
Ferguson, James, 215–16, 240
fertiliser, 160, 177–78, 186–87, 213
FIFA World Cup (South Africa, 2010), 97, 122, 184, 206, 208–9, 237
financial crisis. *See* global financial crisis
Fine, Ben, 154
"fines-and-fences," 83, 96
Finland, 37
Firestone Tires, 164
Fisher, Jonathan, 52
Fletcher, Robert, 161
flooding, 8
FoE Ghana, 227
FoEI. *See* Friends of the Earth International
food aid, 134, 165
Food and Agriculture Organisation (FAO), 121, 191, 199; Voluntary Guidelines on the Responsible Governance of Tenure of Land, Fisheries and Forests in the Context of National Food Security, 102
food-for-work programmes, 119
food security, 8, 33, 40, 70, 134–35, 171, 212; reform proposals for global food system, 188
forests: deforestation, 118; and oxygen provision, 160; reforestation, 119–21, 206. *See also* trees and tree-planting
fortress conservation, 13, 83–89
fossil fuel sectors, 32
Foucault, Michel: anthropological and ethnographic approach to work of, 56; *The Birth of Biopolitics,* 58; on care of the self, 281n110; on challenges faced by modern man, 245; on critical ethos of danger, 240; on economy as field of political regulation, 65; on governmentalisation of the state,

57–59; on imagination of national economies, 157; on neoliberal rationalities of government, 127–28; on pastoral power, 119–20, 139; on power relationships, 240; on state theory, 12–13, 45, 233

France, 20, 53, 115

Frankfurt School of Critical Theory, 24

fraud, 162

free markets, 155

Friends of the Earth International (FoEI): on accountability of Chinese firms, 226; Bassey as chair, 7; Doherty and Doyle study of, 227; ecological movements receiving support from, 145; potential of, 243; reporting government harassment, 218, 221; and Shell pollution and cleanup of Niger Delta, 193, 196; southern members' role in, 41

Frynas, Jedrzej George, 162, 215, 218

G77 countries+China, 172, 222, 223

Gabon NGO campaign against Chinese development projects, 226

Gambia: environmental education in, 140; reforestation in, 121

game reserves. *See* national parks and reserves

genetically modified organisms (GMOs): cotton trials, 214; foods, 41, 134–35, 187

genocide in Rwanda, 115–16, 118, 136–37, 263n22

geographical information systems (GIS), 81, 98

Geothermal Development Project (Kenya), 175

Germany: colonialism's effect on, 53; development aid from, 199, 200; environmental performance indexes on, 37; as green state, 10; neoliberalism in, 58; and Serengeti road dispute, 70

Ghana: corporate social responsibility charters in, 162–63; development projects in, 40; electricity usage in, 128; FoEI general meeting in, 227; green economy strategies in, 173; indigenous knowledge in, 239; invasive alien species in, 135; land mapping in, 81; mining in, 8, 217; natural resource extraction in, 175; PACJA activities in, 227; renewable energy in, 6, 40, 176; sustainable development in, 7

GHGs (greenhouse gases). *See* carbon emissions

Gibe III dam (Ethiopia), 176

Gill, Stephen, 203

Global Environment Facility, 28, 121, 199

global financial crisis (2008), 21, 156, 167, 181; South Africa's stimulus package, 183

Global Green Congress (Dakar 2012), 7, 41, 146, *147*

Global Green Economy Index, 207

Global Green New Deal, 166, 170, 192

global heritage represented by Serengeti, 71

globalisation, 23, 27–30, 132–43; anxieties and xenophobic attitudes created by, 132–33, 136, 242; and consumption issues, 125; contemporary aspects of, 54–55; as corollary to sovereignty, 49; denationalisation due to, 49; emergence of global economy, 157–58; green state literature's focus on, 76; idealists' views on, 198

Global Mechanism of the UN Convention to Combat Desertification, 121

Global Witness, 8, 196

Gola, Loyiso, 150–51

Goldman, Michael, 128, 201

Goldman Environmental Prize, 145

Gomera, Maxwell, 160

Gordimer, Nadine, 152

Gore, Al: *Earth in the Balance,* 118
governance. *See* state formation and role
governing markets, 161–63
governmentality framework for analysis, 57–60
Gramsci, Antonio, 26, 46, 53
Grand Inga dam (DRC), 40
Grand Renaissance dam (Ethiopia), 176
Great Depression, 157
Great Green Wall (Sahel), 121
Great Lakes region (east Africa), 115, 137
Great Limpopo Trans-frontier Conservation Park (South Africa, Zimbabwe, and Mozambique), 96, 98, 99
Green Action Fund, 129
Green Banking Innovation Awards (2010), 215
Green Belt Movement (Kenya), 14, 40, 108–14, 140, 144–45, 239
green consumers, 127–32
green economy, 14–15, 166–72; in Africa, 173–79, 192; and agriculture, 177–78, 191; discourses in, 166–68, 206, 242–43; as driver of African growth, 181–84; global enthusiasm for, 156; green growth, 14, 165–67, 170–71, 181–84, 242; green resilience, 14, 156, 171–72, 179–81, 192, 242; green revolution, 14, 17, 168–69, 188–91, 242–43; green transformation, 14, 17, 156, 169–70, 191–92, 245; national strategies, 153; negativity toward, 172; sustainable development, transformation of African economies and, 184–88
Green Economy Accord (South Africa), 183, 237
Green Economy Index, 203
Green Economy Summit (2010), 173
green growth, 14, 165–67, 170–71, 181–84, 242; compared to green transformation, 171
greenhouse gases (GHGs). *See* carbon emissions
green parties, 41, 146. *See also specific party by name*
Green Party of Benin, 147
Green Party of Egypt, 147
Green Party of Mozambique, 147
Green Party of Rwanda, 148
Green Party of South Africa, 148
Greenpeace International, 7, 196, 226–28
green resilience, 14, 156, 171–72, 179–81, 192, 242
green revolution, 14, 17, 156, 168–69, 188–91, 242–43; unique aspects in Africa, 235
green states: alternative methodology to study, 55–60; authoritarian states as, 236–37; characterisation of, 4–5, 10, 234–39; conceptual framework for, 63–66, 234, 238; empirical dimension, 32–35; as environmental laggards, 216–21, 230; as exemplary environmental leaders, 206–16, 243; and land issues in Africa, 13; leadership roles of, 206–16, 230; meaning of term "green state," 22, 59, 234–35; micropractices and discourses of, 166–68, 206, 233, 242–43; and modes of governance, 241; more than bureaucratic administrations, 71; normative dimension, 31–32, 237; from postcolonial perspective, 239; and realist tradition of international relations, 33; "state greening" features, 32–33; and transformation of African economies, 191–92, 238–39; unique aspects of green states in Africa, 235–36; warfare producing, 197–98. *See also* green economy; territorialisation
green states literature, 4, 10, 12, 30, 33, 36, 234–35, 245
green transformation, 14, 17, 156, 169–70, 191–92; compared to green growth, 171; importance of, 238–39, 245
Groenewald, Pieter, 190

GroundWork, 219, 227
Grove, Richard, 40, 133
Guinea: agricultural economy in, 191; dam construction in, 177; environmental education in, 140; green party in, 147
Gupta, Akhil, 66
Guyana, 94

Haas, Peter, 24
Habitat Council (South Africa), 142
Habyarimana, Juvenal, 116
The Hague district court ruling against Shell (2013), 194
Haile Selassie, 119
Hall, Ruth, 182
Hansen, Thomas Blom, 240
Happy Planet Index (HPI), 8–9, 37, 203–6, 204*t*, 238
Hardin, Garrett, 24
Harley, Jon, 82
Harrison, Graham, 201–2
Harvey, David, 88
Haynes, Jeff, 91
HDI (Human Development Index), 130
health concerns, 133, 219; health budget cuts due to SAPs, 165
Hegel, Georg Wilhelm Friedrich, 20, 32, 44, 68
hegemony, 26, 30, 201
Heilbroner, Robert, 24
Herbst, Jeffrey, 50
hermaphrodite landscapes of slums, 104–5, 242
heterogeneity of Africa, 55, 71, 75, 78, 149, 202–3, 205, 216, 221, 230, 235
Hicks, Robert L., 200
Hirst, Paul, 48
HIV/AIDS, 133–34
Hluhluwe–Umfolozi game reserve (South Africa), 84–85
homogeneity as effect of international cooperation and conflict, 198–202, 230–31, 235
homosexuality, 134
Horkheimer, Max, 25
Horn of Africa and famine, 118, 124
hot spots, 216
HPI. *See* Happy Planet Index
Hughes, David, 74
Hu Jintao, 226
Human Development Index (HDI), 130
human rights, 60, 148, 228, 237
Hutton, Jon, 97
Hyden, Goran, 123
hydropower, 40, 176, 180. *See also* dams

IAS (invasive alien species), 59, 62, 133–39
ICT (information and communication technology), 184
idealists vs. realists, 198
IFIs (international financial institutions), 53, 165
Igoe, Jim, 148
Iliffe, John, 2–3, 7, 115
ILO (International Labour Organisation), 170, 187
IMF (International Monetary Fund), 164
immigrants: climate change increasing future number of, 138; refugees from Burundi, 137–38; and xenophobia, 136–37
Indalo Yethu Trust, 131
India: carbon credits in, 160; carbon emissions in, 219, 224; and Copenhagen Accord, 6; in green states literature, 36; lending for dam construction from, 176; weak environmental reforms in, 38
indigenous peoples: advocacy movements, 41; indigenous knowledge's effect on government and environment, 239–40; lack of involvement in environmental education programmes, 143; lack of involvement in TFCA management, 98; prioritisation of indigenous knowledge in agriculture, 188

inequality. *See* equity and equality
information and communication technology (ICT), 184
infrastructure investment projects, 15, 27, 178. *See also* dams; mining; power plants
Inga Falls (DRC), 176
innovation, 201, 211
intellectual property rights, 188
Inter-Governmental Panel on Climate Change (IPCC), 28; 4th Assessment Report, 223; 5th Assessment Report, 7
International Congress for the Protection of Nature (Paris 1909), 197
international financial institutions (IFIs), 53, 165
International Labour Organisation (ILO), 170, 187
international law, 50, 197; international environmental law, 28, 197; multilateral legal regimes, 199, 201
International Monetary Fund (IMF), 164
international relations (IR), 15, 30, 193–232; and environmental leaders, 206–21, 230; and green states, 66; liberal and institutionalist IR theorists, 34; overview, 193–96; realist tradition of, 33; sovereignty, 54, 196–206; and state theorizing, 47–48, 54–55; transnational environmental solidarity, 221–29; uneven international topography, 15, 100, 202, 221, 229–32, 235
International Rivers, 226
International Union for the Conservation of Nature (IUCN), 70, 142; on Africa's leadership role in reforestation, 206; on invasive alien species, 135; Protected Areas Categories System, 79, 79–80*f*; and Tanzania, 84. *See also* World Parks Congress
Inuit movements for Arctic protection, 41
invasive alien species (IAS), 59, 62, 133–39
IPCC. *See* Inter-Governmental Panel on Climate Change
"iron cage of rationality," 23, 24
Islamic insurgents, 21, 55
IUCN. *See* International Union for the Conservation of Nature

Jackson, Stephen, 136, 150
Jackson, Tim: *Prosperity Without Growth,* 169
James, Deborah, 104
Japan: development aid from, 200; and environmental performance indexes, 37; green economy favored in, 173; mitigation targets in, 224
Jessop, Bob, 13, 45, 46, 48, 49, 56–57, 64, 65
Johannesburg, 125, 127
Jonathan, Goodluck, 206
Jones, Lindsey, 185
Jordan, Andrew, 29
Joseph, Jonathan, 37
Juma, Calestous, 212

Kagame, Paul, 173, 212, 236
Kalala, Bruno Kapandji, 176
Kanchory, Saitabao Ole, 70
Kaplan, Robert D., 73
Kapuściński, Ryszard, 108
Karkkainnen, Bradley, 99
Katse dam (Lesotho), 177
Kaudia, Alice, 174
Kavango–Zambezi Trans-Frontier Conservation Area (KAZA-TFCA), 7, 96–98
Keeley, James, 200, 201
Keep South Africa Tidy/Keep South Africa Beautiful, 132, 142
Keller, Edmond J., 118
Kelsall, Tim, 148
Kenya: Agricultural Carbon Project, 178; bottom-up initiatives in, 121; China's investments in, 225; economic growth projection in, 181; environmental education in, 140, 142; German development aid to, 199–200; Green

Belt Movement and Maathai, 14, 40, 108–14, 140, 144–45, 148, 239; green economy strategies in, 14, 174, 181; green parties in, 7, 146; invasive alien species in, 135; land grabs and exclusive territorialisation in, 89; legacy of colonialism in, 188; national parks in, 86–87; PACJA activities in, 227; population density in, 115, 116; regreening of, 116; renewable energy in, 6, 40, 175–76; and Serengeti road dispute, 69–71; social change in, 187; tree-planting in, 14, 121; World Bank loans to, 165; youth programs in, 187
Keohane, Robert, 20, 21, 34, 42
Kepe, Thembela, 139
Keynesian economics, 49, 157, 165, 169, 243
Kibaki, Mwai, 110, 145
Kibera Community Youth Program (Kenya), 187
killings of environmental activists, 8
Kingsley, Mary, 217
Kitchener, Walter, 88
Klein, Naomi, 3, 196, 216, 221–22, 243
Kleinmond Ecological Society (South Africa), 142
Kruger National Park (KNP; South Africa), 62, 85–86, 91, 93, 96, 208
Kuehls, Thom, 45, 49, 64, 65
Kuloba, John, 70
Kusile Power Station (South Africa), 8, 155, 184
Kyoto Protocol, 6, 160, 167, 224

Lachmann, Richard, 198
lack of fit between environmental issues and geographic boundaries of states, 22–23, 28
Lagos (Nigeria), 82, 125; Urban Transport Project, 40
Lake Turkana Wind Power Project (Kenya), 40, 176
Lake Victoria, Nile perch in, 135
land degradation, 62, 90, 117, 120, 143, 217, 228
land disputes, 70–71
land grabbing, 8, 13, 89–91, 100–104, 138, 189–90, 241
land reform, 102–3; Fast Track Land Reform (Zimbabwe), 15, 189–91, 192, 243
Larner, Wendy, 66
Latin America: calls for ecological limits in, 169; protected areas in, 79; rapidly growing economy of, 171; revolutionary discourse in, 189
Latour, Bruno, 65
La Via Campesina, 41
leadership of Africa in environmental performance, 206–16, 230, 237
lead smelters and blood poisoning, 145
LeBaron, Genevieve, 132
Lefebvre, Henri, 73
Lekgetho, Japhta, 141
Lemke, Thomas, 155
Leopold, Aldo, 24, 133
Lesotho: dam construction in, 177; food aid to, 212
Lesotho Highlands Water Project (LHWP), 177
Lever Brothers (Unilever), 164
liberalism: feminist critique of, 27; vs. totalitarianism, 25. *See also* neoliberalism
Liberia, rubber trees in, 164
Li Bingbing, 212
Libya, carbon footprint in, 130
life expectancies, 205
lighthouse projects, 211
Limpopo National Park (Mozambique), 86
Loango National Park (Gabon), 226
Local Agenda 21 movement, 28
localism, 133, 143
logging companies' corporate social responsibility, 162–63
longue durée, 2, 10, 247n1

Lund, Christian, 81, 106, 239

Maasai and access to Serengeti National Park lands, 84, 87
Maathai, Wangari, 1, 108–14, 144–46; caricature of, 146; *The Challenge for Africa,* 111; on education trivializing indigenous culture, 143; Green Belt Movement of, 14, 109–11, 239; as inspirational model, 18, 148, 149, 242; photograph of, *109*
MacGregor, Sherilyn, 128
Machakos District (Kenya), 121
Madagascar: biofuel projects in, 182; environmental education in, 140; environmental indexes on, 204*t,* 205; green party in, 7, 147; invasive alien species in, 135; mining in, 95, 175; NGOs in, 95
Maine, Kas, 152–53, 155, 191
Majimbo movement, 90
Makhathini Flats (South Africa), 214
Makuleke (South Africa), 93–94, 208
Malawi: economic growth and contraction in, 182, 213; environmental education in, 140; environmental indexes on, 7, 204*t,* 205; famine in, 8, 124; Farm Input Subsidy Program, 212; green economy strategies in, 174; Mutharika as a good example of leadership in, 212–13
Mali: environmental impact assessments (EIA) in, 178; famine in, 8; FoEI branch in, 227; green party in, 147; reforestation in, 121; Wetland of International Importance in, 178
Malthus, Thomas Robert, 24, 114. *See also* overpopulation issues
Mamase, Max, 122
Mamdani, Mahmood, 11, 136–37
Mandela, Nelson, 96
manhood, association with wilderness and frontier, 83
Mann, Michael, 34, 38
Mannheim, Karl, 162
Mapfura-Makhura Incubator (South Africa), 122–23
mapping of terrain, 81–82; *Carte d'Afrique* (Delisle), 73, 74*f*; colonial Egypt, 61; slums, 105–6
Mapushi, Luckson, 134
Markandya, Anil: *A New Blueprint for a Green Economy* (with Barbier), 166
Marx, Karl, 46, 53
Marxist theory, 23, 26–27, 46–48, 50, 53–55, 88, 202
Mathiane, Nomavenda, 126, 219
Mau Mau movement, 90
Mauritania: carbon footprint in, 130; reforestation in, 121
Mauritius: carbon footprint in, 130; ecological footprint in, 203; green economy strategy in, 129, 173; green party in, 146; invasive alien species in, 135; PACJA activities in, 227
maximum sustainable yield, 156
Mazingira Green Party (Kenya), 146
Mbeki, Thabo, 1, 127, 136, 185, 208
Mbembe, Achille, 13, 45, 54, 55, 98, 104, 233
McCann, James, 118
McCarthy, James, 165
McDuff, Mallory, 142
McGregor, JoAnn, 91, 92
McInnes, Colin, 134
McMichael, Philip, 165
Mda, Zakes, 108
Meadowcroft, James, 162, 163, 235
MEC (minerals–energy complex), 183–84
Mediterranean Solar Plan, 175
Medupi Power Station (South Africa), 8, 155, 184
MEND. *See* Movement for the Emancipation of the Niger Delta
Merowe dam (Sudan), 176
metrology and metrological regimes, 65
Mgahinga National Park (Uganda), 78

Michel, Silvio, 146
microinsurance, 180
Middle Ages, 48
Middle East's agribusiness in Africa, 100
Middlemiss, Lucie, 129
Miliband, Ralph, 26
Millennium Development Goals (MDGs), 8, 124, 163, 213, 222
Millennium Villages Programme, 213
Miller, Marian, 199
mining: Chinese mining operations in Zambia, 226; effects of, 8; green mining, 95; minerals–energy complex (MEC), 154–55, 183–84; pollution surrounding, 217
Mitchell, Timothy: on colonial Egypt, 60–61; on economy as field of political regulation, 65; on Egyptian overpopulation, 115; on national borders, 77–78; on nineteenth century theories of moral and political economy, 157; on private property demarcation, 81; on state–society distinction, 47; on state theory, 13, 45, 56; on warfare and creation of states, 197
Mobutu Sese Seko, 54
modernisation theory, 10–11, 12, 30–31, 34, 35–36; agricultural modernisation, 119–20; applied to Africa, 39–43, 164, 181, 236, 237; ecological modernisation theory, 158–59, 198, 202, 235, 237, 243; green state literature's focus on, 76; weak states in, 37–38
Mofokeng, Santu, 151. *See also* photographs
Mohale dam (Lesotho), 177
Moi, Daniel Arap, 109, 111
Mokomazi game reserve (Tanzania), 137
Mol, Arthur P. J., 35–36, 39, 162, 164, 215, 225–26, 230
Monsanto, 101, 214
Moore, Henrietta L., 117, 118
Mori, President, 111
Moroccan Integrated Solar and Wind Energy Programs, 175
Morocco: environmental index on, 205; green party in, 147; renewable energy in, 6, 40, 175–76
Mottiar, Shauna, 219
Movement for the Emancipation of the Niger Delta (MEND), 194–96, 218, 226
Movement for the Survival of the Ogoni People (MOSOP), 41, 193–96, 218
Mozambique: activism and government harassment in, 221; agricultural economy in, 191; biofuel projects in, 182; borders of, 74, 78, 88, 96; dam in, 177; environmental education in, 140; environmental indexes on, 7, 8, 204*t*, 205; environmental marketing and branding of, 184; FoEI branch in, 227; green economy strategies in, 40, 173–74; green party in, 147; land grabs and relocation in, 89; land mapping in, 81; sustainable development in, 185; Trans-Frontier Conservation Areas (TFCAs), 96
Mphanda Nkuwa dam (Mozambique), 177
Mugabe, Robert, 189–90, 228
Muir, John, 24
multilateral legal regimes, 199, 201
multinational corporations, 164, 175
Musyoki, Agnes, 122
Mutharika, Bingu wa, 212–13
Mwambene, Asa, 138
Myers, Norman, 138

Naidoo, Kumi, 7, 18, 152, 227, 228
Nairobi, 82, 110, 125, 127, 141
Nally, David, 118, 155
Namibia: borders of, 96, 99; climate adaptation in, 211; environmental education in, 140; environmental indexes on, 7, 42, 204*t*, 205; green economy strategies in, 174; land

Namibia (*cont.*)
reform in, 190; protected land in, 13, 71
Nanyunja, Robinah, 147
Nasser, Gamal Abdel, 157
National Climate Change Response Paper (2004), 207
National Environmental Awareness Campaign, 141
national parks and reserves, 7; antipoaching efforts, 86–87; developers vs. preservationists in disputes over, 70; exclusivity of, 84–86; in North America and Europe vs. in Africa, 76–77; people and parks movement, 92–93; "post-sovereign" environmental management of, 99; rituals associated with, 78; in South Africa, 62; Trans-Frontier Conservation Areas (TFCAs), 95–100
National Veld Trust (South Africa), 142
natural resource extraction, 3, 32, 164, 175, 178, 217; highly polluting industry, 216
Nature Conservancy, 94
nature conservation and biodiversity: Africa Living Planet Index, 203; biodiversity hot spots, 103; coercive conservation, 241; conservation biology, 144; diversity of practices, 82; "dream of Africa without fences," 96; "fines-and-fences" policies, 83, 96; fortress conservation, 13, 83–89; framed as "win–win opportunity" offering employment and empowerment, 92, 94; globalised interest in, 216; human management of biodiversity, 114; importance to environmental movement of 1960s and 1970s, 75; South Africa's leadership role, 207–8, 237; Tanzania's leadership role, 210. *See also* national parks and reserves
Ndebele, Njabulo, 69
Nedbank (South African bank), 175
Neely, Abigail H., 136
Nelson, Fred, 75, 93, 104
neocolonialism, 163–64
neoliberalism, 164, 165, 202, 241; disciplinary neoliberalism, 203; globalisation, 23, 27–30, 47, 53
neo-Malthusian perspective, 24
neopatrimonialism, 37, 51–52, 165, 213
neo-Weberian perspective, 22, 34
NEPAD (New Partnership for African Development), 222
Netherlands: and antipoaching initiatives, 87; courts in, 196; environmental performance indexes on, 37
Neumann, Iver B., 231
Neumann, Roderick, 53, 84
New Alliance for Food Security and Nutrition, 177
New Deal, 166, 169–70, 222
New Economics Foundation. *See* Happy Planet Index
Newell, Peter, 32, 159, 161, 199
"new-medievalism," 76
New Partnership for African Development (NEPAD), 222
Ngonyo, Josphat, 70
Ngorogoro conservation area, 84
NGOs. *See* nongovernmental organisations
Nhema, Francis, 174
Niger: agricultural economy in, 191; Chinese projects and concerns about, 225; environmental indexes on, 7, 9, 42, 204*t*, 205; famine in, 124; floods in, 8; green party in, 147; reforestation in, 121, 141; regreening of, 122
Niger Delta: activist violence in, 226; militants in, 145; Movement for the Emancipation of the Niger Delta (MEND), 193–96, 218; pollution and degradation of, 8, 15, 175, 217–18, 238; Shell cleanup of, 193–96, 229. *See also* Movement for the Survival of the Ogoni People

Nigeria: borders of, 78; carbon credits in, 160; civil war in, 90–91, 238; climate intervention leadership of, 206; development projects in, 40; environmental indexes on, 39, 204*t*; as environmental laggard, 217–18, 230, 237–38; Federal Ministry of the Environment, 217; floods in, 8; FoEI activities in, 227; Green Revolution strategy in, 177; overview, 237–38; PACJA and FoEI in, 227–28; palm oil business in, 164; population density in, 115; reforestation in, 121; satellites launched by, 206; and Shell pollution and cleanup of Niger Delta, 193–96; sustainable development in, 7; territorial control in, 51
Nigeria–Cameroon Boundary Commission, 81
Nile River, 60–61, 176; Aswan Dam, 61, 157, 176
Nile River Valley: overpopulation in, 115; private property demarcation in, 81
Nixon, Rob, 110
Nkrumah, Kwame, 90
Nkwinti, Gugile, 190
Nobel Peace Prize, 108
nongovernmental organisations (NGOs), 28, 57, 69, 71; and carbon market, 159; conservation initiatives of, 86, 87, 93, 99, 141–42; environmental education programmes, 140; environmental governance communities sharing same personnel and funding as, 200–201; and hybrid practices of territorialisation, 94–95; in South Durban (South Africa), 219
North Africa: mining in, 8; renewable energy in, 40
North America: and agribusiness and land grabs in Africa, 100; conservation in, 76; environmental politics in, 106; green economy in, 129, 173; and green states literature, 33; postmaterialist environmentalism in, 38
Norway: development aid from, 200; and environmental performance indexes, 37; funding for forestry development, 182; as green state, 10
Nossob River as South Africa–Botswana border, 99
nuclear disasters, 25
nuclear power, 178
Nyéléni Forum for Food Sovereignty (Mali 2007), 188
Nyerere, Julius, 90
Nyungwe National Park (Rwanda), 78
Nzema solar photovoltaic plant (Ghana), 6, 40, 176

Oakland Institute, 100, 178
OAU (Organisation for African Unity), 222
Occupy Wall Street (film), 220
O'Connor, James, 26–27
OECD (Organisation for Economic Cooperation and Development), 52, 166
Ofosu, Alfred, 128
Ogoni Nine, execution of, 194
oil pollution sites, 25. *See also* Niger Delta
Okri, Ben: *Famished Road*, 112
Omido, Phyllis, 18, 145
Ophuls, William, 24
organic farming, 187
Organisation for African Unity (OAU), 222
Organisation for Economic Cooperation and Development (OECD), 52, 166
O'Riordan, Tim, 26
Oteng-Agyei, Joe, 173
Ouarzazate solar complex (Morocco), 40, 175–76
Ouédraogo, Ram, 147
overconsumption issues, 123–32
overpopulation issues, 24, 114–16, 130

pacifism, 25
Pan-African Climate Justice Alliance (PACJA), 226–27
Pan-African unity, 3, 15, 90, 97, 222, 224, 236; and environmental solidarity, 17, 221–29; potential of, 243
Panasonic, 182
Paris Agreement (2015), 6, 224
Partido da Terra (Portugal), 147
Partido Nacional Ecológico de Angola, 146–47
Le Parti Écologiste Congolais, 147
Patel, Ebrahim, 173, 183
Paterson, Matthew, 27, 32, 129, 159, 161, 171
Patey, Luke, 39
patriarchy, 22, 26, 47, 111, 134, 169, 202, 228
patrimonialism, 21, 51–52, 126, 165
patriotism, 143
Payments for Ecosystem Services (PES), 159–60, 201
Peace of Augsburg (1555), 48
Peace Parks Foundation (PPF), 87, 96–99, 142
Pearce, David: *Blueprint for a Green Economy*, 166
peasant question, 236
Peek, Bobby, 44, 219
Peluso, Nancy Lee, 86, 119
people and parks movement, 92–95
people in environmental politics, 108–51; contesting biopolitical subjectivities, 148–51; educated entrepreneurial farmer, 14, 118–23, 143; environmental citizen, 139–43, 242; and environmental education programmes, 140–43; environmental laggards, 216–21; exemplary environmental leaders, 206–16, 243; foreign body and invasive alien species (IAS), 133–39, 143; globalisation and anxieties, 132–33; green consumer, 127–32, 143; and HIV/AIDS, 133–34; marginalized peoples, 151, 217, 221, 224, 239–40; missing from green state literature, 111; overconsumption issues, 123–25; overpopulation issues, 114–16; as part of solutions and planning, 242; prolific peasants, 116–18, 143; UNEP goodwill ambassadors, 212; unruly urban masses, 125–27. *See also* activism; Maathai, Wangari
PES (Payments for Ecosystem Services), 159–60, 201
Petersen, Nicole, 180–81
philanthropy, 211
photographs: "Chief More's Funeral, GaMogopa" (Mofokeng), *9*; "Dust storms at noon on the R34 between Welkom and Hennenman, Free State" (Mofokeng), *105*; Global Green Congress, Dakar 2012, *147*; Maathai (Blumenkrantz), *109*; "Old Man, Dukathole" (Mofokeng), *126*; "Police with Sjamboks, Plein Street" (Mofokeng), *67*; "Prayer Service at the Altar on the Easter Weekend at Motouleng Cave" (Mofokeng), *41*; "Samburu boy, Maralal, Kenya" (Blumenkrantz), *113*; South African Green Goal project (Death), *209*; Tea pickers, Murang'a District, Kenya (Blumenkrantz), *244*; "Wine-route—RDP houses on the N7, Western Cape" (Mofokeng), *186*; "Winter in Soweto, Central Western Jabavu" (Mofokeng), *241*; "Winter in Tembisa" (Mofokeng), *17*
Phuhlisani Solutions, 103
Pieterse, Edgar, 105
Player, Ian, 85
poaching, 86–87, 96, 97, 197, 218
Polanyi, Karl, 65, 157
Polihali dam (Lesotho and South Africa), 177
pollution enclaves in South Africa, 218–20
population: conceptual framework for green states based on government of,

64–65; new markets from growth in, 171; overpopulation issues, 24, 114–16, 138, 236; Rwanda, population forecasts for, 186
postcolonial theory, 11, 12–13, 44–68; biopolitical state in Africa, 66–68; colonial Egypt's biopolitics, 60–63; disparities produced by language, race, and religion, 202; and green state effects, 63–66, 239–43; state assemblages and analytics of governmentality, 55–60, 245; and state in Africa, 50–55, 75, 237; and urbanisation, 105
postgrowth economy, 169
postmaterialist environmentalism, 38–39
Poulantzas, Nicos, 26, 46, 53, 56, 57, 64
poverty: critical solidarity over, 228; extreme, 124, 163; free water supply in Durban, 208; priority of poverty reduction in global South, 172; pro-poor orientation, 170; in South Africa, 191; trends in, 124; and World Bank's Lighting Africa initiative, 187; and Zimbabwe Fast Track Land Reform, 191
Poverty Reduction Strategy Papers (PRSP), 201, 210, 236
power plants, 8, 15, 155, 184
PPF. *See* Peace Parks Foundation
precious metals mining, 8. *See also extractive industries*
private property, designation of, 81, 89–90; vs. community ownership over land, 91; encroachment of the commons, 188; restitution to Makuleke community (South Africa), 93–94
pro-poor orientation, 170
protected areas, 79–80, 79–80*f*. *See also* national parks and reserves; nature conservation and biodiversity
Protected Areas Categories System (IUCN), 79, 79–80*f*
PRSP (Poverty Reduction Strategy Papers), 201, 210, 236
Prudham, Scott, 165
public works programs, 139, 185, 236, 237. *See also* New Deal

quasi-states, 51

racism: biopolitics of apartheid South Africa, 60, 62–63; critical solidarity over, 228; disparities produced by language, race, and religion, 202; of environmentalism, 138–39; land redistribution in Zimbabwe, 189
Ragab, Hassan, 147
Rahmato, Dessalegn, 120
Ramsar Convention, 178
Ramutsindela, Maano, 96, 98, 99
Ranger, Terence, 145, 239
Rassemblement des Ecologistes du Burkina Faso, 147
Ravalomanana, Marc, 95
Reagan, Ronald, 28
realists vs. idealists, 198
recycling, 132, 141
Reducing Emissions from Deforestation and Forest Degradation (REDD+), 6, 101, 160–61, 182, 201
reforestation, 119–21, 206. *See also* trees and tree-planting
Regional Environmental Education Programme, 140
Reinfeldt, Frederik, 223
religious sites, 80, 239
relocation of indigenous people: due to land grabs for agribusiness, 101; due to land grabs of colonial settlers, 89–90
renewable energy, 40, 160, 173; initiatives in Africa, 6, 175–76, 183–84
resilience. *See* green resilience
resistance, 144, 145. *See also* activism
Resnick, Danielle, 165, 182, 213
resource curse, 175
revolution. *See* green revolution

Rhodesia: land grabs and exclusive territorialisation in, 89; Native Land Husbandry Act (1952), 93; Natural Resources Act (1942), 93; wildlife management and conservation in, 93. *See now* Zimbabwe
Richards, Audrey, 117
Rio Conference on Environment and Development (1992), 200
Rio Declaration (1992), 172
Rio del Rey, 78
Rio+10. *See* World Summit on Sustainable Development (Johannesburg)
Rio+20 Conference on Sustainable Development (2012), 166, 169, 172, *229*; "African Consensus Statement to Rio+20," 184
Rio Tinto, 95, 175
River Omo, 176
road construction, symbolism of, 71–72, 241–42. *See also* Serengeti National Park
Robins, Steven, 94
Roosevelt, Franklin D., 166, 169–70
Rosenberg, Justin, 202
Rossdale, Chris, 228
Rossport Five trial (Ireland 2005), 228–29
Rousseau, Jean-Jacques, 139
Royal Society for the Protection of Birds, 69
Ruhiira village (Uganda), 213
rule of law, 20, 37, 81
Rupert Nature Foundation, 96
Ruppel, Oliver C., 7
rural areas: customary rule in, 75; exclusive territorialisation of, 89–90; little state intervention in, 51. *See also* agriculture
Rwanda: agricultural economy in, 191; authoritarian regime in, 21; economic growth in, 163; environmental indexes on, 7, 204*t*, 205; environmental marketing and branding of, 184; genocide as racial cleansing in, 136–37; genocide linked to overpopulation in, 115–16, 118, 263n22; green economy strategies in, 7, 14–15, 40, 173, 236–37; green party in, 8, 147, 148; land mapping in, 81; national parks in, 78; National Strategy for Climate Change and Low-Carbon Development, 173, 185–86; overview, 236–37; public works participation required of citizens in, 139; reforestation in, 236; sustainable development in, 185–87
Rwisereka, André Kagwa, 8, 148

Sachs, Jeffrey, 193, 213
sacred groves, 80, 239
"sacrifice zones," 216
SADC (Southern African Development Community), 140, 174, 182
Sahel: Great Green Wall, 121
St Francis Bay–Kromme Trust (South Africa), 142
Sall, Macky, 146
SANP (South African National Parks), 93–94, 142
SAPs (structural adjustment programmes), 37, 53, 164–65
Sarkozy, Nicholas, 19, 20–21, 32, 37, 42, 233
Saro-Wiwa, Ken, 8, 18, 91, 194, 217, 218
Sassen, Saskia, 49
Save Gordons Bay Society (South Africa), 142
Save the Garden Route Committee (South Africa), 142
Scandinavia: development aid from, 200; and environmental performance indexes, 37; funding of Regional Environmental Education Programme, 140; green states in, 10
Schmitt, Carl, 112
Schneider Electric, 182
Scholfield, Katherine, 141–42, 216
Schroeder, Mark, 73
Schroeder, Richard, 82
Schumpeter, Joseph, 170; Schumpeterian workfare post-national regime, 49

Scoones, Ian, 90, 190, 200, 201
Scott, James C., 13, 65–66, 201, 232, 278n38
SDCEA (South Durban Community Environmental Alliance), 219–20
SDGs (Sustainable Development Goals), 141
Seagle, Caroline, 95
Security Council (UN), 33, 167
security issues involving environment, 33, 86, 198
SEED Awards, 129
self-determination, 75
self-regulation, 57
Sending, Ole Jacob, 231
Senegal: climate adaptation in, 211; green economy strategies in, 174; reforestation in, 121; Sarkozy speech in, 19, 20–21, 32, 37, 42, 233
Serengeti, 82, 114; as UNESCO World Heritage Site, 69
Serengeti National Park: establishment of, 84; Maasai's access to, 84, 87; park rangers killing local people (1998), 70; road dispute, 13, 69–71, 82, 84, 104–6, 236
Serengeti Watch, 70
Shaka (Zulu king), 85
Sharma, Aradhana, 66
Shell: political instability and, 218; pollution and clean-up of Niger Delta, 193–96; protests against, 220
Shell-to-Sea campaign, 229
Shilliam, Robbie, 49
Shivji, Issa, 70
Shukuza. *See* Stephenson-Hamilton, James
Sierra Leone: environmental impact assessments (EIA) in, 178; environmental indexes on, 7, 9, 42, 204*t*, 205; FoEI branch in, 227; mining in, 217; war in, 198
Sinopec (Chinese oil company), 226
Sioka, Doreen, 174
slash-and-burn cultivation, 117
slums, 104–6, 217, 242
Smith, Mick, 24, 231
Smuts, Jan, 143
Sneddon, Chris, 230
social change: and green economy, 188; and green states, 197, 243; in Kenya, 187; in Malawi, 213
social conflicts, 70
social justice, 170, 188
Society for the Protection of the Fauna of the Empire, 84
solar energy, 40, 175, 176, 184, 211. *See also* renewable energy
Solar Sister program (Uganda), 211
solidarity: critical solidarity, 227, 228, 245, 281n110; of heads of state, 228; transnational environmental solidarity, 17, 221–29, 236, 243. *See also* Pan-African unity
Somalia: borders of, 78; chaos in, 55; famine in, 8, 124; green party in, 147; PACJA activities in, 227; territorial control in, 51; as weak state, 38
Sonnenfeld, David A., 35–36
South Africa: agriculture in, 122–23; arts and culture of, 150–51; biofuel projects in, 122–23, 182; biopolitics of apartheid South Africa, 60, 62–63, 67, 88, 93, 126; borders of, 78, 87–88, 96, 99; carbon credits in, 160; carbon footprint in, 130; carbon-neutral economy as goal for, 185; carbon tax proposal in, 14, 153–55, 269n3; Climate Change Strategy (2011), 130–32; climate intervention leadership of, 15, 182–83, 206; coal-fired power plants in, 8, 155, 184; and Copenhagen Accord, 6, 223–24; dam in, 177; Department of Education and Department of Labour report, 141; Department of Rural Development and Land Reform report, 102–3; development projects in, 40;

South Africa (*cont.*)
economy described by Mbeki, 185; environmental education/citizenship in, 140–43; environmental indexes on, 9, 39, 204*t*, 204–5; environmental leadership of, 207–9, 218, 230, 237–38; environmental marketing and branding of, 184, 206, 230; environmental NGOs in, 142; environmental politics in, 18, 76; "environmental racialisation" in, 139; FoEI branch in, 227; game and forest stewards in, 14; GMO technology in, 134, 214; green economy strategies in, 7, 14–15, 40, 155, 160–61; Green Goal 2010 programme, 208; greenhouse gas emissions in, 8; green parties in, 147–48; in green states literature, 36; HIV/AIDS in, 134; immigrants and xenophobia in, 136; inequality in, 191; infrastructure development in, 178; Integrated Coastal Management Act, 179; invasive alien species in, 135; Keep South Africa Tidy/Keep South Africa Beautiful, 132, 142; land grabs and exclusive territorialisation in, 89–91, 93–94; land reform in, 190; legacy of colonialism in, 188; mining in, 8, 217; national parks and conservation/biodiversity protection in, 84–87, 93–94, 207–8, 237; National Treasury's Carbon Tax Discussion Paper (2015), 153, 269n3; overview, 237; PACJA activities in, 227; pollution enclaves in, 218–20; population density in, 115; poverty in, 191; public works programmes in, 185, 237; renewable energy in, 6, 176, 183–84; Renewable Energy Independent Power Producer Procurement Programme (RE IPPPP), 176, 183; South African Natives (Urban Areas) Act (1923), 127; stimulus package, 183; sustainable development in, 185; Trans-Frontier Conservation Areas (TFCAs), 96, 98–99; "Treepreneur" programme in, 122; and UNESCO, 216; urban conditions in, 126, 127; weak status for environmental reforms in, 38; Xhosa in, 239

South African Industrial Policy Action Plan, 172

South African National Parks (SANP), 93–94, 142

South Asia, 124

South Durban (South Africa), 15, 145, 219–20

South Durban Community Environmental Alliance (SDCEA), 219–20

southern Africa: Devil weed, effect of introduction into, 135; green politics in, 11; national parks and reserves in, 71; poverty in, 124; trans-frontier park (TFP) in, 96

Southern African Development Community (SADC), 140, 174, 182

Southern African Nature Foundation, 142

Southern Cape, fire costs in, 103

South Korea, green economy favored in, 173

South Sudan: Bangladesh agricultural land lease in, 100; famine in, 8; secession of, 91

sovereignty, 48–49, 196–206, 231; and independence of African states, 75; letter-box sovereignty, 54; policies of, 57–58; in Serengeti road dispute, 71; and territorialisation, 74–75; and Trans-Frontier Conservation Areas (TFCAs), 98

Sowers, Jeannie L., 41

space and spatial theory: Africa as blank space, 73; private property, designation of, 81; protected areas, 79–80, 79–80*f*; symbolism of African wild spaces, 71, 111, 233, 242; territory's abstract form, 73; zoning of spaces, 78–81. *See also* borderline creation

Spain, development aid targeting sustainable development from, 200
Spierenburg, Marja, 98
SSI (Sustainable Society Index), 7, 203–6, 204*t*
Standard Chartered Bank sustainable development index, 7, 8
state effects, 63–66, 111, 236, 239–44, 278n38
state formation and role, 16, 19–43; in Africa's developing states, 36–37, 53; anti-instrumentalist critique, 23, 24–26, 27, 31; antistatist perspectives in, 21, 22–23; ecological modernisers, 30–31, 34, 35–36; failed states, 51–52; governmentality framework for analysis of, 57–60; green ecologist critique, 23–24; importance of the state in environmental realm, 238–39; interaction between external and domestic actors in, 67; and Marxist theory, 46, 53; meaning of "state," 22, 45–46; and modes of governance, 241; neoliberal or globalist critique, 27–30; neo-Weberian account of, 22, 34; political ecology critique, 26–27; possibilities for modernity in Africa, 39–43; and postmaterialist environmentalism, 38–39; quasi-states, 51; rhizome metaphor for, 55, 242; theories of the state, 45–50; as "ultimate attainment of the human spirit," 32; and war making, 25; in weak states, 37–38; Weberian perspective on, 10, 12, 26, 30, 35, 38; Westphalian ideal of territorially sovereign entities, 75; and whole–part paradox, 56. *See also* colonialism, history of; green states
state imperatives linked to environmental issues, 61, 75–76, 235, 237
statist perspectives, 24
Stebbing, E. P., 117
Stephenson-Hamilton, James, 85
Stepputat, Finn, 240
stereotypes of African peasants, 116–17
Stern, Nicholas, 158, 167
Strange, Susan, 28, 76, 106
Stripple, Johannes, 129
structural adjustment programmes (SAPs), 37, 53, 164–65
Sub-Saharan Africa: China's trade with, 225; commercial farmers in, 181–82; large-scale agricultural land deals in, 100; Millennium Villages Programme, 213, 214; national parks and reserves in, 7, 71; World Heritage Sites in, 7
Sudan: development projects in, 40; natural resource extraction in, 175; reforestation in, 121
Sudan–Uganda Boundary Commission, 81
Sukhdev, Pavan, 212
Suriname, 94
sustainable development: challenges of, 17; costs vs. benefits of, 170, 192; development aid targeting, 200; entrepreneurship for, 129; G77 countries' view on, 172; green economy strategies for, 7; and national boundaries, 99; nonparticipation in UN programme, 217; public involvement in, 139–40, 143; sustainable capitalism, 158; transforming African economies via, 184–88; and water utilities, 128; in West Africa and the Sahel, 121
Sustainable Development Commission (UK), 169
Sustainable Development Goals (SDGs), 141
sustainable harvesting, 156
Sustainable Society Index (SSI), 7, 203–6, 204*t*
Swatuk, Larry, 99
Swaziland: activism and government harassment in, 221; FoEI branch in,

Swaziland (*cont.*)
227; food aid to, 212; invasive alien species in, 135
symbolism of African wild spaces (empty of people), 71, 111, 233, 242

Table Mountain fires, 135–36
Tanganyikan reaction to British colonial creation of Serengeti National Park, 84
Tanzania: biofuel projects in, 182; borders of, 78; Chinese trade with, 225; and climate financing, 182; colonialism's effect on, 53; conservation and resource management in, 13, 76, 93, 95, 206, 210, 236; development aid to, 199; environmental education in, 140–41; environmental indexes on, 7, 8, 204*t*, 205; environmental leadership of, 207, 210, 230, 236; environmental marketing and branding of, 184, 230; environmental politics in, 76; FoEI branch in, 227; green economy strategies in, 14–15; as green state politics example, 236; infrastructure development in, 178; land grabs and relocation in, 89; land mapping in, 81; large-scale agricultural land deal in, 100; Ministry of Environment, 199; Mokomazi game reserve, 137; National Environmental Management Act (1983), 140–41; national parks in, 84, 86; National Strategy for Growth and the Reduction of Poverty (2005), 210; National Strategy for Urgent Action on Land Degradation and Water Catchments, 120; NGOs in, 95; population density in, 115; reforestation initiatives in, 112, 120; refugee camps, disposition of land from, 137–38; and Serengeti road dispute, 13, 69–71, 84, 104–6, 236; Southern Agricultural Growth Corridor, 101; State of the Environment report (2006), 84, 125, 137; sustainable development in, 185, 210; urban conditions in, 125, 126; *Vision* 2025 (national development strategy), 210; Wildlife Conservation Act (2009), 93; Wildlife Management Areas, 93
Tanzania Consumer Advocacy Society, 225
tariffs, 172
taxation, proposal for carbon tax, 14, 153–55, 172, 269n3
Tekeze canyon dam (Ethiopia), 176
territorialisation, 13, 71–104; and Berlin Conference (1884–85), 74–75, 77; borderline creation, 77–78; conceptual framework for green states based on, 63–64; definition of "territory," 63; exclusive practices of, 13, 72, 82–83; fortress conservation, 13, 83–89; general practices of, 77–82; and hermaphrodite landscapes, 104–5; hybrid practices of, 13, 17, 72, 91–92, 245; land grabs and land politics, 89–91, 100–104; mapping of terrain, 81–82; neglected concept in green state literature, 76–77; people and parks movement, 92–95; and the state, 71–77, 106; territory distinguished from land, 73; Trans-Frontier Conservation Areas (TFCAs), 95–100; unlikely to diminish in importance, 76; zoning of spaces, 78–81
TFCAs (Trans-Frontier Conservation Areas), 95–100
TFPs (trans-frontier parks), 96–100
Thatcher, Margaret, 28
theories of the state, 45–50
Think Global, Act Local (slogan), 29
Thompson, Grahame, 48
Three Gorges Dam (China), 176
Tienhaara, Kyla, 168
Tiffen, Mary: *More People, Less Erosion,* 116, 121
Tilly, Charles, 25, 67–68, 197, 230
Togo, FoEI activities in, 227

TOTAL, 182
totalitarianism, 25
Touré, Yaya, 212
tourism. *See* ecotourism
Trafigura (Dutch shipping company), 217
transformation. *See* green transformation
Trans-Frontier Conservation Areas (TFCAs), 95–100
trans-frontier parks (TFPs), 96–100
transnational dynamics, 5–6, 28; environmental solidarity, 17, 221–29, 236, 243; non-territorial nature of, 76; role in making African states, 68; and South African protests, 220. *See also* international relations (IR)
Treaty of Westphalia (1648), 48, 72
trees and tree-planting: Australian trees introduced into South Africa, 135; common environmental activity in Africa, 121; Ethiopia program, 236; Kenya campaign (Green Belt Movement), 109–14, 144–45; Madagascar program, 175; Niger program, 141; Rwanda program, 236; South African Green Goal project, 208; South African "Treepreneur" programme, 122
Treverton College environmental education conference (1982), 141
Tunisia: environmental index on, 205; FoEI branch in, 227; green party in, 147
Tutu, Desmond, 18, 209
Twain, Mark, 212

Ubongwa Farmers' Association, 214
Uganda: activism and government harassment in, 221; dam in, 176; environmental education in, 140; Export Promotion Board, 187; FoEI branch in, 227; fragile state agenda in, 52; green party in, 147; HIV/AIDS in, 134; model village (Ruhiira) in, 213; National Bureau of Standards, 187; national parks in, 78; natural resource extraction in, 175; organic farming in, 187; PACJA activities in, 227; reforestation in, 112, 121; solar energy project in, 211; sustainable development in, 7, 129
Umfolozi game reserve, 85
UN Conference on Sustainable Development (Rio de Janeiro 2012), 173–74
UN Conference on Trade and Development (UNCTAD), 170; Economic Development in Africa Report (2012), 192
UNEP. *See* United Nations Environment Programme
UNESCO World Heritage Sites, 69, 71, 79, 216
UNFCCC. *See* United Nations Framework Convention on Climate Change
United Kingdom: *Blueprint for a Green Economy* (Pearce et al.), 166; British colonialism in Africa, 53, 93, 95; carbon emissions in, 219; and environmental performance indexes, 37; pollution and hot spots in, 216; population density in, 115; Transition Towns in, 61
United Nations: agencies of, 28; conference on New and Renewable Sources of Energy (Nairobi 1981), 6–7; Convention to Combat Desertification, 121; Global Compact, 214–15; High Commission for Refugees, 137; recognition of legal regimes, 49
United Nations Development Programme's Human Development Report (2013), 225
United Nations Environment Assembly, 197
United Nations Environment Programme (UNEP): Global Green New Deal/

UNEP (*cont.*)
Green Economy Initiative, 166, 167, 192; goodwill ambassadors of, 212; on green economy and growth, 165–67, 170, 188; green economy defined by, 156; headquarters of, 197; on microinsurance, 180; on need to revise green growth model, 171; Niger Delta pollution report, 193, 218; on pollination's importance, 160; recognition of Maathai as heroine, 109; role of, 6; on Senegal, 174; and Zimbabwe, 190
United Nations Framework Convention on Climate Change (UNFCCC), 222, 224; Climate Adaptation Fund, 181; conferences of the parties (COPs) to, 6; Gold Standard Programme of Activities, 160; Momentum for Change programme, 211; National Adaptation Programmes of Action, 199
United States: and Copenhagen Accord, 6; and environmental markets, 156; environmental performance indexes on, 37; environmental politics in, 76; food aid from, 119, 134; and global financial crisis, 167; hegemony of, 26; negativity toward green economy in, 172; neoliberalism in, 58; and politics of conservation, 76; politics of environmentalists in, 133; pollution and hot spots in, 216; population density in, 115
United States Agency for International Development (USAID), 140, 177, 199; Productive Safety Net Programme, 180
urbanisation, 105; unruly urban masses, 125–27; urban pollution, 145
Utting, Peter, 215

Vandergeest, Peter, 119
van der Waal, Kees, 94
van Onselen, Charles, 152, 191
van Rensburg, Eureta Janse, 140
Vaughan, Megan, 117, 118
Vaughan-Williams, Nick, 75
Vavi, Zwelinzima, 190
Veracini, Lorenzo, 150
Verts Fraternels (Mauritius), 146
Victoria Falls, 177
Vietnam, 205
Vincent, Andrew, 240
violence: activists using in Nigeria, 226; and environmental struggles, 195; immigrants, xenophobic attacks on, 136; and land redistribution in Zimbabwe, 189; perpetuation of, facilitated by cooperation of elites, 202, 221
Vision 2025 (Tanzania), 210
vulnerability: of Africa to climate change, 5, 7, 8; monitoring of, 206; resilience as response to, 172

Walters, William, 66
Waltz, Kenneth, 47, 198, 210, 231
warfare, 25, 50, 90–91, 197–98, 238
Warner, Rosalind, 35
Washington Consensus, 27
water resources, 248n21; purification by wetlands, 160
water scarcity, 218
water utilities, 128; free water supply in Durban, 208
Weber, Max, and Weberian perspective, 10, 12, 22, 25, 26, 30, 34, 35, 38, 45, 47, 50, 51; and black-boxed states, 54; definition of state, 72
Weidner, Helmut, 33, 34
Weiss, Edith, 34
Wele River, 176–77
well-being, in environmental indexes, 205
Wels, Harry, 98
West Africa: cocoa plantations in, 164; dam construction in, 177; Devil weed, effect of introduction into, 135; national parks and reserves in, 71; poverty in, 124; sustainable land

management in, 121; urbanisation in, 125
Westphalian ideal of territorially sovereign entities, 75, 197
whaling, 199
wildlife: South Africa capitalizing on association with, 62; South Africa NGOs and local groups' activities to preserve, 62, 142; and trans-frontier parks (TFPs), 97
Wildlife and Environment Society of South Africa, 140, 142
Wildlife Clubs of Kenya, 142
Wildlife Conservation Society, 94
Wildlife Conservation Society of Tanzania, 69
Wildlife Society (South Africa), 142
Williams, Michael C., 53
Wilson, Japhy, 213
wind energy. *See* renewable energy
wise use movement, 156
Wiwa, Owens, 228–29
women: and climate change migration, 138; feminist critique, 27; gender inequality, 148; household responsibility of, 128; Kenya tree planting (Green Belt Movement), 110–11, 144–45
Working for Water (South Africa), 185, 237
World Bank: BioCarbon Fund, 178; on carbon dioxide capture in Kenya, 108; on climate-smart agriculture, 178; coal-fired plants in South Africa funded by, 155; cost-recovery policies of, 128; on CSR initiatives, 215; and dam construction, 176; on economic growth as the key, 171; embedded staff in African states, 201; as global knowledge bank, 201; Green Economy Initiative supported by, 166; Green Revolution strategy, 177; *Inclusive Green Growth,* 170; on large-scale agricultural land deals in sub-Saharan Africa, 100; Lighting Africa initiative, 187; *Making Development Climate Resilient in Sub-Saharan Africa,* 179; Poverty Reduction Strategy Papers (PRSP), 201, 210, 236; on Serengeti road development, 70; South Africa classified as upper-middle-income country by, 185; and structural adjustment programmes, 164; Tanzania environmental funding from, 199; on Tanzania's carbon sequestration services, 182; trans-frontier park (TFP) funding from, 96
World Commission on Environment and Development. *See* Brundtland Report
World Cup. *See* FIFA World Cup
World Heritage Sites, 7, 69, 71, 216
World Parks Congress (Durban 2003), 96, 207, 237
World Rain Forest Action Group, 196
World Resources Institute, 203
World Summit on Sustainable Development (Johannesburg 2002) (Rio+10), 131, 154, 184, 206, 207, 237
World Trade Organisation, 28, 188
World War II, 157
World Wide Fund for Nature, 93
World Wildlife Fund (WWF): on accountability of Chinese firms, 226; on Africa's carbon footprint, 115, 130; antipoaching operations of, 86; on biocapacity deficit in Africa, 8; on green growth in Mozambique, 174; on pollution "hot spots," 216; in South Africa, 96, 142; in Tanzania, 94–95

xenophobic attitudes, 136, 242
Xhosa (South African tribe), 239

Yale University EPI. *See* Environmental Performance Index
Young, Crawford, 21
Young, Oran, 24, 34
youth programs: in Kenya, 187; wildlife clubs, 142

Zafy, Albert, 147
Zambezi River, 177
Zambia: agricultural practices in, 117, 118; biofuel projects in, 182; borders of, 78; Chinese projects and concerns about, 225–26; copper belt in, 217, 225; environmental education in, 140; genetically modified foods in, 134–35; green economy strategies in, 174; mining in, 8, 217; protected land in, 13, 71
Zarsky, Lyuba, 42
Zenawi, Meles, 212, 223, 236
Zimbabwe: African National Union–Patriotic Front (ZANU–PF) government, 189–90; biofuel projects in, 182; borders of, 74, 88, 96; Communal Areas Management Programme for Indigenous Resources (CAMPFIRE), 92–93; ecological movements in, 145; environmental education in, 140; environmental indexes on, 204*t*, 205; famine in, 8; Fast Track Land Reform, 15, 189–91, 192, 243; food aid to, 212; green economy strategies in, 174; indigenous knowledge in, 239; invasive alien species in, 135; killing of environmental activists in, 8; land grabs in, 91; legacy of colonialism in, 188; national parks in, 86, 92–93; Trans-Frontier Conservation Areas (TFCAs), 96
Zimbabwe Trust, 93
zoning of spaces, 78–81
Zululand, 85
Zuma, Jacob, 223